CANADA
TRANSFORMED

CANADA TRANSFORMED

THE SPEECHES OF

SIR JOHN A. MACDONALD

A BICENTENNIAL CELEBRATION

Edited by Sarah Katherine Gibson & Arthur Milnes

McCLELLAND & STEWART

Library and Archives of Canada Cataloguing in Publication
is available upon request

Published simultaneously in the United States of America by
McClelland & Stewart, a division of Random House of Canada Limited

Library of Congress Control Number available upon request

ISBN: 978-0-7710-5719-9
ebook ISBN: 978-0-7710-5720-5

Cover image: Sir John A. Macdonald, the Harold Daly Collections,
Library and Archives Canada / C-002829

Typeset in Bembo by M&S, Toronto
Printed and bound in the United States of America

McClelland & Stewart,
a division of Random House of Canada Limited,
a Penguin Random House Company
www.randomhouse.ca

1 2 3 4 5   18 17 16 15 14

CONTENTS

PART ONE: BIRTH OF A PARLIAMENTARIAN

PART TWO: RISE OF A STATESMAN

PART THREE: NATION MAKER

PART FOUR: STEADFAST VISIONARY

DIRECTORY OF KEY NAMES

THE UNITED PROVINCE OF CANADA (1841–1867)—
The Union Act of 1841 united the legislatures of Upper and
Lower Canada, creating Canada West (Ontario) and Canada
East (Quebec). The terms Upper and Lower Canada continued
to be used after the union.

THE DOMINION OF CANADA (1867)—The British
North America Act of 1867 created the Dominion of Canada
from Canada East, Canada West, Nova Scotia, and New
Brunswick. It expanded during Macdonald's lifetime to include
Manitoba (1870), British Columbia (1871), and Prince Edward
Island (1873).

HEADS OF STATE THROUGHOUT SIR JOHN A. MACDONALD'S CAREER (1844–1891)

UNITED PROVINCE OF CANADA

TENURE	REIGNING MONARCH
1837–1901	Victoria, Queen of the United Kingdom of Great Britain and Ireland and Empress of India (1819–1901)
	GOVERNOR GENERAL
1843–1845	Metcalfe, Charles Theophilus, 1st Baron Metcalfe (1785–1846)
1846–1847	Cathcart, Charles Murray, 2nd Earl Cathcart (1783–1859)
1847–1854	Bruce, James, 8th Earl of Elgin and 12th Earl of Kincardine (1811–1863)
1854–1861	Head, Sir Edmund Walker (1805–1868)
1861–1867	Monck, Charles Stanley, 4th Viscount Monck (1819–1894)

DOMINION OF CANADA

1867–1868	Monck, Charles Stanley, 4th Viscount Monck (1819–1894)
1869–1872	Young, Sir John, Baron Lisgar (1807–1876)
1872–1878	Blackwood, Frederick Temple, 1st Marquess of Dufferin and Ava (1826–1902)
1878–1883	Campbell, John George Edward Henry Douglas Sutherland, Marquess of Lorne and 9th Duke of Argyll (1845–1914)

| 1883–1888 | Petty-Fitzmaurice, Henry Charles Keith, 5th Marquess of Lansdowne (1845–1927) |
| 1888–1893 | Stanley, Frederick Arthur, 1st Baron Stanley, and 16th Earl of Derby (1841–1908) |

FREQUENTLY MENTIONED NAMES

BALDWIN, ROBERT (1804–1858)

Leader of colonial reform in Canada West in the 1830s, he joined forces with Louis-Hippolyte La Fontaine and his French-Canadian reformers to push for responsible government. In 1843, they participated in a mass resignation from Lord Metcalfe's ministry. In 1849, La Fontaine and Baldwin created a Reform Ministry, and Lord Elgin allowed their ministry to distribute patronage, thereby largely resolving the question of responsible government.

BLAKE, EDWARD (1833–1912)

An Upper Canadian lawyer and Reformer, Blake gained recognition for challenging the constitutionality of the "double shuffle" in 1858. In 1867 he ran in both provincial and federal elections, winning the seats for Bruce South and Durham West. He became premier of Ontario in 1871, and was a prominent voice in the provincial rights movement. He also served in Alexander Mackenzie's federal Liberal government, but bitterly opposed its railway deal with British Columbia. He took a leading role in challenging Macdonald's franchise bill of 1885. In 1892, the Irish Nationalist party invited Blake to run for a seat in the British House of Commons, which he won.

BROWN, GEORGE (1818–1880)

After launching *The Globe* in 1844, Brown rose to prominence as an Upper Canadian politician on its success; by 1853 the newspaper was reputed to have the widest circulation in British North America. Brown entered the legislature of the United Province of Canada in 1851, and in 1853 put his weight behind the representation by population campaign and the sectarian interests of Protestant Ontario. His "Two-Day Administration" in 1858 with Antoine-Aimé Dorion became the butt of jokes, but in 1864 he rose to prominence again as a member of the Great Coalition that sought the confederation of the British North American colonies. Brown retired from political life in October 1867.

CARTIER, SIR GEORGE-ÉTIENNE (1814–1873)

Cartier was a French-Canadian businessman, lawyer, and politician deeply committed to economic progress for Canada East. In 1854 he became a minister in the United Province of Canada, making him the most influential politician among the moderate-Conservative *Bleus*. In 1858 he began promoting a British North American federation. After the idea gained support from the Colonial Office, he became part of the Great Coalition and of the Canadian delegation at the Confederation conferences. In 1868, he helped negotiate the acquisition of Rupert's Land and the North-West Territory. In 1871 he helped negotiate British Columbia's entry into Confederation.

CARTWRIGHT, SIR RICHARD (1835–1912)

An Upper Canadian businessman, politician, and author from a prominent Loyalist family in Kingston, Cartwright entered politics in 1863 as a Tory, but by 1869 he had left the party. In 1873, he sat as an independent. His complete break with the Tories came during the Pacific Scandal and he formed strong ties with the Liberals. He gained office in Alexander Mackenzie's government as minister of finance. He opposed the Conservatives' National Policy tariff as "anti-British," because it rejected free trade. After the defeat of the Liberals in 1878 he sat in opposition.

DORION, SIR ANTOINE-AIMÉ (1818–1891)

A Lower Canadian lawyer, newspaperman, and politician, Dorion cut his political teeth in the turmoil of 1849, founding the Montreal Annexation Association, which called for Canada's annexation by the United States. By 1851, he was a prominent member of the *Rouges,* although he did not personally support the party's anticlericalism and radicalism. In 1854, he was elected to a seat in the legislature of the United Province of Canada, where he allied himself with George Brown, and they eventually formed the "Two-Day Administration." However, Dorion opposed Brown's project of the Great Coalition of 1864 and its aim of Confederation. Nevertheless, after Confederation he represented the ridings of Hochelaga and later Napierville in the House of Commons, where he helped renew and reconstruct the Liberal Party and promoted Wilfrid Laurier's career. He retired from politics in 1874 when he accepted the position of chief justice in Quebec.

DRAPER, WILLIAM HENRY (1801–1877)

An Upper Canadian politician and lawyer, he began his legal career in the offices of prominent members of the Family Compact, who later supported his political career. He gained political traction under Governor General Sir Charles Bagot (1781–1843). He retired from politics, but was summoned back by Lord Metcalfe, the new governor general, after the mass resignation of his ministry in the infamous "Metcalfe Crisis." The Tories took the ensuing election in 1844, and until 1847 Draper was effectively premier of the province and helped nurture Macdonald's career. His role in shaping the Conservative Party far outweighed the political success of his government. He left politics to become the puisne judge for the Queen's Bench of Canada West in 1847.

GALT, SIR ALEXANDER TILLOCH (1817–1893)

A Scottish-born businessman, author, and politician, Galt began his career as a high-level functionary for the British American Land Company, and spent several years in Canada in the 1840s, particularly in the Eastern Townships of Lower Canada, where he promoted industrial development and railways. In the 1850s, he participated in the construction of part of the Grand Trunk Railway. He entered the legislature in 1849 by acclamation. Galt would often sit as an independent, but he became a strong member of Macdonald and Cartier's Conservative ministry and was appointed inspector general. One of the earliest advocates of Confederation, he made the ministry's adoption of this plan his condition for joining. A delegate to the Confederation conferences in Charlottetown, Quebec, and London between 1864 and 1866, he was by then minister of finance. In London he played a role in securing the educational rights of minorities. After Confederation, Galt resigned over disagreements with Macdonald. He avoided politics thereafter, continuing his career as a businessman and author.

HINCKS, SIR FRANCIS (1807–1885)

A moderate reform politician and newspaper man in Canada West, Hincks sat in the first Parliament of the United Province of Canada and helped orchestrate the alliance between Robert Baldwin and Louis-Hippolyte La Fontaine. He accepted leadership of the Reformers after Baldwin retired. After La Fontaine also retired, Hincks was co-premier with Augustin-Norbert Morin (1803–1865) in 1851, with a platform to secularize the clergy reserves, abolish seigneurial tenure, extend the franchise and increase representation, and have an elected Legislative Council. He lost his place at the head of government after the "£10,000 Job" scandal alleged he improperly used his office to benefit personally from a railway deal. He resigned in 1855. In 1869, Macdonald offered him the post of finance minister, and he accepted, but within five years he withdrew from politics.

HOWE, JOSEPH (1804–1873)

An ardent imperialist, publisher, and Nova Scotia legislator, he was first elected in 1836 and was speaker of the province's Assembly in 1841. His newspaper, the *Novascotian,* was an influential reform paper and its support helped elect the Reformers in 1847, which led to his appointment as provincial secretary. He advocated for bringing responsible government to Nova Scotia and for expanding the role of government. In 1853 he became chief commissioner of railways, overseeing the initial construction of the Nova Scotia Railway. In 1855 his government lost to Charles Tupper's Tories, but Howe became Liberal premier in 1860. Howe initially opposed Confederation, and spearheaded a repeal movement, but later joined Macdonald's government as president of the Privy Council and minister of the interior. He was responsible for arranging Manitoba's entry into Confederation. In 1873 he became lieutenant-governor of Nova Scotia but died soon after.

LA FONTAINE, SIR LOUIS-HIPPOLYTE (1807–1864)

A Lower Canadian politician and judge, La Fontaine helped create a united Reform Party. He believed that the creation of a single party across Upper and Lower Canada would best serve the interests of French Canadians. He united with Baldwin and together they secured responsible government in the 1840s. He helped provoke the "Metcalfe Crisis" of 1843, by insisting that the governor devolve to his responsible ministers the prerogative to dispense patronage. He and his party were to be in opposition between 1843 and 1847. In 1848 he and Baldwin led a Reform government and won responsible government when Governor General Lord Elgin allowed their ministers to dispense patronage. La Fontaine became attorney general of the United Province of Canada and embarked on a wide-ranging program of reform. He resigned in 1851 and returned to his law practice.

LANGEVIN, SIR HECTOR-LOUIS (1826–1906)

A Lower Canadian lawyer, Langevin began his political career as a journalist in the 1840s and was an early supporter of Confederation. Elected in 1857 to the House of Assembly, he tended to vote as an independent, but was linked ideologically with the Conservatives. A member of the Great Coalition of 1864, he participated in the Confederation conferences, promoting Canada East's claims to being a distinct society. After Confederation he held posts as secretary of state, superintendent general of Indian affairs, and minister of public works. After the death of Cartier, he became Macdonald's right-hand man in French Canada and leader of the Quebec wing of the

Conservatives. He ended his career in disgrace, under the shadow of alleged corruption.

LAURIER, SIR WILFRID (1841–1919)

A Lower Canadian lawyer, newspaperman, politician, and masterful orator, Laurier joined the Liberals of Canada East in 1864. He first ran for a seat in the House of Commons in 1874 and for the next four years set about gaining the confidence of his fellow Liberals, winning the portfolio of inland revenue in 1877. In 1878 Macdonald and the Conservatives returned to power. The next six years were difficult for Laurier, but in 1885, he rose to prominence again on the tide of the Louis Riel affair and the North-West Rebellion, and joined forces with Mercier's provincial Liberals. He spoke at the Champ de Mars gathering, a crowd of 50,000 that protested Riel's hanging. In 1887 he became leader of the Liberals, but he did not become prime minister until 1896.

MACDONALD, JOHN SANDFIELD (1812–1872)

An Upper Canadian lawyer and politician, Macdonald served on the Court of the King's Bench in the late 1830s. With Tory backing, he ran successfully in the first election of the United Province of Canada, but later declared himself a Reformer during the "Metcalfe Crisis" of 1843. He fell into conflict with Francis Hincks, but retained his seat as an independent Reformer in 1851 and by 1854 became the leader of a disunited Reform opposition. After the Macdonald-Cartier government fell in 1862, he entered the ministry with the portfolio of attorney general for Canada West and was premier until 1864. After Confederation, he became the first premier and attorney general of Ontario.

MACKENZIE, ALEXANDER (1822–1892)

An Upper Canadian businessman, journalist, and Canada's second prime minister, Mackenzie emerged as a leader of the Reformers in the early 1850s. In 1861 he was elected as a Reform member for the riding of Lambton, where he served until 1867. He supported Confederation, but not the Great Coalition of 1864. He had supported George Brown, but tended to act on the interests of his constituents over abstract principles, such as free trade. The Reform movement, long defined by local, sectarian interests struggled to establish itself as a party with a national vision in the Confederation period. Brown's departure from politics in 1867 created a vacuum that Mackenzie filled, first as a party manager, and then in 1873 as leader, taking the Liberal Party into federal office in the wake of the Pacific Scandal. Their platform reflected key liberal ideologies of free trade and free enterprise, although the party never developed strong cohesion under his leadership. He lost the election of 1878, but continued to sit in opposition and frequently crossed swords with Macdonald.

MACNAB, SIR ALLAN NAPIER (1798–1862)

An Upper Canadian politician and businessman, MacNab was a prominent member of the Family Compact and after the 1841 Act of Union he maintained a leading role in the Tory party. He helped reconstitute the party and nurtured Macdonald's political career. He proclaimed that "all my politics are railroads," and his questionable dealings in this business earned him political enemies. In 1854 the governor general invited him to be co-premier with Augustin-Norbert Morin (1803–1865), a position he held until cabinet resignations, in which Macdonald participated, forced him from office. He retired from Canadian politics for several years, but was elected to the legislative council for the Western division in 1860, and became its speaker in 1862.

MERCIER, HONORÉ (1840–1894)

A journalist, lawyer, and politician born in Canada East, Mercier was at first opposed to Confederation, but he eventually supported the idea, with some reservations. In 1871 he helped develop the platform of the Parti National, promoting unity in French Canada across political divides. Because of the Parti's still embryonic status, he sat as a Liberal in the House of Commons in 1872 and spoke on the issue of disallowance of the New Brunswick's Common Schools Act of 1871. He was not invited back into the Liberal fold for the election of 1874 and returned instead in an 1879 by-election, after which he became a rising star for the Liberals. By the mid-1880s he had became a key proponent of the "compact theory of Confederation" that emerged as a counter to Macdonald's centrist vision of Confederation. In the spontaneous assembly at Champ de Mars after Louis Riel's execution in 1885, Mercier promoted his vision of French-Canadian unity. Mercier was elected premier of Quebec in 1887.

MILLS, DAVID (1831–1903)

Originally an Upper Canadian teacher and school inspector, Mills acquired an interest in politics while supporting the Reformers' initiatives. In the 1860s he received a degree from the University of Michigan School of Law. His main aim appears to have been a political career and in 1867 he won the seat for Bothwell in the House of Commons as a Reform (later Liberal) candidate. He held the seat until 1882 and again from 1884 to 1896. He gained prominence as a defender of provincial rights from the opposition benches. In Alexander Mackenzie's government, he became the minister of the interior responsible for the North-West Territories and for Indian affairs. Back in opposition, he led many of the Liberals' attacks on the National Policy, and the Franchise Bill. He also criticized Macdonald's government in his capacity as editor-in-chief of the *London Advertiser* in the late 1880s. However, Mills did depart from Liberal views to support (in part) Macdonald's refusal to disallow the Jesuits' Estates Act in 1889. He also defended language rights in the west and supported separate schooling in Manitoba.

MOWAT, SIR OLIVER (1820–1903)

A former school-fellow of Macdonald at Kingston's Midland District Grammar School, Mowat began his law career in Macdonald's office, only leaving in 1840. Their political careers, however, followed different lines. He rose to public prominence as one of the prosecutors of Francis Hincks over the "£10,000 Job" affair. His political career grew as he participated in municipal politics in Toronto as a Reformer (later, as a Liberal). In 1858 he held a seat in the legislature for the first time. In 1861, he ran for two seats, and lost the Kingston seat to Macdonald. But in 1863 and 1864 he twice held the post of postmaster general. He served on George Brown's constitutional committee of 1864 and he participated in the Quebec Conference in October 1864. However, as the Liberal premier of Ontario between 1872 and 1896, he led the challenge to the British North America Act, as a key theorist in the provincial rights movement. In 1896 he joined Laurier's federal Liberals first as minister of justice and then as government leader in the Senate.

RIEL, LOUIS (1844–1885)

A Métis leader from the Red River Settlement, Louis Riel rose to prominence in 1869–1870 on the occasion of the transfer of Rupert's Land to the new Dominion of Canada. A Catholic French speaker, Riel had been educated at the Petit Séminaire de Montréal and returned to St. Boniface in 1868. While he had been gone, the ultra-Protestant Canadian Party of annexationists had exacerbated religious tensions within the colony. He led the Métis opposition to the survey party working to advance the transfer of the territory and orchestrated the resistance to the designate lieutenant-governor William McDougall (1822–1905), who prematurely declared the territory's transfer. The Métis' position, supported by other residents of Red River, was that they had not been properly consulted. Macdonald sent Special Commissioner Donald Alexander Smith to present the federal government's terms, and the resisters responded with a proposition to send a special delegation to Ottawa to negotiate the creation of Manitoba. The settlers at Red River organized a provisional representative government with Riel as its president, to articulate their terms of entry into Confederation. Members of the Canadian Party took the offensive, determined to undermine Métis influence in the region.

The creation of Manitoba went forward and Lieutenant-Governor Adams George Archibald (1814–1892) arrived in 1870 to establish the new government. Riel had begun to suffer from mental exhaustion while seeking a seat as a representative. In 1875 he was banished and fled south for five years over the Scott affair, and his mental condition deteriorated. He eventually settled down in Montana, until the Métis called him back in 1884. They were unhappy about the Canadian Pacific Railway and the threat it appeared to pose to their land titles and semi-nomadic way of life. Plains Cree leaders were also concerned. The call to action appealed to Riel's now almost messianic sense of vision for his people; however, events spiralled out of control into the violence of the North-West Rebellion. Riel was hanged for his part, on November 16, 1885.

SMITH, DONALD ALEXANDER, 1ST BARON STRATHCONA AND MOUNT ROYAL (1820–1914)

As a young man, Smith was a clerk with the Hudson's Bay Company (HBC), eventually attaining the position of commissioner of the Montreal department in 1868. In 1869, Macdonald appointed Smith a special commissioner for the federal government to help allay Métis fears about the transfer of Rupert's Land to Canada. He presented the government's intentions for the region and promised to confirm Métis land titles and grant representation on a territorial council. Riel accepted the proposition, and suggested a convention of forty representatives to consider the offer. Following the Red River negotiations, Smith accepted a post as president of the HBC's Council of the Northern Department and served for a short time as the governor of Assiniboia until the arrival of Lieutenant-Governor Adams George Archibald. He helped topple Macdonald's hold on power over the Pacific Scandal. Smith withdrew from politics in 1880 and was a junior partner in George Stephen's Canadian Pacific Railway bid.

SMITH, GOLDWIN (1823–1910)

A British-born writer, historian, and journalist, Smith rose to prominence as a proponent of the Manchester School—a group of thinkers who espoused free trade and anti-imperialism. In the mid-1860s, he resigned his position at Oxford University to travel to North America, where he taught at Cornell University for two years. In 1871 he moved to Toronto and helped found the *Canadian Monthly and National Review*, the *Evening Telegraph* newspaper, and other publications. His belief in classical liberalism was muted by his equal if not more vigorous belief in a nationalism focused on an Anglo-Saxon destiny. He rejected universal male suffrage and female suffrage, and believed the French Revolution to have been a calamity, and democracy a threat. He did, with great reluctance, support Macdonald's views on the National Policy.

TILLEY, SIR SAMUEL LEONARD (1818–1896)

A New Brunswick druggist, Tilley entered the political arena as a social reformer and temperance supporter. In 1854 he became the provincial secretary in a Reform government, giving him wide-ranging responsibilities until the government's dissolution in 1856. In 1857 he returned to government as a Reformer and became involved in the intercolonial railway scheme. Allied with his grand railway schemes was an equally expansionist vision of a North American union that extended beyond a Maritime union, which he outlined at the Confederation conferences. In 1865 Albert Smith (1822–1883) and the anti-confederates won the election, but when New Brunswickers returned to the polls in 1866, sentiment had turned in favour of Confederation in the wake of a Fenian invasion. Tilley's government passed the Quebec Resolutions and he participated in the London Conference, where he was credited with suggesting the name Dominion of Canada based upon Psalm 72:8, "His dominion shall be also from sea to sea." After Confederation, Tilley was minister of customs, and a two-time minister of finance. He served as lieutenant-governor of New Brunswick from 1873 to 1878 and from 1885 to 1893.

TUPPER, SIR CHARLES (1821–1915)

A Nova Scotian physician and politician, Tupper rose to prominence during the Confederation conferences. As a Conservative member in Nova Scotia, he advanced the interests of medicine and education. He helped negotiate the intercolonial railway with the Province of Canada, and paved the way to Confederation by opening discussions with Canada and the other Maritime colonies. He headed the Nova Scotia delegations to Charlottetown and Quebec, supporting Macdonald's vision of a highly centralized federation. In the negotiations, he surrendered Nova Scotia's right to collect customs duties, which left the province in a weakened financial position, embittering attitudes towards Confederation. Rather than risk losing a vote over the Quebec Resolutions in 1865, Tupper waited for a year. In 1866, by promising changes to the terms, he persuaded a positive vote by the legislature. He entered the federal government in 1867, where he helped reconcile Howe and the anti-confederates to Confederation. He became president of the Privy Council and minister of inland revenue in 1872, and minister of customs in 1873. Thrust into opposition in 1873, he distinguished himself as a Conservative critic of Mackenzie's Liberals.

When Macdonald returned to power in 1878, he made Tupper minister of public works, and in 1879, minister of railways and canals, and the Nova Scotian helped secure the contract for the Canadian Pacific Railway. In 1883 he accepted the unpaid postion of high commissioner in London, while still holding a cabinet post. In 1884 he resigned from cabinet and accepted a salary as high commissioner but remained active in Canadian politics, to the consternation of the Liberals.

In May 1896 Tupper was named prime minister of Canada after the Conservative government of Sir Mackenzie Bowell (1824–1917) foundered and Parliament was dissolved, but his party went down to defeat in a June election.

PREFACE

His loss overwhelms us. For my part, I say, with all truth, his loss overwhelms me, and that it also overwhelms this Parliament, as if indeed one of the institutions of the land had given way. Sir John A. Macdonald now belongs to the ages, and it can be said with certainty that the career which has just been closed is one of the most remarkable careers of this century.

— HON. WILFRID LAURIER

TRIBUTE TO SIR JOHN A. MACDONALD IN THE HOUSE OF COMMONS, 1891

Over the decades, Canadians have gathered at the foot of Sir John A. Macdonald's commanding statue in Kingston to commemorate our first prime minister.

Visiting there in 1941, Arthur Meighen summed up why Canadians honour Macdonald as we do. "We turn aside for a mere moment," he said, "to pay tribute where tribute is due and to gain inspiration if we can, courage if we can, wisdom if we can, at the fountain of history."

We still find all of these qualities in the study of Macdonald's life and legacy. In particular, his public addresses serve, even today, as a guide to Canadian nationhood, and we are pleased they are now being published.

The two-hundredth anniversary of our first prime minister's birth is now upon us. This special celebration is led by the non-profit, non-partisan Sir John A. Macdonald Bicentennial Commission, on which we serve jointly as honorary commissioners. It provides all Canadians—particularly young people—with an important opportunity to share Canada's national story with each other.

And what an inspirational story it is.

It tells of a man who arrived on our shores as an immigrant boy with his family, just as so many thousands do today, and who went on to found a transcontinental nation. With the able assistance of such partners as George Brown, George-Étienne Cartier, Thomas D'Arcy McGee, and others, Macdonald overcame so many imported differences and so much geography to bind us as one.

Lacking the great eloquence of his worthy opponent Wilfrid Laurier, Macdonald chose blunt words when presenting his challenge to the citizens of his day: "If we do not take advantage of the time, if we should ourselves be unequal to the occasion, it may never return," he said. "And we shall hereafter bitterly and unavailingly regret having failed to embrace the happy opportunity now offered of founding a great nation."

Canadians answered the call, and the nation the Father of Confederation envisioned is now nearing the dawn of its 150th year.

But the task of renewing and building Canada, as Macdonald's speeches remind us, is never complete. Nation-building in this new century will require new leaders, new visions of Canada, and new participants in the democratic process he bequeathed us.

This is why we encourage students and teachers from coast to coast to coast to study these addresses and become involved in the Macdonald bicentennial. By learning more about what first united Canadians in 1867, we can continue to strengthen those ties as Canada moves forward. This volume will serve as an excellent road map for Canadian students today and for generations to come.

In Sir John A.'s speeches are found the compromises, partnerships, and historical realities that continue to shape and refine Canada. But there are also great omissions. Aboriginal peoples were, in effect, left out of the nation-building exercise. Understanding such mistakes will help lead us to the reconciliation and healing our country so urgently requires.

Tomorrow's leaders are now hard at work in classrooms across the land. As they prepare to assume the mantle of leadership, we are confident that Macdonald's story will provide a steady guide.

"We are a great country, and shall become one of the greatest in the universe if we preserve it," he said. "We shall sink into insignificance and adversity if we suffer it to be broken."

Just as Macdonald was in his time, Canada's youth are up to the task ahead.

We commend these speeches by the first and founding prime minister to all Canadians.

KIM CAMPBELL
JEAN CHRÉTIEN
JOE CLARK
PAUL MARTIN
BRIAN MULRONEY
JOHN TURNER

As originally published in the Globe and Mail, *January 10, 2014*

INTRODUCTION

The non-partisan Sir John A. Macdonald Bicentennial Commission was established in Kingston in 2010, five years before the 200th anniversary of the birth of Canada's Father of Confederation. Members of the commission's steering committee, led by Robert P. Tchegus, carefully crafted our group's mandate. It was our pledge to "inspire a greater appreciation of the life and achievements of Sir John A. Macdonald of Kingston, Canada's Father of Confederation, by promoting events in the arts, education, tourism; and other sectors locally, regionally; and nationally in the countdown to the 2015 Bicentennial of Macdonald's birth, and to create an ongoing celebration befitting Canada's greatest statesman."

We believe that with the publication of *Canada Transformed* our commission has fulfilled what is the most important part of our mandate. I speak, of course, about education.

We are confident that in the years ahead students of Canadian history will often turn to this volume as they study Canada's earliest days as a nation, and that they will be joined by academics and other citizens in exploring these addresses.

In so doing, today's Canadians will embark upon a journey

of discovery, just as Sir John A. Macdonald did, which will remind them of the compromises made and challenges faced by our founders in creating a great nation. They will see that whatever the political or personal ups and downs Sir John A. encountered along the way, his confidence in Canada's future constantly shone through his addresses.

Canada was his cause and Canada was worth it.

"For twenty long years I have been dragging myself through the dreary waste of colonial politics," he said in Halifax in 1864. "I thought there was no end, nothing worthy of ambition; but now I see something is well worthy of all I have suffered in the cause of my little country. This question has now assumed a position that demands and commands the attention of all the colonies of British America. There may be obstructions, local difficulties may arise, disputes may occur, local jealousies may intervene, but it matters not—the wheel is now revolving, and we are only the fly on the wheel, we cannot delay it—the union of the colonies of British America under one Sovereign, is a fixed fact."

Almost thirty years later, in 1891, when placing his final election manifesto before the Canadian people, Sir John A. reminds them that their nation is a transcontinental reality. Canadians had achieved the impossible. "The Canadian Pacific Railway now extends from ocean to ocean, opening up and developing the country at a marvellous rate," he wrote. "The dream of our public men was an accomplished fact, and I myself experienced the proud satisfaction of looking back from the steps of my car upon the Rocky Mountains fringing the eastern sky."

No attempt has been made by the editors to ignore addresses by Macdonald that make unpleasant reading today, in modern Canada. A product of his times, Sir John A. was far from perfect.

As noted by Canada's former Prime Ministers already in this book, by studying the first Prime Minister's speeches concerning Aboriginal Canadians and Chinese Canadians we can all learn from past mistakes and devise a better future.

Finally, we hope that many readers of this volume will consider donating their copies to their local school, public, or post-secondary institution libraries, to help ensure that Sir John A. Macdonald's story will continue to be available to the leaders of tomorrow.

Wilfrid Laurier, in his tribute to Macdonald delivered in the House of Commons two days after Sir John A.'s death, put it best: "Before the grave of him who, above all, was the Father of Confederation, let not grief be barren grief; but let grief be coupled with resolution, the determination, that the work . . . shall not perish, but that though United Canada may be deprived of the services of her greatest men, still Canada shall and will live."

Sir John A. would agree that Laurier's challenge remains our challenge today. We believe that in the study of the Father of Confederation's most important public addresses will be found some of the inspiration and vision to inspire today's Canadians to take up the challenges of the future.

ARTHUR MILNES
Commissioner, Sir John A. Macdonald Bicentennial Commission
Kingston and Scarborough
April 2014

EDITOR'S NOTE

CEASELESS MOTION

With word and deed we insert ourselves into the human world and this insertion is like a second birth . . .

— HANNAH ARENDT
The Human Condition

REPRESENTING CANADA

The speeches collected here catch Sir John A. Macdonald (1815–1891) on the fly, and history off guard. Portraits and statues of Macdonald only hint at the peculiar coiled energy of his being. In life, Macdonald was a man in motion, a "thin spare form in ceaseless motion," as the *Globe* reported in 1860.[1] Too restless for the fine arts of oration, he "dashed" into "his speeches with the force of a whirlwind," wrote another reporter in 1861.[2] Macdonald talked for a living: beginning in 1844, he spoke to voters in seven elections held in the United Province of Canada (1841–1867), and in another seven in the Dominion of Canada before his death in office in 1891; he debated with the other elected representatives in fourteen Parliaments.[3] Macdonald's was the open-ended arena of politics, of contests as unpredictable and fateful as any battle. He fixed his life at the dynamic centre of a spinning-top Canada in a globalizing world, a nation transforming.

"The life of Sir John Macdonald," said his rival, Wilfrid Laurier, "from the date he entered Parliament, is the history of Canada; he was connected to and associated with all the events, all the facts which brought Canada" to its state in 1891. Laurier may have intended his words to cut two ways—Canada in the 1890s was still a nation of promise. But, Macdonald would probably have taken it as a compliment. Only the year before he had said, "If you look back upon the history of Canada since 1841, you will find that all the real progress that has been made by Canada, be it material or social, was made during the time when the Conservative influence was predominant." The future at his back, Macdonald watched the past recede.[4]

The speeches here provide a retrospective of Macdonald's role in shaping Canada. The editors allowed Macdonald's own interests to guide the selection of speeches. As a young politician, Macdonald spoke infrequently in the legislature. His private secretary, Joseph Pope (1854–1926), reported that Macdonald did "not think he [had] made more than five speeches during his first five sessions."[5] So, the speeches in the volume before 1854 are a fairly exhaustive record of the issues that brought him to his feet. After 1854, when he gained more responsibility and prominence, Macdonald did not necessarily choose the subject of his speeches and he spoke more often. The editors selected speeches where Macdonald transcended the topic at hand, to articulate his vision for Canada and of political leadership.

As a collection, Macdonald's statements and visions for Canada do read like a history of the country before and after Confederation. In the 1840s, he participated in the shaping of

responsible government in Canada. In the 1850s, he participated in the debates which indirectly marked a rapidly changing relationship between governments and their people. By the
mid-century, the colonial state had evolved to legislate in more
intensive ways in society—creating asylums, school systems and
other social institutions—and to help society absorb growing
numbers of immigrants.[6] It also took a directing role in public
works. By 1859, the Canadian government had helped finance
2,250 kilometres of track in Canada West.[7] The debates of the
era, however, continued to focus on constitutional matters and in
particular on the question of "representation by population"—
legislators, aware of their role in setting the moral foundations
of society, focused as much on establishing the representa-
tiveness of the values embodied in their laws, as on the laws
themselves. Should a government dominated by representatives in Canada East pass legislation for Canada West, or vice
versa? These were the pressing questions of a rapidly changing
society.[8] Macdonald's speeches of the 1860s connected with
the forging and consolidation of Confederation show that he
viewed the process much as historians have; as a multifaceted
philosophical, cultural, social, and personal affair, not just as a
legislative act.[9]

The speeches representing Macdonald after Confederation
were selected to show Macdonald fighting to fulfill a vision for
the country.[10] We see him at the centre of the struggle to incor-
porate the west in his transcontinental nation, and building
the Canadian Pacific Railway, nurturing the economy, defending the federal structure of Confederation against the growing
provincial rights movement, and imagining the future of the
British Empire. Macdonald's post-Confederation speeches also
show him as a cultivator of Canadian identity, as he reached out

to different social groups and provided means for public education and commemoration.

The book's limited space means that unwieldy or difficult speeches that did not provide clear statements about his vision for the nation were regretfully set aside. Likewise, this volume of speeches cannot represent aspects of Macdonald's career that he did not choose to make a matter of the public record.[11]

The chronological presentation of Macdonald's speeches allows us to appreciate his words for what they are—ephemeral acts, addressing an open-ended, unknown future. We can see Canada's transformations through his eyes, and we can even see a little past his own horizons, to appreciate and value what he could not.

We cannot hear, however, Macdonald's voice speaking directly through time in these pages. Rather, these are Macdonald's words as they fell on a reporter's ear, and were then printed and circulated in the press and semi-official government publications.

Harried, underpaid reporters sat into the wee hours of the morning taking shorthand notes of election speeches and the debates in the legislatures. Rushing against deadlines, they grappled rambling orations into condensed (usually by about one-third), third-person accounts. The later the hour or the nearer the printing deadline, the more abbreviated the text, but in general, one hour of speech filled three standard newspaper columns. Not until 1875 were parliamentary debates in Canada officially recorded. Not until 1909 were they recorded verbatim.[12]

REPRESENTATIVE GOVERNMENT

So, the form in which these speeches reach you, as printed transcriptions, is as important as their content. The very act of reading these speeches is to become Macdonald's audience, a member of the public that shaped representative government in Canada. Macdonald knew that his spoken words would circulate in print beyond his immediate interlocutors.

Political news and the printed legislative debates fed the Canadian press. By mid-century, Canada West supported 159 newspapers, and Canada East, 54.[13] They were local, and highly partisan, and survived by reporting politics.[14] Susannah (Moodie) Strickland (1803–1885), the celebrated observer of Canadian life, called the colony's papers "a strange mélange of politics, religion, abuse, and general information," which historians agree was a fair description. "The Canadian," she said, "cannot get on without his newspaper any more than an American without his tobacco."[15] This public insistence on monitoring Parliament helped reshape the structures of representative government so that it was more responsible to the elected chamber.[16]

Historian Jeffrey McNairn has shown that an informed, reading public created the conditions for responsible government to emerge in Canada.[17] The idea's genesis lay in the Rebellions of 1837–1838 and the resulting legislative union of Upper and Lower Canada into the United Province of Canada in 1841. Lord Durham (1792–1840), architect of the new government, recommended that the governor choose as his advisors—members of the executive council—men who could command a majority of the elected representatives in the legislative assembly. The printed gloss in the margin of his recommendations called it responsible government. Quite how this idea would be implemented was not known.[18]

Fatefully, Macdonald launched his political career in 1843, a turning point in the debate about responsible government in Canada. It was the contest where he declared his moderate Tory beliefs. It was the year of the "Metcalfe Crisis," as described in the first speech presented in this volume. In the twelve-month debate that ensued, Canadians rejected the idea of a constitution that balanced power between the Commons, the Lords, and the Crown as a living representation of society. Rather, intense discussion and debate in the press and face-to-face meetings at local associations revealed that society had changed too much. Democratic and republican ideals had infiltrated society too thoroughly. A landed aristocracy did not exist in Canada. But what did exist was a society with numerous land owners able to meet the threshold of the franchise—males over the age of twenty-one with property, who made up about twenty percent of the population. Many of them were literate and keen to take part in government and society.[19]

So, while nationalist and democratic movements swept across Europe and Latin America, post-Rebellion Canada further developed a deliberative democracy practised by a reading public (not all of whom had the right to vote); a consensus emerged in the debate about responsible government that parliamentary government—focused upon the debates of the elected representatives and the relationship between the representatives and the public—was best suited for Canada. The representative chamber, the house of assembly and later the House of Commons, increased in importance, while the other (traditionally hereditary or appointed) chamber, the legislative council and later the Senate, decreased. A role for the monarchy was retained in the figure of a governor general, who took advice on Canadian matters from leaders of majority in Assembly and their ministers.[20]

REPRESENTING MACDONALD

Macdonald's style of oratory and his vision of the elected representative's role must be understood in the context of the public's growing power through their consumption of the press. It helps to explain the sometimes pedantic style of his orations and shows a dynamic, rather than a reactionary, quality to his Conservatism.

Macdonald embraced traditional Tory views about social leadership. "Sir," he said, "in this House we are representatives of the people, and not mere delegates." He rejected the republican view that an elected representative was a mouthpiece for his constituency. Edmund Burke (1729–1797) best explains Macdonald's view: "Your [elected] representative owes you, not his industry only, but his judgment; and he betrays, instead of serving you, if he sacrifices it to your opinion."[21] However, without a landed aristocracy there was no structure to support a socially deferential confidence in elected members of Parliament among Canadians.

So Macdonald adopted other techniques in his speeches to win the voters' confidence in his judgment. Knowing that his words could be misconstrued, he avoided rhetorical flourishes, and his reasoning appears calculated to reach the reporter's notebook unedited. He spoke with the dry, evidence-based logic of the lawyer. He also spoke using the terms of Scottish moral philosophy, a social theory of sympathy, tolerance, and forbearance.

Macdonald used evidence from the past in order to convince the public of his sound judgment. Historical narratives and historical precedence still carried their own special authority in the nineteenth century, particularly because it was the basis for common law, as Macdonald well knew. His speeches often began with long historical preambles. He peppered them with references to events, past and contemporary, across the British Empire and the United States and cited directly from newspapers, books, and letters. Macdonald deployed evidence and the history in order to keep the record straight, to frame his reversals of position, to highlight his consistency. Macdonald worked very hard to make sure that voters saw the logic and consistency of his actions, as they unfolded over time.

He worked just as hard to demonstrate that he understood his voters and drew from a deep understanding of human nature informed by Scottish moral philosophy. Historians have tended to interpret Macdonald's facility with people and his tolerance for human foibles as a facet of his personality.[22] This may have been the case. But, it was also his expression of an eighteenth-century social philosophy that he applied to the rapidly evolving political arena in Canada.

He reached for an authentic speaking style best suited to this philosophical outlook. As one reporter for *The Leader* in 1861 explained:

> His delivery is the overflowing of a sensitive and powerful mind wholly given up to the subject and carried irresistibly along with the enthusiasm of honest conviction. A [D'Arcy] McGee may roar in polished phrases to an almost unattainable height, in the lofty branches of studied eloquence, and a [Lewis Thomas] Drummond* may descend to the no less powerful work of the drama, and clothe his enunciation in and borrow his style from the tragic—but both styles sink

---

* Presumably the reporter is referring to Lewis Thomas Drummond (1813–1882), an Irish-born Lower Canadian politician with notable powers of oratory. (Little, "Drummond, Lewis Thomas," *DCB*)

beneath the overwhelming avalanche of unstudied eloquence which bursts from the full heart, which scorns
all conventionalities and carries conviction to every
heart by the sheer force of sincerity, which speaks in
every sentence.[23]

Macdonald's "sensitive" mind and sincere delivery was a culti-
var of the Scottish moral philosophy. Popularized in Scotland,
the land of Macdonald's birth, by Adam Smith (1723–1790) in
his *Theory of Moral Sentiments*, the philosophy offered a theory
of community and society well into the nineteenth century. It
posited that guidelines for human behaviour, a sense of propriety and morality, sprang from the emotions. The exercise of
sympathy, and the imaginative understanding of another's expe-
riences, helped individuals perceive and calibrate collectively
held values and to form a moral community. Smith, according
to historian John Dwyer, "likened" the process, "to the tuning
of musical instruments." Sentimental attunement to the distress
and plight of others became an important aspect of sentimental-
ism that sustained movements for social justice like abolition-
ism. Smith, however, focused upon command of the self and its
desires as the avenue to this social understanding, such that self-
education and self-cultivation became lifelong responsibilities
for any social participant. When Macdonald, in these speeches,
urges others "to bear and forbear," promotes tolerance, speaks
of sympathy, and advocates sociability to drive the "crotchets"
out of men's minds, he is speaking this language.[24]

An eyewitness account published in 1883 described
Macdonald's sympathetic and imaginative understanding of
his Kingston voters in action in 1844. "Never," says the eyewitness, "did [Macdonald] lose temper, but good naturedly

waited till there was a lull in the disturbances." Later, "when silence was restored, [Macdonald] said he knew most of the electors, and they were all manly fellows—too manly, indeed, to refuse another fair play. They were opposed to him, he said, and they had a right to be, and he would not give much for them if they would not stand up for their own candidate; but if they had a right to their opinions—he had also a right to his. He only wished to present his side of the case, and if his hearers did not agree with him they might afterwards vote for whom they chose."[25] The capacity to educate the mind and to exercise social forbearance was a personal standard to which he held himself.

Used to being discussed in the press, Macdonald also spoke in the knowledge that his audience knew some basic facts of his biography. His near duel in 1849 with William Hume Blake (1809–1870), depicted in the "Fighting the Rebellion Losses Bill, 1849" speech in this book, was likely a matter of public knowledge if not scandalized gossip. As was his love of drink. Both biographical facts are important backdrops to the logic of his speech presented here as "Rejecting the Temperance Bill, 1853." Likewise, his (relative) poverty was an important statement. He did not enrich himself by his political career. Rather, he viewed his poverty as a statement of public-spirit- edness. Drawing attention to his modest means was a way of demonstrating his self-sacrifice for the nation; he referred, for example, in 1873 to "the enormous sacrifice of his personal and pecuniary interests" to politics. It was also the bar of civic engagement and hard work against which he judged the behav- iour of others, and the context for some of his intolerant and impatient remarks towards Canada's Aboriginal peoples who did not appear to embrace membership in the polity; people intent upon personal enrichment at the expense of the country; and, the Chinese, whom he did not understand at all.[26]

Creating a moral community lay at the heart of his leadership and his vision for Canada and he understood morality in eighteenth-century terms, as a dynamic, constantly renewing force. He created bounded spaces for renewal and progress— spaces such as the debating floor of the House of Commons, the arena of the British Empire, the national market protected behind the tariff walls of the National Policy, the transcontinental nation bound by the Canadian Pacific Railway. Political historian Janet Ajzenstat has argued that the Fathers of Confederation probably viewed parliamentary democracy itself as a source of identity for the new nation because it created an arena for renewal and reinvention.[27] For Macdonald, the entire nation was an arena for renewal.

PRESENTING MACDONALD'S SPEECHES

This presentation of Macdonald's speeches aims to preserve, as far as possible, the nineteenth-century reading experience. Such a collected volume did not then exist and a reader would have followed Macdonald's speaking career through a variety of published sources if he or she could not hear him speak in person on the hustings or in the legislative arena. The newspapers and semi-official publications were the main sources, but small collections of speeches were also published, and often reproduced in biographies. So, this volume has clearly indicated the sources of each speech to provide readers with more insight into the varied avenues by which Macdonald's spoken words entered the cultural arena.

The cross-section of sources used for the pre-Confederation period of his career in particular reflect the dynamic and varied sources of parliamentary and political knowledge. This volume includes examples from the three main colonial newspapers of the day—*The Globe, The Leader,* and the Montreal *Gazette*—and the smaller, but influential, Kingston *Chronicle and Gazette,* and *Chronicle and News,* and Ottawa *Daily Citizen.* It also includes speeches reproduced from semi-official parliamentary publications, *The Mirror of Canadian Parliament* and *Thompson's Mirror of Parliament.*

The colonial newspapers, and even the semi-official parliamentary organs, were partisan enterprises. For example, among the leading reporters of parliamentary news, Toronto's *Globe* tended to represent a Reform, or Liberal perspective, and Toronto's *The Leader* and the Montreal *Gazette,* a moderate conservative perspective. Macdonald for one complained that a person had to read "the *Colonist,* the *Leader,* as well as the *Globe,* in order to see fully both sides of the question under debate."[28] All ignored the debates given in French, and the French press appeared uninterested in printing political speeches from the legislature. The *Mirror of Parliament* publications were widely abused by the politicians for their inaccuracy. Historian Peter Waite, however, an expert on the colonial newspapers, reports that there was little to distinguish between a Reform report of a speech printed in the *Globe* and a Conservative report of the same speech printed in the *Leader.*[29] Excerpts from Macdonald's self-printed speeches are also included in this volume, to focus attention on his own words, just as the excepts were intended to do in the nineteenth century.

The Confederation-era speeches were drawn from a narrower array of sources, reflecting the increased stability and the search for authority in parliamentary reporting. Until 1875, the parliamentary debates were not officially published, but twentieth-century reconstructions of the debates have been produced, and they were used as the sources for this volume.[30] Also included are texts that were reproduced and circulated within contemporary publications, demonstrating the wider cultural reach of orations made on the legislature floor.

The speeches have been arranged to reflect the stages of Macdonald's career. Part One showcases his early career, beginning with his entry into provincial politics between 1843 and 1844, which beginning was termed a "birth" in the speech reproduced here as "Celebrating Forty Years in Politics, 1885." Part Two documents Macdonald's emergence as one of the leading statesmen of the United Province of Canada between 1854 and 1864. He held the portfolio of attorney general for Canada West between 1854 and 1862 and again from 1864 to 1867. He was co-premier between 1856 and 1857 and between 1864 and 1865 with Sir Étienne-Paschal Taché (1795–1865), and in 1857 and between 1858 and 1862 with George-Étienne Cartier. He was also a member of the Great Coalition of 1864 that helped to forge Confederation, as depicted in Part Three. Parts Four and Five showcase Macdonald's career as Canada's prime minister between 1867 and 1873 and between 1878 and 1891, and offer glimpses of his years in opposition during that period.

The speeches are presented as a series of self-contained portraits of an issue or episode in the story of Macdonald's relationship with Canada. They are meant to be like open windows onto a subject, and to complement other histories of Canada or the reader's basic knowledge. Brief endnotes and footnotes help place each speech in its wider historical context. The notes are all fully referenced and can suggest further reading; however, to save space, only the short titles of the referenced works are provided in the notes. The bibliography provides full references.

Over his career, Macdonald met and worked with a large number of people—mostly men. Where possible, these individuals have been identified and their lifespans indicated; within the speeches themselves, identities and lifespans are indicated in square brackets. Round brackets present within the speeches are original to the sources. Most of the individuals not identified by a lifespan are included in the "Directory of Key Names," which distils brief sketches from the *Dictionary of Canadian Biography (DCB)*.

The speeches from all the sources have been faithfully excerpted and transcribed. Spelling has not been modernized or standardized, and it varies between British and American forms—sometimes within the same speech—which was characteristic of the age. Macdonald himself attempted to impose some order in Canada's "official documents" in 1890 by directing that publications such as "the Canada *Gazette*" and "the Dominion Statutes," "uniformly" use the English "spelling of such words as 'honour,' 'favour,' 'labour,' 'honourable,' and the like," as he put it.[31]

A few obvious typographical errors in the original printed material have been corrected, and the spelling of Macdonald's name standardized, but where the meaning was not clearly evident, the errors are marked by [sic]. Where any text was illegible, a suggested text is presented in square brackets or the text is omitted with an ellipsis within square brackets ([. . .]). For particularly long and complex speeches, modern paragraphing has been introduced to help the reader, as has modern punctuation. Otherwise, the original text has been reproduced to give the flavour of the times.

Readers may notice that the meaning of some words shift over time—words such as "culture" and "race." The concept of culture, as a self-evident body of art or way of life, emerged over the nineteenth century. During Macdonald's lifetime, the word "culture," together with the word "civilize," still referred to a process of training—whether of nature or people. As the meaning of the word "culture" shifted, so did the word "race." At the outset of Macdonald's life, "race" tended to be used to mean "culture" in its emerging meaning—as a distinctive way of life. He uses it this way, for example, in the speeches collected here as "Thoughts on the Secret Ballot, 1846," or "'Best Speech Mr. Macdonald Ever Delivered,' 1861." But, towards the end of the century, "race" acquired a newer meaning, denoting unchangeable and determining biological differences specific to human groups. Macdonald himself offers a vivid explanation of this later nineteenth-century concept of "race" when he debated the merits of extending the franchise to the Chinese, reproduced here as part of "The Franchise Debates, 1885." The shift in the term's use did not happen abruptly, and it was often used in its cultural and biological senses within the same period. So, Macdonald did not necessarily have an idea of biological race when he uses the word at other times, even in 1885. Finally, the word "Indian" has also undergone an evolution, over a much longer timeframe. The readers will find the term "Indian" used throughout this book in the speeches themselves, and when specific historical events are discussed, but the term "Aboriginal" is used to denote the group's broad historical experience and identity.[32]

Many of the speeches have also been excerpted from larger debates and longer statements. For the sake of space, many of the preambles have been removed, but enough exist in the present volume to give the reader an idea of Macdonald's historical style of constructing arguments. Would that the speeches assembled here serve the same function as these historical preambles and assemble a historical accounting of Macdonald's life as he spoke it to Canadians past.

DR. SARAH KATHERINE GIBSON
Queen's University, Department of History, Kingston Ontario

PART ONE

BIRTH OF A
PARLIAMENTARIAN

DECLARING FOR THE CROWN
AND FOR BRITAIN, 1843

KINGSTON, CANADA WEST, DECEMBER 4

The mayor of Kingston called a public meeting on December 4, 1843. A pall of mourning still hung thick. The Legislative Assembly had voted to remove the capital from Kingston to Montreal. Then Governor General Lord Metcalfe's ministers resigned, in a demonstration of emerging party organization in Canada, after he denied Reformers Robert Baldwin and Louis-Hippolyte La Fontaine a request to allow the ministers to dispense patronage. Government was at a standstill. That day, many Kingstonians rallied to support Metcalfe's vision of responsible government that included the governor's prerogative in dispensing patronage. Macdonald, a newly married and up-and-coming lawyer and a recently elected alderman, rose to decry the Reformers; he gained the attention of the Tories in the ensuing election campaign Metcalfe helped orchestrate.[1]

Kingston's Chronicle and Gazette *reported on December 6, 1843:*

J. A. MACDONALD: proposed the second resolution and remarked that after the long speeches which had been made, he would not detain the meeting. The heart of the matter at issue was of great importance and both parties should consider it with calmness. [. . .] British supremacy was involved in the question before them, and if they did not support the Governor General [Lord Metcalfe] they would be giving their adherence to Republicanism.

All the defences of the country and the advantages enjoyed by its inhabitants from their connection with the Mother Country would be cut off. It was very naturally supposed that after having been so long without legislation the late Ministry would have effected some good for the country—these hopes have been disappointed, and he [Macdonald] thought the Ministry had taken their recent step for the purpose of embarrassing the Governor.

An antagonism had long existed and the Council knew the fact well. Their resignation on the principle of Responsible Government was mere clap-trap—patronage was the true cause. Mr. [Robert] Baldwin thought that after having carried the Seat of Government measure, he was to have every thing his own way. When the Seat of Government was removed to Lower Canada, the Executive would be surrounded by Mr. [Louis-Hippolyte] Lafontaine's favourites and all the offices would be filled from those ranks.

Was not His Excellency as good a judge of the claims and qualifications of Candidates for office as the Ministry. If, for instance, an office were to become vacant in the Midland District, would that Ministry which had done everything in its power to ruin us, be the proper body to fill those offices— would they not be desirous of making appointments disadvantageous to our best interests? And if there was one prerogative more than another which His Excellency should freely exercise it was that of giving his assent to Acts of Parliaments. (The learned gentleman was here interrupted by the noisy conduct of the meeting).

He [Macdonald] concluded by moving the 2d Resolution, which was seconded by John Walkins, Esq.

2nd resolved, That the firm, manly and vigorous way in which His Excellency has maintained the Prerogative of the Crown and at the same time upheld the just rights of all classes of the people, entitles him to our confidence, and we entertain a confident hope that the Province at large will uphold His Excellency in the course of policy avowed by him.

UPHOLDING THE ELECTION LAW, 1844

HOUSE OF ASSEMBLY,
MONTREAL, DECEMBER 19

Macdonald took his first seat in Canada's Legislative Assembly on November 28, 1844.[2] Tory and Conservative forces had carried the election. Three weeks later he made his first speech, and it was to challenge Robert Baldwin himself. Macdonald rose to question the legality of a petition challenging the elections of the Conservative-leaning George Moffatt (1787–1865) and Clément-Charles Sabrevois de Bleury (1798–1862) to the Montreal city riding; the two men were accused of winning their seats by bribery and corruption.[3] The Montreal Gazette *reporting a few days later wrote, "Mr. Macdonald, who moved the adjournment is evidently not used to parliamentary debate, but he as evidently has the stuff in him. He gathered up the scattered strands of argument with great dexterity, and knitted them up like a man used to the work of reply."[4]*

The Montreal Gazette *of December 21, 1844, reported:*

MR. MACDONALD, (Kingston,) in reply to the observations of the Hon. Member for the Fourth Riding of York [Robert Baldwin], contended that the Hon. and learned gentleman was mistaken in supposing that the law did not require parties petitioning, to be resident at the place where the election took place, and that if afterwards they become residents it would be sufficient.

The Hon. and learned Member for Quebec [Thomas Cushing Aylwin (1806–1871)] did not adopt that line of argument, because he saw it was an unsound one. He (Mr. Macdonald) contended that the whole of the argument upon this subject used by Sir William Follett, which had been referred to, was sustained, and it was a principle not only of law but of common sense; that parties not residing at the place of election cannot be aggrieved by the return.* It could not be contended that they had sustained a wrong, and it would be out of their power to make the affidavit which is required by the statute. He contended that the first ground of objection was not answered for this way, [for] the law of Lower Canada [in this regard] was the same as the law of England. And the argument used must apply with equal force in the one case as in the other; the second ground of objection, he thought, was equally unanswerable. It was true that the Magistrate had taken it upon himself to state that the oath which had been taken was according to law, but

---

* Macdonald is referring to Sir William Webb Follett (1796–1845), British solicitor general twice in the 1830s and 1840s and attorney general from 1844 to 1845. The report of Macdonald's speech published in the *British Whig* of December 24, 1844, indicates Sir Robert Peel (1788–1850) as the authority mentioned, suggesting Macdonald is referring to a similar debate in Britain's House of Commons over the Controverted Elections Act of 1839. Sir Robert Peel, prime minister of Britain from 1834 to 1835 and 1841 to 1846, argued that the House should judge its own cases, rather than involve another body, in order to preserve historical rights in the matter, primacy within Parliament, and "moral authority" in public. Peel believed that representatives trying their own cases impartially, without descending into messy partisan politics, would reinforce the House's moral authority to lead, rather than be led by, public opinion. (Prest, "Sir Robert Peel, second baronet, prime minister," *ODNB*; Cragoe, "Sir Robert Peel and the 'Moral Authority' of the House of Commons, 1832–41," 55, 57, 66, 69; Hamilton, *rev.* Pugsley, "Follett, Sir William Webb," *ODNB*; http://hansard.millbanksystems.com/people/sir-william-follett/; *Debates of the United Province of Canada*, vol. iv, pt. 1, 524)

he contended that that House was the only competent judge as to whether the oath had been administered according to law. The last objection which had been taken was that the parties entering into recognizances had not [been] justified according to law, and it was fully sustained by reference to the Law itself, which requires that parties entering into recognizances in Lower Canada must be freeholders, no matter what amount of personal property they might possess. It seemed to him, therefore, upon all these grounds, that the petition could not be supported, and to settle the precedent, he would move that the further considerations of the question be deferred until the 11th day of January next.

DEFENDING PRIMOGENITURE, 1845

HOUSE OF ASSEMBLY, MONTREAL,
JANUARY 30

In January 1845 the leading reformer in Canada West, Robert Baldwin, urged a debate on the issue of primogeniture, saying that "the sooner the great principles of the social system" in the United Province of Canada "were settled, the better." He believed that the people of Canada West, inspired by their neighbours to the south, wished to change the inheritance laws. At issue was a bill proposed by John Roblin (1799–1874) to distribute equally the estates of parents who died without wills. Baldwin saw the debate as a signal occasion for responsible government in the Province of Canada, where the legislature could be guided by public opinion. Macdonald did not agree with Baldwin's proposal.[5]

The Montreal Gazette *of February 1, 1845, reported:**

MR. MACDONALD of Kingston had heard, with surprise, and regret, the Hon. Member for the 4th Riding of York [Robert Baldwin], after declaring that the system, now attempted to be

---

* The blurred text in the *Gazette* was reconstructed from the *Debates of the Legislative Assembly of United Canada*, vol. 4, 1844-5.

introduced, was liable to great objections which were not applicable to the old one, state his intention to support it. He had thought that his motto was "*Fiat justicia, rual caelum.*" And after this acknowledgement he would vote for a measure which he knew to be a bad one, because he had taken it into his head that the people of Upper Canada required it. In what manner had he obtained the opinion of which he had spoken? Had any pledge in favour of this measure been exacted by any constituency in Upper Canada? There were but two legal and Parliamentary means of learning what were the opinions of the people—petitions and public meetings, and there had been neither of these in its favour. The great majority of the people were against this measure as anti-British and anti-Monarchical; it ought not to be introduced here, for the very reason that it had been introduced into the United States; it was folly to raise a Monarchical structure upon Republican foundation. The law of primogeniture was the great bulwark between the people and the Crown, and the Crown and the people. The measure intended to be introduced was against the first principles of political economy, it was calculated to make the poor poorer, that which was a comfortable farm-house in one generation, a cottage in the second, and a hovel in the third; and under it, agriculture, instead of becoming a science, would be degraded, as it was in Ireland and France, to a mere means of life. He [Macdonald] would refer honourable gentlemen opposite to an article contained in *Blackwood's Magazine*, a publication not much given to Tory principles, upon this very subject. It quotes the opinions of three travellers; Birkbeck,* in speaking of France, says, "The

---

* Presumably Morris Birkbeck (1764–1825), whose two books about the agricultural promise of Illinois became sensationally popular in Western Europe. (Erickson, "Birkbeck, Morris," ODNB)

partition of farms goes on from generation to generation, as the people increase in numbers, society is constantly retrograding, there is no improvement, and no hope of it." Arthur Young,[*] whose travels through France became the means of improving the agriculture of England, and raising it to its present position, gives as strong testimony upon the subject; and the son of William Cobbett[†] writing from France in 1823, says:—"I hear on all sides, the greatest complaints of this Revolutionary Law, by its action society is disgraced in the extreme, and some persons, in spite of the Act, are returning to their ancient custom." Chancellor Kent,[‡] of the United States, says:—"Large properties continuing in the same hands, tend to the advancement and improvement of the people." The evil of the partition law in the United States has not been generally felt, because of the safety valve of the West; but in some of the older States it had been felt already, and the Legislatures of Maryland and Connecticut had been compelled to alter it, and assimilate it to the law of Scotland, giving the estate to the oldest, subject to the charge of annuities to the younger. The greatness of England was owing to its younger sons, it was they who had spread the name, the fame, and the glory of England over the world; they formed its colonies, led its armies and navies, they were its statesmen and its scholars. Yes, it was the youngest sons of England, that

---

* Arthur Young (1741–1820) was a celebrated and influential promoter of agricultural reform in Britain. In 1793 he published an account of his observations about farming practices in France and other countries, gleaned during a three-year tour in the 1780s. (Mingay, "Young, Arthur," *ODNB*)

† William Cobbett (1763–1835) was an English pamphleteer, farmer, and journalist. (Dyck, "Cobbett, William," *ODNB*)

‡ James Kent (1763–1847) was chancellor of New York in 1814 and published *Commentaries on American Law* (1826–1830). (Butler, "Kent, James," *DEAP*)

had made her great in peace and war. What would have been the younger Pitt or Fox,* if, instead of being sent forth to seek their fortunes, the estate of their father had been divided? They would have been mere country squires, instead of becoming, as they did, the lights of the world. What would the Duke of Wellington have been, if the paternal estate had been divided? It was fortunate for him, for this country, and the world, that he was left with his sword in his hand, and that sword was all he had. The Members of Upper Canada would be madmen to support an alteration in the law of primogeniture, an alteration which it was acknowledged by its supporters to be contrary to justice and quality, but expedient because it pleased the people.

---

* William Pitt (1759–1806), "Pitt the Younger," a second son, became prime minister of Britain. Charles James Fox (1749–1806), also a second son, became a celebrated politician and leader of the Whigs. (Ehrman and Smith, "Pitt, William," ODNB; Mitchell, "Charles James Fox," ODNB)

CHALLENGING THE USURY LAWS, 1846

Macdonald regarded his first speech in the legislative assembly as his address advocating the repeal of usury laws, during which he demonstrated his understanding of contemporary British philosophy and of utilitarianism. The moral stigma against usury meant that, in Britain, at least, politicians allowed usury laws to fall into disuse rather than risk difficult debates, and the laws were not repealed there until 1854. Macdonald's liberal, pragmatic views on the subject were in keeping with the trend in the Province of Canada towards liberalizing the lending and debt laws.[6]

As recorded in the Mirror of Parliament of the Province of Canada, being the 2nd Session of the 2nd Parliament, *April 27, 1846:*

MR. MACDONALD of Kingston—In this case like all other innovations upon old prejudices, (and it was purely prejudice that enacted these laws) it would have to be a long time before the public before this principle as well as unshackled trade, would be received with favour.

That great English writer, Jeremy Bentham, whose work

on the subject of the Usury Laws,* Sir James Macintosh† pronounced unanswered and unanswerable, laid it down as a
proposition that could not be disputed, that every adult of a
sane mind has a right to lend money on any terms he pleases;
and every adult of a sane mind has a right to borrow money on
any terms he pleases; and any restriction upon this liberty is an
infringement of natural right.

It is said of this, Oh! this sounds very well in theory, but
it will never do to practice. He [Macdonald] could not understand how—when a theory was correct, the practice of that
theory would not be correct also. At the present time usury
was practised secretly, and the borrower had to pay not only for
the value of the money, but also for the risk run by the usurer,
in consequence of the penalties. Many properties were sold by
Sheriff's sale for the sixth of their value, which would have been
saved to their owners, if they had been allowed to pay a higher
rate of interest than six per cent, and thus obtain money.

Many such instances had occurred within his knowledge.
It was a common thing among young merchants, when pressed
for money, to send part of their stock to auction, and sell it at
a ruinous sacrifice, which they would not have been obliged
to do, if the usury laws were abolished. He referred to several
instances that are mentioned in Kelly on Insurance of the bad
and ruinous effect of the Usury laws upon the merchants.

---

* Jeremy Bentham (1748–1832) was a British philosopher noted for his contributions to the
philosophy of utilitarianism, along with James Mill (1773–1836), John Stuart Mill (1806–1873),
and Henry Sidgwick (1838–1900). The book is Bentham's *Defence of Usury: Shewing the impolicy
of the present legal restraints on the terms of pecuniary bargains in a letter to a friend to which is added a
letter to Adam Smith* (London, 1787). (Scruton, *A Dictionary of Political Thought*, 38, 298-9, 480)

† Sir James Mackintosh (1765–1832) was a British political writer and Whig politician who
gained recognition in the era of the French Revolution; in 1830 he published *Dissertation
on the Progress of Ethical Philosophy*. (Finlay, "Mackintosh, Sir James, of Kyllachy," *ODNB*)

ARGUING FOR IMPORT DUTIES, 1846

In the spring of 1846 the system of preferential trade laws that had shaped the Canadian economy started to crumble. Britain's Conservative government led by Sir Robert Peel (1788–1850) repealed the Corn Laws at the height of the potato blight in Ireland. The subsequent Whig government of Lord John Russell (1792–1878) also promoted free trade, repealing it and other protective laws gradually until 1849. The colonies scrambled to maintain their balance in a new economic order. The issue at hand on April 28, 1846, was a prior decision by the House to levy duties on leather goods entering Canada by the United States. William Henry Draper's conservative followers still holding the House proposed to protect the leather industry with a differential duty on leather goods entering by sea (5%) or by Toronto or Kingston (25% or 30%).The opposition noted its differential effects on Upper and Lower Canada. Macdonald rose to offer his analysis.[7]

As reported in the Mirror of Parliament of the Province of Canada, being the 3nd session of the 2nd Parliament, *for April 28, 1846:*

MR. MACDONALD, Kingston, said that a bill was passed last
session giving protection to the manufactures of this colony,
and the measure now proposed by the Administration was
expressly for the purpose of making the bill of last session effectual, and if hon. members did not make up their minds to carry
it through, then they must give up all they had fought for, all
they had gained, and resolve to put our manufactures in competition with the convict labour of the American Penitentiary.
With respect to Mr. Gladstone's despatch at which hon. gentlemen seemed to take so much umbrage, whether the principles
enunciated in that despatch were right or wrong, they must
be governed by it.* (Mr. Aylwin†—we know that.) And he
[Macdonald] hoped hon. gentlemen would not now raise the
question, whether they must submit to the dictation of that
despatch. They must do so. They were bound to do so, and
as a mere matter of interest, leaving aside altogether a higher
principle they would find they would have to submit to it. The
danger to our markets was not from British but American manufactures, and whilst British manufactures coming through the
United States must of course pay the high duty, coming by the
St. Lawrence they would pay an *ad valorem* duty of five per cent,
and if hon. gentlemen wished the country to enjoy that protection they must vote with the Ministry.

---

* Macdonald may have been referring to a dispatch of February 13, 1846, from the secretary of the colonies, William Ewart Gladstone (1809–1898), in which he insisted that
the duties imposed by the colonial legislature on leather goods be reduced. He raised
the possibility of disallowing the Canadian law. That February, Gladstone also followed
through on the new British laissez-faire ethos and did not guarantee further Canadian
loans for large projects like railways. He also called the legislature's attention to the need
to make payments into Britain's Sinking Fund. (Piva, *The Borrowing Process 1840–1867*,
62; *Mirror of Parliament*, April 28, 1846, 109)

† Mr. Thomas Cushing Aylwin (1806–1871)

THOUGHTS ON THE SECRET BALLOT, 1846

Turbulence at election time in Canada East and Canada West begged for electoral reform. Riots and fatalities often occurred; betting happened publicly at open-air polls. Fraud and intimidation were rife. The Reformers were keen to institute practices used in the United States to diminish voting problems. An 1842 election act minimized some problems, but the polls still tended to be overcrowded and prone to violence. In Montreal in particular, riots marred city and federal elections in 1844. By 1846, electoral violence there had become routine. After yet another episode, the Assembly began debating a "bill for establishing vote by ballot at Municipal Elections in Montreal." Macdonald looked at the issue from another perspective.[8]

As reported in the Mirror of Parliament of Canada, being the 2nd session of the 2nd Parliament, *May 13, 1846*:

MR. MACDONALD, Kingston, said if the system of voting by ballot was beneficial to Montreal, it would be equally so in all parts of the Province and in the House. What is the principle which the ballot system advocates? To obtain secrecy of a vote.

This he [Macdonald] contended the system would be unable to perform in Canada. The people there had no one exercising an illegitimate influence over them, as in England and other European countries. Every man in Canada would, and did, make public his opinions, and therefore defeated the object of the ballot. By that system the innocent would frequently suffer with guilty. When there were such a connexion of different races, each would be expected to vote for his countryman, and treated accordingly by the party in opposition. In New York the grossest frauds in voting were practised by that system. Should any person be charged of being elected by false votes, it could be examined by the House.

LEARNING THE LESSONS ON EDUCATION: HIS FIRST BILL, 1847

HOUSE OF ASSEMBLY,
MONTREAL, JULY 9

In May 1847, a disorganized and crumbling party of moderate Conservatives offered Macdonald the position of receiver general. He accepted, but only on the condition, as he wrote, that he address an issue "which operates on the principles or prejudices of the public, if Conservatives hope to retain power, they must settle it before the general election." He meant the university endowment question—the vexing question of the just distribution, in a religiously plural society, of an 1828 grant (of about 91,469 hectares) for an Anglican institution, King's College, chartered in 1827. While King's College was relatively liberal, fierce opposition to state support of one denomination revealed the extent to which Canadians continued to view religion as a key organizing principle of the arts and sciences.

On July 9 Macdonald tabled his first bills, both relating to the "University Question," as it was informally called. They restored King's College to Anglican control and placed the university endowment under the joint control of King's College, the Methodist Victoria College of Cobourg, and Roman Catholic Regiopolis College and Presbyterian

*Queen's College at Kingston. Funds were apportioned to each institu-
tion. They also made provisions for an agricultural college. So intense
were the feelings aroused that the debate happened on the first reading.
The bills went no further and Parliament was prorogued and the 1848
election called.9*

*Macdonald's long-term private secretary recorded Macdonald's
brief speech on the occasion:10*

MR. MACDONALD SAID: At an early date [in 1798], out of
the Crown Lands of the Province, Government set apart a large
amount of 500,000 acres for District School[s] and [University]
Instruction; but the intentions of the Government of that day,
in this respect, were not carried out. The Government set apart
half of the best of these Lands for the support of a University,
which obtained its Charter under the name of King's College.
Afterwards,* the Charter was amended, for the purpose of liberalizing it, as the former Charter was strongly objected to, on
the grounds that the College would be altogether too exclusive;
but, instead of healing the rancorous feeling that was then exhibited, it has been made the subject of religious discussion, and all
parties are now loudly demanding a settlement of the Question.
Several attempts had been made to settle it; but they have all
failed, because the schemes that were proposed did not come
home to the people: and the people had no interest in them. The
Government were now prepared to propose a Measure, which,
he [Macdonald] hoped would meet the assent of all parties.

---

* In 1837, the institution's charter was amended to remove the College from Anglican
control and make the Crown's largesse available to other religious denominations and
their colleges, which emerged by the early 1840s. In 1843 Robert Baldwin had proposed
a 108-clause bill aimed to create one large nonsectarian university and to turn the other
colleges, including King's, into constituent parts. (Moir, *Church and State in Canada
West*, 83-4, 88).

WINNING THE VOTER WITH
THE UNIVERSITY QUESTION, 1847

LAMBTON HOUSE,
KINGSTON, DECEMBER 20

*Macdonald's first bill had failed to pass legislature, but he made the
University Question his signature cause during the campaign of 1847,
which he ran against a young reform candidate, Kenneth Mackenzie.
On December 20, "electors of the City" of Kingston, "favorable to the
return of the Hon. John A. Macdonald, crowded into Lambton House
to hear him speak."*

The Kingston Chronicle and News *reported on December 22,
1847:*

The HON. JOHN A. MACDONALD rose, amidst loud
cheers, to address the meeting. The hon. gentleman [Macdonald]
stated that on two former occasions he had appeared before the
electors of the City as a candidate for their suffrages: on the first
he was elected by an overwhelming majority to represent them
in Parliament: on the second he was returned without opposition. In the first contest he had stood before them unknown as

a public man, and untried, and yet they had reposed sufficient confidence in him to charge him with the care of their particular interests, and with a share in the general legislation of the country. He now appeared as a candidate under different circumstances.

During his brief career he had borne some part in the government of the province, and he was now to be judged by his acts, not by any hopes which might be entertained of his willingness or ability to serve them. It was by their judgment upon these acts that he was prepared to stand or fall. It would certainly afford him matter of sincere regret if the event should prove that he had forfeited their confidence, but he had not the slightest reason to believe such to be the case.

When he first took his seat within the walls of the House of Assembly, and for a period of two years, he occupied the position of an independent member: at the expiration of that period, however, he was called upon to assume the highly responsible post of Receiver General, with a seat in the Executive Council; and since the time of his entry into administration he held himself responsible to his constituents and the country, not only for his individual acts, but for the general conduct of the government; and as an individual, and as a member of the government, he was prepared to show that his own exertions and those of the Council of which he formed a part, had been directed to measures calculated to benefit the whole province, at the same time that he had neglected no available opportunity of advancing the interests of this city and district.

He had already, on several occasions, in ward meetings, entered into those explanations which the fact of a dissolution of the House and an appeal to the country seemed to require at his hands, and he had no doubt that many who were now around him had been present on one or more of these occasions; but this more general assemblage of the electors, although called together for the purpose of making necessary arrangements for the nomination day, afforded him an opportunity of exhibiting more fully than he had hitherto done the nature of the great question in issue, and the course which he had pursued in reference to the University question.

He need hardly tell them that if his colleagues and himself had so determined, they might have continued in office for another twelvemonth; they might have permitted the existence of the late Parliament during its full legal term. If ministers were justly amenable to the charge made against them by their opponents, that their only desire was to retain office, this would certainly have been the case; but the ministry pursued a different course, and in their determination they were strengthened by the fact, that whatever part the conduct of the government bore in the pacification of the country—whether or not it had produced or aided it—certain it was, that never in the history of the colony was there exhibited a greater absence of political strife, and the bitterness of feeling which it engendered. And no time was better fitted than the present for that calm consideration and unprejudiced determination of political questions which the ministry desired to be extended to the policy of their government than the present. Then there was another consideration almost of equal importance, arising as it did in the convenience of the people. By the dissolution, the elections will take place at a period of the year of all others the best suited to the convenience of the great body of the people, especially to that of the farmers of the country, whereas had Parliament continued until the end of its constitutional existence, the Elections would have taken place next August or September, when the inconvenience of attending to them would be very great. All that his colleagues and himself desired, was a full, free and fair expression of the opinion of the country. They did not cling to office—they desired not to retain office by resort to any quirk or dodge or anything of the kind. They afforded the best possible proof of this in offering the fairest chance, the greatest facilities to the exercise of opinion. They threw themselves unreservedly upon the people of the country. He was aware that it had been said that ministers were compelled to a dissolution by Lord Elgin.* The assertion was a foul, wanton falsehood. He (Mr. Macdonald) stated boldly upon his word of honor as a gentleman—he asserted as a member of the administration, that Lord Elgin had not the slightest knowledge of the intentions of ministers on this point until they were laid before his lordship—nor had his lordship expressed any desire that they should resort to a dissolution, or interfered in the matter in any way. The resolution to dissolve parliament and appeal to the people was the act of the ministry alone. They had been frequently challenged by their opponents to place themselves at the bar of public opinion, and they determined to accept the challenge. (Hear, and cheers.) When the University Bill was brought in, they were told that so important a measure should not be decided without a direct appeal to the country, and the assertion was accompanied with the taunt that ministers dare not submit their scheme to such a test. But what was their answer? The dissolution and the appeal were the answer. (Cheers.) That question is now fairly before the country. Ministers claim the

---

* Lord Elgin was newly installed as governor general for the Province of Canada in 1847 when the administration of William Henry Draper (1801–1877) requested dissolution due to the lack of support from French-speaking Reform members. Elgin had tried to mend the breach and avoid the dissolution. (Morton, "Bruce, James, 8th Earl of Elgin," *DCB*)

support or the opposition of the people of Upper Canada on that bill.

He [Macdonald] said he would enter into some details to show to the meeting the real nature of the question before them. In 1798 there was an appropriation of the School Lands in the Province for the establishment, first, of Grammar Schools in the several districts, and afterwards of an University. It was arranged at that period that there should be four of these grammar schools put in operation, one at Newark (now Niagara), one at Sandwich, one at Kingston, and one at Cornwall. The University was to be established at York. There was a grammar school established in this District, and for some time it was in a most flourishing condition. He (Mr. Macdonald), his friend Mr. Smith, and others, had been educated there. But when the idea of a great University at Toronto was entertained and acted upon, the Grammar School here was broken up, or at least so reduced in its resources as to be altogether unlike what it was intended to be. King's College was established, but on a basis so exclusive as to give offence to a great portion of the people, and the consequence was, public meetings and protests, laying the foundation of an agitation which has been long maintained. King's College was undoubtedly a noble institution, an ornament to the country, and one of the best schools of learning on the continent. That was generally admitted. Yet it did not afford those facilities for education which it was very evident the great body of the people desired. The necessity of sending youth to Toronto to obtain the advantages of an University education formed a great barrier to the utility of the system. Mr. [Robert] Baldwin, during his administration, introduced a bill to change the character of the institution. But that bill did not propose to remedy what was really the evil. He proposed to establish a great godless university; in which it was proposed to teach men everything but that which it most concerned them to know—that religious morality which formed at once the bond of social union in this life, and was in some measure a preparation for that hereafter. The attempt hitherto made to create and maintain such institutions had been very few in number, and they had failed. On this continent Girard College [in Philadelphia, U.S.] was the only institution which formed an exception to the rule that its educational establishments are under the guidance of some one religious denomination. Mr. Baldwin's bill failed, as did likewise the bill introduced by that gentleman's successor, Mr. [William] Draper. He (Mr. Macdonald) has supported Mr. Draper's bill through two sessions, but the discussion to which these measures had given rise convinced him that a bill materially different was required to satisfy the people of the country, and when he came into the government he applied himself to the maturing of a measure which would in his opinion suit their requirements. He felt, indeed, that unless the question was so settled; unless that the settlement was such as to command the assent of the great mass of the people, there would be no peace; and he entered upon the task in that spirit. He felt that, in proposing a measure, he had some personal advantage in not having been previously in any way mixed up with the parties, and as a presbyterian, he would not be considered as having an undue partiality to those in whose hands the University was placed. And when he had matured that bill which was now before the people, and presented it to gentlemen in the House connected with the Church of England, he was pleased to say it to their credit, that although of the members of the House representing Upper Canada, upwards of thirty were attached to the Church of England—although that bill proposed to take from them an income now amounting to £11,000, and one which in five years will amount to £16,000, and gave them in lieu but £3,000, they readily assented, for the sake of peace, to a settlement upon that basis. He then consulted others. The Rev. Mr. McNab, the Principal of Victoria College, who was then in Montreal, at once gave his approval of the plan, observing, however, that from their numbers the Methodist body were entitled to a somewhat larger portion. He (Mr. Macdonald) also met the Roman Catholic bishop of Kingston, who likewise gave the scheme his approval. He also wrote to the Synod of the Presbyterian Church in connection with the Church of Scotland, and resolutions in favour of the ministerial plan were adopted by that body. He had thus obtained an expression of opinion from the four existing Colleges, in favor of his bill. Had ministers not a right then, to anticipate that the measure would be acceptable to the majority of the people of Canada. It had been said that other bodies of Christians than those named were excluded from participating in the benefit of the measure. He most solemnly declared that no such exclusion was intended or existed. The bill distinctly provides for giving proportionate assistance to other Colleges, as they shall arise and place themselves in a position by means of charters, to participate in the endowment. He extended his remarks on this subject to a greater length than the particular business of the meeting warranted him in doing, but as the University Bill, was the great question before the country, he was anxious that they should give it their most serious consideration. And he was moreover anxious that he should not be misunderstood. The distinction, then, between the bill which he had introduced for the settlement of the University Question, and those which preceded it, was, that while the latter designed only one great institution at

Toronto, inaccessible to the great body of the people, he (Mr. Macdonald) aimed at placing the advantages of an University education within their reach. People, he knew, would much prefer having their sons educated under their own surveillance than to send them from all parts of the Province to Toronto, and maintain them there at increased expense. He was desirous also of having a more regular gradation of education than at present. It was true that there existed District Schools, but with the miserable pittance allotted to these it was not to be expected that they should be of much positive advantage to the country. Under the best possible direction they could ill supply the wants of each district. It was more than any one man could do to impart effectively such an education as was designed in the original endowment of Grammar schools. And there consequently existed a very wide gap between these schools and the University. He proposed to lessen this. The ministerial measure embraced the establishment in each district of a Grammar school, with a fund sufficient to maintain four masters. It was designed, in the first place, on the District Council of any district advancing £250, to add to it £500 for the purpose of the erection of a suitable building; then to give £350 towards the salaries of the masters, which, with say £150 presumed tuition fees, would yield £500 per annum for this purpose, and would probably pay for the services of two classical, one mathematical and an English master. In such an institution an education could be obtained equal to that which has fallen to the lot of the greater number of public men in Canada—and the facilities for such an education would, as he had before pointed out, be almost at every man's door. Then it has been justly urged that with only one University as proposed by Mr. Baldwin, the son of the poor man would be literally excluded from the higher walks and pursuits of life, for the poor man could not afford to send his son to Toronto for the purpose of receiving an University education. How did ministers meet this objection? Did they propose to continue this system, as some of those did who were very fond of crying "Justice to all classes"? No. There are now twenty-two districts in Upper Canada, and in a short time there will be twenty-four. It is proposed that at the annual examination in each of these district grammar schools, the two scholars who shall prove their superior advancement shall be sent to the University of their choice and educated at the public expense. Thus, for instance, if the youth belonged to the Church of England, he would prefer King's College, and be sent there: if a Roman Catholic, he would desire to go to Regiopolis; if a Presbyterian, to Queen's College; if a Methodist, to Victoria; and in like manner with reference to other colleges which may be established. This looked a little more like "justice to all," than the establishment of one great institution under circumstances which would amount to a virtual exclusion of the poorer class of society. And it could not be justly said that the son of the farmer, or the mechanic, should be excluded—that high education should be confined to high rank, for some of the brightest names on the pages of the world's history are those of men who by the force of genius rose from the lowest to fill the highest stations in society. But ministers have gone yet further in their endeavor to bring education within the reach of the mass of the people. We are all used to look upon the pursuits of agriculture as of the highest importance; we speak of the farmers as forming the "bone and sinew" of the country; yet it is well known that few are acquainted with Agriculture as a science. Of the importance of its study as such, however, there cannot exist a doubt. But how is such a description of knowledge to be obtained?

How many farmers are there in the country who would send their sons to Toronto to study agricultural science under the direction of a Professor? Perhaps not a dozen. But the measure now before the country embraces the institution of a model farm and school in the neighborhood of every capital town, under the direction of a scientific man—where a scientific knowledge of agriculture will be imparted to the youth who attend it, as well as a good practical education. Such was the nature of the measure which ministers submitted to the consideration of the people of the country, and by their verdict upon its fitness or unfitness, he repeated they were ready to stand or fall.

Mr. Macdonald proceeded to remark upon the advantage which Kingston would derive from the maintenance in this city of two Colleges. He complained of the misrepresentations of his opponent, who, he said, went to his (Mr. Macdonald's) Roman Catholic friends and alleged that he was only endeavoring to buy them; then visited his Protestant supporters and accused him of endeavoring to build up Popery. Mr. Macdonald also read the resolutions moved by Mr. Mackenzie in July last, in which he denounced the scheme of division among the different denominations of Christians and sectarian Colleges, and then read his answer to certain questions addressed to him on behalf of the Roman Catholic electors of Kingston, in which Mr. Mackenzie announced his readiness to vote the public monies to support denominational Colleges! Mr. Macdonald then read his own answer to the same queries, and this was received with shouts of applause. In conclusion Mr. Macdonald stated fully the exertions which he had made for the benefit of Kingston and the Midland District—exertions made in the face of the most strenuous opposition from east and west, and especially from Mr. Mackenzie's particular friend, Mr. Baldwin. He reviewed also the general policy of the administration, and claimed credit for their having placed Upper Canada on a footing of equality with Lower Canada, and removing the injustice of which the former justly complained under the Lafontaine-Baldwin administration. But the hon. gentleman's remarks upon the University Bill occupy so much space that we are obliged to forego a detailed report.

Mr. Macdonald resumed his seat amidst loud applause, and resolutions approving of his conduct, and expressing a determination to support him, were passed by acclamation. A vote of thanks was given to the Chairman and the Secretary, and after a few hearty rounds of cheers for the Queen, and Mr. Macdonald, the meeting broke up.

Macdonald won Kingston 386 to 84 votes on December 29. The Conservative Party did not fare as well, and Macdonald returned to the Assembly in opposition, which would last until 1854—a "long and apparently hopeless opposition," a friend would later remark.[11]

FIGHTING THE REBELLION
LOSSES BILL, 1849

HOUSE OF ASSEMBLY,
MONTREAL, FEBRUARY 16

In 1849, the Province of Canada was on the brink of crisis. The air crack-led with tension. The debate over the Rebellion Losses bill threatened the fragile union of the Canadas. A harsh winter strained the province's poor-relief system and the colony was adjusting to the final repeal of the preferential trade laws. In 1848, revolutions had washed across Europe, Karl Marx (1818–1883) and Friedrich Engels (1820–1895) published The Communist Manifesto, *and in Canada, Louis-Hippolyte La Fontaine and Robert Baldwin swept the Reformers to victory. Lord Elgin, the new governor general, entrenched responsible government by committing his office to working with the party chosen by the voters and allowing them to distribute patronage. Riots marked the social disloca-tion of a colonial society struggling to accommodate new arrivals and a new program of reform. That year, La Fontaine proposed the Rebellion Losses bill to compensate Lower Canadians for damage sustained in the Rebellions of 1837 and 1838; tension spiked to a fever pitch with the prospect of rewarding the rebels. Macdonald took little part in the*

debate, but when solicitor general William Hume Blake (1809–1870)
echoed the challenge that the Tories were the real "rebels" of 1837 and
1838, Macdonald challenged him on the floor, and, by private message,
called him to a duel.[12]

As the Montreal Gazette reported, February 19, 1849:

MR. MACDONALD (Kingston) said that he would feel
obliged by the hon. member [William Hume Blake] reading
all the words [from the documents he was citing].

MR. BLAKE asked him what he meant.

MR. MACDONALD said that he wanted him to read the
whole of it, and would do it for him if he wished. He asked if
it were Parliamentary, in reading documents, to leave out sentences and parts of sentences?

Asserting "a right to read any parts he liked," Blake began his conclu-
sion. Meanwhile, Macdonald had also sent Blake a "threatening com-
munication," containing a challenge to a duel. He and Blake left the
floor of the House.

The Journal for the Legislative Assembly of the Province of
Canada *for February 16, 1849, records that:*

Mr. Speaker informed the House, That, according to information he had received, a hostile meeting was intended between
Mr. Solicitor General *Blake* and the Honorable Mr. *Macdonald,*
two of the Members of this House, in consequence of some
words of heat which had passed in the Debate of this day, but
which had not been taken notice of at the time, and that he

had ineffectually sent a message to Mr. *Blake* to come to the Chair; and Mr. *Blake* and Mr. *Macdonald* not being found in the House;

The Serjeant at Arms went with the Mace, by Order of the House, to the lodgings of Mr. *Blake* and Mr. *Macdonald*, to require their immediate attendance in their places.

The Honorable Mr. *Macdonald* took his place in the House.

The Serjeant at Arms reported that Mr. *Blake* could not be found.

The Honorable Mr. *Macdonald* submitted himself to the House, and declared that he would be in his place at the next sitting; and that in the meantime no collision would take place.

On the motion of the Honorable Mr. Attorney General *Baldwin*, seconded by the Honorable Mr. *Badgley*, Ordered, That Mr. Speaker do issue his Warrant to the Serjeant at Arms, or his Deputy, to take into his custody *William Hume Blake*, Esquire, and that he be brought to the House in custody.

BONSECOURS MARKET, MONTREAL, FEBRUARY 17

The next day, as reported by the Montreal Gazette, another kind of meeting took place. One short month before, the report said, people "of all classes and origins" had "assembled to express their opinions upon the peaceable subject of Protection to their industry." But now, the bill had roused all the burning passions of the Rebellions, of "Anglo Saxon" divided from "French Canadian," of "almost a state of civil war." In the hall at the Bonsecours Market, "thousands and thousands of Anglo-Saxons"—"the wealthy merchant, the intelligent mechanic, and industrious artisan"—met. "[P]eaceable in their conduct," the report said, "but burning with the fire of an insulted nationality, and breathing the determination of resistance to a nefarious attempt at their robbery as loyalists" they met to define their position in a series of resolutions. Responding to the third resolution on "pecuniary compensation" for the rebels, Macdonald spoke, as reported by the Gazette *on February 19, 1849.*[13]

MR. MACDONALD MPP (Kingston) had never seen in all his life such a meeting as that, although he had seen many meetings in Upper Canada. To reward traitors and rebels, at the expense of those who put them down, could never be submitted to by them. They saw by every mail, and every newspaper that came from Upper Canada what the feeling was there. As a newspaper in Montreal had truly said, the heather was on fire. In 1837, they the Upper Canadians had also had their rebellion in Upper C. of scoundrels and traitors, and they had put them down. What had been their reward? They had been told by ministers of the government, that they were the rebels, traitors and murderers. He told them (the government) to their teeth that they lied before that meeting it was as well to use plain terms, and he told them again that they lied. Then was not the time to talk lightly; he [Macdonald] told them [the government], that they would never submit to oppression. They would not put their hands in their pockets to reward traitors. He was satisfied that there was no man in that meeting which would do anything contrary to the wishes of his venerable friend the chairman of the meeting [George Moffatt (1787–1865)], and who stood as the representative of the loyalty of Lower Canada. If these men were in want, they would give them money out of charity, but there was not one man, that would suffer money to be taken from him, to reward them.

Macdonald was one of the last speakers recorded in the Gazette's *report. "The people afterwards," the description concluded, "retired quietly to their homes."*

HOUSE OF ASSEMBLY, MONTREAL, FEBRUARY 22

On February 22, the debate over the Rebellion Losses bill in the House of Assembly moved forward. The Reformers amended the resolutions to prohibit anyone convicted or banished to Bermuda for their activities during the Rebellions from receiving compensation. Macdonald intervened again that evening.[14]

On February 26 the Montreal Gazette *reported:*

MR. MACDONALD (Kingston) considered that the members on his side of the House had been shamefully treated by the Ministry. They had been hurried into the consideration of the Resolutions without any notice, or without any explanation being given of the measure. And now, because the members opposite had found that the people of the country were indignant at the measure, they were afraid to wait until the people had an opportunity of expressing their opinions of it, for fear that some of their supporters might become unwilling to vote for the measure after they were informed of the views of their constituents upon it. The measure was a most shameful one, and one which ought not to be forced on in the manner which it had been done; and the members on his side, considering the way in which they had been treated, would enter into no compromise; they would speak when they liked, as long as they liked, and as often as they liked. (Cheers.)

The House sat until noon the next day. The bill was voted in, and Lord Elgin, recognizing responsible government in the first test of the principle, did not countenance disallowing it, and signed it on April 25, 1849.

Macdonald had left Montreal when Tory discontent spilled into the streets, angry voters blind to ideals of deliberative democracy. In their eyes, the advent of responsible government had only empowered the Reformers and the French Canadians, making a mockery of their loyalty during the Rebellions. This, combined with Tory bewilderment about the Empire's withdrawal of preferential trade, snapped their loyalty in two. The protests turned violent. They invaded the House of Assembly, ripping and tearing, and set the whole alight. Some later joined a movement to annex the province to the United States. The protests swept across Canada West as well, and a petition was mounted to recall Lord Elgin. The seat of government was removed from Montreal, and it began its perambulations, alternating between Toronto and Quebec City.[15]

REJECTING THE TEMPERANCE BILL, 1853

HOUSE OF ASSEMBLY,
QUEBEC CITY, APRIL 13

When the member for Lincoln, William Hamilton Merritt (1793–1862), proposed to tax liquor in order to support the temperance movement, Macdonald was moved to irony and sarcasm. Temperance movements of the mid-Victorian era reflected the social turmoil of the industrializing world. In keeping with the liberal views of the era, the temperance societies promoted voluntary self-governance by drinkers and civic institutions. However, by the 1850s the growing problem of alcoholism alerted philosophers and emerging social scientists to the limits of individual self-control and to the reality of systemic causes of some social distress. Macdonald had a well-known proclivity for the increasingly—but not yet totally, as he would argue—unacceptable habit.[16]

On May 3, 1853, a reporter for The Globe *wrote:*

HON. J. A. MACDONALD ridiculed the remarks of the hon. member for Lincoln, who looked on ardent spirits as a poison, and although he would not have it here for himself, would send it abroad to poison his friends, or else would have it all drunk up in the next eighteen months. This bill struck at the very root of the excise altogether; and what was most strange was, that the hon. gentleman who had introduced it, and wanted to make it out a crime almost to manufacture spirits at all, came down with the budget.

Now, he was a minister responsible for that budget, and he wanted to go in for all laws repealing license, except in relation to the duties on distilleries. (Hear, hear.) How could that hon. gentleman come forward and propose that all excise duties in Upper Canada should be repealed, except the duty on whiskey? He preserved those duties where he really advocated their existence, for the most mean purpose, namely, that of augmentation of the revenue; *that* appeared palpably from the course which that hon. gentleman had pursued; but he would ask, did he not state, when he introduced his bill, that the question was one far above pecuniary considerations? When the hon. member for Simcoe [William Benjamin Robinson (1797–1873)] said that it was a revenue question, the hon. Inspector General [Francis Hincks] said that the hon. member ought to be ashamed of himself to bring forward such a statement, for that the welfare of the country depended upon the carrying of the bill, but *he* brings forward a measure by which he wishes to wipe away excise duties, and still preserve his distillery duties; and what for? For the sake of about £16,000. What is the effect of this measure? To prohibit not only the use of ardent spirits, but the use of any liquors that will intoxicate. Wine was one of those liquors, (at least *he* was told so and he believed it was) and yet that hon. gentleman according to his measure wished to make wine cheaper to everybody, so that whereas a man formerly paid 3s. for a bottle of Medeira, he should be enabled to get it for 6d.

Now, he would ask the hon. Inspector General whether the

measure for altering the duties on wine was not for the sake of reducing its price in the market? Undoubtedly it was.

But there was a contradiction—there had been a total desertion of the great principles of responsible government by the minister of the day. It was like those gentlemen who declared that they never belonged to Temperance Societies,* and the only grounds of justice they brought forward for advocating the measure in the House, were, that in their little miserable municipalities, there were a lot of men who joined together upon this question, those hon. gentlemen were therefore willing to sacrifice their own principles, for the sake of courting a support of that kind. He held, that the policy of the Government was bad. The Inspector General could no more legislate a man to be a sober man, anymore than a religious man, and with all those resolutions of his, he would say that in order to raise man, the influence must proceed from the action of man upon man, and not by the operation of a statute—it is only by the force of public opinion, and by the force of the public mind being directed and laid on as it had been in England, Ireland and the United States, against a particular vice, weakness and frenzy, that you can succeed—the moment you trust to the law, that moment your exertions cease.

He would take one instance to establish the truth of his assertion. When his hon. and gallant friend, Sir Allan MacNab was a young man, and in His Majesty's service what was the law in relation to dueling? If the one felt his honour injured, or himself insulted, he would send a challenge, the parties went out, and they might shoot one another, and what was the consequence

---

* The temperance movement gained prominence in the 1840s with some religious groups. By the 1850s, it began to be secularized. (Noel, "Temperance Movement," OCCH)

if one party did shoot the other and left him weltering in his blood, leaving a family behind him, what did the law declare? It declared that the man should be strung by the neck until he was dead.

Did the existence of that law prevent the crime of dueling? No! How was it now? Duelling is considered out of date; the fashion has gone out; public opinion has declared against it.* A man now who has had two affairs in his life is considered no longer within the pale of civilized society.

The fact of the matter is, that public opinion is strongly against such wicked contests, and therefore it has almost ceased and is bound by the opinion of society. Read the memoirs of the last six years about the people in Ireland. You had a duty on spirits which almost rendered it prohibitory—they could not get it legally, and what was the consequence? I would ask whether the bottle of whisky was not as before present at the wakes night after night? Why, what was the law there?—when Father Mathew† went there, he did not go with the Maine Liquor Law in his hand, he prevailed upon them, and gained upon them, and by that moral suasion he was enabled to use in Ireland, he produced a revolution which all the King's laws and all the King's troops for the last hundreds of years were unable to obtain. Why endeavour to make people feel oppressed, injured, and irritated by such means? I hope this bill will be thrown out, and that the House will not go so far as to admit that there ought to be an absurd law like this, an oppressive law

---

* Duelling did fall out of favour in Britain and the Canada in the 1840s. (Morgan, "Duelling in Upper Canada," *CHR* 1995, 561)

† Theobald Mathew (1790–1856), an Irish Catholic teetotalist reformer, popularly known as Father Mathew. ("Temperances and total abstinence," OCIH)

like this, and a futile law like this; for it has been proved by every gentleman who spoke, even by the advocates of it, that so futile a law as that could not be allowed to exist. The hon. member for Kent [George Brown] (who had made, he thought, the strongest speech against it) said that any law introduced at a time when the people were not prepared for it was a futile law, and he said, "put it off till 1855."

MR. [GEORGE] BROWN—no, the hon. gentleman was mistaken. He said, that for his own part he would like to have heard from the special committee, clear evidence as to the state of the public mind upon the question, for he considered that the bill should not be put into operation until public opinion was clearly in favor of it. He was quite willing to vote for the bill now, with the proviso that it should come into force upon the first of January, 1855.

MR. MACDONALD—Then he saw that the hon. member for Kent was of the same opinion as the hon. member for Lincoln, to have the stock already in hand, drank up first. He thought that it would be doing a great injury to the community to pass this bill, and he should therefore vote against the second reading of it.

REPRESENTATION BILL, 1853

HOUSE OF ASSEMBLY, QUEBEC CITY, MARCH 23

George Brown, editor of The Globe, *so often hostile to Macdonald and the Conservatives, entered a new arena in 1852. He was elected into the House of Assembly, as an independent Reformer, signalling a shift in the shape of the Reform movement in Canada. While the Clear Grits brought strong populist sentiments to the table, Francis Hincks thought about railways. The Reformers, however, did share a desire (together with some Conservatives) for democratic reforms along American lines, and advocated an elected legislative council. Brown, meanwhile, expressing his mistrust of the Catholic Church's increasing role in social welfare, pursued an agenda of separating church and state and advocated increased political representation for fast-growing Protestant Canada West. His Representation Bill of 1853 moderately reduced the ratio of elected representatives to voters and increased the seats in Canada West and Canada East to 65 for each.[17] Brown and the Clear Grits would remain hostile to Macdonald until the Great Coalition of 1864.*

The Globe *reported on April 12, 1853:*

HON J. A. MACDONALD (Kingston)—If there is one thing to be avoided, it is meddling with the constitution of the country, which should not be altered till it is evident that the people are suffering from the effects of that constitution as it actually exists.

I say (he continued) that the Government have never been called upon to bring forward this measure. The voice of the country has been silent upon it, and why? Because the people have, under the present system, always been fairly and thoroughly represented by those whom they sent to Parliament. The representatives for the time being have always fairly represented the people by whom they were elected, and there never has been any want of sympathy between the people and their representatives. The people have always been fully represented by their 84 members. The best evidence of this is that we have no petition before us in favour of this measure; no one has asked for it. A sacrilegious hand has been placed upon our constitution, and I say that in every question put to the people, Clergy Reserves, Rectories, or what not, the people of Canada have told their representatives what course they wished them to take. Look at all the other great questions of the day that have been put to the people of Canada—are not our tables loaded with petitions regarding them? Where is there a single petition in favour of this measure from Upper Canada or from Lower Canada? (Echo answers, where?) It has been said that this has been made a test question at the elections: but if that is the real state of the case the people would have made their intentions known by petitions. I say that it is an unpardonable meddling with our constitution, to say that the members who sit here do not fairly represent the people.

The Inspector General [Francis Hincks] introduced a bill which nearly doubles the number of representatives, and yet he says that the Government had no intention of putting it into effect. The only reason of that can be that he sees that the people are fairly represented by the members now sitting here. There is no reason for such a course but this, which is the only one that has ever been assigned: that the Government can buy up the members and can exercise more influence over them.

The hon. the Inspector General has a most winning way of exercising an influence over the members of this House—a way much more potent than is possessed by any hon. member on this side of the house. When I had the honour of a seat in the Cabinet, I found hon. members on the other side of the House a most impracticable set, but the hon. Inspector General is a much better hand at that sort of thing. He is carrying this measure just as Lord Castlereagh* carried the Union in Ireland—doing precisely the same thing. He goes about giving a member here and a member there, just picking up votes whenever he can get them, and yet the only reason ever given for this measure was that it would prevent corruption by the government. I am not afraid of this undue influence of the government, because I believe the people of Upper Canada can take as good care of her own interests, even with only 84 members, as they could with three times the number.

I think also that I could not vote for this measure on account of the injustice of its details. Why, sir, to think that 60,000 persons in one place are to have six members, while 60,000 next to them are to have but three members!—there must be some strong reason for this extraordinary inconsistency. It is evident that the country has been cut and carved in all directions, without any regard to fairness or justice, just to obtain the requisite

---

* Robert Stewart, Viscount Castlereagh (1769–1822), campaigned for the union of Britain and Ireland in 1800. (Thorne, "Stewart, Robert, Viscount Castlereagh and second marquess of Londonderry," *ODNB*)

number of votes to carry the measure. I know that the Inspector General, if left to himself, would have done what is just and right, but he is under the influence of men to whom he dare not refuse to grant their wishes.

As I have made up my mind to vote against this bill, it is perhaps not fair that I should refer to the details, but there is one great reason why I should vote against this bill, and that is that it is not now to go into effect. Why should we now pass a bill of this import and nature which is not to come into force for three years? But I tell the Inspector General that he dare not, according to the constitution of the country, carry this idea into effect. He dare not continue the present House one moment after this bill comes into force. You not only declare that there are not a sufficient number of representatives, but you declare by the Franchise Bill that there are a large number of persons in Upper Canada who are not represented, but who ought to be represented, and yet you say now, after declaring that their rights exist, that they are not to be granted for three years to come!

The Inspector General cannot give this advice to the representative of the Crown, and if he does he is unworthy of the place that he holds; and if he gives it, it will not be received. Look at the Reform Bill in England [of 1832]. That was passed by a Parliament that has been elected only one year before, and the moment it was passed Lord John Russell* declared that the House could not continue after it had declared that the country was not properly represented. How can we legislate on the Clergy Reserves until another house is assembled, if this bill

---

* John Russell, first Earl Russell (1792–1878), Whig politician who later became two-time prime minister of Britain. (Prest, "Russell, John [formerly Lord John Russell], first Earl Russell," *ODNB*)

passes? A great question like this cannot be left to be decided by an accidental majority. We can legislate upon no great question after we have ourselves declared that we do not represent the country. Do hon. gentlemen opposite mean to say that they will legislate on a question affecting the rights of people yet unborn, with the fag end of a Parliament dishonoured by its own confessions of incapacity. He (Mr. Macdonald) had only one thing more to say, and that was, that he would recommend my hon. friend the Attorney General* to look carefully into the Union Act† before he consented to allow this bill to pass.

---

* William Buell Richards (1815–1889) was attorney general for Canada West between 1851 and 1853. Lewis Thomas Drummond (1813–1882) was attorney general for Canada East between 1851 and 1856. (MacPherson, "Richards, Sir William Buell," *DCB*; Little, "Drummond, Lewis Thomas," *DCB*)

† Macdonald is referring to the 1841 act that created the United Province of Canada.

COMPENSATION TO THE SEIGNEURS, 1853

HOUSE OF ASSEMBLY,
QUEBEC CITY, APRIL 27

Macdonald, still sitting in the opposition benches, applied his legal reasoning and grasp of historical precedent to argue that Canada West should not be called upon to compensate the seigneurs of Canada East when legislation abolishing seigneurial tenure was debated. Later in his career, he would explain the close economic connection he saw between the two provinces, but here he is focused upon the nature of the scheme, not the principle of it. The Reformers, still dominant, sought to modernize the social-economic system of Canada East by abolishing the seigneurial system and bringing property law in line with that of Canada West.[18]

The Globe *reported on May 12, 1853:*

The Chairman of the committee of the whole to which was referred certain resolutions to provide for indemnity to Seigniors, and for other purposes, reported the following resolutions:—

1. *Resolved*—That it is expedient to appropriate for the payment of the Indemnity to be awarded to Seigniors, and other expenses to be incurred under the bill to define Seigniorial rights and to facilitate the redemption thereof,

a sum equal to that coming into the Consolidated Revenue Fund of this Province [i.e., the United Province of Canada] from the following Lower Canadian sources of revenue; that is to say:—From *Quint*, and other dues which are now or hereafter shall become payable to the Crown in or upon the Seigniories in Lower Canada, of which the Crown is the Seignior Dominant, as well as from all arrears of such dues:—From the revenues of the Seigniory of Lauzon, and the proceeds of the sale of any part of the said Seigniory which may hereafter be sold and all arrears of such revenues:—From all monies arising from action duties and auctioneer's licenses in Lower Canada:—From all monies arising in Lower Canada from licenses to sell spirituous, vinous or fermented liquors by retail in places other than places of public entertainment, commonly called shop or store licenses.

2. *Resolved*—That it is expedient that the sums required to pay the said Indemnity and expenses, be raised by debentures to be issued under the authority of the Governor in Council and chargeable on the Consolidated Revenue Fund; but that separate accounts be kept of the monies coming into the said Consolidated Revenue Fund from the several Lower Canadian source of revenue aforesaid; and that if the sums payable out of the Consolidated Revenue Fund for the principal and interest of such debentures, shall exceed the amount arising from the several source of revenue men mentioned in the preceding resolution, it will in the opinion of this House, be expedient to appropriate a sum equal to such excess for some local purpose or purposes in Upper Canada.

HON. MR. MACDONALD moved in amendment thereto, "That is it inexpedient and unjust to the tax payers of Canada to appropriate any portion of the territorial revenues of this Province to the payment of the Indemnity to be awarded to the Seigniors of Lower Canada, inasmuch as the proposed legislation under the bill as now framed is of local interest only, and such Indemnity should be paid by the parties immediately benefitted thereby."

A vote was taken for "concurrence in the amendment" and it was 14 "Yeas" and 35 "Nays" so that the 1st Resolution was agreed to. The 2nd Resolution was read.

HON. MR. MACDONALD moved in amendment thereto, "That it is expedient and unjust to the people of Canada to charge the Consolidated Revenue Fund of the whole Province with the payment of any portion of the said Indemnity to Seigniors, and that such indemnity should be paid by that section of the Province immediately benefitted by the proposed measure."

A discussion and vote followed. The count was nearly the same, 14 "Yeas" and 36 "Nays."

HON. MR. MACDONALD again moved in amendment to the 2nd Resolution, "That the proposition to pledge the Consolidated Revenue Fund for the payment of the said indemnity, or any portion thereof, and thereby to increase the Provincial Debt and taxation to an unknown and unlimited amount, is improper, unprecedented and dangerous; that it deprives this House of the necessary check over the Public Expenditure and the Public burdens; and that this House will fail in its duty to the people of Canada if it assents to any such proposition."

MR. MACDONALD [the reporter continued] in proposing this amendment went on to say, that is was a most unprecedented course that was now proposed by the Government with regard to this matter. That the Legislature of this country who are the guardians of the public purse, should be called on to impose upon the people and their children a burden, the amount of which they did not know, was a most objectionable as well as inconsistent course of procedure. They had no security whatever that the amount they were now called upon to secure for this purpose might not be one hundred thousand pounds, or that it might not be twice as much as that sum. He would ask the Inspector General if he could find a precedent for the course he now proposed?

It was true that a vote of credit had been given on occasion, but that was under extreme circumstances, and for one year only. Again they had undertaken great public works to advance the material interests of the country, and how could they go on with their undertaking with a burden of this kind upon their resources, the amount of which could not be told, which the Government themselves did not know, and which they said they could not find out.

The hon. gentleman then went on to allude to the slavery question in England, which he contended was analogous to this. When it was proposed to indemnify the slaveowners for their property, the Government did not ask Parliament to pledge the revenues of the country to an unlimited extent, but the Secretary of the Colonies, Lord Stanley,* came down with

---

* Macdonald is referring to Edward George Geoffrey Smith-Stanley (1799–1869) who was the secretary of state for war and the colonies between 1833 and 1834, and who drew up the Abolition of Slavery Bill that offered £20 million to plantation owners in compensation for freeing their slaves. Smith-Stanley served again as colonial secretary

minute and elaborate calculations of the value of each slave, and an exact estimate of the sum required, and the Inspector General should have done the same in this case. He should have formed an estimate of the amount required for every seigniory, and then come down with an exact statement of the whole sum that would be required. A finance minister in England would be laughed at if he proposed to tax the people for an unlimited amount; and then what a miserable proposition was this that was laid down in these resolutions. Two-thirds of the whole taxation of the country is paid by the people of Upper Canada and here they talk of asking [for] a certain amount out of the Consolidated Fund for the benefit of Lower Canada, and then remunerating Upper Canada by paying her a similar sum out of her own resources. The Government have already refused to reduce the customs' duties on account of the present burden arising from the public works, and yet they ask us to take on ourselves another burden the amount of which we do not know; and as far as the remuneration to Upper Canada is concerned it just amounts to telling her to tax herself for her own benefit.

---

between 1841 and 1845 and as Britain's prime minister for three separate terms in the 1850s and 1860s. (Hawkins, "Edward George Geoffrey Smith-Stanley, 14th Earl of Derby," *ODNB*)

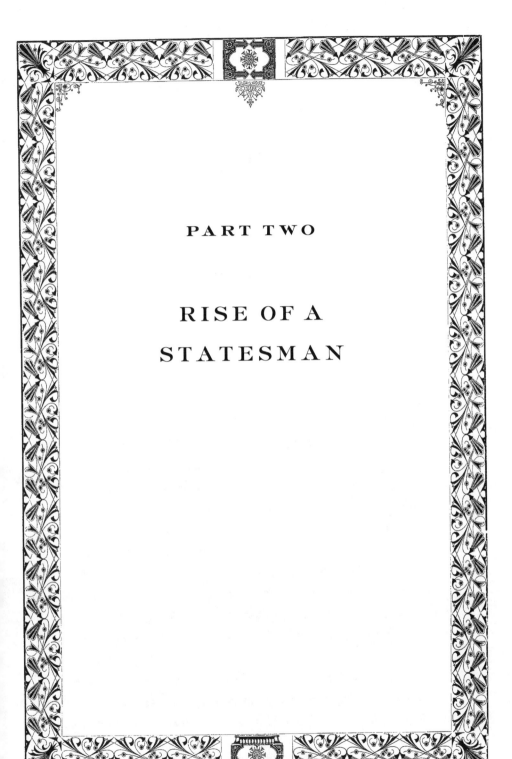

PART TWO

RISE OF A
STATESMAN

"YIELDING TO THE TIMES":
SECULAR CLERGY RESERVES, 1854

The MacNab-Morin ministry that came to power in 1854 grew into a Liberal-Conservative coalition. It brought old-guard Tories, led by Allan Napier MacNab, into alignment with Macdonald's moderate vision by accepting the reform platform of Augustin-Norbert Morin (1803–1865), which included the secularization of the clergy reserves, an elected legislative council, and the abolition of the seigneurial regime.

The ministers divided the bills between them for introduction into the legislature. Macdonald, who had been appointed attorney general for Canada West, took responsibility for the clergy reserves bill. The reserves were Crown lands set aside for the support of Protestant churches and had proved an intractable political issue since their establishment in 1791. By 1850 they continued to be a political liability because they incited competition among churches and drew criticism from those who desired separation of church and state. The bill Macdonald introduced protected the incomes of clergymen already supported by the clergy reserves, but diverted the funds towards municipal improvement and railway schemes.

Macdonald's bill marked the end of this question in Canadian politics, and it passed on the third reading on November 23, 62 votes to 39. In defending it, Macdonald met opposition from all sides, but speaking particularly to John Hillyard Cameron (1817–1876), a fellow Tory for Toronto, Macdonald explained why the old-guard Tories and moderate Conservatives should embrace this reform.[1]

The Globe *reported on November 10, 1854:*

HON. MR. MACDONALD (Kingston) said,—The honorable gentleman [John Hillyard Cameron] who has just spoken, widely though his views differ from those of the Government on this subject, has discussed it calmly, and while I regret that on this occasion and on this subject he should be found on a different side from those with whom he has formerly acted, I think he has done credit to himself in the manner in which he has laid his views before the House, and that in defining his own position, he has defined it ably and well. But it appears to me that the honorable gentleman is defeating his own purpose. It is well known that hon. gentleman feels that the Church [of England] of which he is a member, and other Churches which are in a like position, are attacked, are injured by the whole measure emanating from the Government. He feels that, and he speaks under the influence of that feeling, but while I respect that feeling not only in him but in others who take a similar view of the subject, I sincerely believe that he is not doing his Church, or his friends, or his principles a service by the course which he takes. I believe, from my experience in this country, from my recollection of the history of this whole question, that the course which has all along been adopted by the anti-secularizers, if I may use the expression, by the Church of England in Canada, has been seriously detrimental to themselves, and has been the cause of all the excitement and all the agitation which have so long disturbed this country. (Hear, hear.) There is no maxim which experience teaches more clearly than this, that you must yield to the times. Resistance may be protracted until it produces revolution. Resistance was protracted in this country until it produced rebellion. (Hear, hear.) Do we not hear the honourable member for Haldimand [William Lyon Mackenzie* (1795–1861)] get up in his place and state day after day, and in a debate after debate—ever since his return to this country have we not heard him allege that the cause of [rebellion was the Clergy Reserves?] [The honourable member] from Toronto (Hon. Cameron) talked about finding the people religious, contented and happy, and leaving them bereft of their religious consolations and miserable. But on looking back, is it really the case that we find them contented and happy? I view this subject from the same point of view as the honorable gentleman.

I view the whole question of right from the same point of view with that honourable gentleman. I have never disguised my opinion on that subject, but still I cannot hide from myself the conviction that this measure did not find the people contented and happy, but that the question from the time it was first agitated until now has been a source of trouble and contention, setting man against man, neighbour against neighbour, Church against Church. Has there not been blood-shed

---

* William Lyon Mackenzie (1795–1861) had returned to Canada after a few years in the United States and was sitting in the House as the member for Haldimand. He had led the Upper Canadian rebels in 1837 and 1838 and cited grievances over the reserve lands, including the clergy reserves, as a source of discontent. Lord Durham (1792–1840), whose report helped create the United Province of Canada, called the reserves the key question for the "pacification of Canada." Mackenzie supported the abolition of the clergy reserves. (Greer, "1837-38: Rebellion Reconsidered," 9; Armstrong and Stagg, "Mackenzie, William Lyon," *DCB*)

in Upper Canada?—have we not seen the most disgraceful, the most disastrous scenes enacted in Upper Canada, in consequence of the agitation of this question?* We thought in 1840 that it was settled forever.† Those hopes were shared by such men as the honorable Robert Baldwin and his party, but those hopes were disappointed, and the agitation re-opened. Mr. Baldwin was not responsible for the re-agitation of the question. It was re-opened from causes far beyond his control, and now we meet the subject—I mean the Conservative members of the present administration—we approach the subject from this point of view, that it is a matter of necessity that no matter what may be the right or the wrong of the question, the people have determined it, the people will have it, and the people must have it. We might as well attempt to stop the swellings of the tide, as to stay the deliberately expressed opinion of Upper Canada on this question.

I do not disguise that I feel the taunts which have been thrown upon us for the course we have taken. It is one of the penalties of the course we took that we should have those taunts to endure. We will receive the taunts of our enemies and *quondam* friends, and kiss the rod, conscious of the purity of our motives. We are willing to abide the consequences, and though our course may make some friends cold and give enemies an opportunity of attacking us, we believe that in after days when this question has through our means been settled, we will receive the thanks of all parties for having been the means, no

---

* Macdonald is referring to the Rebellions of Upper and Lower Canada in 1837 and 1838.

† In 1840 the revenue from the clergy reserves was distributed among several Protestant churches. (Westfall, *Two Worlds*, 106)

matter what our alleged or supposed motives may be, of laying this demon which has so long disturbed this country.

I believe it is a great mistake in politics and in private life to resist when resistance is hopeless. I believe there may be an affected heroism and bravado in sinking with the ship, but no man can be charged with cowardice, if, when he finds the ship sinking, he betakes himself to the boat. And I believe that, in taking the course we did, we are doing good service even to the Churches which are affected by the measure, because the measure must come, the measure will come, the measure cannot be delayed, and I believe we are actually doing service by settling the question while we can protect any interest whatever.

Do we not even read at this moment in the extreme papers of a renewed agitation even against this measure? Do we not see that a very influential paper in Upper Canada has stated that, instead of these incumbents having any right to be protected, they have robbed the people of Canada of upwards of a million, and that the Churches which have received that money ought to return it?—And so sure as I speak, so sure it will be that, if this question is protracted for five years more, not only would the Clergy Reserves be secularized, but there would be a loud call from the extreme and fanatical party which the honorable member for Lambton [George Brown] represents, (Hear, hear.) there would be such a pressure from that party as even that hon. member with all his strength of will would not be able to restrain, and the incumbents would be called upon to give up everything in the world, and there would be a general confiscation of Church and Clergy property.

I said that resistance to an inevitable necessity is no virtue. If the necessity is obvious, if it is clear that a measure must become law, then resistance ceases to be a merit and becomes a mere factious obstruction. We all remember the course taken by the Duke of Wellington and Sir Robert Peel on the Catholic Emancipation Bill.* It has been said—had you changed your opinion conscientiously, had you really become secularizers, it would be all well enough; but you still avow that your former opinions, you still avow that you would avoid the consequences if you could, and yet for the sake of office, you have agreed to secularize. Those arguments were used in exactly the same way against the Imperial government on the occasion to which I have referred. It was not until they saw bloodshed in Ireland, Ribbon Lodges in every village and Whiteboys† in every county, that the Duke of Wellington came to this conclusion which he avowed manfully—I have not changed my opinion at all, but we must have Emancipation in Ireland or civil war. He was then subject to precisely the same taunts, to precisely the same insults that have been offered to us, but he bore them patiently and lived through them. Had Charles the First‡ yielded betimes to the popular cry, his head would not have rolled on the scaffold. And in France, when the first attempt was made to make the property of the Church contribute to the necessities of the State, if that attempt had not been resisted, the property would not have been confiscated. And on this very

---

* The Duke of Wellington (1769–1852) and Sir Robert Peel (1788–1850) bowed to the inevitable and, reversing their previous positions, announced a decision in 1829 in favour of Catholic political emancipation. (Hilton, *Mad, Bad People?*, 387)

† "Ribbonmen" referred to the members of secret networks, dating from the 1810s, of farmers and shopkeepers who promoted Catholic values and Irish independence, by violent means if necessary. "Whiteboys" were members of Irish agrarian protest movements of the late seventeenth and early eighteenth centuries, and by the nineteenth century the term was used to signify agricultural or rural protesters in general. ("Ribbonism," and "Whiteboys," *OCIH*)

‡ Charles I (1600–1649) was executed in January 1649. (Kishlansky and Morrill, "Charles I," *ODNB*.)

question, had the Church of England not resisted the claim of the Church of Scotland, when first raised in 1824, the question would have been settled. And had the Churches of England and Scotland not resisted the pressure from without, after they were mutual shares of the fund, the question then would have been settled.*

By continually resisting and not yielding in time, they prevented the question from being settled long ago, instead of being left as now a matter of struggle and contention. Now we are offering our humble aid to the question, and if our measure becomes law, the question will be finally and for ever settled. The first resolution of the hon. member for Toronto attacks the expression about the semblance of connection between Church and State. I have no hesitation in stating my own opinion, that in a country where the majority of the people are of one religion, and that a Christian religion, the State should acknowledge itself a Christian State, and make provision for the maintenance of religion. In England I believe that the connection between Church and State has been beneficial, but as certainly it has been injurious in Ireland. And I believe that in a country like this, it is of the greatest consequence to destroy the very semblance of connection between Church and State; for I believe it is nothing more than a semblance. In our country the people belong to so many various sects, and the balance in favor of any one Church is so uncertain, that it would be only rousing and continuing feelings of jealousy and dissention similar to those which exist in Ireland, to keep up any semblance of such connection.—The hon. member for Toronto had spoken

---

* In 1824, the Church of Scotland, as an establishment church in Britain with the Church of England, was included as a beneficiary of the lands reserved for "a Protestant clergy." Other denominations began asking for a share of the reserves. (Craig, *Upper Canada*, 171-2)

with his usual ability and with his usual legal ingenuity as to
the effect of the Imperial Act of 1853, and he endeavours to
establish that by the Act of 7 and 8 George IV and the Act of 3
and 4 Victoria there has been an appropriation of a certain portion of the Clergy Reserves for the two Churches of England
and Scotland, and as those Reserves or a large portion of them
have been sold and invested, he argues that the proceeds have
become the final property of those Churches.

There is a great deal of ingenuity in the argument. I see it
is pressed with equal ingenuity in a letter addressed to the hon.
Commissioner of Crown Lands by the Bishop of Toronto, and
that secularization, if secularization there must be, can only
affect unsold property, and cannot affect those proceeds of lands
sold, which have already been invested. Without discussing the
mere law of the question—and I dare say my hon. friend took
a strictly legal view of the subject, avoiding the open view in
which this subject should be approached—I would say that one
thing is clear that if the Imperial Legislature meant that, they
were practising a delusion, a mockery, and a snare on the people
of Canada. (Hear, hear.) If they meant that the proceeds of the
sale of all the Clergy Reserve Lands sold up to 1853, three-
fourths of the value of the whole, for it is the most valuable lands
that have been sold, belonged inalienably to those Churches and
that all we have been disputing is about a mere fraction of the
whole, a million of acres worth perhaps as many dollars, then
I say they were actually practising an imposition on the people
of Canada. (Hear, hear.) Every statesman in England as well as
here knew that the whole Clergy Reserve fund was the subject
of controversy, and the Imperial Act was passed for the purpose
of allowing us to legislate upon it.—What would be the sense
of the clause that the Incumbents were to be indemnified, but

for this. It is evident that the present fund is a capital sufficient to satisfy the demands of those men to the last farthing, and if they were to receive that it was idle to talk about indemnifying them. And the very language of the statute itself does not support my hon. friend in his view of the case.—If that statute does not give this Legislature the power of legislating on the whole fund, whether vestable or invested, then I must say that I do not understand what words in the English language mean.

The hon. gentleman has attempted to draw an analogy between the Trinity Corporation of New York and the Clergy Reserve question. I cannot see any analogy between the two cases, for the Act of 1791 merely reserves those lands for future appropriation, and creates no vested right in them in the Protestant Clergy or any body whatever. On any other supposition, the Act of 1840 was as much an act of spoliation as the present bill. If there be sacrilege at all, the sacrilege was committed in 1840, and all the clergy, from the Bishop of Toronto down to the last Methodist clergyman who has drawn out of the fund, have been all guilty of sacrilege by receiving the stipends under the authority of an Act, which was the first act of sacrilege. (Hear, hear.) I think that even the hon. gentleman who had proposed those resolutions does not hope to carry them. He knows that the majority of the people of Upper Canada are opposed to his views whether rightly or wrongly. It is quite clear that, if what the honorable gentleman wishes were carried out, Upper Canada would again be agitated as it has been for years past, and it is quite clear that, if the hon. gentleman wished to inflict upon Canada a curse, he could not inflict upon it a greater curse than the continued agitation of this question. I call upon the hon. gentleman and upon the Church whose interests he advocates, to yield. I call upon them to cease this agitation.

They may smart under a sense of wrong, and may feel that they are deprived of rights, but no matter whether proceeding from the member for Lambton, or the member for Haldimand, or from this government, one thing is clear that the blow must fall, the secularization must take place. Why then resist against all hope? Why continue to agitate the public mind? Why not yield to inevitable necessity? If a person receives a wrong, there is always a consolation that it is a wrong without a desert. I believe that those Churches who will suffer from this Act will receive in some [. . .]* but we give it up for the sake of peace, we give it up for the sake of settling those quarrels for ever, we give it up in the name of charity, and that it may not be said that we are the disturbers of the public peace. This may be strong language, but I use it in no offensive sense. They are not disturbers of the public peace in asserting their own rights, but the effect of the demanding their rights is that the public peace is disturbed, and we ask them to yield and accept our measure. We introduce this measure as a measure of peace, peace at any sacrifice, and for peace in this question no price too great can be paid.

---

* The government's settlement provided for the clergy's salaries by paying a one-time sum to their churches; in the following lines of this speech Macdonald imagines the clergy saying that they were doing it for the sake of peace. (Westfall, *Two Worlds*, 111)

DEFENDING SEPARATE SCHOOLS, 1855

It fell to Macdonald to introduce the contentious new Separate Schools bill of 1855 to the Assembly at the tail end of a long parliamentary session. Étienne-Paschal Taché (1795–1865) had already tabled it in the legislative council. Assembly members who rose to speak expressed annoyance that such an important bill had been introduced so late in the session after many members had left Quebec City. They also complained that it had been introduced in council first, which prohbited amendments to the bill.[2]

Separate schooling had been established in Canada West in 1841, but since the mid-1840s, the superintendent of education, Egerton Ryerson (1803–1882), had worked towards a common system of non-denominational Christian education. The number of separate schools tended to decline, but their provision remained protected by law upon request of twelve families to a board of trustees in a city or town. The Catholic Church, however, was struggling to minister to a vast diocese of 80,000 congregants in and beyond Toronto, expanded by the immigrant Irish. Armand-François-Marie de Charbonnel (1802–1891), the Roman Catholic Bishop of Toronto, found himself particularly disturbed by the "ignorance and intemperance," as he saw it, of the distressed immigrants. Seized with the spirit of institutional assertion coming from Rome, he pushed for the new bill of 1855 in order to increase the Church control of schools—control that rested at that time in the hands of individual Catholic families. The new bill did not go as far as the bishop wanted, but it did provide for Catholic teachers in the common schools, and exempted the separate school supporters from paying rates to the common schools and lowered the number of families necessary to request a school from twelve to five. The passage of the bill by a bloc of legislative members from Canada East alienated many in Canada West and intensified demands for constitutional change.³ Discussion opened, with members questioning the very existence of separate schooling.

The Globe *reported on June 11, 1855:*

ATTY. GEN. MACDONALD proceeded to say that the question was not whether they should have Separate Schools or not, but that principle having already been established by law, and this Bill being introduced to make it more workable, he did not think it fair that its details should be attacked on the ground that we should not have Separate Schools at all. That question ought to have come up in another form and then he would have been quite prepared to say that he was strongly in favour of Separate Schools, and to give his reasons for being of that opinion. He believed that the Roman Catholics, the laity as well as the priesthood, wished to have Separate Schools, or at least the power to establish them if they chose, and he was in favour of granting them that power. If they could make the world all of one way of thinking, it might work more harmoniously, but yet he doubted very much if things would go on a bit better on that account. The severance of opinion, the right of private judgment, tended to the elevation of man, and he should be sorry if a Legislature, the majority of whose members were Protestants professing to recognize the great Protestant principle of right of private judgment, should yet seek to deprive Roman Catholics of the power to educate their children according to their own principles, or, if they chose to term it so, according to their own religious prejudices. He believed it was the duty of the State to educate every child, and to make him a civilized being, by affording the readiest means of opening the avenues of knowledge to the mind, and communicating the elementary principles of education. With the religious faith of the child they had nothing whatever to do. (Mr. [George] Brown.—Hear! hear!) All the State had to do was to teach the children to read, write and cipher and when they did so, they advanced them in the scale of civilized beings. But because it happened that a large class of our fellow subjects could not conscientiously approve of the Common School system, thought that the faith of their children would be endangered by it, and believed that education should go hand in hand with religion, was the State to deny to those parties the blessings of education? If they would not receive un-sectarian education, he would say, let them be allowed to educate their children in their own way.

"DOUBLE MAJORITY," 1858

1857 was a signal year for Macdonald. He had replaced Sir Allan Napier MacNab at the head of government, first in a co-premiership with Sir Étienne-Paschal Taché (1795–1865), and then with George-Étienne Cartier, who replaced Taché. Legislation streamed through the hands of the Macdonald-Cartier coalition, shaping the province's penitentiaries, asylums, civil service, and justice system and creating the "Act to encourage the gradual civilization of the Indians in this Province, and to amend the laws respecting Indians," which entitled Indians who demonstrated certain property qualifications to vote.[4] But constitutional questions continued to dominate the legislature. The idea of government by a "double majority" had been the modus operandi of the legislature between 1848 and 1856—creating, in effect, a "quasi-federal question," as Sir Edmund Head, the governor general, observed—because it sought a majority of votes from Canada West and Canada East to pass laws, and raised the question of whether laws affecting one portion of the United Province of Canada should hold the majority of votes from members of that portion.

As George Brown and the Clear Grits grew in power in Canada West to join forces with the Reformers, this system became less stable.

In the summer of 1858, the question of the "double majority" principle had arisen again. Alexander Galt began proposing a formal federal structure for the provinces and even the whole of British North America. In this debate, George Brown, representing Toronto, encapsulated the general view that "in Canada, two races, two languages, two religions, and two different social systems, and the diversity of sentiment between the two nations were beginning to make themselves felt in the management of public affairs, whilst local jealousies were everywhere seen." He rejected the "Will o' the Wisp" idea of the "double majority," promoting instead representation by population and the implicit idea of universal suffrage, which would give more votes to the more heavily populated Canada West.[5]

The Globe *reported on July 20, 1858:*

ATTY. GEN. MACDONALD: . . . As to the Double Majority principle, he [Macdonald] looked upon it as in every respect opposed to the principle of Responsible Government, and as such he should always oppose and vote against it. The true method was to have a Government, the members of which agreed on the principles of legislation applicable to the whole country, and not one divided into two sections, under local influences of east and west, to the sacrifice of the great and general interests of the Province. This country is one, and nearly all the questions of local import are unimportant. And was it for the sake of these that an Administration which commanded the confidence of a large majority of the House was to be set aside for the sake of a principle which the hon. member for Toronto himself had declared to be unwholesome? The position of the Government in England was similar to that of the Upper Canada section of the Government in this Province. Lord Derby had the largest following of any man in the House of Commons, but he had not a majority. If the old Whigs under Palmerston and Russell, and the Liberals under Bright and the Peelites under Gladstone, were to unite their forces, they could [out]number Lord Derby's following, but it was not objected to him on that he ruled by a minority.* The member for Toronto said the Government had been afraid to go on with their measures. Was it not the fact that they had occupied fully the whole time assigned to the Government? They had used their own discretion as to the order in which they should be brought up, but the House had not been left a moment idle, by the Government failing to give them measures to consider. All of them were well advanced, there being only one, the Land Bill, which had not had a second reading. That also would be forward in due time. He [Macdonald] had no hesitation in admitting that, in consequence of the temporary excitement created in Upper Canada by the course he and his colleagues thought it their duty to take on Lower Canada matters, there was a prejudice against them in Upper Canada, and they suffered severely at many of the elections, but any one who went over the returns would find that the majority of votes polled through the country were in favour of persons known to be friends of the Administration. (Incredulous laughter from the Opposition.) And in this House he claimed that the Government had the majority of religions and creeds. He had made a calculation, and what was the result, not claiming [i.e., including or counting] the member for Huron and the member for South Waterloo, (Messrs. Holmes

---

* In 1858 Lord Derby (Edward Smith-Stanley), prime minister of Britain, had created a majority Conservative government from a minority position by exploiting an opposition fragmented between Lord John Russell (1792–1878), Henry John Temple, third Viscount Palmerston (1784–1865), radicals and liberals associated with John Bright (1811–1889) and Peelite supporters. (Hawkins, *British Party Politics, 1852–1886*, 66-9)

and W. Scott) neither of whom had much sympathy with the member for Toronto?

MR. BROWN: It would be strange if you did claim them, when they voted non-confidence in you two or three days ago.

ATTY. GEN. MACDONALD then concluded his speech by giving, as the result of his calculations, that there were in the House 42 Protestants who supported the Government, and 36 who opposed it; 33 Roman Catholics, Ministerialists, and 17 Opposition; 47 of British origin, Ministerialists, and 38 Opposition; 28 of French origin, Ministerialists, and 14 Opposition.

FINDING THE SEAT OF GOVERNMENT, 1858

Like the constitutional questions, the "seat of government" question had tended to monopolize debate in the House of Assembly, since 1843. Moving the capital between cities—the so-called perambulating system started after 1849—was proving tiresome. Debate on the issue in 1856 had lasted a week and led to Macdonald's resignation from office in a move that compelled the removal of Sir Allan Napier MacNab as head of the Conservatives,[6] eventually leaving Étienne-Paschal Taché (1795–1865) as the first minister and Macdonald installed as his co-premier. In 1857 an agreement to make Quebec City the capital had been unexpectedly overturned, prompting Macdonald to suggest that Queen Victoria be asked to choose the seat of government, and she agreed.[7]

At this moment in 1858, the House was discussing amendments to an address to the Queen, asking that she rescind her choice of Ottawa, which carried by 64 votes to 50. George-Étienne Cartier had replaced Taché as co-premier with Macdonald in 1857. This Macdonald-Cartier ministry chose to treat it as a vote of non-confidence (despite surviving a vote of adjournment on the issue) and resigned. Governor General

Sir Edmund Head asked George Brown to form the ministry, setting the stage for the "two-day administration," and the "double shuffle."[8] The Leader *reported on July 29, 1858:*

HON. ATTORNEY GENERAL MACDONALD said that the hon. member for Toronto [George Brown] had previously acceded to the policy of the Government in fixing the Seat of Government. Yet now he would unfix it until some great questions of public policy were settled. The only question of great public importance remaining unsettled was the Representation question. So far as the vote of that House could go, he might remark that that question had for the present session been decided by the House. Former Governments feeling the difficulty of this question had made it an open one. It was impossible for any Government to submit any one place [for the seat of government]—as on such a proposition all the other local interests would unite against that place. In order to get over this difficulty Government came down to the House and fully and fairly stated the case, asking an appropriation and recommending that Her Majesty [Queen Victoria] be asked to select the Seat of Government. The Legislature of that day agreed as to the advisability of this course, and Her Majesty was asked to give her decision. He [Macdonald] presumed that in assenting to that course, every hon. member had acted in good faith. He for one had done so, though he felt that his constituency had strong claims for the Seat of Government. Her Majesty, it was arranged, was not to be advised on the subject by the Canadian Government, and accordingly no such advice had been tendered. Her Majesty gave her decision; and although strictly speaking that despatch ought not to have been made public till laid before the House, still the Government knowing that there was room in a matter of this kind for the charge that the despatch had been concealed to allow for speculation,* at once made it public through the Press. That decision had been subsequently ratified by the Legislature and the appropriation for the necessary buildings had been passed. He [Macdonald] thought the amendment of the hon. member for Berthier [Eugène-Urgel Piché] a brusque and uncourteous insult to Her Majesty and one which decidedly negatived the pretensions of Montreal. The House had already strongly decided in favor of a permanent seat of Government, and in the last Parliament there was such an overwhelming opinion in favor of it, that a motion affirming it was carried without a division. As he [Macdonald] said before the effect of the motion of the hon. member for Berthier was merely to declare in the rudest and boldest manner that the House regretted Her Majesty's decision. If the hon. member for Montreal [Antoine-Aimé Dorion] had taken the more open course of fighting for Montreal and not entered into the present party arrangement, that hon. member would have averted the consequences of the vote on the hon. member for Berthier's motion—which would undoubtedly be against the interests of Montreal. He [Macdonald] would vote for sustaining the decision of Her Majesty, and against the amendments of the hon. members for Berthier and Toronto.

---

* Presumably, Macdonald meant land speculation, as the choice of Ottawa as the capital would raise the value of land in the area.

DEFINING A HOMELAND WITH
THE HOMESTEAD ACT, 1860

LEGISLATIVE ASSEMBLY,
QUEBEC CITY, APRIL 19

In the spring of 1860 the House of Assembly was debating whether to study in a "Committee of the Whole" a bill "to Exempt Homesteads and certain other property, under certain value, for sale under execution." The constitutional crisis of the "double shuffle" in 1858 had passed, and the government's "quiet and peaceable" activities vindicated Governor General Head's assessment of the province's need for stability. The government completed its full legal term, with a practical program for the province.9

As Thompson's Mirror of Parliament for the 3rd session of the 6th Parliament *reported on April 19, 1860*:

MR. [LEWIS THOMAS] DRUMMOND [member for Lotbinière] said, this Bill would seriously affect the interests of Lower Canada by attracting all the Immigrants to Upper Canada, where every man could hold £200 worth of Real Estate in defiance of his creditors. Even the *habitants* of Lower Canada would desert their country with such a temptation. If this Bill passed, he should feel obliged, though opposed to the measure in principle, to introduce a similar Bill for Lower Canada.

HON. ATTORNEY GENERAL MACDONALD understood the Hon. gentleman to oppose the Bill because it would render Upper Canada too popular. He hoped he would lose no time in repudiating such sentiments, for they were certainly not the sentiments of other Hon. members from Lower Canada, who were not in the habit of opposing Bills because they were to add to the prosperity of Upper Canada. The relations between Upper and Lower Canada were so intimate, that it was impossible to pass any Bill affecting the one that did not affect the other. If a measure regarding the trade, or Commerce, or Agriculture, or any of the material interests of the country was good for Upper Canada, it was also good for Lower Canada, and if it was bad for one section, it would inevitably redouble the prejudice of the other section. (Hear, hear.) That was the salvation of the country; that was the all sufficient answer to the resolutions touching the Dissolution of the Union which all were so anxious to hear discussed. (Hear, hear.) We were one people; one in necessity, one in business, one in trade, one in prosperity, and one in our prospects of the future. (Hear, hear.) This fact would show, when the question arose, how wicked and infamous was the attempt to separate what nature had joined together. (Hear, hear, and laughter.) Hon. gentlemen opposite might laugh, but it was because they had played with the question until they had become familiarized with it, but none trembled more than they did at the mere idea of those resolutions being successful. He [Macdonald] would not then discuss the principle of this Bill, but he could shew to the satisfaction of every Hon. member that it would not work at all. It was faulty in every clause. If a Property Exemption Bill was needed, it must be of a different nature altogether. He [Macdonald] would suggest that the consideration of the Bill be postponed for a week or so, to give opportunities to examine it in detail. He was, however, opposed to it in principle, but he was also opposed to having persons turned out of doors and deprived of everything they possessed. He thought that property now exempted was insufficient. A larger exemption should be granted by the Division, than by the Superior Courts, but at present it was just the reverse.

TALKING ON TOUR, 1860

Macdonald stumbled and fell politically on the occasion of the royal tour in the late summer of 1860. The occasion began well enough. The legislators at Quebec primped and prepared the city to welcome the Prince of Wales, Albert Edward, later Edward VII (1841–1910). The Globe reported that a "great deal of time has been wasted by John A. Macdonald in learning to walk, for the sword suspended to his waist has an awkward knack of getting between his legs, especially after dinner," later drawing a portrait of Macdonald's "thin, spare frame" in "ceaseless motion."[10] The royal tour was important on a number of different fronts. For Canada, it was an opportunity to be on the world stage. For the Conservatives, it presented an opportunity to reinforce their commitment to Britain. For Aboriginal peoples it presented an occasion for the Crown to investigate their concerns about the Indian Department. For the Orange Order it was an opportunity to express their Protestant loyalties.[11]

The royal tour progressed from city to town to city in repeating pattern of "spruce arches, cannon, procession, levee, lunch, ball, departure; cheers, crowds, men, women, enthusiasm, militia, Sunday school children, illuminations, fire works, etcetera, etcetera, ad infinitum," as one exhausted reporter described.

At Kingston there were triumphal arches, but no parade. Henry Pelham Fiennes Pelham-Clinton, fifth duke of Newcastle (1811–1864) and then colonial secretary, travelling with the nineteen-year-old prince, declined to allow his charge to acknowledge the Orange Order displays planned in Kingston. The Irish order, suppressed in Britain, but legal in Canada, held strong anti-Catholic views that stemmed from their commitment to the idea of Protestantism as integral to the British constitution. So, the royal party remained on a ship in the harbour. When no compromise emerged, the ship steamed away, but Macdonald stayed in Kingston to keep faith with his constituents and supporters among the Order and to express his annoyance that Newcastle had not recognized Canadian law.[12]

Still worried, Macdonald embarked on a speaking tour to repair any damage. He began in Brantford on November 9, and visited St. Thomas, London, Hamilton, Toronto, Guelph, Kingston, Belleville, Caledonia, St. Catharines, Simcoe, and Millbrook, finishing on December 7. Upwards of eight hundred people would turn out to hear him speak.

After the tour, Macdonald printed a collation of excerpts from his speeches. His addresses in Brantford explaining the royal tour and in St. Catharines recalling the "double shuffle" of 1858 show a politician preparing to meet the voters. Macdonald and Cartier were voted back into power in June 1861. A new governor general, Lord Monck, arrived that November.[13] Macdonald asked the Kingston electors to read the speeches that he had delivered to the people of Brantford on November 9, 1860.

The Address of the Hon. John A. Macdonald to the Electors of the City of Kingston . . . of 1861 *reports:*

[HON. MR. MACDONALD:] This has been a great year for Canada. The chairman [of the Brantford gathering] has alluded in graceful terms to the auspicious visit to Canada of the son of our present Sovereign—our future Sovereign. He has spoken of Her Majesty as she deserves; she is not merely a Queen appointed by law, but she reigns in the hearts and affections of all her subjects. We are proud that we live in the times of such a Queen; and our happiness is increased by a knowledge of the fact that our children will in all human probability live under a king [Prince Albert Edward, later King Edward VII (1841–1910)] who, from his visit to this country, has satisfied us that he has all the virtues of his royal mother. (Cheers.) Why, he carried the hearts of Canada by storm. The people were loyal before his visit, but their hearts swelled within them when they saw the son of their Sovereign—so kind, so considerate, and always willing and anxious to please every body. If loyal before, they are twenty times more so, if possible, now. (Loud cheers.)

And it is particularly gratifying to me that the day selected by the gentlemen of the County of Brant for this dinner should be the birthday of our future sovereign and son of our beloved Queen. This is not a mere temporary gratification, but one of lasting remembrance. As for His Royal Highness the Prince of Wales, his visit to Canada formed a most important epoch in his life; as long as he lived he would remember it as his first act of royalty. Before he came here he had been laboring to form himself for the government of the country, but he had been undergoing a course of training only until he came to this country; and here first he had assumed the position and taken stand as sovereign of Canada. (Applause.)

He did not come, as we are proud to know, simply as the heir to the Crown of British Empire; but with the added dignity of the direct representative of Her Majesty, who, unable to come herself and gratify the wishes of the Canadian people, appointed him to be for the time her *locum tenens*, giving him for the time all her powers, all her position, as far as granting honor to this country was concerned; and we have the gratification of knowing that not only our future sovereign, but the direct representative of Her Majesty has visited this large, great and magnificent Colony of ours. Besides the great honor conferred, the people of Canada must feel that the visit will be of great and permanent advantage. It has called the attention of the world to the position and prospects of Canada; and it will have a lasting effect upon all our great national interests. The country will be sought after; its great resources and wealth thought of in a manner never known before; and if much of the riches of the mother country pours into Canada—if we find as I believe we shall find, that our character, our resources, and our position are much better understood in Europe than formerly—it will all be owing to the visit of the Prince of Wales to this country. (Applause.)

It is quite true that in this world we have no perfect happiness; and we have an instance of it in this case. We know that the visit of His Royal Highness was in some respects accompanied by mistakes and heartburnings, for which, however, the Prince was not responsible; from which he was perfectly free. If there has been any feeling of discomfort or annoyance, we all know that His Royal Highness was not the cause of it; if any interest of any character has been insulted or neglected, he was not responsible for it. On the contrary, we hold the Prince as dear to us as ever, and felt more proud of him the day he left Canada to visit the United States than the day he first put his foot on our soil. (Loud cheers.)

But there has been, I grieve to say, an unpleasantness to which the chairman has alluded; there has been a source of discontent and heartburning; there has been a source of a feeling in Canada that a large and respectable Association of men [the

Orangemen] has been neglected and their position ignored, that a wanton insult has been offered to them, that their dignity has been wounded. (Cheers.) That feeling the chairman has given expression to in no equivocal language and that feeling is entertained by the great majority of the people of Upper Canada. (Applause.)

When it was announced that His Royal Highness was to come to Canada in place of Her Majesty, we all received the announcement with the greatest pride and satisfaction, and did not anticipate that any of the difficulties that subsequently occurred would have taken place. We hoped that the whole of His Royal Highness's course through Canada would be one unbroken triumph; and I fear that if that prospect was destroyed, it was because the Prince's progress was advised and directed by an individual high in position, high in power, and occupying a high post in the Imperial Government [the Duke of Newcastle, the colonial secretary], but who unfortunately was not acquainted with Canada, who did not know our people and their social and religious relations, and who judged of things in this country by the position and bearing of things in the country in which he lived. It follows, as a matter of course, that when Her Majesty sent her son to represent Her, She took the same course with respect to him that She would have taken with respect to Herself. Had she come to this country Herself She would have been accompanied by some member or members of Her Ministry, to whom She would have looked for advice; and by whom Her progress would have been directed. As you well know, when Her Majesty visits her Scottish residence at Balmoral, She is always accompanied by one or more ministers, and the same is the case when She goes to Ireland. It was only the other day that She returned from Prussia, whither she had been accompanied by Lord John Russell, Minister for Foreign Affairs, in order that he might be at hand to give Her advice should circumstances arise requiring it.

In carrying out this political practice and usage, when She sent her son here to represent herself, She sent with him as She would have brought with herself one of the members of Her cabinet—that member who was most particularly connected with the colonies, His Grace the Duke of Newcastle—to give him advice as to how he should proceed during his royal progress in Canada. Any one acquainted with British constitutional practice will see that She was only literally carrying out a recognized principle. No one has so strictly observed constitutional usage as the Queen. She has never made a mistake in this respect. In this case She certainly did what She has always done—acted in accordance with the constitution of the country. (Applause.)

I know that it has been attempted to make the Provincial Administration responsible for the progress of the Prince of Wales, for the advice given to him; and for the course adopted by him in this country. But you will see from what I have stated, that his Royal Highness could not be advised by the Provincial Administration and by the Imperial Administration at the same time. The Duke of Newcastle came here on behalf of the Imperial Ministry, was endowed with all the powers and responsibilities; and such being the case, there could not possibly exist two separate bodies to advise, who might not have agreed, and certainly would not have agreed as to the course the Prince finally took. (Loud cheers.) It should be borne in mind that the members of the Canadian Ministry have taken precisely the same oath as that the Duke of Newcastle took with respect to the laws and the liberty of the subject. The Provincial government, as a government, are bound to give advice to the Governor General. That is their duty—nothing more and nothing less. In any case affecting the interests of Canada they are bound to give advice to His Excellency the Governor General, or to the Administrator of the Government; and they cannot, without a dereliction of duty, shrink from it; but they cannot, without an assumption of undue power, exceed it. (Cheers.)

This being the case, I show the whole argument against us to be fallacious. We were bound to give advice to the person who administered the affairs of this country; but the Prince of Wales no more administered the affairs of this country than the most humble man in it. He came out here as the representative of Her Majesty, but did not exercise the functions of a Governor General. The Provincial Government had no power therefore to advise him. We were bound to advise the Governor General; we could not go beyond our duty and advise one who was not the Governor General. (Applause.)

You know we are in a state of Colonial dependence; and long may the connection between this and the mother country exist. But the people of this country have rights to sustain; they have their own position to uphold. It is within the recollection of every man among us that it is only lately we became possessed of the rights we now enjoy. It is only within a few years that after a long agitation and stubborn contest, we were accorded the privilege of governing our own affairs as we think proper. But while we enjoy our own rights, we must take care not to trench upon those of others; and it would have been a great mistake to force advice upon the Prince of Wales when he was to be guided by Imperial considerations and by the officer of Her Majesty sent with him for the purpose. It is only by respecting Imperial rights that we can claim and enjoy our own and be able to say that we possess all the same rights in this country as the members of the Imperial Government in Great Britain. That is the view taken by the Provincial Government of which I am a member.

You may remember in reading the debates of last season—not very profitable or interesting matter—(a laugh)—that the subject of the Prince's visit was discussed; and there was a very natural anxiety that his Royal Highness should be received in a manner worthy of his position and of the country. At that time—I call the particular attention of those who hear me to this point, for it is made a ground of party attack upon the Government, that they neglected their duty in not giving their advice with regard to the Prince's progress;—at that time, the whole of the Opposition party in Parliament took the ground that the Provincial Government were not and ought not to be responsible for the progress of the Prince of Wales. (Cheers.) It was an afterthought to hold them responsible, induced by the natural desire to fasten a charge of dereliction of duty upon the Ministry, and thus lead to a forfeiture of the confidence of the people.

Why, if you remember the speeches that were made in the House at the time, you must recollect one made by Mr. [D'Arcy] McGee. You must remember the language that hon. gentleman used with regard to the visit, and to the impropriety of the Governor General and the Ministry interfering in the matter at all. And lest it should be said that this was merely an individual opinion, I will refer to the motion of Mr. [George] Brown, who in the absence of Hon. J[ohn] S[andfield] Macdonald, moved the appointment of a committee *chosen from both sides of the House*, to consider the most fitting manner of receiving the Prince of Wales. The fact is, the Opposition felt the Prince of Wales would rouse to enthusiasm the feeling of every man in this country, and feared John A. Macdonald and [George-Étienne] Cartier would take advantage of that feeling to destroy the influence of the Opposition and build up themselves. (Applause.) They then argued that it was not the duty of the Government, but of the Legislature, to receive the Prince; and that it would only make it a matter of party political triumph if the Government interfered at all. That this was the feeling of the Opposition then is clearly apparent. In the speech that was delivered from the throne in the beginning of the present Session an allusion was made to the happy prospect of the Prince of Wales' visit; and the address being before the House, Mr. McGee, the hon. member for Montreal, made the following remarks.—I quote from the *Mirror of Parliament*:—

"Mr. McGee said he did not intend to speak, and should not have spoken, had it not been the impression on many minds that the first paragraph of the address should not go to the public without an expression of opinion from hon. gentlemen generally. That paragraph, as they were all aware, had reference to the visit to Canada of His Royal Highness the Prince of Wales. It would be in the recollection of Mr. Speaker—for no one had been more concerned in bringing about this desirable result than himself—that the address of both Houses was agreed to with great unanimity on all sides. Therefore, what he would desire to express now—he did not care whether hon. gentlemen on this side of the House would agree with him—was that, if His Royal Highness the Prince of Wales should, *by the command of Her Majesty and under the advice of Her constitutional advisers*, visit Canada, it was highly desirable that he should be received by all classes of Her Majesty's subjects with invariable good will—not, he would say, with perfunctory kindness, but with hearty good will. In the Imperial point of view the object of His Royal Highness' visit was, no doubt, to increase the good feeling existing between this Colony and the mother country and also to impress the people of the United States with the value of monarchical institutions. As regarded ourselves the object of the visit could no doubt be to make an advertisement. As regarded the Grand Trunk Railroad Company their object was no doubt to make money. (Cries of "oh.") There was no question about the matter, although hon. gentlemen might cry "oh," but whatever might be their object, the object of Imperial statesmen—the men who looked before and after—was to increase the attachment between Canada and the mother country. Well, that being so, he wished to say, as one of the representatives of the city where His Royal Highness would probably be first and most prominently introduced to the people, that if His Royal Highness was to be chaperoned by a person standing between the people and His Royal Highness, and whom the people thoroughly detested; if His Royal Highness' visit was merely made the instrument for rebuilding the popularity of an unpopular Governor General, it were really better that His Royal Highness should not visit the Province. (Cries of "shame.")

SPEAKER: There must be no allusion to His Excellency the Governor General.

McGEE: Why, it was His Excellency's speech that was the order of the day and he was speaking to it. (A laugh.) He did not raise this question; but he wished to say that if an unpopular Governor General [Sir Edmund Head] were to stand between the Prince and the people—if they were to see His Royal Highness made the instrument for whitewashing the double shuffle and the two sets of oaths taken by Hon. gentlemen opposite—if, in short, they were to see the visit converted into a political object and a display of flunkeyism, instead of an expression of loyalty to the throne and to the person of the Queen—if they were to see an unpopular Governor General standing between the Prince and people, then a great deal more mischief than good would be the result.

SPEAKER: Order. (Cries of "chair.")

McGEE: Well it should be understood that if His Royal Highness came here under the present circumstances under the advice and protection of gentlemen opposite, and with a Governor General who had a historic name or an actual name—his reception would not be such as every loyal subject and every attached subject would desire it to be."*

Here was a distinct announcement of those members of Parliament who spoke on the subject, against the Government interfering at all, and I have no doubt these same gentlemen

---

* This is an accurate transcription of the passage as printed in Thompson's *Mirror of Parliament* (Quebec, 1860), for February 29, 1860, 13-4.

will now denounce us as traitors to the country for not advising the Prince, forcing him to go where we wished, and to act
as we choose. In answer to Mr. McGee's, the only notice taken
of it was by Mr. Gowan* who had intended to reply but said
"He had been advised that the best way to treat it would be by
passing it over in silence." And I would have passed it over in
silence also, and not raked it from the ashes in which it lay, had
not the very party to which I belong now said that we were
guilty of a violation of the constitution because we did not
interfere. (Loud applause.) I will now refer to the motion of Mr.
J. S. Macdonald, who wished to have a committee chosen from
both sides of the House to make arrangements for the visit. My
answer was, of course, that the Prince of Wales would come
to this country attended by his own Imperial advisers, and that
the Provincial Government would have no right to interfere as
to His Royal Highness' course, and that if they did they would
probably be told it was none of their business. But I objected to
a committee of that kind because it involved the expenditure
of the public moneys. You all know that the Government of
the day are alone responsible for the disbursement of the public
money. I pointed out that under the constitution we could not
hand that responsibility over to any body, whether a member
of the Legislature or not; and that we could not, as long as we
possessed the confidence of Parliament, entrust to any one the
expenditure of the large sum of money that would be required
for the purpose of receiving the heir apparent to the British
throne in a manner worthy of Canada, and as he ought to be

---

* Ogle Robert Gowan (1803–1876) was grand master of the Grand Orange Lodge of
British North America, a Macdonald ally in the 1840s and a George Brown antagonist in
the late 1850s when he sat for North Leeds. He retired from provincial politics in 1861.
(Senior, "Gowan, Ogle Robert," DCB)

received by the people of this country. On the 14th of May Mr. Brown, in the absence of Mr. J. S. Macdonald, moved the appointment of the committee.

> Mr. Brown said "the Legislature had invited the Prince and the Legislature, as representing the people of Canada, ought to receive him. It was not a political matter and the Government ought not to take the entire control out of the hands of the Legislature."

> "Mr. Cauchon said it was desirable that the demonstration should not be a party affair, but thought it would be saved from that character by some member of the opposition seconding the address to be moved by the government.

> "Mr. Brown said his motion went further than that. The Prince was a guest of the Legislature and they were the proper body to take action in regard to his progress through the Province. If the reception were left in the hands of the Executive, there was danger of it being regarded as a party affair."

There, gentlemen, you will see, that before the Prince came, when the opposition were naturally as anxious to do honor to His Royal Highness as the majority of the House, and to claim that they were as loyal subjects and as sincere in their desire that Canada should give a worthy reception to the Prince— they were at the same time anxious to prevent what they feared, namely, that the government would take advantage of the enthusiasm created by the Prince's presence and make political capital out of it, and to avoid this proposed that the whole of the royal progress should be under the management of a committee chosen equally from both sides of the House.—And they now say that the government ought to have assumed the responsibility, and that we were guilty of a dereliction of duty in not doing what they then said we ought not to do. (Loud applause.)

Now, supposing the government had, for the sake of avoiding responsibility, consented to the appointment of a committee, what would have been the position of the committee? They would have held no position in the state, being a mere voluntary body without administrative powers. Supposing these difficulties had arisen, as they probably would, would the committee have advised the Duke of Newcastle? Were they constitutional and responsible advisers? And what would the Duke of Newcastle have said to them had they offered their advice?—"Pray who are you?" (Laughter.) He would, of course, have paid no attention to their suggestions. And this was the course the opposition would have adopted; and now they denounce the government for not having interfered, for not having stood between the Prince and the people, for having allowed every body, whether of high or low degree, a free opportunity of approaching the foot of the throne, and without respect to party politics of any kind whatever, paying their loyal duty to the Crown. (Applause.)

When Mr. J. S. Macdonald's motion was before the House, I said "the Prince during his visit would not be directed by the Government or the Legislature but would be accompanied by his own advisers, and would consult Her Majesty's Representative here, the Governor General, and of course the Governor General could not receive advice from gentlemen who had no confidence in his Government. The Ministry could not admit the unconstitutional principle that this money should be voted and expended, except on their responsibility." I said that the Government were responsible for the expenditure of the money, but as to where the Prince would go, how long he would stay in the country, and as to his line of progress, he was to be governed entirely by the advisers who would come with him; and if those advisers had not come, Her Majesty would have been guilty of that which she had never before been guilty of, a violation of constitutional usage. And the doctrine which I laid down was accepted by the Legislature; the motion was lost, and the matter was left just as the Governor had put it—that, as a Ministry, we should see to the disbursement of the funds, and that it should be done handsomely. We should never have been able to stand up before Parliament and the country if we had received the Prince in a mean, sordid manner. (Applause.)

And I may say now—I am happy to inform you—that, while it is admitted by everybody, and while we have the pleasure of knowing His Royal Highness was gratified, pleased and surprised by the handsome and magnificent reception he had met, the people of Canada will be surprised to learn at the proper time the economical way in which they have given that admittedly grand reception. (Loud cheers.)

Well, returning to the constitutional question—the course of Government was clear. We were acquainted with the outlines of his progress. We knew he would go to Quebec, the capital of the Province; to Ottawa, the future capital; to Montreal, to visit the magnificent Victoria Bridge; and to the other principal cities and the great wonders of nature in the country. We knew the main points at which he would stop, and made arrangements to give him a worthy reception at each place. We made suggestions as to what was to be done, but merely suggestions, as we had no authority to advise. There our duty ended; and when His Royal Highness came he was accompanied by the Duke of Newcastle, his constitutional adviser.

Now I must say I think it unfortunate that the Prince was advised by the Duke of Newcastle. He was a man of undoubted integrity and honor, and of high rank and position; but liable to look at things from an Imperial point of view. He was like myself a member of an administration, depending upon Parliament for support, and had to consider what effect the progress of the Prince would have upon the mother country and the Palmerston Administration.* (Applause.) He did look upon things from an Imperial point of view; and from his course upon the Orange question, I am quite certain that the Duke of Newcastle thought more of the condition and prospects of the Palmerston Government than of the Province. Why, we know that at the very time the Duke of Newcastle was saying he would not recognize the Orange Institution in any manner, a bill was being passed through the Imperial Parliament, with the sanction of the Government, declaring it criminal to wear the badge or colors of the Orange Order. That fact, no doubt, was pressing upon His Grace, and we can easily understand what his feelings were when asked if it would be convenient for His Royal Highness to receive an address from the members of the Order in this country. He felt that by giving his consent, he would be practically opposed to the legislation of the Imperial Parliament, in which he and his Government had a very small majority—and that majority he was liable at any moment to lose. Whatever effect that might have upon his

---

* Henry John Temple, third Viscount Palmerston (1784–1865), a British Liberal with former Tory sympathies, was prime minister between 1855 and 1859 and 1860 and 1865. (Steele, "Temple, Henry John, third Viscount Palmerston," *ODNB*)

mind, he evidently never thought of the effect of his course upon Canada. I must say that His Grace acted in a most manly and straightforward manner, assuming the responsibility where he alone was responsible.

I believe the letter he wrote to the Mayor of Kingston was most injudicious and dictatorial. I am satisfied that had he made the request, in the name of the Prince, that the Orangemen would not appear in badges and regalia; from one end of the country to the other they would have abandoned them, and I am convinced that had His Grace pursued this course, there would have been no difficulty. (Cheers.) It is one thing to lead a man by kindness and courtesy, and another to shake a halter and say "come along." (Laughter and applause.) But while his course was dictatorial and injudicious, while he sacrificed the good feeling of the people of Canada, I must say that His Grace manfully took all the responsibility upon himself, and I will explain how. The Prince had reached Ottawa when the news arrived that there was likely to be difficulty at Kingston. Of course, I was exceedingly anxious that every thing should pass over well at that place; and therefore, while His Royal Highness went up the Upper Ottawa, I left for Prescott, for the purpose of meeting a deputation sent specially down to come to some arrangement with the Duke of Newcastle. I accompanied them back and introduced them to His Grace, with whom they had a long, earnest and animated conversation on the matter. We pressed, in stronger and more emphatic language than His Grace was probably accustomed to hear, what we thought it was his duty to do and what might be the consequence if he persisted in his threatened course. In doing so, I did not act as a member of the Government, but as representative of Kingston, whose interests I had at heart.

I am not going to enter into a discussion as to the propriety or impropriety of the conduct of the Orange Association. One thing is quite clear, that they had a legal right to assemble in the streets; that like any other loyal subjects—and God knows there were none more loyal—they had the right of presenting their humble duty to the son of their Sovereign. Whether they chose to do so in the peculiar garb of the Order or not, depended upon themselves; there being no law to prevent their appearance in such regalia. It may not have been in good taste to do so, but the way to avoid it was not by writing that letter, but to ask them to refrain for the sake of the Prince. When they were told that they must act in such a manner as was agreeable to His Grace, and if they did not, the place where they assembled would not be honored by a visit from the Prince, they naturally felt deeply wounded and annoyed.

All this was pressed strongly upon the Duke of Newcastle. He admitted the truth of it. He said he was quite aware of the difference of the law in England and in Canada; he was quite aware that the Mayor had no right to prevent the Orangemen appearing in procession; that if he did attempt to use force to prevent them, he would be committing a breach of the law for which he would be held answerable; but His Grace said—and I am exceedingly grieved that he persisted in the course—"as the Prince of Wales may visit Ireland next year, I cannot and will not advise him to take a course here that he cannot take there." For this determination and the results of it the Duke of Newcastle rests responsible. In speaking of this conversation, I speak with confidence as to the meaning of his statements, because there were four gentlemen of character and standing present who are quite ready to vouch for the truth of them.

We pressed upon His Grace also these considerations: The

Orange Association were not forcing their way unduly into the presence of the Prince, but the committee of reception had notified them and given them a place in the procession; and the different lodges in the country had gone to great trouble and considerable expense in making preparations. The Mayor stated also that when the Duke of Newcastle's letter was received, announcing that the Prince would not land if Orangemen took part in the procession, he informed the committee, who, although they had assigned the lodges a place in the procession, came to the conclusion that there should be no procession of any kind; and asked whether under these circumstances the Prince might not land and see the people, and yet not be held to give up the position taken or held to recognize officially the Orange institution? The Duke in reply stated that as long as there was an Orange arch or banner or badge in the streets he could not allow His Royal Highness to land. He was fixed in this determination; and the deputation, after exhausting every argument in vain, finally left: and as I had no official duty to perform, I resolved to cast in my lot with my own people at Kingston. I therefore returned there with the deputation and stayed there. I felt it would be very bad taste to enter into the festivities at other places, nor did I see His Royal Highness again until the moment he was leaving the country, when I went to pay him my respectful duties and bid him farewell. (Applause.)

I have said before and now repeat that the course taken by the Duke of Newcastle was highly injudicious. Had the Prince landed in Kingston under the circumstances stated by the Mayor, what would have been the consequences? He would have pleased the Orange institution, because, although not recognized officially their rights would have been vindicated; and on the other hand, the Roman Catholics would have been pleased, because they would have succeeded so far that the Duke of Newcastle would not have carried out the recognition of the Order. The people of Kingston would have been pleased, because the Prince had honored them with a visit and accepted of their hospitalities. But as it was every body was displeased. The people of Kingston were annoyed because their city was avoided; and the Duke of Newcastle had left behind him a rankling wound which would require all the temper and moderation of the public mind to soothe; where we expected, and if he had acted judiciously there would have been, gratification and pride. All that was lost by the injudicious and dictatorial conduct of the Duke of Newcastle, and upon him alone rests the responsibility.

As far as the Government is concerned, we feel we have carried out the constitution literally; as far as I personally am concerned, I stood by the rights of the people and vindicated them as strongly as I could. I entreat the pardon of gentlemen present for dwelling upon this matter; but it is of great importance that I should put the views of myself and my colleagues in the Administration fairly before them and through them before the country. (Cheers.) Well, having done so, I will glance at the position taken by the Opposition on the subject. They said "Oh, you should have resigned. You should have advised the Prince of Wales, and if your advice was not respected, you should have resigned." The constitutional maxim with regard to advice was this: if the Government gave advice to the Governor General, and if in his discretion that advice were rejected, then they would give place to those whose advice he could act upon. But supposing we had offered advice to His Excellency on this subject, what might his answer have been? "Well, gentlemen, I agree with you." Suppose His Excellency said that—

HON. MR. [PHILIP] VANKOUGHNET:* (interruptingly)
Perhaps he did.

HON. MR. MACDONALD: Yes, perhaps he did. Well, the
Governor General would say, "The Prince of Wales will not
take my advice." Should we resign in that case? But supposing for
the moment that the Governor General had said to the Prince
"I advise you to land." The Prince would have at once replied, "I
cannot do that, because it would be contrary to the advice of the
Duke of Newcastle, who is here as my constitutional adviser."
Were we to resign and hand over the Government of this country to "joint authority," Brown, Dorion and McGee, because
the Prince of Wales preferred to take the advice of the Duke of
Newcastle to that of Sir Edmund Head? (Laughter and cheers.)
Why, the whole thing can be made so ridiculous that you will
see at once the absurdity of the argument of the Opposition.
Supposing we had resigned because the Duke of Newcastle
would not take our advice. What then? The Governor General
would have sent for Mr. Brown, who would have spent a couple
of weeks in forming his ministry, scattered all over the country.
Was the Prince of Wales to remain in the harbor of Kingston for
a fortnight, having his meals conveyed to him in a small boat,
till Mr. Brown had succeeded in making an Administration?
And then, supposing he had remained; what would Mr. Brown
have done? He would then have had to advise—it would
have been his business to advise; and the Duke of Newcastle
would have said, "I refused Cartier and Macdonald, and I can't
agree with you." (Laughter.) Mr. Brown would, of course, in

---

* Probably, Philip Michael Matthew Scott VanKoughnet (or Vankoughnet) (1822–1869),
who became chancellor of the Court of Chancery of Upper Canada in 1862. (Morton,
"VanKoughnet, Philip Michael Matthew Scott," DCB)

virtuous indignation, have resigned at once; and the Prince of Wales would have been at Kingston till the present day. (Great laughter.) This is precisely the line of argument adopted by the Opposition. I know that with all their faults, gentlemen would prefer the present Government to one hurried together under the circumstances pointed out—they would rather have the devil they knew than the devil they didn't know (laughter); they would rather have the present Administration with the sins of seven years on their heads, than trust their interests to the untutored zeal of a Brown and of a McGee. (Great applause.)

I know many of my own friends are as ardent Protestants as myself. Well, these very friends would have been the first to say, had I resigned, "You should have stuck to the ship to the last." The Government are quite ready, when they receive constitutional notice, gracefully to walk out; but until then it would be cowardly, and treasonable to the party who have so long sustained us, to break up that party and throw them into unexpected opposition, in return for the generous and hearty support they have given us, through good and evil report, for seven long years. (Loud and prolonged cheering.) I trust you will pardon me for occupying so much of your time. (Cries of "go on.") No; I think I have said enough; that I have exposed the fallacies of the Opposition, and run the fox to earth. (Cheers.) And no one knows the absurdity of their arguments more than the leaders of the Opposition, who are exceedingly anxious to take the places of the Government now that the Prince of Wales is gone and there is no advice to be tendered.

The effects of the "double shuffle" lingered into the 1860s. Governor General Sir Edmund Walker Head continued to defend his actions. So did Macdonald. After the Macdonald-Cartier ministry resigned over the seat-of-government question in 1858, Head had invited George Brown to form a ministry. Macdonald thought Brown overconfident and watched him "jump like a fish at the chance." After two days of negotiations with Antoine-Aimé Dorion from Canada East, Brown entered into a coalition, showing himself amenable to co-operation and moderation. The government fell on a non-confidence vote (71 to 31 votes) within hours of being in office, in a late-night debate after many had left the legislature floor. But the votes of the 28 missing members would not have changed the outcome, Head pointed out.

Sensing the tenuousness of Brown's position, Head had warned Brown that he would not likely grant a dissolution of the new coalition government. It was August, and harvest season was an inconvenient time for a new election and the people had already been to the polls that winter. So when the Brown-Dorion "two-day administration" fell, Head turned to George-Étienne Cartier to form the new government, who then turned to Macdonald; together they formed the Cartier-Macdonald ministry. Keen to avoid sending their selected ministers to the polls to run in by-elections for their seats, the two leaders availed themselves of the recent Independence of Parliament Act, which stated that office-holders who resigned could change portfolios within a month without having to seek election. So, they switched their portfolios and then switched them back in a "double shuffle."[14] Two court challenges supported its legality.

The Address of the Hon. John A. Macdonald to the Electors of the City of Kingston . . . of 1861 *reports Macdonald's speech at St. Catharines on December 3, 1860:*

[HON. MR. MACDONALD:] If there is one thing, gentlemen, that has been trumpeted from one end of the country to the other, it is the course the Government pursued when they resumed office after the disastrous and humiliating defeat of the

Two-Days administration [in 1858]. (Hear, hear.) I allude to
what has been called the "double shuffle." (Laughter.) I wish
our course on that occasion to be distinctly understood, and I
think, when you hear the position we were placed in, you will
feel that we were fully justified in acting as we did.

Sir, when we resigned our positions in 1858, we had a large
majority in Parliament. We were not then driven out because
we had lost the confidence of the House; on the contrary, we
had a very large working majority; but we, who "cling to office
for the sake of public plunder," resigned our places at once,
rather than see our Queen insulted on the Seat of Government
question. We might have retained our position without difficulty, for that very day, half an hour after the vote was taken,
I appealed to the House on the question of confidence, which
Mr. [George] Brown, with his usual want of judgment, brought
up, and when I accepted the vote on the adjournment as one of
confidence or want of confidence, a majority of 14 sustained us.

You all remember how greedily Mr. Brown clutched office,
how he tried to form a government, how he could only do so by
abandoning all his principles, how the Governor General could
not within the constitution grant him a dissolution, how he
was forced to resign, and the present Government was formed.
Well, the law says, in the first place, that any man holds office
until his successor is appointed, and that any minister can return
to his office within a month of his resignation without going to
the people for re-election, and in the second place, it provides
that any member of the administration can exchange office with
his fellow ministers, also without going back to his constituents.
Now there was no necessity for our making that exchange of
offices at all, and I as an individual and other members as individuals, expressed as lawyers our opinions that we were not

obliged to do it; but there was a difference of opinion, and in order to bring ourselves as clearly under the second clause of the law as we were under the first, we did effect the exchange. In going back without re-election, we complied with the spirit of the law; in exchanging offices we complied with every letter of it too. (Hear, hear.)

They say, however, that we were wrong in thus occupying offices whose duties we did not intend to perform, and it is the general impression that if there was anything wrong, it was in the exchange. But the same kind of procedure is common in England. If any member there desires to leave Parliament, he cannot resign as he can here, but he accepts the office of Steward of the Chiltern Hundreds, gets his commission, whose duties he never intends to perform, vacates his seat by becoming an office holder, and then resigns his office for the next man who wishes to do likewise. It was in a precisely similar spirit that our exchange was made, and the malignantly foul charge that we swore to what was false is so evidently untrue, that it is hardly necessary to say any thing about it. (Hear.)

What, Sir, is perjury? It is stating as a fact what is not a fact, and swearing to it. But when we took office for the sake of holding it but momentarily, all we stated was, that while we held office we would perform its duties, and this we intended to do, whether we held our position for one minute or for 20 years. (Applause.)

And it comes with a bad grace from Mr. Brown to make this charge—from him, I say, more than from some of his colleagues, for they were *entrapped* by him—for he knew that on the very first day he accepted power, the Governor told him he could give no promise of a Dissolution, expressed or implied, and although he knew he could not retain his place for more than two days, yet he swore to discharge offices he knew he could not perform. (Hear, hear.)

I can prove this out of his own mouth, for with his usual want of policy and judgment, he told the people of Galt the other day, that one of the reasons for his accepting office was, that he should drive us back to our constituents. He said:

> "When the Brown-Dorion Administration consented to be sworn in, it was with the full knowledge that they might not hold office for 24 hours, but there was this among other arguments in favor of our running the risk of Sir Edmund Head's machinations, that if we took office and were kicked out by the Governor General we could all be returned again, while the others would have to undergo the same ordeal but would not have the same success."

What petty trickery this was! Although he knew he could not get a dissolution—although he knew he could never perform the duties of his position as Finance Minister—yet he took office for the sake of sending a few members back to their constituents, and giving them a little trouble and annoyance. But, Sir, what was the result of that course? There are but two tribunals that could judge of our course. The question had a constitutional and a legal aspect. If we acted unconstitutionally, the only tribunal to decide whether we did so, was the High Court of Parliament. If we acted illegally, the courts of law could alone settle that. The subject was solemnly submitted to Parliament, and by a deliberate vote they decided that we had acted quite constitutionally; and I have no doubt we did, for we acted legally too, as was found when the matter came up on two several actions before the two Courts of Queen's Bench and Common Pleas. (Hear.)

And just mark another bit of petty cheating. The great Grit party could not risk a farthing upon the issue, but they got a man to bring the actions who was insolvent. (Laughter.) So that if they could not punish us, they at least cheated us. (Great laughter.) They sued us, not in one action, which would have settled the whole case, but they brought several actions, for £5,000 a piece, one against me, one against Mr. Smith, Mr. Vankoughnet,* and others, and took care that when they failed we should have a pauper to look to for our costs. (Applause and laughter.) The judges did not differ in the case. The six judges gave their judgments that we were right in retaining and exchanging our offices. Constitutional and legal tribunals having thus decided the matter, is it not absurd to charge us with a breach either of the Constitution or the law? (Loud cheers.) But these courts of law, it appears, are of no value now-a-days. (Oh!)

If there is one thing more disgraceful than another in Mr. Brown's course, it is the attacks he has lately made upon myself and the bench of justice in Upper Canada. On the occasion to which I have alluded, *The Globe*, Mr. Brown's organ, did not hesitate, day after day, to insinuate that our judges were under my thumb, that I could get them to give judgment as I liked, thus aspersing their honesty as arbiters of justice. ("Shame.")

Now I believe that Upper Canada is proud and has good reason to be proud of the high character, both for honesty

---

* Sidney Smith (1823–1889) was postmaster general in the Cartier-Macdonald ministry between 1858 and 1862. Philip Michael Matthew Scott VanKoughnet (1822–1869) became commissioner of Crown lands following the "double shuffle" of 1858 and chief superintendent of Indian Affairs in 1860. (Smith, "Smith, Sidney," *DCB*; "VanKoughnet, Philip Michael Matthew Scott," *DCB*)

and learning of her Bench. (Cheers.) No honest Liberal, no honest Reformer, no honest Radical, however extreme may be his political opinions, will cast a stain on the ermine of Sir John Robinson or the other Conservative judges, and no Conservative will breathe a word against Mr. Justice [William Buell] Richards [1815–1889] or the other Reformers on the Bench. We all know that they are honest, that they are beyond all price and all purchase. (Hear, hear.) Yet the *Globe* did not hesitate to assail them, and it assails them this very day in connection with the extradition case, insinuating that they are under my control, that I have an underhand connection with them. It is almost needless to say that I have had no communication with them about this Anderson case,* and that I had none with them, either direct or indirect, about the resumption of our seats. (Hear, hear, and cries of "So it is.")

---

* Sir John Beverly Robinson (1791–1863) was the chief justice of the Court of Queen's Bench, a careful, steady man whose judgments only "excited controversy" twice in his career, notably in the internationally known extradition case of John Anderson (born 1831), a Missouri Slave, who, aided by abolitionists, fled to Canada, after committing a murder. When the United States demanded his return, Lord Elgin refused. Meanwhile, Anderson faced charges in Canada West, but retained the support of abolitionists, and when Robinson's court granted the extradition, it roused public hostility. (Saunders, "Robinson, Sir John Beverly," *DCB*; Reinders, "Anderson, John," *DCB*)

"BEST SPEECH MR. MACDONALD
EVER DELIVERED," 1861

The Leader *reported that on April 19, 1861, Macdonald delivered "without exception, the best speech" he "ever had." "Those who are acquainted with his style," the report continued, "need not be told that he is not what is called a 'flowery orator.' Metaphor and metaphysics be alike flung to the dogs, and [he] dashes into debate with the suddenness and strength of a whirlewind." Newspaper reports that spring of the 1861 census results again opened constitutional discussions in the legislature, as the Reformers with Brown and some of Macdonald's own Conservative supporters began insisting upon representation by population in light of the confirmed numerical superiority of Canada West. Macdonald continued to resist the idea. Added to the news of the census was the breaking event of the United States' collapse into civil war, on April 12. Macdonald assessed the constitutional crises of the two countries, providing a lucid account of his vision of representative government, the implications of the American Civil War for the Province of Canada, and his general vision for good government and the limitations of the American-style federalism.*[15]

The Leader *published Macdonald's speech on April 30, 1861, referring to him in various ways, but mostly as Attorney General Macdonald, or as Hon. Mr. J. A. Macdonald:*

ATTY. GEN. MACDONALD—This important question had been fully and fairly discussed by members on all sides of the House. He had been in Parliament for seventeen years, and had never heard any subject so ably debated, from every point of view. So much so had this been the case, that if the speeches had been fully reported, or, better still, if each member would take the trouble to prepare his speech, a volume would be formed which would be, for all time to come, a faithful repertory of all that could be said on the subject and almost a hand-book to our constitution. (Hear.)

His honorable friend the member for South Simcoe [Thomas Roberts Ferguson (1818–1879)] could say that the attempt, if attempt there had been, to prevent ample discussion of his bill, had been a signal failure, and he had received the just reward of the zeal and sincerity with which he had pressed it forward. He had forever connected his name with Representation by Population. He was no trading politician—he had not used the question for the purpose of exalting himself individually or attacking a Government, but impressed with the importance of the subject, he had brought it forward on its merits. It could be no longer said that discussion had been stifled. And it would be a criminal waste of the public time to let it go to a second reading for the sake of courtesy, when the whole debate would be had over again. (Hear.)

For the subject had been exhausted, every argument had been used, every clause, of the bill was understood, and its merits and defects were known. He, for one, should give his vote on the merits of his honorable friend's bill. (Hear.) Well, looking at the bill thus, he could not give his vote for it. (Hear, hear.) He would give the same vote as in July, 1855, against the introduction of a measure of this kind. It seemed to him that the measure was premature, until such time as the census was completed, fully showing in what manner we could deal with the question fairly. If there was to be a readjustment of the representation of the country, it must be done with an accurate knowledge of all the facts. (Hear.)

But there were serious objections to the bill itself. In the first place there was no limit to the amount of representation. If the measure was carried out, we should soon have a parliament as numerous and as cumbrous as that of Great Britain. There was no maximum set down. It was said that, as the counties increased in population, so must the number of representatives increase. That was a vicious principle, which had been disallowed last session by this very House. The principle of allowing a constituency to have more than one representative was disallowed in the bill to divide Montreal, Quebec, and Toronto into separate electoral districts. The only principle by which the true relation between the constituency and the representative could be established was by having one representative to one constituency.

MR. [MICHAEL] FOLEY*—That is a matter of detail.

HON. J. A. MACDONALD—It went to the very principle of the bill. In fact, to adopt the measure would be to take a

---

* Michael Hamilton Foley (1820–1870) was a journalist who sat for North Waterloo as a Reformer and backed George Brown's campaign for representation by population. (Hodgins, "Foley, Michael Hamilton," DCB)

retrograde step. Well, looking further than the bill, and at the principle of representation according to population, he would say now what he had always said, he was opposed to it, and always voted against it. His honorable friend from Cornwall [John Sandfield Macdonald] had charged the Conservative party, the other day, with having commenced the agitation of the subject. That was not the case. The question was never mooted until it was brought up by the Baldwin administration in 1849. From 1840 to 1849, the country accepted the constitution. It had been adopted by the representatives of the people of Upper Canada and by the governing power in Lower Canada. There was a great deal of doubt and hesitation in the mind of Upper Canada at the time, and almost universal dislike to it on the part of Lower Canada, but both set themselves honestly to work it out to the best advantage. And so they went on until 1849, when a measure to increase the number of representatives in the House was introduced by the Lafontaine-Baldwin Government. He defied his honorable friend to show that in any way whatever the Conservative party had supported that measure; on the contrary, they had always adopted a contrary course. In 1849, '50, '51, and '52, the Conservative party had voted against it as one man, and were, in fact, so close driven that if one of them had changed his vote, the measure would have been carried. It depended, they might remember, on the question whether the Speaker had a casting vote or not, under the two-thirds clause, and Mr. [Augustin-Norbert] Morin [1803–1865] decided that, under the act of Union, he had not.

MR. [OGLE] GOWAN—That bill did not involve Representation by Population.

HON. J. A. MACDONALD—He knew that. But at that time M. Chauveau,[*] an *élève* of M. Papineau, moved an amendment involving Representation by Population. They would find, on the 18th of March, 1849, that he moved two resolutions.

First, M. Chauveau moved, seconded by M. Laurin, and the question was put.

> "That it is to be regretted the inhabitants of the late Province of Lower Canada have not been constitutionally consulted with respect to the passing of the Act of the Imperial parliament re-uniting the two late provinces of Upper and Lower Canada, and that the said Act contains provisions contrary to justice, and to the rights of British subjects.

"The only yeas on this were Messrs. Chauveau, Laurin and Papineau.

Second, M. Chauveau moved,

> "That among the provisions which are contrary to justice and the rights of British subjects, is that which establishes an equal number of Representatives for each section of the Province formerly constituting

---

[*] Pierre-Joseph-Olivier Chauveau (1820–1890) was a lawyer and writer deeply interested in the vibrancy of French-Canadian letters and identity. He had supported La Fontaine's Reformers when he had entered legislature in the 1840s but denounced the union. Prominent among Reformers, he nonetheless lost the speakership of the assembly to Louis-Joseph Papineau (1786–1871), leader of the Lower Canadian Rebellions of 1837 and 1838, returned from exile. He held various offices in the Reform ministries of the early 1850s until he was ousted and fell back on a literary career. (Hamelin and Paulin, "Chauveau, Pierre-Joseph Olivier," *DCB*)

the Province of Lower Canada, without taking into consideration their respective population."

The division was the same.

MR. FOLEY—Everyone knew what that was for.

HON. MR. MACDONALD—He did not know what the hon. member meant by that. There were two resolutions on the solemn record of the House proposing a change in the quantity of the Representatives of Upper and Lower Canada, and the Conservative party voted against them in the most distinct way, showing that not a single member of the party was in favor of altering the basis of the Union. The only motions from which it might be inferred that they were in favor of a change were one made by Mr. John Gamble,* and another by Sir Allan MacNab, that, if a constituency had more than 20,000 people it should have two representatives. These resolutions were however moved as amendments, for the purpose of defeating the second reading of the bill to increase the number of members of Parliament. He had said, and urged it in his humble way, and warned the Lower Canadians at the time against such legislation. True, the increase was based on the principle of equality, but he had pointed out as strongly as he could that if they were at liberty to discuss the question at all, they could not fetter themselves to the question of equality. The Union was a distinct bargain, a solemn contract, reduced to writing, and if it were meddled with at all—if they could exercise their independent

---

* John William Gamble (1799–1873) was an old-guard "Constitutional" Tory who opposed the 1841 union of the Canadas as a threat to the Protestant order. He sat in the legislative assembly in the early 1850s. (Oyster, "Gamble, John William," *DCB*)

judgment with regard to it—if they could alter it in the slightest degree, they could not bind the Colonial Legislature; but must leave several questions open to be discussed; the principle of equality being as liable to be brought up as the principle of increase. (Hear.) And so it had proved. (Hear, hear.)

He was directly opposed to the principle of Representation by Population as a conservative, because it led, by logical sequence, to universal suffrage. His hon. friend the member for North York [Adam Wilson (1814–1891)] had attempted the other night to draw a distinction between the constituent body and the Representative body, and said the alteration in the one did not involve the alteration of the other. That was not a correct argument. In this bill, the Representative body was to be altered as the members in the constituent bodies increased. But that was not all. The representation was not to be based on the number of electors but in the number of the people, men, women and children, which brought up the whole subject of universal suffrage at once. It led directly to it, and as a conservative, he must oppose it with all his might.

DR. [SKEFFINGTON] CONNOR—Absurd, absurd!

HON. J. A. MACDONALD—The hon. member might think it absurd, but there were here gentlemen even on the Opposition benches who, though they might not agree with the argument, would not think it absurd. (Hear.) He was opposed to universal suffrage, he repeated it. Experience had shown that it left a nation weak and led it towards anarchy and despotism. Unless there was a middle power, unless property was protected and made one of the principles on which representation was based, they might perhaps have a people altogether equal, but they would soon cease to have a people altogether free. (Hear.)

MR. FOLEY—Perhaps before the Attorney General went further, he would allow him to read a resolution expressive of his views on Representation by Population at a particular time. When the measure was before the House to equalize the representation of Upper Canada, Mr. Gamble moved in amendment, seconded by Sir Allan MacNab—"That all the words after 'That' be left out, and the bill be recommitted for the purpose of inserting the following words:

> "And be it enacted, that whenever the population of either section of the Province shall exceed that of the other by one-third, every county or riding then containing within its limits a population of 30,000, shall be entitled to send a second member to represent the county or riding in the Legislative Assembly. And it shall be the duty of the Governor in Council to divide such county or riding into two ridings of compact and adjacent territory as nearly as can be of equal numbers in relation to population, for the purpose of such representation, and to designate the boundaries of such ridings as shall be entitled to be represented, &c."

Among the yeas taken down was the name of the hon. Attorney General West, and almost all the other Conservatives. (Hear, hear.) Still, the hon. gentleman affected to place the House under the impression that he never voted for Representation by Population. (Hear, hear.)

HON. J. A. MACDONALD—The hon. gentleman might as well have saved himself the trouble of reading that resolution. He had previously mentioned the reason for which Mr. Gamble brought it forward. (Hear.) Another objection he had to the principle involved in his hon. friend's bill was this—that if Representation by Population were adopted, it must either increase indefinitely the number of representatives, or else it compelled adoption of the vicious system of altering the territorial limits of constituencies every time there had to be a readjustment. Now, it was of the very greatest importance, of primary importance, indeed, that the English system should be kept up in this country—that there should not be frequent changes in the limits of constituencies, and the people having a common interest should send persons to Parliament to represent that local interest, as well as to deliberate on the state of the country at large. (Hear.)

See what the consequence was of the adoption of the contrary principle in the United States, where instead of a cluster of municipalities sending a representative to Congress on whom they could rely, they had more geographical divisions, and had the horrid system of party caucuses or conventions at which those men were chosen to be returned by the divisions who were the most available for party purposes.

There was another reason favorable to county organizations. It was that, in them, men were trained to the duties of administration—learned to bear and forbear—learned how to make judicious compromises—and got all sorts of crotchets driven out of their minds. Let all these be thought of before we talked of introducing a general system of breaking up counties into squares, to which system such a principle as that of this bill must infallibly lead. (Hear.)

He was satisfied that the best means of securing good government was representative institutions, but representative institutions being merely a means to an end were liable to be altered, just as the experience of the country might dictate. There was no inalienable right in any man as such to exercise the franchise. Otherwise on what principle could we say as we did say, that one man had a right to the franchise because he was assessed for £50 of real estate, while we deprived of the right a man who was assessed for £49, a man whose natural capacity might be greater in every way? Yet no one in this House objected to that arrangement, unless, indeed, the junior member for Montreal [Thomas D'Arcy McGee], who, if he understood him rightly, had expressed himself, in favor of universal suffrage. The objection to that system was obvious, though perhaps on this continent, from the general diffusion of wealth among the people, it was less obvious than in Europe. If the principle of representation by universal suffrage was adopted, the result would be in this country as it had been in other countries, that those who had no property would come to have the governing power, the power of imposing the burdens on those who had the property. In all countries where universal suffrage had been introduced, it amounted in the long run to a confiscation of property, and men of property had been obliged as in France, to seek refuge in despotism, to rescue them from the tyrannical power of mere numbers. While population was one of the chief elements on which representation should be based, it was still only one of the elements, and the true principle by which representation should be regulated, was that all interests should be represented. (Hear, hear.)

That was the principle of representation in England, and under it England had flourished, and had withstood the storms of revolution, of foreign war, and domestic dissension. From the time that England had representative institutions in their present form, the principle that all interests should be protected had been the protection and safeguard of England, even during periods when the storm of revolution was sweeping over Europe. England had stood in that position because all interests and all classes found protection in her legislature, and so he would have it to be in this country. Our representation of counties might be fairly said to protect the agricultural interest. So the members for our cities and towns might be held to represent the great commercial and manufacturing interests, and those of our artisans and mechanics. And if it were thought proper to enlarge still further the representation in parliament, he would not only continue but increase the system of burgh representation, giving a member to every considerable town having vitality. He would not choose places like Niagara, although he hoped his hon. friend the member for that town would not consider he was speaking in disparagement of Niagara. Just as old Sarum and Gotton in England, when one was an old tree and another an old house, were the means of introducing great men into parliament, so Niagara had returned an hon. gentleman, who was worthy to represent the most important constituency in a country. He would be strongly in favor of increasing the burgh representation and giving representatives to such towns as Brantford, St. Hyacinthe, &c. Now, as regarded the question of representation by population so strongly pressed upon the attention of the House, while he believed his hon. friend, the member for South Simcoe was sincerely and truly, heart and soul, attached to the advocacy of that principle, he could not pay the same compliment to the great body of hon. gentlemen opposite who formed Her Majesty's opposition. The member for

North Oxford [William McDougall (1822–1905)], in the most candid manner, announced his opinions, and not his own opinions alone, but those of the great body of reformers of Upper Canada, when he said that representation by population was not a sufficient remedy, was not *the* remedy. That was settled long ago, not only by that hon. gentleman, but by the whole body of the reformers of Upper Canada, at the Convention in 1859.

MR. J[OHN] S[ANDFIELD] MACDONALD—No[t] all the Reformers of Upper Canada.

HONORABLE J. A. MACDONALD said he understood the member for Cornwall was not present. But at all events it was a very large, very numerous, very respectable, and most influential collection of Reformers from Upper Canada, and the results they arrived at might be held to be a fair indication of the opinions of the Reformers of Upper Canada on important questions. The Reformers in that convention came to the conclusion that representation by population was, to use the language of hon. gentlemen opposite, no efficient remedy for the evils under which Upper Canada suffered, and the other day the hon. member for North Oxford repeated that statement. He (Atty. Gen. Macdonald) made bold to deny that Upper Canada had been suffering under evils. When they asked what these evils were, they were told that the interests of Lower Canada were mainly consulted, and that the ministry of the day, having a majority from Lower Canada, had overridden Upper Canadian interests, had prevented Upper Canadian legislation in an Upper Canadian spirit, had introduced a system of French domination and had enforced French principles generally upon the people of Upper Canada against their will. But when hon. gentlemen opposite were asked to give an instance of French domination, they could not give one. The member for North Waterloo, being pressed on one occasion, instanced the Jury Bill.

MR. FOLEY—I could instance fifty others.

HON. J. A. MACDONALD—defied the hon. gentleman to point to a single measure carried by the present Government since they took office in September, 1854, which had given dissatisfaction in Upper Canada.

MR. FOLEY—I will mention one at once—the Clergy Reserves Act.

HON. J. A. MACDONALD—If there was one measure of the whole of those passed by this Government, which had met with universal acceptance throughout the whole of Upper Canada, it was the Clergy Reserve Bill, and when he retired from politics altogether, he should be glad and proud to have it said that he had been, in his small way, instrumental in having helped in the settlement of that question which was stated to have caused the rebellion of 1837, setting father against son and family against family. Whatever other dispute might arise, that great question had been settled for ever, and has been settled in a manner satisfactory—aye without exception—to everyone.

MR. FOLEY—No! No!

HON. J. A. MACDONALD—The hon. gentleman might say no, but he was willing to meet him in the presence of the hon. gentleman's own constituents, and ask them if they were not satisfied. He was sure he would receive from them an affirmative answer. The people of Upper Canada were satisfied with that measure; in the first place, because it settled the question for ever; in the second place, the different religious denominations and their clergy were satisfied; and then in the next place, instead of that enormous property, being a matter of dispute and covetousness between different sects and denominations in Upper Canada, it had been wisely distributed among all the municipalities of Upper Canada to be used by them for such useful purposes as they saw fit, to pay their honest debts, to educate their children, or to improve their roads. The question had been removed from the arena of party dispute, and had been settled in such a manner as to satisfy every party and every interest. (Cheers.) But the hon. gentleman also quoted the Jury Law. And what was the complaint in that case? One complaint had reference to a bill which came down from the Upper House, permitting juries to render verdicts, although the jury was not unanimous.

HON. MR. FOLEY—That was not the bill at all, I voted with you on that bill.

HON. J. A. MACDONALD—went on to say that because he made a speech declaring that the jury ought to be unanimous, and the majority of the House went with him and threw out the bill, wishing to preserve the old Saxon principle which had prevailed from the time of King Alfred upwards, that the unanimous verdict of a jury of twelve men should be required and because the French actually voted that the law of England which had come down to us from our Anglo-Saxon ancestors should be maintained that was French domination!

The other jury Bill to which the member for Waterloo had referred, was introduced for the purpose of cutting down the enormous expenses of the old system, and it had been effectual in reducing them to a most remarkable extent. This had again and again been proved. His hon. friend from Kent (Mr. [Archibald] McKellar) when he first got the Bill, rose in his place and said it was a great improvement on the old system. And yet he was sorry to say for the independence of that hon. member he was afterwards whipped in by the hon. member for Toronto, his leader, and compelled to vote against the Bill at its third reading. And why? Because he was told it was an Upper Canadian measure, introduced by an Upper Canadian member of a Government which had not a majority in Upper Canada, and no matter how good it might be, it must be voted against, in order to resist French domination, although it reduced the expenses of the Jury system by at least one-third or one-half. And so it was with other measures he had introduced in one instance when he introduced a Bill which had met with universal approval in the profession,—that effecting an alteration of the Surrogate Courts, he saw his hon. Friend from South Ontario (Mr. [Oliver] Mowat), and the member for South Oxford (Dr. [Skeffington] Connor [1810–1863]), engaged in eagerly cutting up the Bill, as the word was passed along to oppose it—cutting it up and hurriedly reading the marginal notes, in order to see if they could find nothing, on account of which to oppose the Bill; and the member for Cornwall then rose and said—"Good Bill or bad Bill, law or no law, we will vote against every Bill the Government introduces," because forsooth they are not supported by a majority of Upper Canada.

MR. FOLEY—And a cumbrous bill it is.

HON. J. A. MACDONALD—I venture to say the hon. gentleman knows nothing about the working of the Bill.

MR. FOLEY—I venture to say I know a great deal more about it than you do.

HON. J. A. MACDONALD—believed the hon. gentleman opposed the bill without reading it, and he was pretty well satisfied he had not read it since. (Laughter.) This, however, had become a grave matter, from the manner in which hon. gentlemen opposite had treated it. Threats, most disloyal threats, had been held out, in order to prevent hon. members from exercising their own judgment on the subject. (Hear, hear.) There had been threatening statements that the people of Upper Canada would rise in their might and push him and his colleagues from their stools and put others in their place. Was that a right argument? Was it becoming for hon. gentlemen to rise and threaten this House with an appeal to arms, that would set man against man, introduce a state of civil war, and repeat in this country the dreadful scenes which were now being enacted across the border—and they had all heard the awful news that had come tonight of men of the same blood killing each other, as in the first French revolution. The member for North Oxford (Mr. McDougall) rose in his place and threatened this House and the country with a resort to arms, and why? Because we chose to have our own opinions about the readjustment of representation in Parliament. These hon. gentlemen ought to consider well the effect of such appeals, which would be wicked, were they not absurd. He asserted there was no feeling among the people of Upper Canada, which would warrant such appeals, whatever might be their feeling on the principle of Representation by Population, or their desire to have an adjustment made. If there was a loyal people in the world, it was the people of Upper Canada, and he was confident they would not look to Washington (Cheers)—notwithstanding that they were invited by the member for North Oxford and by the member for North York to look to Washington.

MR. MCDOUGALL—I will not allow the hon. gentleman to misrepresent me. My argument was that if this course of policy was pursued, the people of Upper Canada might be driven to look to Washington.

HON. J. A. MACDONALD—The hon. gentleman threatened that the country would rebel, and he was not alone in making such a threat—the member for North York distinctly told the House the same thing. They knew too that the honorable and able member for North Oxford was not only taking a high position in this House, but was connected with the public press, with what might perhaps be called the leading paper in Upper Canada, the *Globe*. They knew that that hon. member, as much almost, if not more than the hon. gentleman who leads the Opposition, guided the counsels of that paper, and they found the same thing announced in its columns. In an article in the *Globe* of the 18th September, 1860, while the Prince of Wales was here, the following passage occurred:—

"Let the *Times*, let the Duke of Newcastle [Colonial Secretary] and his colleagues be assured, that we have reached a crisis in this country which must end and that speedily, in one of two ways; either in a change of the Union Act, with the aid and assent of the Imperial

Parliament, that will secure the rights and immunities to the people of Upper Canada in proportion to their numbers, or in a violent disruption of the present political relations of the provinces towards each other, and possibly towards Great Britain." (Sensation.)

And what made it still more wicked, was that those hon. gentlemen rose in their places, one after another, and threatened us with rebellion, because forsooth the majority in Parliament would not accede to a principle which they themselves said was no remedy. What did the hon. member for North Oxford, and those who acted with him say? "Upper Canada, labors under great evils; Representation by Population is no remedy for those evils; and, therefore, if you don't concede Representation by Population, we will deluge the country in blood." (Sensation.)

Did not this show clearly that those hon. gentlemen were not sincere, and that they were making this question simply a means of agitating the public mind, without caring about the injury they would bring upon the prospects of Upper Canada? When people set the wheels of revolution rolling, though it were merely for temporary and party purpose—perhaps to carry an election, perhaps to obtain possession of power—there was no saying when or where the revolution might stop. And deep would be the criminality and sin of those men who, for any purpose of that kind, would announce to the world that the people of Upper Canada were going to throw off their allegiance to their Sovereign, and look to Washington, introducing a civil war of man against man and brother against brother, because forsooth we will not agree to a principle which these very men themselves say now is no remedy at all for the evils under which the country labours. (Cheers.)

Could political profligacy go farther? This, it appeared, was to be their cry at the next general election, but they would find that wherever there was a sin of that kind, there was a corresponding retribution, a corresponding punishment. (Cheers.)

The member for North Oxford was the only member of the Opposition who had risen in his place and candidly and straight forwardly stated his opinions on Representation by Population. He gave the hon. gentleman every credit for his candour. But we had found the member for North York rising and threatening us with war unless Representation by Population be conceded, while the hon. gentleman had himself declared that it is no remedy. So the member for South Ontario—and he was sorry to include that hon. gentleman in the category—though he announced at the Toronto Convention that Representation by Population was no remedy for the evils in question, he too joined in the cry that the people of Upper Canada would rise and rebel because of the refusal of what he himself had declared was no remedy. This was the language of the member for South Ontario:

> "It is plain that if we desire the interests of this country—
> if we wish to secure ourselves against bankruptcy—if we
> are not ready to submit to the grossest degradation—we
> must look out for some other measures than representa-
> tion according to population to obtain relief."

HON. MR. MOWAT—That is a false statement of my speech. If he takes my whole speech you will find that I took this ground, that Representation by Population is a good thing, but that the difficulties of our position were pressing, that it might take considerable time to obtain it, and that we might add to our demands other things still more valuable than Representation by Population.

ATTY. GEN. MACDONALD—I merely ask, were not those words uttered?

HON. MR. MOWAT—It is unfair to pick out one sentence.

HON. MR. FOLEY—Read the whole speech. (Laughter.)

ATTY. GEN. MACDONALD—then read the whole paragraph, of which the above sentence formed a part, and said the hon. gentleman pointed the evils under which Upper Canada laboured, and stated that from all those evils Representation by Population would be no relief. The hon. gentleman could neither evade nor explain away his own words. In the "Globe" of the 19th May, 1859, he found the following words:

> "How comes it? ask certain crab like reformers, that Representation by Population is now treated as a minor measure, and that larger organic changes 'are pressed for as of greater importance.'"

The interrogatory admits of an easy reply. We urged Representation by Population so long as we regarded that measure sufficient to secure the rights of Upper Canada, and afford a reasonable guarantee for the good government of the Province. Having learned by experience that the grievances complained of by the people spring from sources beyond the mere numbers in the Legislature, we now advocate more searching and comprehensive reforms.

Again on the 16th June the same paper said—

"Not the men alone, but the system must be changed. And the system wanted in lieu of that in operation; does not consist of a single measure, as those who try to misrepresent us would persuade the public.

"Give us Representation by Population to-day;— to-day we would press for larger reforms not because Representation based upon Population is less just now than of old, but because the march of events has brought the country to a position in which other and more vigorous methods of securing good government must needs be brought into requisition."

MR. FOLEY—There is nothing extraordinary in that.

HON. J. A. MACDONALD—The hon. member for North York, who threatened us with fire, famine and slaughter, the other night, (Laughter.) said to his constituents on the 4th January, 1860, that "it was idle to talk of Representation by Population, as we never should get it till there was a change and then we need care very little about it." In other words, that when it was got, it was not worth having. (Laughter.) Yet this was the remedy which the hon. member told us yesterday was a matter of such vital importance that the people of Upper Canada were going to rise in their might and carry it at the point of the bayonet. (Hear.)

In a speech on the 22nd December, 1860, the hon. member for North Wellington, (Mr. James Ross) said of representation by population, "he thought it would prove not quite the thing, and therefore let it be dropped." (Laughter.) It had been dropped, and hon. gentlemen opposite had taken it up again, not, he believed, in any sincere spirit, but for the purpose of being used at the next general election, in order to strengthen their party, and damage the present government. He (Mr. Macdonald) would not object to the party using every legitimate means to defeat their opponents; but he would appeal to the patriotism of the hon. gentlemen opposite, for the sake of their common country not to persevere in the course indicated by the speeches of their leaders in this House. They knew that Mr. [William H.] Seward [1801–1872], the Secretary of State for the United States, had declared that he would look to the acquisition of Canada as a means of indemnifying that Republic for the loss of the Southern States. They knew that in consequence of the unhappy war which was now raging in the United States, there was every prospect of the emigration and wealth from the old world—the great bulk of which found its way to the Western Prairies of a foreign country—now finding a home in Canada. They knew that in consequence of this fratricidal war, and this inevitable disruption, Canada had every prospect of being the great nation of this continent. They knew all this, and yet they saw that the hon. gentlemen opposite for factious and party purposes, for the mere lust of office, were ready and willing to blight all this fair prospect, to prejudice if not ruin our hopes, our well grounded hopes, just at the moment of fruition, by the factious insanity of their course. (Hear.)

Let them imagine the feelings of the emigrants just landing in our country. He would come here because he had been informed that it was a land of law and order, of peace and prosperity, and he therefore had changed his original intention of settling in the United States—now become a prey to intestine war—and what would first salute his ears? He would hear that the leaders of a great party in the Province had openly avowed that unless a Reform Bill was carried, unless there was a re-adjustment of the

Representation, unless the majority would yield to the minority, they would cause the very foundations of society to be broken up, and the scenes, the bloody scenes now enacting in the United States repeated in this country. (Hear, hear.)

And when they thought that these threats were held and used by a party not sincere in their desire for this reform for they had formally abandoned it in Convention as a remedy, surely they must feel that that party was committing the greatest of political sins. (Loud applause.)

He (Mr. Macdonald) could understand an enthusiast, a one-dealed fanatic acting in this manner, and he might respect his sincerity—but when all these evils were to be inflicted on the country, when the stream of wealth and healthy emigration was to be diverted from us, when we were to have no longer peace in our borders, when all this ruin was to happen from the factiousness of a party, for partisan purposes only, the country must believe with him that the depth of political wickedness had been reached by them. And verily, verily, they would have their reward! Whenever a member of that party went to the polls in U.C. and were opposed by a Ministerial candidate, whether Conservative or Reform, the Opposition candidate would find himself confronted by the damning evidence of the political hypocrisy of his party and his party leaders, in such a manner, as would overwhelm him with shame and convince the honest farmers of his constituency of the propriety, nay, the necessity of repudiating him, his pernicious doctrines, and his disloyal principles. (Applause.)

The yeomanry of Upper Canada were too intelligent and too loyal to their Sovereign and the best interests of their country, to allow themselves to be made the dupes of a parcel of political hacks, or calmly to suffer those great interests to be sacrificed for selfish and party ends. (Loud cheers.) On the heads and on the consciences of that party rested the responsibility of the evils which must result from the revolutionary sentiments which had been uttered, the unpatriotic threats, the disloyal language which they had heard, and the risk of ruin to our material and social progress. The people of Upper Canada would mark it, and as the crime was great, signal and condign would be the consequent punishment. (Hear, hear, hear.)

HON. MR. FOLEY—Call spirits from the vasty deep, and they will come.

HON. J. A. MACDONALD—did not doubt the people of Upper Canada would see the force of his argument, and that gentleman opposite would discover, when they went to the polls, the woeful mistake which they had committed.

MR. CONNOR—You are fond of prophesying.

HON. J. A. MACDONALD—The hon. gentleman would see that he was a true prophet. (Hear, hear.) The hon. gentleman from North Oxford had referred to the platform of the Toronto Convention, according to which each section of the Province was to have a local Parliament for the purpose of managing its own affairs, with some "joint authority" for some other inexplicable purpose, which no mortal man knew. This "joint authority" he took it, must not be a mere governing power, but a legislative power. It must be so, if it had to settle the great questions which affected the whole country, and he gleaned as much from the speech of Mr. Brown at the Convention, where he said "the collection of Revenue to meet the necessary expenditure of the general government and the interest and the sinking fund of the public debt—the management of the Post Office—the control of the navigation of the St. Lawrence from Lake Superior to the Gulf, and the enactment of common commercial and criminal laws, would I apprehend, embrace the main if not the sole duties entrusted to the central government." That was to say, every possible subject connected with life, freedom and property must be legislated upon by the governing body; so that, to all practical intents and purposes, the scheme was a most unwieldy one, for it resolved itself into one large Parliament and two smaller ones. In other words, it would be exactly the same body that was now sitting here, with two others holding their sessions, the members from Upper and Lower Canada sitting in separate Committee rooms, as overgrown County Councils and settling about roads, bridges, &c. And after all, the question of Representation by Population would then present the same difficulty which it did now. (Hear, hear.)

It had been alleged that Upper Canada paid 70 per cent of the Revenue and would it not still insist upon having a proportionate representation in this Joint Parliament as it insisted upon having a preponderance now. (Loud cheers.) But they had a right to complain of hon. gentlemen, because if they sincerely thought that the "joint authority" scheme was a good one, it was their duty to press it on the Government, and this they had not done. The only feasible scheme which presented itself to his mind, as a remedy for the evils complained of, was a confederation of all the provinces. But in speaking of a confederation he must not be understood as alluding to it in the sense of the one on the other side of the line. For that had not been successful. But when he said this, he did not say so from any feeling of satisfaction at such a result. Far from him be any such idea.

He heartily agreed with the junior member for Montreal (Mr. McGee) in every word of regret which he had expressed at the unhappy and lamentable state of things which they now witnessed in the States, for he remembered that they were of the same blood as ourselves. He still looked hopefully to the future of the United States. He believed there was a vigor, a vitality, in the Anglo-Saxon character and the Anglo-Saxon institutions of the United States, that would carry them through this great convulsion, as they had carried through our mother country in days of old. (Loud cheers from both sides of the House.) He hoped with that hon. gentleman (Mr. McGee) that if they were to be severed in two, as severed in two he believed they would be, two great, two noble, two free nations would exist in place of one. (Hear, hear.) But while he thus sympathised with them, he must say, let it be a warning to ourselves that we do not split on the same rock as they. The fatal error which they had committed—and it was perhaps unavoidable from the state of the colonies at the time of the revolution, was in making each state a distinct sovereignty, and giving to each a distinct sovereign power, except in those instances where they were specially reserved by the constitution and conferred upon the general government. The true principle of a confederation lay in giving to the general government all the principles and powers of sovereignty, and that the subordinate or individual States should have no powers but those expressly bestowed on them. We should thus have a powerful Central Government—a powerful Central Legislature, and a powerful centralized system of minor Legislatures for local purposes. (Hear, hear.)

Take the plan of dividing Upper and Lower Canada as proposed by the Toronto Convention, and where would be all their hopes of an assimilation of our laws? (Hear.) We were one people, having all our interests in common. An assimilation of our laws was being rapidly effected. Indeed, during the twenty years that the two Provinces had been united together, there had been a closer union effected than had been effected between England and Scotland with all the long years of union [since 1707] that existed between those two countries. (Hear, hear.) Besides having a common Parliament and a common Government, we had a common municipal law—a common educational system, and the same criminal and commercial law; and by the abolition of the Seignorial tenure we were slowly but surely approaching the same manner of holding lands. By slow but sure degrees, they were becoming rapidly amalgamated; and when he looked back for twenty years, he was surprised and gratified to feel that the experiment had been eminently successful. Hon. gentlemen boasted of the majority obtained by them in Upper Canada at the last election—obtained by an influence against the present Government, which he had already referred to and pressed on the attention of the House and through the House on the Country. Yet he had no hesitation in saying, as there were not two but three parties in Upper Canada, that he was not only at the head of the largest party in the House, but he commanded the largest united majority in Upper Canada. ("Hear, hear," from several members, and "oh, oh," from Mr. Foley.)

The hon. gentleman might cry "oh," but the fact was, nevertheless, as he stated. Our first great consideration should be to calm this agitation. The true way to deal with the question was to consider it solely on its merits. Let every man who was in favor of Representation by Population go to the poll and fearlessly declare it, and every man who was against it, go likewise to the poll and make the declaration; no matter what their politics might be, let them fairly and candidly state, irrespective of every other consideration, whether they were or were not in favor of this principle. He would even go so far as to say, with the hon. member for East Durham (Mr. [Francis Henry] Burton [1817–1872]) that no matter what a man's political antecedents might be if he was strongly impressed with the necessity of the principle, he ought to support any ministry which would undertake to carry it, and secure a majority in Parliament for that purpose. This question, like every other great question must be left to work its way on its own merits. His hon. friend, the Postmaster General, had adduced proofs, which need not be again repeated, to the House, that all subjects of great public interest in England—Reform in Parliament, Free Trade, Catholic Emancipation, Repeal of the Corn Laws and the abolition of the Slave Trade—every great question had been removed from the arena of party struggles and strife, and had worked their way upon their own merits. (Hear, hear.) So must this question; and after it had fairly worked its way by discussion in Parliament, by discussion at the polls, by discussion in the Press, they could fairly assume that the public mind had been educated upon it, and that it was ripe for a verdict to be passed upon it one way or the other. But he must admit that it was in vain to hope that the question could be settled in the present temper of the two Provinces. The hon. gentleman opposite had laughed and jeered during the whole of this debate at the Postmaster General [Sidney Smith (1823–1889)], because, being in favor of Representation by Population, he remained a member of the Government. Why, just look back to the 12th day of July, 1858 and see what took place then. A motion was made on that day, similar to that now before the House, for the introduction of a bill for readjusting the representation of the people in Parliament on the basis of population, and on the same day they found the majority of the hon. gentlemen opposite who voted with the hon. member for Toronto, voting in its support, and the whole of the hon. gentlemen who formed the Lower Canada section of the Brown-Dorion administration voting against it. A motion was at that time made to give the bill the three months' hoist, and Messrs. [Joseph-Élie] Thibaudeau [1822–1878], [Lewis-Thomas] Drummond [1813–1882], [Antoine-Aimé] Dorion, in fact the whole of the Lower Canada members of Mr. Brown's Government, and the hon. member for Cornwall, one of the members from Upper Canada, voting to throw out the bill on the first reading.

HON. M. DORION—Not on the first reading.

HON. M. CARTIER—Yes, it was the very same motion.

MR. DUNKIN—And moved by the same member.

HON. MR. MACDONALD—Yes, they all voted to throw out the bill at once, without even giving it the consideration of a second reading. On the 30th day of July—but a few days after this vote was taken—they found the hon. Mr. Brown and the hon. M. Dorion forming an administration and attempting to grapple with the question on which they had just before been seen to be hopelessly divided. How they did grapple with it might be inferred from the fact that after two years' experience, after two years' cogitation, the hon. member for Montreal would give precisely the same vote that he gave on the 12th day of July, 1858. Although on the 30th July he formed a government to settle the question he was now about to vote against representation by population, and in favour of the motion for the six months' hoist, which had been seconded by his former colleague, the hon. member for Portneuf [Joseph-Élie Thibaudeau]. (Hear, hear.)

So that it was quite clear that the present government, no, nor any other government having a majority in the House, as at present constituted, could take up this question and settle it. He defied hon. gentlemen opposite to form an administration possessing the confidence of a majority in the House, whatever might be the result of the next election, no matter what might be the character of the administration, whether it was formed exclusively by hon. gentlemen on the Opposition Benches, or whether it was a combination of parties of different political opinions, under the feeling at present existing between Upper and Lower Canada, it was impossible that they could carry out the principle of representation by population. It must, therefore, be left to work its own way on its own merits. If it had real merits, if it had vitality, if it was a correct principle, if it was just alike to the people of Upper and Lower Canada, whatever might be the temporary feeling or prejudice against it, it would be found that in the long run, truth was strong and must prevail. As was the case in the other great questions it might take a long time to make a proper impression, but if it had truth on its side it certainly must and would become sooner or later the law of the land. If hon. gentlemen opposite would but reflect for a single moment, they would see that by the course they were taking, making this a question of party, they were causing this to be a matter impossible to be carried out, and declaring to a certain extent that they themselves and those connected with them must for ever remain in hopeless opposition. Surely there were questions enough besides this for them to quarrel about and make the subjects of party strife—surely they might put this one question aside, like the Slave Trade question in England, and not regard it as a question affecting one party more than another. They might leave this question to fight its own way. They could take up other issues on which to quarrel and divide; and if they would only adopt this course, they would prevent the unwholesome, the unholy agitation now going on; they would avoid all the injury which would otherwise result to the national interests of the country; they would avoid all the agitation on this subject as a matter of party consideration at the polls. By setting it aside from party politics, they would preserve peace, prosperity and quiet to the land; but by making it a matter of party strife, they agitated the country from end to end, and frustrated every possibility of its becoming the law of the country. Agitation would set interest against interest, section against section, race against race, and prevent the possibility of its passing into law. (Hear.)

Dissolution of the Union had been spoken of. But he really hoped that this had been held out as an empty threat. He believed that the best interests of the Province were dependent on the continuance of the Union, and that our national prosperity and future greatness were involved in its being preserved intact. But before enlarging on this point, he desired to say a word on another subject. It was most unreasonable to expect the majority to yield to the minority. He believed that the majority of the people of Central Canada would be found to act with the Lower Canadians on this point. (Loud cheers from the Ottawa members,) if even, unfortunately, a dissolution of the Union were to take place, the people of Central Canada could not be expected to remain with Upper Canada. Supposing a dissolution to take place to-morrow, Upper Canada could not for a moment insist that the line should be run as in 1791. If the people of Central Canada desired to be connected with Lower

Canada, Upper Canada must yield. The whole of the interests of the country from Kingston to the old Province line, the whole country lying between the St. Lawrence and the Ottawa, and the whole Valley of the Ottawa were inseparably connected with Lower Canada. Central Canada neither bought nor sold in the West. Montreal and Quebec were her markets, and indeed, every element of her prosperity was bound up with the prosperity of Lower Canada. They could not expect for a moment that with all the advantages of trade and commerce in the East, Central Canada would consent to be joined to Upper Canada and allow herself to be cut off from the sea, and be separated from the sources of her prosperity, that, in short, she would look North and South, and West, and everywhere, but in the quarter from which her only help would come. (Hear, hear.) Draw a line between the two Provinces, and Upper Canada would be obliged to surrender this large and growing portion of her country, and it would also be found that the agitation for representation by population was worse than useless, for Central Canada would have given a preponderance of population to Lower Canada. Such must be the result of this cry of dissolution. (Hear, hear.)

But he believed that that cry was a mere empty threat. He could not bring himself to believe that those by whom it was used were sincere. God and nature had joined us together. Stretched the full length along the Northern Shore of the great lakes and commanding the mighty St. Lawrence, we possessed the same common interests—interests which were only now beginning to be developed. Rapidly and steadily Lower Canada was becoming one of the most important manufacturing countries in the world. Upper Canada was increasing in an equal ratio in agricultural prosperity. Such was the rapid increase of this western world—such the productive power of the west, that no European market would be found for its immense cereal productions, and Upper Canada must therefore look for a wholesome interchange of commodities with the Eastern Province. Upper Canada being the producer and Lower Canada the consumer, Upper Canada would send to Lower Canada the products of her soil, and Lower Canada return the fruits of her manufacturing industry, and thus, year by year, the Union would become a greater and still greater necessity. Would they consent to forego all these benefits, to scatter all these advantages, because of their determination to impose Representation by Population upon Lower Canada? Who could lay his hand on any serious evils that had occurred under the Union? For his part he was surprised at its marvellous success. When they considered that at the time of the Union the country was torn by domestic dissensions, and Upper Canada overwhelmed with debt, and that now because of the Union the country possessed the best credit in the world after the mother country, would they consent to a severance of that Union, because Upper Canada had a population of a tenth or thereabouts over Lower Canada? We were now approaching to a population of three millions of people—we were approaching to the population of the United States at the time they declared their independence, we were standing at the very threshold of nations, and when admitted we should occupy no unimportant position amongst the nations of the world. Long might we remain connected with Great Britain. He hoped for ages for ever Canada might remain united with the mother country. But we were fast ceasing to be a dependency and assuming the position of an ally of Great Britain—England would be the centre, surrounded and sustained by an alliance not only with Canada but Australia, and all her other possessions; and there would thus be formed an immense confederation of freemen, the greatest confederacy of civilisation and intelligent men that ever had an existence on the face of the Globe. (Cheers.)

He hoped to live to see that day; and it would surely come, if our statesmen would only be patriotic enough to lay aside all desire to do that which tended to rend the existing Union and allowed us to continue to progress as we had progressed since 1840. He believed his hon. friend from North Waterloo was one of those who entertained feelings of patriotism and love of country, and that though a strong party man he could, when occasion demanded, lay aside all party feeling for the good of the Province. He asked the hon. gentleman to carry out that principle on this question. Let him and all others return home, to the sphere of their influence and usefulness; let them use every legitimate means for the purpose of carrying out their views on the other subjects on which they had set their minds; but do not in the name of our common country, do not make this a matter of party agitation and party strife. Let each go home and imbue his neighbours as far as he could with his particular views on other matters; but let them all set aside party feeling in a matter of such vital consequences as this, and work together for the common good on the principle of Union, and not on the principle of one section fighting and striving against and seeking to annihilate the other. (Loud cheers.)

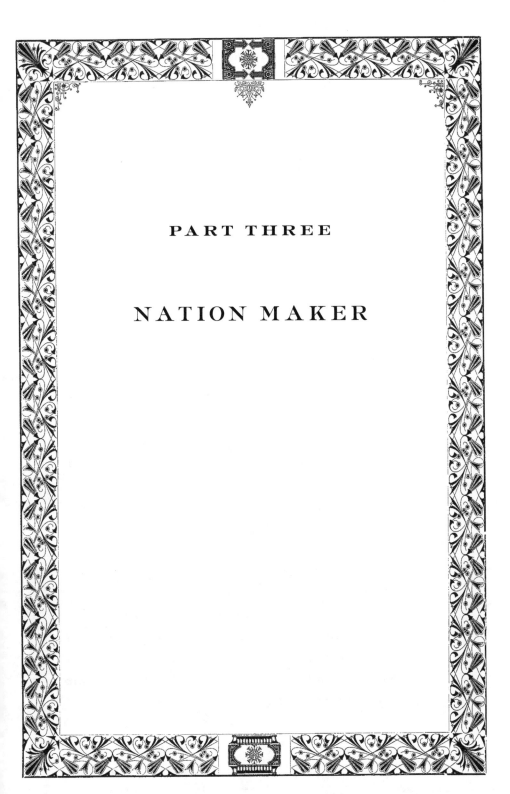

PART THREE

NATION MAKER

TOAST TO COLONIAL UNION, 1864

The delegates from Canada, New Brunswick, Prince Edward Island, and Nova Scotia met at Charlottetown, in the first week of September 1864. When the discussions were over, they stopped at the Halifax Hotel in Halifax. The idea of Confederation had been discussed in principle at the recent conference, but the real work would begin on the opening of the legislature at Quebec City in October. Until then, the delegates continued to explain and promote their vision of a British North American federation.

A public dinner on a rain-drenched evening in Halifax provided a convivial stage for Macdonald. Inside the hotel, the delegates from the Charlottetown Conference—Tupper, Tilley, Cartier, Brown, Galt— all spoke. After a call to toast "on colonial union" had rung out, Macdonald rose.[1]

Edward Whelan (1824–1867), a delegate for Prince Edward Island, compiled the public speeches given that fall from newspaper reports and edited them in consultation with their authors. Macdonald's speech on this occasion is included in the resulting book, The Union of the British Provinces, *published in 1865:*

[JOHN A. MACDONALD:] My friends and colleagues, Messrs. [George-Étienne] Cartier and [George] Brown, have returned their thanks on behalf of the Canadians for the kindness bestowed upon us, and I shall therefore not say one word on that subject, but shall approach the question more immediately before us. I must confess to you, sir, and to you, gentlemen, that I approach it with the deepest emotion. The question of "Colonial Union" is one of such magnitude that it dwarfs every other question on this portion of the continent. It absorbs every idea as far as I am concerned.

For twenty long years I have been dragging myself through the dreary waste of Colonial politics. I thought there was no end, nothing worthy of ambition, but now I see something which is well worthy of all I have suffered in the cause of my little country. This question has now assumed a position that demands and commands the attention of all the Colonies of British America. There may be obstructions, local difficulties may arise, disputes may occur, local jealousies may intervene, but it matters not—the wheel is now revolving, and we are only the fly on the wheel, we cannot delay it—the union of the colonies of British America, under one sovereign, is a fixed fact. (Cheers.) Sir, this meeting in Halifax will be ever remembered in the history of British America, for here the delegates from the several provinces had the first opportunity of expressing their sentiments. We have been unable to announce them before, but now let me say that we have arrived unanimously at the opinion that the union of the provinces is for the advantage of all, and that the only question that remains to be settled is, whether that union can be arranged with a due regard to sectional and local interests. I have no doubt that such an arrangement can be effected, that every difficulty will be found susceptible of solution, and that the great project will be successfully and happily realized.

What were we before this question was brought before the public mind? Here we were in the neighbourhood of a large nation—of one that has developed its military power in a most marvellous degree—here we are connected by one tie only, that of common allegiance. True it was we were states of one Sovereign, we all paid allegiance to the great central authority, but as far as ourselves were concerned there was no political connection, and we were as wide apart as British America is from Australia. We had only the mere sentiment of a common allegiance, and we were liable, in case England and the United States were pleased to differ, to be cut off, one by one, not having any common means of defence. I believe we shall have at length an organization that will enable us to be a nation and protect ourselves as we should. Look at the gallant defence that is being made by the Southern Republic—at this moment they have not much more than four millions of men—not much exceeding our own numbers—yet what a brave fight they have made, notwithstanding the stern bravery of the New Englander, or the fierce *elan* of the Irishman. (Cheers.) We are now nearly four millions of inhabitants, and in the next decennial period of taking the census, perhaps we shall have eight millions of people, able to defend their country against all comers. (Cheers.)

But we must have one common organization—one political government. It has been said that the United States Government is a failure. I don't go so far. On the contrary I consider it a marvellous exhibition of human wisdom. It was as perfect as human wisdom could make it, and under it the American States greatly prospered until very recently; but being the work of men it had its defects, and it is for us to take advantage by experience, and endeavor to see if we cannot arrive by careful study at such a plan as will avoid the mistakes of our neighbors.

In the first place, we know that every individual state was an individual sovereignty—that each had its own army and navy and political organization—and when they formed themselves into a confederation they only gave the central authority certain specific powers, reserving to the individual states all the other rights appertaining to sovereign powers. The dangers that have arisen from this system we will avoid if we can agree upon forming a strong central government—a great central legislature—a constitution for a Union which will have all the rights of sovereignty except those that are given to the local governments. Then we shall have taken a great step in advance of the American Republic. If we can only attain that object—a vigorous general government—we shall not be New Brunswickers, nor Nova Scotians, nor Canadians, but British Americans, under the sway of the British Sovereign. In discussing the question of colonial union, we must consider what is desirable and practicable; we must consult local prejudices and aspirations. It is our desire to do so. I hope that we will be enabled to work out a constitution that will have a strong central Government, able to offer a powerful resistance to any foe whatever, and at the same time will preserve for each Province its own identity—and will protect every local ambition; and if we cannot do this, we shall not be able to carry out the object we have now in view.

In the Conference we have had, we have been united as one man—there was no difference of feeling—no sectional prejudices or selfishness exhibited by any one;—we all approached the subject feeling its importance; feeling that in our hands were the destinies of a nation; and great would be our sin and shame if any different motives had intervened to prevent us carrying out the noble object of founding a great British Monarchy, in connection with the British Empire, and under the British Queen. (Cheers.)

That there are difficulties in the way would be folly for me to deny; that there are important questions to be settled before the project can be consummated is obvious; but what great subject that has ever attracted the attention of mankind has not been fraught with difficulties? We would not be worthy of the position in which we have been placed by the people if we did not meet and overcome these obstacles. I will not continue to detain you at this late period of the evening, but will merely say that we are desirous of a union with the Maritime Provinces on a fair and equitable basis: that we desire no advantage of any kind, that we believe the object in view will be as much in favor as against these Maritime Colonies. We are ready to come at once into the most intimate connection with you. This cannot be fully procured, I admit, by political union simply.

I don't hesitate to say that with respect to the Intercolonial Railway,* it is understood by the people of Canada that it can only be built as a means of political union for the Colonies. It cannot be denied that the Railway, as a commercial enterprise, would be of comparatively little commercial advantage to the people of Canada. Whilst we have the St. Lawrence in Summer, and the American ports in time of peace, we have all that is requisite for our purposes. We recognize, however, the fact that peace may not always exist, and that we must have some other

---

* Canada and the maritime colonies were then discussing the creation of an intercolonial railway between Halifax or Saint John and Quebec City as an economic link and means of mutual defence. Agreement to build the railway became part of the Confederation deal and Britain helped support its construction. It was completed in 1867. (Cruikshank, "Intercolonial Railway," OCCH)

means of outlet if we do not wish to be cut off from the ocean for some months in the year. We wish to feel greater security—to know that we can have assistance readily in the hour of danger. In the case of a union, this Railway must be a national work, and Canada will cheerfully contribute to the utmost extent in order to make that important link without which no political connection can be complete. What will be the consequence to this city, prosperous as it is, from that communication? Montreal is at this moment competing with New York for the trade of the great West. Build the road and Halifax will soon become one of the great emporiums of the world. All the great resources of the West will come over the immense railways of Canada to the bosom of your harbor.

But there are even greater advantages for us all in view. We will become a great nation, and God forbid that it should be one separate from the United Kingdom of Great Britain and Ireland. (Cheers.) There has been a feeling that because the old colonies were lost by the misrule of the British Government, every colony must be lost when it assumes the reins of self-government. I believe, however, as stated by the gallant Admiral, that England will hold her position in every colony—she will not enforce an unwilling obedience by her arms; but as long as British Americans shall retain that same allegiance which they feel now, England will spend her last shilling, and spill her best blood like wine in their defence. (Cheers.)

In 1812 there was an American war because England empressed American seamen.* Canadians had nothing to do

---

* Britain enforced a trade embargo by stopping and searching American vessels for contraband and impressing any seamen believed to have deserted from the Royal Navy, actions that helped bring the two nations into conflict in 1812. (Oliver and Granatstein, "War of 1812," OCCMH)

with the cause of the quarrel, yet their militia came out bravely and did all they could for the cause of England. Again, we have had the Oregon question, the Trent difficulty*—question after question in which the colonies had no interest—yet we were ready to shoulder the musket and fight for the honor of the mother country. It has been said that England wishes to throw us off.† There may be a few *doctrinaires* who argue for it, but it is not the feeling of the people of England. Their feeling is this—that we have not been true to ourselves, that we have not put ourselves in an attitude of defence, that we have not done in Canada as the English have done at home. It is a mistake: Canada is ready to do her part. She is organizing a militia, she is expending an enormous amount of money for the purpose of doing her best for self-protection. I am happy to know that the militia of Nova Scotia occupies a front rank; I understand by a judicious administration you have formed here a large and

---

* The Oregon Crisis of 1845 threatened hostilities between Britain and the U.S. in North America. The U.S. president, James Knox Polk (1795–1849), claimed control of the Oregon Territory shared by British North America up to the same latitude—54° 40'— as the Russian boundary in Alaska. Britain fortified the eastern end of Lake Ontario at Kingston—Macdonald's hometown—to meet any outbreak in hostilities. The *Trent* affair of November 1861 also threatened to bring Britain to the brink of conflict with the United States. The captain of the USS *San Jacinto* had stopped the British ship, the RMS *Trent*, seizing two Confederate diplomats. Britain demanded satisfaction and sent troops to British North America in preparation for conflict. The U.S. returned the Confederate diplomats. The following year, the British government gravely considered intervening in the American conflict to help mediate an end, an involvement which was eventually rejected. (Oliver and Granatstein, "Oregon Crisis (1845)," *OCCMH;* Careless, *Union of the Canadas,* 103; Oliver and Granatstein, "Trent Affair," *OCCMH;* Steele "Temple, Henry John, third Viscount Palmerston (1784–1865)," *ODNB;* Cannon, "Foreign Policy," *OCBH*)

† By the 1860s a growing voice of colonial reformers in the British Parliament called for reductions of, if not complete withdrawal from, military obligations in the colonies. (Burroughs, "Defence and Imperial Disunity," *OHBE,* vol. 3, 327; Morton, *Critical Years,* 74-5)

efficient volunteer and militia organization.* We are following your example and are forming an effective body of militia, so that we shall be able to say to England, that if she should send her arms to our rescue at a time of peril, she would be assisted by a well disciplined body of men. Everything, gentlemen, is to be gained by Union, and everything to be lost by disunion. Everybody admits that union must take place some time. I say now is the time.

Here we are now, in a state of peace and prosperity—now we can sit down without any danger threatening us, and consider and frame a scheme advantageous to each of these colonies. If we allow so favorable an opportunity to pass, it may never come again; but I believe we have arrived at such a conclusion in our deliberations that I may state without any breach of confidence—that we all unitedly agree that such a measure is a matter of the first necessity, and that only a few (imaginary, I believe) obstacles stand in the way of its consummation. I will feel that I shall not have served in public life without a reward, if before I enter into private life, I am a subject of a great British American nation, under the government of Her Majesty, and in connection with the Empire of Great Britain and Ireland. (Loud cheers.)

---

* In August, the Canadians had several bills to improve colonial defence readiness, including a new militia bill and amendments to the Volunteer Act of 1862 that increased their number to twenty-five thousand. John Sandfield Macdonald noted that "it was evident that the time had come when we should betake ourselves to the efficient defence of the country!" Since the late 1850s, the Maritime provinces had been under pressure to improve their contributions to colonial defence. (Morton, *Critical Years*, 134-5 with citation, 74-5)

DEBATING CONFEDERATION, 1865

By the end of the Quebec Conference (October 10–27, 1865), the delegates had agreed upon seventy-two resolutions. Some beliefs about parliamentary government were so fundamental that they did not even enter into the discussions. Rather, the delegates focused upon patching together benefits of federalism from perceived American mistakes and the British imperial model.

The Quebec Resolutions envisaged a federation along American lines insofar as it divided powers between two levels of government with an aim, as Macdonald put it, of preserving the provinces' "individuality." They also embraced an American-style scheme of political representation—representation by population in a lower house, and equal provincial representation in an upper house.² The dreadful scenes of the United States at war with itself raised fears of a weak state, with two factions warring at its bosom, and swung the shape of the federation in favour of Macdonald's vision.

Macdonald fought for a centralized federal model along imperial lines. He got his way. The nation devised in Quebec City would have a strong central government with powers that turned the American model on its head. Where the American federal model saw sovereign states devolving specific powers to a federal government and reserving the rest for themselves, the Canadian model located the residual powers in the central government; it was empowered to legislate for "the peace, order and good government" of the nation and in "all matters of a general character, not specially and exclusively reserved for the Local Governments and Legislatures." However, a reserve clause did grant the provinces authority over matters of a "private or local nature," as they should arise.[3]

The Quebec Resolutions also strengthened the central government by borrowing from Britain's own governance of British North America. The advent of responsible government saw the British government move away from interfering with local legislative matters, and by the late 1850s the "colonial reformers" and "Little Englanders" were advocating that Britain withdraw even more from colonial obligations and were promoting or supporting "self-reliance."[4]

The imperial connection supplied the model for the power of disallowance and the reservation mechanism accorded to the central government over provincial legislation.[5] Likewise, the powers of central appointment of provincial governors and the right to identify local works as being in the national interest also strengthened the central government.

At the same time, the empire itself would contain Canada's central government. By preserving the seat of sovereignty in the "fostering care of Great Britain" and Queen Victoria, the Confederation plan prevented the central government from encroaching upon the provinces. The imperial government, not the federal government, created the provinces, so what the federal government did not create, it could not destroy, nor alter, nor could it serve as the final judge in case of dispute.[6]

The language of the Quebec Conference debates was vague, as were the Confederation debates that followed—the thirty or so delegates at

Quebec City drafted the resolutions, but the provincial assemblies would have to ratify them. They could not change or alter their contents. The vote was a yes or a no.[7]

The 3rd Session of the 8th Parliament of the United Province of Canada opened on February 3, 1865, and the premier, Sir Étienne-Paschal Taché (1795–1865), read out the seventy-two resolutions. On February 6, Macdonald spoke to them.

ATTORNEY GENERAL [JOHN ALEXANDER] MAC-DONALD moved,

> "That an humble Address be presented to Her Majesty, praying that She may be graciously pleased to cause a measure to be submitted to the Imperial Parliament, for the purpose of uniting the Colonies of Canada, Nova Scotia, New Brunswick, Newfoundland, and Prince Edward Island in one Government, with provisions based on certain Resolutions, which were adopted at a Conference of Delegates from the said Colonies, held at the city of Quebec, on the 10th October, 1864."

[MACDONALD]:—Mr. Speaker [Hon. Ulric-Joseph Tessier], in fulfilment of the promise made by the Government to Parliament at its last session, I have moved this resolution. I have had the honor of being charged, on behalf of the Government, to submit a scheme for the Confederation of all the British North American Provinces—a scheme which has been received, I am glad to say, with general, if not universal, approbation in Canada. The scheme, as propounded through the press, has received almost no opposition.* While there may be occasionally, here and there, expressions of dissent from some of the details, yet the scheme as a whole has met with almost universal approval, and the Government has the greatest satisfaction in presenting it to this House.

This subject, which now absorbs the attention of the people of Canada, and of the whole of British North America, is not a new one. For years it has more or less attracted the attention of every statesman and politician in these provinces, and has been looked upon by many far-seeing politicians as being eventually the means of deciding and settling very many of the vexed questions which have retarded the prosperity of the colonies as a whole, and particularly the prosperity of Canada. The subject was pressed upon the public attention by a great many writers and politicians; but I believe the attention of the Legislature was first formally called to it by my honorable friend the Minister of Finance [Alexander Tilloch Galt]. Some years ago, in an elaborate speech, my hon. friend, while an independent member of Parliament, before being connected

---

* Newspapers in Canada West tended to support the Confederation scheme, as did the province's governor general, Lord Monck. In Canada East, strong support for the scheme by the Catholic Church set the tone and tended to drown out critical analysis of Confederation's terms from the Institut canadien de Montréal and from Antoine-Aimé Dorion and Jean-Baptiste-Éric Dorion (1826–1866); Antoine-Aimé Dorion, in particular, worried that the provincial governments would be too weak in the federal system, and in a manifesto he characterized the Quebec Conference as the secret machinations of a government unwilling to consult the people. Opposition in the Maritime provinces was quite vocal. The leading anti-Confederation proponent in Prince Edward Island, Cornelius Howatt (1810–1895), characterized the issue for the island province as "a question of self or no self." In New Brunswick, a negative view of Confederation as the scheme devised by "the oily brains of Canadians," in the words of Albert James Smith (1822–1883), was gaining ascendency. In Nova Scotia, Joseph Howe contributed anti-Confederation pieces to Halifax's *Morning Chronicle* under a thinly veiled anonymity. (Creighton, *Road to Confederation*, 192; Vipond, *Liberty and Community*, 22-3; Lamonde, *Histoire sociale des idées aux Québec*, 345-6, 351-6; Reid, *Six Crucial Decades*, 108-10)

with any Government, pressed his views on the Legislature at great length and with his usual force. But the subject was not taken up by any party as a branch of their policy, until the formation of the Cartier-Macdonald Administration in 1858, when the Confederation of the colonies was announced as one of the measures which they pledged themselves to attempt, if possible, to bring to a satisfactory conclusion. In pursuance of that promise, the letter or despatch, which has been so much and so freely commented upon in the press and in this House, was addressed by three of the members of that Administration to the Colonial Office.* The subject, however, though looked upon with favor by the country, and though there were no distinct expressions of opposition to it from any party, did not begin to assume its present proportions until last session.

Then, men of all parties and all shades of politics became alarmed at the aspect of affairs. They found that such was the opposition between the two sections of the province, such was the danger of impending anarchy, in consequence of the irreconcilable differences of opinion, with respect to representation by population, between Upper and Lower Canada, that unless some solution of the difficulty was arrived at, we would suffer under a succession of weak governments,—weak in numerical support, weak in force, and weak in power of doing good. All were alarmed at this state of affairs. We had election after

---

* Macdonald is probably referring to the October 25, 1858, letter from Conservative members of the Canadian government addressed to the Colonial Office. It outlined a proposal for a confederation and stated "[i]t will be observed that the basis of Confederation now proposed [in 1858] differs from that of the United States in several important particulars. It does not profess to be derived from the people, but would be the Constitution provided by the Imperial Parliament." (Ajzenstat, *Canada's Founding*, 28 with citation)

election,—we had ministry after ministry,—with the same
result.* Parties were so equally balanced, that the vote of one
member might decide the fate of the Administration, and the
course of legislation for a year or a series of years. This condition
of things was well calculated to arouse the earnest consideration
of every lover of his country, and I am happy to say it had that
effect. None were more impressed by this momentous state
of affairs, and the grave apprehensions that existed of a state
of anarchy destroying our credit, destroying our prosperity,
destroying our progress, than were the members of this present House; and the leading statesmen on both sides seemed to
have come to the common conclusion, that some step must be
taken to relieve the country from the dead-lock and impending
anarchy that hung over us.†

---

* "Within three years, four ministries had been compelled to resign." (McArthur, *History
of Canada for High Schools*, 343)

† City of London investors did react positively to the prospect of confederation of
the British North American colonies; by 1860 Britain invested more in British North
America, per capita, than in the United States. In print and private communication,
British businessmen expressed satisfaction about the centralized state outlined in the
Quebec Resolutions (leaked to the press). The bond markets also reacted positively to
the state proposed by the Quebec Resolutions, and the cost of borrowing money for
Canadians tended to fall as the deal gained more coherent political support in Canada.
Like the Fathers of Confederation, many British investors attributed the roots of the
American Civil War to the over-powerful states. Moreover, they regarded the states as
practical impediments to business because each operated under different laws and some
had defaulted on bonds. British investors also believed that the powerful subnational
bodies (states or provinces) drew lower-class people into their political community and
diluted effective government with too much democracy. The results, many assumed,
would be anti-statist voting populations and correspondingly low rates of taxation that
would limit the scope and scale of government activity for the collective benefit of communities. Also, the prospect of nationhood for the colonies fit with a "Little Englander"
ethos among British manufacturers who viewed the colonies as millstones around their
necks. Proponents of liberalism like Goldwin Smith and John Bright (1811–1889), however, denounced the proposed confederation for all these reasons, calling it a "conservative" project that thwarted *laissez-faire* economics as the path to prosperity and gave
free rein to the blind self-interest of British investors. (Smith, "Reaction of the City of
London," 1-24)

With that view, my colleague, the President of the Council [George Brown], made a motion founded on the despatch addressed to the Colonial Minister, to which I have referred, and a committee was struck,* composed of gentlemen of both sides of the House, of all shades of political opinion, without any reference to whether they were supporters of the Administration of the day or belonged to the Opposition, for the purpose of taking into calm and full deliberation the evils which threatened the future of Canada. That motion of my honorable friend resulted most happily. The committee, by a wise provision,—and in order that each member of the committee might have an opportunity of expressing his opinions without being in any way compromised before the public, or with his party, in regard either to his political friends or to his political foes,—agreed that the discussion should be freely entered upon without reference to the political antecedents of any of them, and that they should sit with closed doors, so that they might be able to approach the subject frankly and in a spirit of compromise. The committee included most of the leading members of the House,—I had the honor myself to be one of the number,—and the result was that there was found an ardent desire—a creditable desire, I must say,—displayed by all the members of the committee to approach the subject honestly, and to attempt to work out some solution which might relieve Canada from the evils under which she labored.

---

* George Brown proposed to the Assembly a committee to study the constitutional problems of the United Province of Canada in the summer session of 1864. Brown reported the committee's conclusions on June 14, 1864, stating that "[a] strong feeling was found to exist among the members of the committee in favour of changes in the direction of a federative system, applied either to Canada alone, or to the whole British North American Provinces, and such progress has been made as to warrant the committee in recommending that the subject be again referred to a committee at the next session of Parliament." (Creighton, *Road to Confederation*, 49–51 with citation)

The report of that committee was laid before the House, and then came the political action of the leading men of the two parties in this House, which ended in the formation of the present Government.* The principle upon which that Government was formed has been announced, and is known to all. It was formed for the very purpose of carrying out the object which has now received to a certain degree its completion, by the resolutions [the seventy-two resolutions of the Quebec Conference] I have had the honor to place in your hands. As has been stated, it was not without a great deal of difficulty and reluctance that that Government was formed. The gentlemen who compose this Government had for many years been engaged in political hostilities to such an extent that it affected even their social relations.† But the crisis was great, the danger was imminent, and the gentlemen who now form the present Administration found it to be their duty to lay aside all personal feelings, to sacrifice in some degree their position, and even to run the risk of having their motives impugned, for the sake of arriving at some conclusion that would be satisfactory to the country in general. The present resolutions were the result. And, as I said before, I am proud to believe that the country has sanctioned, as I trust that the representatives of the people in this House will sanction, the scheme which is now submitted for the future government of British North America. (Cheers.) Everything seemed to favor the project, and everything seemed to shew that the present was the time, if ever, when this great union

---

* Macdonald is referring to the Great Coalition of 1864 created by George Brown's Reformers and Macdonald and Cartier and their Conservatives under the leadership of Sir Étienne-Paschal Taché (1795–1865). (Martin, "Great Coalition," *OCCH*)

† Macdonald is referring to the deep antipathy between George Brown and himself.

between all Her Majesty's subjects dwelling in British North America, should be carried out. (Hear, hear.)

When the Government was formed, it was felt that the difficulties in the way of effecting a union between all the British North American Colonies were great—so great as almost, in the opinion of many, to make it hopeless. And with that view it was the policy of the Government, if they could not succeed in procuring a union between all the British North American Colonies, to attempt to free the country from the dead-lock in which we were placed in Upper and Lower Canada, in consequence of the difference of opinion between the two sections, by having a severance to a certain extent of the present union between the two provinces of Upper and Lower Canada, and the substitution of a Federal Union between them. Most of us, however, I may say, all of us, were agreed—and I believe every thinking man will agree—as to the expediency of effecting a union between all the provinces, and the superiority of such a design, if it were only practicable, over the smaller scheme of having a Federal Union between Upper and Lower Canada alone.

By a happy concurrence of events, the time came when that proposition could be made with a hope of success. By a fortunate coincidence the desire for union existed in the Lower Provinces [i.e., the Maritime provinces], and a feeling of the necessity of strengthening themselves by collecting together the scattered colonies on the sea-board,—and induced them to form a convention of their own for the purpose of effecting a union of the Maritime Provinces of Nova Scotia, New Brunswick, and Prince Edward Island, the legislatures of those colonies having formally authorized their respective governments to send a delegation to Prince Edward Island for the purpose of attempting to form a union of some kind.* Whether the union should be federal or legislative was not then indicated, but a union of some kind was sought for the purpose of making of themselves one people instead of three. We, ascertaining that they were about to take such a step, and knowing that if we allowed the occasion to pass, if they did indeed break up all their present political organizations and form a new one, it could not be expected that they would again readily destroy the new organization which they had formed,—the union of the three provinces on the sea-board,—and form another with Canada. Knowing this, we availed ourselves of the opportunity, and asked if they would receive a deputation from Canada, who would go to meet them at Charlottetown, for the purpose of laying before them the advantages of a larger and more extensive union, by the junction of all the provinces in one great government under our common Sovereign.† They at once kindly consented to receive and hear us. They did receive us cordially and generously, and asked us to lay our views before them. We did so at some length, and so satisfactory to them were the reasons we gave; so clearly, in their opinion, did we shew the advantages of the greater union over the lesser, that they at once set aside their own project, and joined heart and hand with us in entering into the larger

---

* In 1862 the lieutenant-governor of New Brunswick, Lord Arthur Hamilton Gordon (1829–1912), proposed to the Colonial Office the unification of New Brunswick, Nova Scotia, and Prince Edward Island. The following summer he began promoting his idea in the Maritimes. Initially the response was tepid, but following the Canadian intentions to reopen the 1862 railway agreement with the Maritimes, a stronger sense of solidarity emerged among the three colonies. By the spring of 1864, the legal framework to discuss a Maritime union had been forged. (Creighton, *Road to Confederation*, 11, 20, 23-5, 35)

† In the summer of 1864, Lord Monck informed Sir Richard Graves MacDonnell (1814–1881), the new lieutenant-governor of Nova Scotia, that a delegation of Canadians wished to attend the proposed discussion of Maritime union. (Creighton, *Road to Confederation*, 37)

scheme, and trying to form, as far as they and we could, a great nation and a strong government. (Cheers.)

Encouraged by this arrangement, which, however, was altogether unofficial and unauthorized, we returned to Quebec, and then the Government of Canada invited the several governments of the sister colonies to send a deputation here from each of them for the purpose of considering the question, with something like authority from their respective governments. The result was, that when we met here on the 10th of October, on the first day on which we assembled, after the full and free discussions which had taken place at Charlottetown, the first resolution now before this House was passed unanimously, being received with acclamation as, in the opinion of every one who heard it, a proposition which ought to receive, and would receive, the sanction of each government and each people. The resolution is, "That the best interests and present and future prosperity of British North America will be promoted by a Federal Union under the Crown of Great Britain, provided such union can be effected on principles just to the several provinces." It seemed to all the statesmen assembled—and there are great statesmen in the Lower Provinces, men who would do honor to any government and to any legislature of any free country enjoying representative institutions—it was clear to them all that the best interests and present and future prosperity of British North America would be promoted by a Federal Union under the Crown of Great Britain. And it seems to me, as to them, and I think it will so appear to the people of this country, that, if we wish to be a great people; if we wish to form—using the expression which was sneered at the other evening—a great nationality, commanding the respect of the world, able to hold our own against all opponents, and to defend those institutions we prize: if we wish to have one system of government, and to establish a commercial union, with unrestricted free trade, between people of the five provinces, belonging, as they do, to the same nation, obeying the same Sovereign, owning the same allegiance, and being, for the most part, of the same blood and lineage: if we wish to be able to afford to each other the means of mutual defence and support against aggression and attack—this can only be obtained by a union of some kind between the scattered and weak boundaries composing the British North American Provinces. (Cheers.)

The very mention of the scheme is fitted to bring with it its own approbation. Supposing that in the spring of the year 1865, half a million of people were coming from the United Kingdom to make Canada their home, although they brought only their strong arms and willing hearts; though they brought neither skill nor experience nor wealth, would we not receive them with open arms, and hail their presence in Canada as an important addition to our strength?* But when, by the proposed union, we not only get nearly a million of people to join us—when they contribute not only their numbers, their physical

---

* At the time of Confederation, the combined population of British North America was 3.5 million. The United States had ten times the number of people. New studies of Canada's immigration records for the second part of the century tend to revise downward the "official" figures, portraying a nation receiving fewer people than had been thought. Evidence of high numbers of people leaving the country suggests that Canada was "a nation of emigration" in the latter half of the nineteenth century. In one notable example, refugee slaves who had settled in Canada West after arriving along the underground railway returned in large numbers to the United States in the 1860s. Of immigrants arriving in Canada from the 1860s until the end of the century, most did originate in Britain, but Chinese labourers were arriving to mine gold on the west coast by the 1860s and in the 1870s Icelanders and German Mennonites from Russia joined the flow and settled in Manitoba. More Chinese arrived in the 1880s to work on the Canadian Pacific Railway. Ukrainian immigrants arrived in greater numbers in the 1890s. (McInnis, "Population of Canada in the Nineteenth Century," 416, 417, 422–4; "Wang, *His Dominion and the 'Yellow Peril,'*" 10-11; Winks, *The Blacks in Canada*, 234, 289)

strength, and their desire to benefit their position, but when we know that they consist of old-established communities, having a large amount of realized wealth,—composed of people possessed of skill, education and experience in the ways of the New World—people who are as much Canadians, I may say, as we are—people who are imbued with the same feelings of loyalty to the Queen, and the same desire for the continuance of the connection with the Mother Country as we are, and at the same time, have a like feeling of ardent attachment for this, our common country, for which they and we would alike fight and shed our blood, if necessary. When all this is considered, argument is needless to prove the advantage of such a union. (Hear, hear.)

There were only three modes,—if I may return for a moment to the difficulties with which Canada was surrounded,—only three modes that were at all suggested, by which the dead lock in our affairs, the anarchy we dreaded, and the evils which retarded our prosperity, could be met or averted. One was the dissolution of the union between Upper and Lower Canada, leaving them as they were before the union of 1841. I believe that that proposition, by itself had no supporters. It was felt by every one that, although it was a course that would do away with the sectional difficulties which existed,—though it would remove the pressure on the part of the people of Upper Canada for the representation based upon population,—and the jealousy of the people of Lower Canada lest their institutions should be attacked and prejudiced by that principle in our representation; yet it was felt by every thinking man in the province that it would be a retrograde step, which would throw back the country to nearly the same position as it occupied before the union,—that it would lower the credit enjoyed by United

Canada,—that it would be the breaking up of the connection which had existed for nearly a quarter of a century, and, under which, although it had not been completely successful, and had not allayed altogether the local jealousies that had their root in circumstances which arose before the union, our province, as a whole, had nevertheless prospered and increased. It was felt that a dissolution of the union would have destroyed all the credit that we had gained by being a united province, and would have left us two weak and ineffective governments, instead of one powerful and united people. (Hear, hear.)

The next mode suggested, was the granting of representation by population. Now, we all know the manner in which that question was and is regarded by Lower Canada; that while in Upper Canada the desire and cry for it was daily augmenting, the resistance to it in Lower Canada was proportionally increasing in strength. Still, if some such means of relieving us from the sectional jealousies which existed between the two Canadas, if some such solution of the difficulties as Confederation had not been found, the representation by population must eventually have been carried; no matter though it might have been felt in Lower Canada, as being a breach of the Treaty of Union, no matter how much it might have been felt by the Lower Canadians that it would sacrifice their local interests, it is certain that in the progress of events representation by population would have been carried; and, had it been carried—I speak here my own individual sentiments—I do not think it would have been for the interest of Upper Canada. For though Upper Canada would have felt that it had received what it claimed as a right, and had succeeded in establishing its right, yet it would have left the Lower Province with a sullen feeling of injury and injustice. The Lower Canadians would not have worked cheerfully under such a change of system, but would have ceased to be what they are now—a nationality, with representatives in Parliament, governed by general principles, and dividing according to their political opinions—and would have been in great danger of becoming a faction, forgetful of national obligations, and only actuated by a desire to defend their own sectional interests, their own laws, and their own institutions. (Hear, hear.)

The third and only means of solution for our difficulties was the junction of the provinces either in a Federal or a Legislative Union. Now, as regards the comparative advantages of a Legislative and a Federal Union, I have never hesitated to state my own opinions. I have again and again stated in the House, that, if practicable, I thought a Legislative Union would be preferable. (Hear, hear.) I have always contended that if we could agree to have one government and one parliament, legislating for the whole of these peoples, it would be the best, the cheapest, the most vigorous, and the strongest system of government we could adopt. (Hear, hear.) But, on looking at the subject in the Conference, and discussing the matter as we did, most unreservedly, and with a desire to arrive at a satisfactory conclusion, we found that such a system was impracticable. In the first place, it would not meet the assent of the people of Lower Canada, because they felt that in their peculiar position—being in a minority, with a different language, nationality and religion from the majority,—in case of a junction with the other provinces, their institutions and their laws might be assailed, and their ancestral associations, on which they prided themselves, attacked and prejudiced; it was found that any proposition which involved the absorption of the individuality of Lower Canada—if I may use the expression—would not be received with favor by her people. We found too, that though their people speak the same language and enjoy the same system of law as the people of Upper Canada, a system founded on the common law of England, there was as great a disinclination on the part of the various Maritime Provinces to lose their individuality, as separate political organizations, as we observed in the case of Lower Canada herself. (Hear, hear.)

Therefore, we were forced to the conclusion that we must either abandon the idea of Union altogether, or devise a system of union in which the separate provincial organizations would be in some degree preserved. So that those who were, like myself, in favor of a Legislative Union, were obliged to modify their views and accept the project of a Federal Union as the only scheme practicable, even for the Maritime Provinces. Because, although the law of those provinces is founded on the common law of England, yet every one of them has a large amount of law of its own—colonial law framed by itself, and affecting every relation of life, such as the laws of property, municipal and assessment laws; laws relating to the liberty of the subject, and to all the great interests contemplated in legislation; we found, in short, that the statutory law of the different provinces was so varied and diversified that it was almost impossible to weld them into a Legislative Union at once. Why, sir, if you only consider the innumerable subjects of legislation peculiar to new countries, and that every one of those five colonies had particular laws of its own, to which its people have been accustomed and are attached, you will see the difficulty of effecting and working a Legislative Union, and bringing about an assimilation of the local as well as general laws of the whole of the provinces. (Hear, hear.)

We in Upper Canada understand from the nature and operation of our peculiar municipal law, of which we know the value, the difficulty of framing a general system of legislation on local matters which would meet the wishes and fulfil the requirements of the several provinces. Even the laws considered the least important, respecting private rights in timber, roads, fencing, and innumerable other matters, small in themselves, but in the aggregate of great interest to the agricultural class, who form the great body of the people, are regarded as of great value by the portion of the community affected by them. And when we consider that every one of the colonies has a body of law of this kind, and that it will take years before those laws can be assimilated, it was felt that at first, at all events, any united legislation would be almost impossible. I am happy to state—and indeed it appears on the face of the resolutions themselves—that as regards the Lower Provinces, a great desire was evinced for the final assimilation of our laws. One of the resolutions provides that an attempt shall be made to assimilate the laws of the Maritime Provinces and those of Upper Canada, for the purpose of eventually establishing one body of statutory law, founded on the common law of England, the parent of the laws of all those provinces. One great objection made to a Federal Union was the expense of an increased number of legislatures.

I will not enter at any length into that subject, because my honorable friends, the Finance Minister and the President of the Council, who are infinitely more competent than myself to deal with matters of this kind—matters of account—will, I think, be able to show that the expenses under a Federal Union will not be greater than those under the existing system of separate governments and legislatures. Here, where we have a joint legislature for Upper and Lower Canada, which deals not only with subjects of a general interest common to all Canada, but with all matters of private right and of sectional interest, and with that class of

measures known as "private bills," we find that one of the greatest sources of expense to the country is the cost of legislation.
We find, from the admixture of subjects of a general, with those
of a private character in legislation, that they mutually interfere
with each other; whereas, if the attention of the Legislature
was confined to measures of one kind or the other alone, the
session of Parliament would not be so protracted and therefore
not so expensive as at present. In the proposed Constitution all
matters of general interest are to be dealt with by the General
Legislature; while the local legislatures will deal with matters of
local interest, which do not affect the Confederation as a whole,
but are of the greatest importance to their particular sections. By
such a division of labor the sittings of the General Legislature
would not be so protracted as even those of Canada alone. And
so with the local legislatures, their attention being confined to
subjects pertaining to their own sections, their sessions would
be shorter and less expensive. Then, when we consider the
enormous saving that will be effected in the administration of
affairs by one General Government—when we reflect that each
of the five colonies have a government of its own with a complete establishment of public departments and all the machinery
required for the transaction of the business of the country—that
each have a separate executive, judicial and militia system—that
each province has a separate ministry, including a Minister of
Militia, with a complete Adjutant General's Department—that
each have a Finance Minister with a full Customs and Excise
staff—that each Colony has as large and complete an administrative organization, with as many Executive officers as the
General Government will have—we can well understand the
enormous saving that will result from a union of all the colonies,
from their having but one head and one central system.

We, in Canada, already know something of the advantages and disadvantages of a Federal Union. Although we have nominally a Legislative Union in Canada—although we sit in one Parliament, supposed constitutionally to represent the people without regard to sections or localities, yet we know, as a matter of fact, that since the union in 1841, we have had a Federal Union; that in matters affecting Upper Canada solely, members from that section claimed and generally exercised the right of exclusive legislation, while members from Lower Canada legislated in matters affecting only their own section. We have had a Federal Union in fact, though a Legislative Union in name; and in the hot contests of late years, if on any occasion a measure affecting any one section were interfered with by the members from the other—if, for instance, a measure locally affecting Upper Canada were carried or defeated against the wishes of its majority, by one from Lower Canada,—my honorable friend the President of the Council, and his friends denounced with all their energy and ability such legislation as an infringement of the rights of the Upper Province. (Hear, hear, and cheers.) Just in the same way, if any act concerning Lower Canada were pressed into law against the wishes of the majority of her representatives, by those from Upper Canada, the Lower Canadians would rise as one man and protest against such a violation of their peculiar rights. (Hear, hear.)

The relations between England and Scotland are very similar to that which obtains between the Canadas. The union between them, in matters of legislation, is of a Federal character, because the Act of Union between the two countries provides that the Scottish law cannot be altered, except for the manifest advantage of the people of Scotland. This stipulation has been held to be so obligatory on the Legislature of Great

Britain, that no measure affecting the law of Scotland is passed unless it receives the sanction of a majority of the Scottish members in Parliament. No matter how important it may be for the interests of the empire as a whole to alter the laws of Scotland—no matter how much it may interfere with the symmetry of the general law of the United Kingdom, that law is not altered, except with the consent of the Scottish people, as expressed by their representatives in Parliament. (Hear, hear.) Thus, we have, in Great Britain, to a limited extent, an example of the working and effects of a Federal Union, as we might expect to witness them in our own Confederation.

The whole scheme of Confederation, as propounded by the Conference, as agreed to and sanctioned by the Canadian Government, and as now presented for the consideration of the people, and the Legislature, bears upon its face the marks of compromise. Of necessity there must have been a great deal of mutual concession. When we think of the representatives of five colonies, all supposed to have different interests, meeting together, charged with the duty of protecting those interests and of pressing the views of their own localities and sections, it must be admitted that had we not met in a spirit of conciliation, and with an anxious desire to promote this union; if we had not been impressed with the idea contained in the words of the resolution—"That the best interests and present and future prosperity of British North America would be promoted by a Federal Union under the Crown of Great Britain,"—all our efforts might have proved to be of no avail. If we had not felt that, after coming to this conclusion, we were bound to set aside our private opinions on matters of detail, if we had not felt ourselves bound to look at what was practicable, not obstinately rejecting the opinions of others nor adhering to our own; if we had not met, I say, in a spirit of conciliation, and with an anxious, overruling desire to form one people under one government, we never would have succeeded. With these views, we press the question on this House and the country.

I say to this House, if you do not believe that the union of the colonies is for the advantage of the country, that the joining of these five peoples into one nation, under one sovereign, is for the benefit of all, then reject the scheme. Reject it if you do not believe it to be for the present advantage and future prosperity of yourselves and your children. But if, after a calm and full consideration of this scheme, it is believed, as a whole, to be for the advantage of this province—if the House and country believe this union to be one which will ensure for us British laws, British connection, and British freedom—and increase and develop the social, political and material prosperity of the country, then I implore this House and the country to lay aside all prejudices, and accept the scheme which we offer. I ask this House to meet the question in the same spirit in which the delegates met it. I ask each member of this House to lay aside his own opinions as to particular details, and to accept the scheme as a whole if he think it beneficial as a whole.

As I stated in the preliminary discussion, we must consider this scheme in the light of a treaty. By a happy coincidence of circumstances, just when an Administration had been formed in Canada [i.e., the Great Coalition of 1864] for the purpose of attempting a solution of the difficulties under which we laboured, at the same time the Lower Provinces, actuated by a similar feeling, appointed a Conference with a view to a union among themselves, without being cognizant of the position the government was taking in Canada. If it had not been for this fortunate coincidence of events, never, perhaps, for a long series of years would we have been able to bring this scheme to a practical conclusion. But we did succeed. We made the arrangement, agreed upon the scheme, and the deputations from the several governments represented at the Conference went back pledged to lay it before their governments, and to ask the legislatures and people of their respective provinces to assent to it. I trust the scheme will be assented to as a whole. I am sure this House will not seek to alter it in its unimportant details; and, if altered in any important provisions, the result must be that the whole will be set aside, and we must begin *de novo*. If any important changes are made, every one of the colonies will feel itself absolved from the implied obligation to deal with it as a Treaty, each province will feel itself at liberty to amend it *ad libitum* so as to suit its own views and interests; in fact, the whole of our labours will have been for nought, and we will have to renew our negotiations with all the colonies for the purpose of establishing some new scheme. I hope the House will not adopt any such a course as will postpone, perhaps for ever, or at all events for a long period, all chances of union.

All the statesmen and public men who have written or spoken on the subject admit the advantages of a union, if it were practicable: and now when it is proved to be practicable, if we do not embrace this opportunity the present favorable time will pass away, and we may never have it again. Because, just so surely as this scheme is defeated, will be revived the original proposition for a union of the Maritime Provinces, irrespective of Canada; they will not remain as they are now, powerless, scattered, helpless communities; they will form themselves into a power, which, though not so strong as if united with Canada, will, nevertheless, be a powerful and considerable community, and it will be then too late for us to attempt to strengthen ourselves by this scheme, which, in the words of the resolution, "is for the best interests, and present and future prosperity of British North America."

If we are not blind to our present position, we must see the hazardous situation in which all the great interests of Canada stand in respect to the United States. I am no alarmist. I do not believe in the prospect of immediate war. I believe that the common sense of the two nations will prevent a war; still we cannot trust to probabilities. The Government and Legislature would be wanting in their duty to the people if they ran any risk. We know that the United States at this moment are engaged in a war of enormous dimensions—that the occasion of a war with Great Britain has again and again arisen, and may at any time in the future again arise. We cannot foresee what may be the result; we cannot say but that the two nations may drift into a war as other nations have done before. It would then be too late when war had commenced to think of measures for strengthening ourselves, or to begin negotiations for a union with the sister provinces.

At this moment, in consequence of the ill-feeling which has arisen between England and the United States—a feeling of which Canada was not the cause—in consequence of the irritation which now exists, owing to the unhappy state of affairs on this continent, the Reciprocity Treaty, it seems probable, is about to be brought to an end—our trade is hampered by the passport system, and at any moment we may be deprived of permission to carry our goods through United States channels—the bonded goods system may be done away with, and the winter trade through the United States put an end to.* Our

---

* The Reciprocity Treaty of 1854 outlined the free trade of specific goods between Canada and the United States and permitted shared access to certain fishing grounds. Canada's governor general, Lord Elgin, negotiated the agreement, which the US Senate terminated abruptly in March 1865. (Forster, "Reciprocity," *OCCH*)

merchants may be obliged to return to the old system of bringing in during the summer months the supplies for the whole year. Ourselves already threatened, our trade interrupted, our intercourse, political and commercial, destroyed, if we do not take warning now when we have the opportunity, and while one avenue is threatened to be closed, open another by taking advantage of the present arrangement and the desire of the Lower Provinces to draw closer the alliance between us, we may suffer commercial and political disadvantages it may take long for us to overcome.

The Conference having come to the conclusion that a legislative union, pure and simple, was impracticable, our next attempt was to form a government upon federal principles, which would give to the General Government the strength of a legislative and administrative union, while at the same time it preserved that liberty of action for the different sections which is allowed by a Federal Union. And I am strong in the belief—that we have hit upon the happy medium in those resolutions, and that we have formed a scheme of government which unites the advantages of both, giving us the strength of a legislative union and the sectional freedom of a federal union, with protection to local interests.

In doing so we had the advantage of the experience of the United States. It is the fashion now to enlarge on the defects of the Constitution of the United States, but I am not one of those who look upon it as a failure. (Hear, hear.) I think and believe that it is one of the most skillful works which human intelligence ever created; is one of the most perfect organizations that ever governed a free people. To say that it has some defects is but to say that it is not the work of Omniscience, but of human intellects. We are happily situated in having had the opportunity of watching its operation, seeing its working from its infancy till now. It was in the main formed on the model of the Constitution of Great Britain, adapted to the circumstances of a new country, and was perhaps the only practicable system that could have been adopted under the circumstances existing at the time of its formation. We can now take advantage of the experience of the last seventy-eight years, during which that Constitution has existed, and I am strongly of the belief that we have, in a great measure, avoided in this system which we propose for the adoption of the people of Canada, the defects which time and events have shown to exist in the American Constitution.

In the first place, by a resolution which meets with the universal approval of the people of this country, we have provided that for all time to come, so far as we can legislate for the future, we shall have as the head of the executive power, the Sovereign of Great Britain. (Hear, hear.) No one can look into futurity and say what will be the destiny of this country. Changes come over nations and peoples in the course of ages. But, so far as we can legislate, we provide that, for all time to come, the Sovereign of Great Britain shall be the Sovereign of British North America. By adhering to the monarchical principle, we avoid one defect inherent in the Constitution of the United States. By the election of the President by a majority and for a short period, he never is the sovereign and chief of the nation. He is never looked up to by the whole people as the head and front of the nation. He is at best but the successful leader of a party. This defect is all the greater on account of the practice of re-election. During his first term of office, he is employed in taking steps to secure his own re-election, and for his party a continuance of power. We avoid this by adhering to the monarchical principle—the Sovereign whom you respect and love. I believe that it is of the utmost importance to have that principle recognized, so that we shall have a Sovereign who is placed above the region or party—to whom all parties look up—who is not elevated by the action of one party nor depressed by the action of another, who is the common head and sovereign of all. (Hear, hear and cheers.)

In the Constitution we propose to continue the system of Responsible Government, which has existed in this province since 1841, and which has long obtained in the Mother Country. This is a feature of our Constitution as we have it now, and as we shall have it in the Federation, in which, I think, we avoid one of the great defects in the Constitution of the United States. There the President, during his term of office, is in a great measure a despot, a one-man power, with the command of the naval and military forces—with an immense amount of patronage as head of the Executive, and with the veto power as a branch of the legislature, perfectly uncontrolled by responsible advisers, his cabinet being departmental officers merely, whom he is not obliged by the Constitution to consult with, unless he chooses to do so. With us the Sovereign, or in this country the Representative of the Sovereign, can act only on the advice of his ministers, those ministers being responsible to the people through Parliament.

Prior to the formation of the American Union, as we all know, the different states which entered into it were separate colonies. They had no connection with each other further than that of having a common sovereign, just as with us at present. Their constitutions and their laws were different. They might and did legislate against each other, and when they revolted against the Mother Country they acted as separate sovereignties, and carried on the war by a kind of treaty of alliance against the common enemy. Ever since the union was formed the difficulty of what is called "State Rights" has existed, and this had much to do in bringing on the present unhappy war in the United States. They commenced, in fact, at the wrong end. They declared by their Constitution that each state was a sovereignty in itself, and that all the powers incident to a sovereignty belonged to each state, except those powers which, by the Constitution, were conferred upon the General Government and Congress. Here we have adopted a different system. We have strengthened the General Government. We have given the General Legislature all the great subjects of legislation. We have conferred on them, not only specifically and in detail, all the powers which are incident to sovereignty, but we have expressly declared that all subjects of general interest not distinctly and exclusively conferred upon the local governments and local legislatures, shall be conferred upon the General Government and Legislature.— We have thus avoided that great source of weakness which has been the cause of the disruption of the United States. We have avoided all conflict of jurisdiction and authority, and if this Constitution is carried out, as it will be in full detail in the Imperial Act to be passed if the colonies adopt the scheme, we will have in fact, as I said before, all the advantages of a legislative union under one administration, with, at the same time the guarantees for local institutions and for local laws, which are insisted upon by so many in the provinces now, I hope, to be united.

I think it is well that, in framing our Constitution— although my honorable friend the member for Hochelaga (Hon. Mr. Dorion) sneered at it the other day, in the discussion on the Address in reply to the speech from the Throne—our first act should have been to recognize the sovereignty of Her Majesty. (Hear, hear.) I believe that, while England has no desire to lose her colonies, but wishes to retain them, while I am satisfied that the public mind of England would deeply regret the loss of these provinces—yet, if the people of British North America after full deliberation had stated that they considered it was for their interest, for the advantage of the future of British North America to sever the tie, such is the generosity of the people of England, that, whatever their desire to keep these colonies, they would not seek to compel us to remain unwilling subjects of the British Crown. If therefore, at the Conference, we had arrived at the conclusion, that it was for the interest of these provinces that a severance should take place, I am sure that Her Majesty and the Imperial Parliament would have sanctioned that severance. We accordingly felt that there was a propriety in giving a distinct declaration of opinion on that point, and that, in framing the Constitution, its first sentence should declare, that "The Executive authority or government shall be vested in the Sovereign of the United Kingdom of Great Britain and Ireland, and be administered according to the well understood principles of the British Constitution, by the Sovereign personally, or by the Representative of the Sovereign duly authorised." That resolution met with the unanimous assent of the Conference. The desire to remain connected with Great Britain and to retain our allegiance to Her Majesty was unanimous. Not a single suggestion was made, that it could, by any possibility, be for the interest of the colonies, or of any section or portion of them, that there should be a severance of our connection. Although we knew it to be possible that Canada, from her position, might be exposed to all the horrors of war, by reason of causes of hostility arising between Great Britain and the United States—causes over which we had no control, and which we had no hand in bringing about—yet there was a unanimous feeling of willingness to run all the hazards of war, if war must come, rather than lose the connection between the Mother Country and these colonies. (Cheers.)

We provide that "the Executive authority shall be administered by the Sovereign personally, or by the Representative of the Sovereign duly authorized." It is too much to expect that the Queen should vouchsafe us her personal governance or presence, except to pay us, as the heir apparent of the Throne, our future Sovereign has already paid us, the graceful compliment of a visit. The Executive authority must therefore be administered by Her Majesty's Representative. We place no restriction on Her Majesty's prerogative in the selection of her representative. As it is now, so it will be if this Constitution is adopted. The Sovereign has unrestricted freedom of choice. Whether in making her selection she may send us one of her own family, a Royal Prince, as a Viceroy to rule over us, or one of the great statesmen of England to represent her, we know not. We leave that to Her Majesty in all confidence. But we may be permitted to hope, that when the union takes place, and we become the great country which British North America is certain to be, it will be an object worthy the ambition of the statesmen of England to be charged with presiding over our destinies. (Hear, hear.) Let me now invite the attention of the House to the provisions in the Constitution respecting the legislative power. The sixth resolution says, "There shall be a general legislature or parliament for the federated provinces, composed of a Legislative Council and a House of Commons." This resolution has been cavilled at in the English press as if it excluded the Sovereign as a portion of the legislature. In one sense, that stricture was just—because in strict constitutional language, the legislature of England consists of King, Lords and Commons. But, on the other hand, in ordinary parlance we speak of "the King and his Parliament," or "the King summoning his Parliament," the three estates—Lords spiritual, temporal Lords, and the House of Commons, and I observe that such a writer as Hallam* occasionally uses the word Parliament in that restricted sense. At best it is merely a verbal criticism.

The legislature of British North America will be composed of King, Lords, and Commons. The Legislative Council will stand in the same relation to the Lower House, as the House of Lords to the House of Commons in England, having the same power of initiating all matters of legislation, except the granting of money. As regards the Lower House, it may not appear to matter much, whether it is called the House of Commons or House of Assembly. It will bear whatever name the Parliament of England may choose to give it, but "The House of Commons" is the name we should prefer, as shewing that it represents the Commons of Canada, in the same way that the English House of Commons represents the Commons of England, with the same privileges, the same parliamentary usage, and the same parliamentary authority.

In settling the constitution of the Lower House, that which peculiarly represents the people, it was agreed that the principle of representation based on population should be adopted, and the mode of applying that principle is fully developed in these resolutions. When I speak of representation by population, the House will of course understand, that universal suffrage is not in

---

* Macdonald may be referring to Henry Hallam (1777–1859), British constitutional historian. (Lang, "Hallam, Henry," ODNB)

any way sanctioned, or admitted by these resolutions, as the basis on which the constitution of the popular branch should rest.

In order to protect local interests, and to prevent sectional jealousies, it was found requisite that the three great divisions into which British North America is separated, should be represented in the Upper House on the principle of equality. There are three great sections, having different interests, in this proposed Confederation. We have Western Canada, an agricultural country far away from the sea, and having the largest population who have agricultural interests principally to guard. We have Lower Canada, with other and separate interests, and especially with institutions and laws which she jealously guards against absorption by any larger, more numerous, or stronger power. And we have the Maritime Provinces, having also different sectional interests of their own, having, from their position, classes and interests which we do not know in Western Canada. Accordingly, in the Upper House— the controlling and regulating, but not the initiating, branch (for we know that here as in England, to the Lower House will practically belong the initiation of matters of great public interest), in the House which has the sober second-thought in legislation—it is provided that each of those great sections shall be represented equally by 24 members. The only exception to that condition of equality is in the case of Newfoundland, which has an interest of its own, lying, as it does, at the mouth of the great river St. Lawrence, and more connected, perhaps, with Canada than with the Lower Provinces. It has, comparatively speaking, no common interest with the other Maritime Provinces, but has sectional interests and sectional claims of its own to be protected. It, therefore has been dealt with separately, and is to have a separate representation in the Upper

House, thus varying from the equality established between the other sections.—

As may be well conceived, great difference of opinion at first existed as to the constitution of the Legislative Council. In Canada the elective principle prevailed; in the Lower Provinces, with the exception of Prince Edward Island, the nominative principle was the rule. We found a general disinclination on the part of the Lower Provinces to adopt the elective principle; indeed, I do not think there was a dissenting voice in the Conference against the adoption of the nominative principle, except from Prince Edward Island. The delegates from New Brunswick, Nova Scotia and Newfoundland, as one man, were in favor of nomination by the Crown. And nomination by the Crown is of course the system which is most in accordance with the British Constitution. We resolved then, that the constitution of the Upper House should be in accordance with the British system as nearly as circumstances would allow. An hereditary Upper House is impracticable in this young country. Here we have none of the elements for the formation of a landlord aristocracy—no men of large territorial positions—no class separated from the mass of the people. An hereditary body is altogether unsuited to our state of society, and would soon dwindle into nothing. The only mode of adapting the English system to the Upper House, is by conferring the power of appointment on the Crown (as the English peers are appointed), but that the appointments should be for life. The arguments for an elective Council are numerous and strong; and I ought to say so, as one of the Administration responsible for introducing the elective principle into Canada. (Hear, hear.)

I hold that this principle has not been a failure in Canada; but there were causes—which we did not take into consideration at the time—why it did not so fully succeed in Canada as we had expected. One great cause was the enormous extent of the constituencies and the immense labor which consequently devolved on those who sought the suffrages of the people for election to the Council. For the same reason the expense—(laughter)—the legitimate expense was so enormous that men of standing in the country, eminently fitted for such a position, were prevented from coming forward. At first, I admit, men of the first standing did come forward, but we have seen that in every succeeding election in both Canadas there has been an increasing disinclination, on the part of men of standing and political experience and weight in the country, to become candidates; while, on the other hand, all the young men, the active politicians, those who have resolved to embrace the life of a statesman, have sought entrance to the House of Assembly.

The nominative system in this country, was to a great extent successful, before the introduction of responsible government. Then the Canadas were to a great extent Crown colonies, and the upper branch of the legislature consisted of gentlemen chosen from among the chief judicial and ecclesiastical dignitaries, the heads of departments, and other men of the first position in the country. Those bodies commanded great respect from the character, standing, and weight of the individuals composing them, but they had little sympathy with the people or their representatives, and collisions with the Lower House frequently occurred, especially in Lower Canada. When responsible government was introduced, it became necessary for the Governor of the day to have a body of advisers who had the confidence of the House of Assembly which could make or unmake ministers as it chose. The Lower House in effect pointed out who should be nominated to the Upper House; for the ministry, being dependent altogether on the lower branch of the legislature for support, selected members for the Upper House from among their political friends at the dictation of the House of Assembly. The Council was becoming less and less a substantial check on the legislation of the Assembly; but under the system now proposed, such will not be the case. No ministry can in future do what they have done in Canada before,—they cannot, with the view of carrying any measure, or of strengthening the party, attempt to overrule the independent opinion of the Upper House, by filling it with a number of its partisans and political supporters.

The provision in the Constitution, that the Legislative Council shall consist of a limited number of members—that each of the great sections shall appoint twenty-four members and no more, will prevent the Upper House from being swamped from time to time by the ministry of the day, for the purpose of carrying out their own schemes or pleasing their partisans. The fact of the government being prevented from exceeding a limited number will preserve the independence of the Upper House, and make it, in reality, a separate and distinct chamber, having a legitimate and controlling influence in the legislation of the country.

The objection has been taken that in consequence of the Crown being deprived of the right of unlimited appointment, there is a chance of a dead lock arising between the two branches of the legislature; a chance that the Upper House being altogether independent of the Sovereign, of the Lower House, and of the advisers of the Crown, may act independently, and so independently as to produce a dead lock. I do not anticipate any such result. In the first place we know that in England it does not arise. There would be no use of an Upper House, if it did not exercise, when it thought proper, the right of opposing or amending or postponing the legislation of the Lower House. It would be of no value whatever were it a mere chamber for registering the decrees of the Lower House. It must be an independent House, having a free action of its own, for it is only valuable as being a regulating body, calmly considering the legislation initiated by the popular branch, and preventing any hasty or ill-considered legislation which may come from that body, but it will never set itself in opposition against the deliberate and understood wishes of the people. Even the House of Lords, which as an hereditary body, is far more independent than one appointed for life can be, whenever it ascertains what is the calm, deliberate will of the people of England, it yields, and never in modern times has there been, in fact or act, any attempt to overrule the decisions of that House by the appointment of new peers, excepting, perhaps, once in the reign of Queen Anne. It is true that in 1832 such an increase was threatened in consequence of the reiterated refusal of the House of Peers to pass the Reform Bill. I have no doubt the threat would have been carried into effect, if necessary; but every one, even the Ministry who advised that step, admitted that it would be a revolutionary net, a breach of the Constitution to do so, and it was because of the necessity of preventing the bloody revolution which hung over the land, if the Reform Bill had been longer refused to the people of England, that they consented to the bloodless revolution of overriding the independent opinion of the House of Lords on that question. (Hear, hear.) Since that time it has never been attempted, and I am satisfied it will never be attempted again. Only a year or two ago the House of Lords rejected the Paper Duties Bill, and they acted quite constitutionally, according to the letter and as many think, according to the spirit of the Constitution in doing so. Yet when they found they had interfered with a subject which the people's house claimed as belonging of right to themselves, the very next session they abandoned their position, not because they were convinced they had done wrong, but because they had ascertained what was the deliberate voice of the representatives of the people on the subject.

In this country, we must remember, that the gentlemen who will be selected for the Legislative Council stand on a very different footing from the peers of England. They have not like them any ancestral associations or position derived from history. They have not that direct influence on the people themselves, or on the popular branch of the Legislature, which the peers of England exercise, from their great wealth, their vast territorial possessions, their numerous tenantry and that prestige with which the exalted position of their class for centuries has invested them. (Hear, hear.) The members of our Upper House will be like those of the Lower, men of the people, and from the people. The man put into the Upper House is as much a man of the people the day after, as the day before his elevation. Springing from the people, and one of them, he takes his seat in the Council with all the sympathies and feelings of a man of the people, and when he returns home, at the end of the session, he mingles with them on equal terms, and is influenced by the same feelings and associations, and events, as those which affect the mass around him. And is it, then, to be supposed that the members of the upper branch of the legislature will set themselves deliberately at work to oppose what they know to be the settled opinions and wishes of the people of the country? They will not do it. There is no fear of a dead lock between the two houses.

There is an infinitely greater chance of a dead lock between the two branches of the legislature, should the elective principle be adopted, than with a nominated chamber—chosen by the Crown, and having no mission from the people. The members of the Upper Chamber would then come from the people as well as those of the Lower House, and should any difference ever arise between both branches, the former could say to the members of the popular branch—"We as much represent the feelings of the people as you do, and even more so; we are not elected from small localities and for a short period; you as a body were elected at a particular time, when the public mind was running in a particular channel: you were returned to Parliament, not so much representing the general views of the country, on general questions, as upon the particular subjects which happened to engage the minds of the people when they went to the polls. We have as much right, or a better right, than you to be considered as representing the deliberate will of the people on general questions, and therefore we will not give way." (Hear, hear.)

There is, I repeat, a greater danger of an irreconcilable difference of opinion between the two branches of the legislature, if the upper be elective, than if it holds its commission from the Crown. Besides, it must be remembered that an Upper House, the members of which are to be appointed for life, would not have the same quality of permanence as the House of Lords; our members would die; strangers would succeed them, whereas son succeeded father in the House of Lords. Thus the changes in the membership and state of opinion in our Upper House would always be more rapid than in the House of Lords. To show how speedily changes have occurred in the Upper House, as regards life members, I will call the attention of the House to the following facts:—At the call of the House, in February, 1856, forty-two life members responded; two years afterwards, in 1858, only thirty-five answered to their names; in 1862 there were only twenty-five life members left, and in 1864, but twenty-one. (Hear, hear.) This shows how speedily changes take place in the life membership. But remarkable as this change has been, it is not so great as that in regard to the elected members. Though the elective principle only came into force in 1856, and although only twelve men were elected that year, and twelve more every two years since, twenty-four changes have already taken place by the decease of members, by the acceptance of office, and by resignation. So it is quite clear that, should there be on any question a difference of opinion between the Upper and Lower Houses, the government of the day being obliged to have the confidence of the majority in the popular branch— would, for the purpose of bringing the former into accord and sympathy with the latter, fill up any vacancies that might occur, with men of the same political feelings and sympathies with the Government, and consequently with those of the majority in the popular branch; and all the appointments of the Administration would be made with the object of maintaining the sympathy and harmony between the two houses. (Hear, hear.)

There is this additional advantage to be expected from the limitation. To the Upper House is to be confided the protection of sectional interests; therefore is it that the three great divisions are there equally represented, for the purpose of defending such interests against the combinations of majorities in the Assembly. It will, therefore, become the interest of each section to be represented by its very best men, and the members of the Administration who belong to each section will see that such men are chosen, in case of a vacancy in their section. For the same reason each state of the American Union sends its two best men to represent its interests in the Senate. (Hear, hear.)

It is provided in the Constitution that in the first selections for the Council, regard shall be had to those who now hold similar positions in the different colonies. This, it appears to me, is a wise provision. In all the provinces, except Prince Edward [Island], there are gentlemen who hold commissions for the Upper House for life. In Canada, there are a number who hold under that commission; but the majority of them hold by a commission, not, perhaps, from a monarchical point of view so honorable, because the Queen is the fountain of honor,—but still, as holding their appointment from the people, they may be considered as standing on a par with those who have Her Majesty's commission. There can be no reason suggested why those who have had experience in legislation, whether they hold their positions by the election of the people or have received preferment from the Crown—there is no valid reason why those men should be passed over, and new men sought for to form the Legislative Council of the Confederation. It is, therefore, provided that the selection shall be made from those gentlemen who are now members of the upper branch of the Legislature in each of the colonies, for seats in the Legislative Council of the General Legislature. The arrangement in this respect is somewhat similar to that by which Representative Peers are chosen from the Peers of Scotland and Ireland, to sit in the Parliament of the United Kingdom. In like manner, the members of the Legislative Council of the proposed Confederation will be first selected from the existing Legislative Councils of the various provinces.

In the formation of the House of Commons, the principle of representation by population has been provided for in a manner equally ingenious and simple. The introduction of this principle presented at first the apparent difficulty of a constantly increasing body until, with the increasing population, it would become inconveniently and expensively large. But by adopting the representation of Lower Canada as a fixed standard—as the pivot on which the whole would turn—that province being the best suited for the purpose, on account of the comparatively permanent character of its population, and from its having neither the largest nor least number of inhabitants—we have been enabled to overcome the difficulty I have mentioned. We have introduced the system of representation by population without the danger of an inconvenient increase in the number of representatives on the recurrence of each decennial period. The whole thing is worked by a simple rule of three. For instance, we have in Upper Canada 1,400,000 of a population; in Lower Canada 1,100,000. Now, the proposition is simply this—if Lower Canada, with its population of 1,100,000, has a right to 65 members, how many members should Upper Canada have, with its larger population of 1,400,000? The same rule applies to the other provinces—the proportion is always observed and the principle of representation by population carried out, while, at the same time, there will not be decennially an inconvenient increase in the numbers of the Lower House. At the same time, there is a constitutional provision that hereafter, if deemed advisable, the total number of representatives may be increased from 194, the number fixed in the first instance. In that case, if an increase is made, Lower Canada is still to remain the pivot on which the whole calculation will turn. If Lower Canada, instead of sixty-five, shall have seventy members, then the calculation will be, if Lower Canada has seventy members, with such a population, how many shall Upper Canada have with a larger population?

I was in favor of a larger House than one hundred and ninety-four, but was overruled. I was perhaps singular in the opinion, but I thought it would be well to commence with a larger representation in the lower branch. The arguments against this were, that, in the first place, it would cause additional expense; in the next place, that in a new country like this, we could not get a sufficient number of qualified men to be representatives. My reply was that the number is rapidly increasing as we increase in education and wealth; that a larger field would be open to political ambition by having a larger body of representatives; that by having numerous and smaller constituencies, more people would be interested in the working of the union, and that there would be a wider field for selection for leaders of governments and leaders of parties. These are my individual sentiments,— which, perhaps, I have no right to express here—but I was overruled, and we fixed on the number of one hundred and ninety-four, which no one will say is large or extensive, when it is considered that our present number in Canada alone is one hundred and thirty. The difference between one hundred and thirty and one hundred and ninety-four is not great, considering the large increase that will be made to our population when Confederation is carried into effect.

While the principle of representation by population is adopted with respect to the popular branch of the legislature, not a single member of the Conference, as I stated before, not a single one of the representatives of the government or of the opposition of any one of the Lower Provinces was in favor of universal suffrage. Every one felt that in this respect the principle of the British Constitution should be carried out, and that classes and property should be represented as well as numbers. Insuperable difficulties would have presented themselves if we had attempted to settle now the qualification for the elective franchise. We have different laws in each of the colonies fixing the qualification of electors for their own local legislatures; and we therefore adopted a similar clause to that which is contained in the Canada Union Act of 1841, viz., that all the laws which affected the qualification of members and of voters, which affected the appointment and conduct of returning officers and the proceedings at elections, as well as the trial of controverted elections in the separate provinces, should obtain in the first election to the Confederate Parliament, so that every man who has now a vote in his own province should continue to have a vote in choosing a representative to the first Federal Parliament.

And it was left to the Parliament of the Confederation, as one of their first duties, to consider and to settle by an act of their own the qualification for the elective franchise, which would apply to the whole Confederation. In considering the question of the duration of Parliament, we came to the conclusion to recommend a period of five years. I was in favor of a longer period. I thought that the duration of the local legislatures should not be shortened so as to be less than four years, as at present, and that the General Parliament should have as long a duration as that of the United Kingdom. I was willing to have gone to the extent of seven years; but a term of five years was preferred, and we had the example of New Zealand carefully considered, not only locally, but by the Imperial Parliament, and which gave the provinces of those islands a general parliament with a duration of five years.* But it was a matter of little importance whether

---

* New Zealand's Constitution Act of 1852 had set out a "quasi-federal system" whereby the central government wielded the balance of power, but provinces retained control over land and development. The British wanted to withdraw imperial troops from around the world and promoted colonial responsibility for internal policy-making and

five years or seven years was the term, the power of dissolution by the Crown having been reserved. I find, on looking at the duration of parliaments since the accession of George III to the Throne, that excluding the present parliament, there have been seventeen parliaments, the average period of whose existence has been about three years and a half. That average is less than the average duration of the parliaments in Canada since the union, so that it was not a matter of much importance whether we fixed upon five or seven years as the period of duration of our General Parliament.

A good deal of misapprehension has arisen from the accidental omission of some words from the 24th resolution. It was thought that by it the local legislatures were to have the power of arranging hereafter, and from time to time of readjusting the different constituencies and settling the size and boundaries of the various electoral districts. The meaning of the resolution is simply this, that for the first General Parliament, the arrangement of constituencies shall be made by the existing local legislatures; that in Canada, for instance, the present Canadian Parliament shall arrange what are to be the constituencies of Upper Canada, and to make such changes as may be necessary in arranging for the seventeen additional members given to it by the Constitution; and that it may also, if it sees fit, alter the boundaries of the existing constituencies of Lower Canada. In short, this Parliament shall settle what shall be the different

---

defence. The new ministry elected in 1864 "accepted [. . .] self-reliance." Conflicts over land helped shape the colony's government over the next decade. The Maori attempted to manage their land settlement through a collective tribal assembly as part of the King Movement and to assert their autonomy. When the movement lurched into violence in 1863, New Zealand's colonial relationship with Britain came into question when Britain was called upon to defend the settlers. (Dalziel, "Southern Islands: New Zealand and Polynesia," *OHBE*, vol. 3, 584-6)

constituencies electing members to the first Federal Parliament. And so the other provinces, the legislatures of which will fix the limits of their several constituencies in the session in which they adopt the new Constitution. Afterwards the local legislatures may alter their own electoral limits as they please, for their own local elections. But it would evidently be unproper to leave to the Local Legislature the power to alter the constituencies sending members to the General Legislature after the General Legislature shall have been called into existence. Were this the case, a member of the General Legislature might at any time find himself ousted from his seat by an alteration of his constituency by the Local Legislature in his section. No, after the General Parliament meets, in order that it may have full control of its own legislation, and be assured of its position, it must have the full power of arranging and re-arranging the electoral limits of its constituencies as it pleases, such being one of the powers essentially necessary to such a Legislature. (Hear, hear.)

I shall not detain the House by entering into a consideration at any length of the different powers conferred upon the General Parliament as contradistinguished from those reserved to the local legislatures; but any honorable member on examining the list of different subjects which are to be assigned to the General and Local Legislatures respectively, will see that all the great questions which affect the general interests of the Confederacy as a whole, are confided to the Federal Parliament, while the local interests and local laws of each section are preserved intact, and entrusted to the care of the local bodies. As a matter of course, the General Parliament must have the power of dealing with the public debt and property of the Confederation. Of course, too, it must have the regulation of trade and commerce, of customs and excise. The Federal Parliament must have the sovereign power of raising money from such sources and by such means as the representatives of the people will allow. It will be seen that the local legislatures have the control of all local works; and it is a matter of great importance, and one of the chief advantages of the Federal Union and of local legislatures, that each province will have the power and means of developing its own resources and aiding its own progress after its own fashion and in its own way. Therefore all the local improvements, all local enterprizes or undertakings of any kind, have been left to the care and management of the local legislatures of each province. (Cheers.)

It is provided that all "lines of steam or other ships, railways, canals and other works, connecting any two or more of the provinces together or extending beyond the limits of any province," shall belong to the General Government, and be under the control of the General Legislature. In like manner "lines of steamships between the Federated Provinces and other countries, telegraph communication and the incorporation of telegraph companies, and all such works as shall, although lying within any province, be specially declared by the Acts authorizing them, to be for the general advantage," shall belong to the General Government. For instance, the Welland Canal, though lying wholly within one section, and the St. Lawrence Canals in two only, may be properly considered national works, and for the general benefit of the whole Federation. Again, the census, the ascertaining of our numbers and the extent of our resources, must, as a matter of general interest, belong to the General Government. So also with the defences of the country. One of the great advantages of Confederation is, that we shall have a united, a concerted, and uniform system of defence. (Hear.)

We are at this moment with a different militia system in each colony—in some of the colonies with an utter want of any system of defence. We have a number of separate staff establishments, without any arrangement between the colonies as to the means, either of defence or offence. But, under the union, we will have one system of defence and one system of militia organization. In the event of the Lower Provinces being threatened, we can send the large militia forces of Upper Canada to their rescue. Should we have to fight on our lakes against a foreign foe, we will have the hardy seamen of the Lower Provinces coming to our assistance and manning our vessels. (Hear, hear.) We will have one system of defence and be one people, acting together alike in peace and in war. (Cheers.)

The criminal law too—the determination of what is a crime and what is not and how crime shall be punished—is left to the General Government. This is a matter almost of necessity. It is of great importance that we should have the same criminal law throughout these provinces—that what is a crime in one part of British America, should be a crime in every part—that there should be the same protection of life and property as in another. It is one of the defects in the United States system, that each separate state has or may have a criminal code of its own,—that what may be a capital offence in one state, may be a venial offence, punishable slightly, in another. But under our Constitution we shall have one body of criminal law, based on the criminal law of England, and operating equally throughout British America, so that a British American, belonging to what province he may, or going to any other part of the Confederation, knows what his rights are in that respect, and what his punishment will be if an offender against the criminal laws of the land. I think this is one of the most marked instances in which we take advantage of the experience derived from our observations of the defects in the Constitution of the neighboring Republic. (Hear, hear.) The 33rd provision is of very great importance to the future well-being of these colonies. It commits to the General Parliament the "rendering uniform all or any of the laws relative to property and civil rights in Upper Canada, Nova Scotia, New Brunswick, Newfoundland and Prince Edward Island, and rendering uniform the procedure of all or any of the courts in these provinces." The great principles which govern the laws of all the provinces, with the single exception of Lower Canada, are the same, although there may be a divergence in details; and it is gratifying to find, on the part of the Lower Provinces, a general desire to join together with Upper Canada in this matter, and to procure, as soon as possible, an assimilation of the statutory laws and the procedure in the courts, of all these provinces.

At present there is a good deal of diversity. In one of the colonies, for instance, they have no municipal system at all. In another, the municipal system is merely permissive, and has not been adopted to any extent. Although, therefore, a legislative union was found to be almost impracticable, it was understood, so far as we could influence the future, that the first act of the Confederate Government should be to procure an assimilation of the statutory law of all those provinces, which has, as its root and foundation, the common law of England. But to prevent local interests from being over-ridden, the same section makes provision, that, while power is given to the General Legislature to deal with this subject, no change in this respect should have the force and authority of law in any province until sanctioned by the Legislature of that province. (Hear, hear.)

The General Legislature is to have power to establish a

general Court of Appeal for the Federated Provinces. Although the Canadian Legislature has always had the power to establish a Court of Appeal, to which appeals may be made from the courts of Upper and Lower Canada, we have never availed ourselves of the power. Upper Canada has its own Court of Appeal, so has Lower Canada. And this system will continue until a General Court of Appeal shall be established by the General Legislature. The Constitution does not provide that such a court shall be established. There are many arguments for and against the establishment of such a court. But it was thought wise and expedient to put into the Constitution a power to the General Legislature, that, if after full consideration they think it advisable to establish a General Court of Appeal from all the Superior Courts of all the provinces, they may do so. (Hear, hear.)

I shall not go over the other powers that are conferred on the General Parliament. Most of them refer to matters of financial and commercial interest, and I leave those subjects in other and better hands. Besides all the powers that are specifically given in the 37th and last item of this portion of the Constitution, confers on the General Legislature the general mass of sovereign legislation, the power to legislate on "all matters of a general character, not specially and exclusively reserved for the local governments and legislatures." This is precisely the provision which is wanting in the Constitution of the United States. It is here that we find the weakness of the American system—the point where the American Constitution breaks down. (Hear, hear.) It is in itself a wise and necessary provision. We thereby strengthen the Central Parliament, and make the Confederation one people and one government, instead of five peoples and five governments, with merely a point of authority connecting us to a limited and insufficient extent.

With respect to the local governments, it is provided that each shall be governed by a chief executive officer, who shall be nominated by the General Government. As this is to be one united province, with the local governments and legislatures subordinate to the General Government and Legislature, it is obvious that the chief executive officer in each of the provinces must be subordinate as well. The General Government assumes towards the local governments precisely the same position as the Imperial Government holds with respect to each of the colonies now: so that as the Lieutenant Governor of each of the different provinces is now appointed directly by the Queen, and is directly responsible, and reports directly to Her, so will the executives of the local governments hereafter be subordinate to the Representative of the Queen, and be responsible and report to him. Objection has been taken that there is an infringement of the Royal prerogative in giving the pardoning power to the local governors, who are not appointed directly by the Crown, but only indirectly by the Chief Executive of the Confederation, who is appointed by the Crown. This provision was inserted in the Constitution on account of the practical difficulty which must arise if the power is confined to the Governor General. For example, if a question arose about the discharge of a prisoner convicted of a minor offence, say in Newfoundland, who might be in imminent danger of losing his life if he remained in confinement, the exercise of the pardoning power might come too late if it were necessary to wait for the action of the Governor General. It must be remembered that the pardoning power not only extends to capital cases, but to every case of conviction and sentence, no matter how trifling—even to the case of a fine in the nature of a sentence on a criminal conviction. It extends to innumerable cases, where, if the responsibility for its exercise were thrown on the General Executive, it could not be so satisfactorily discharged. Of course there must be, in each province, a legal adviser of the Executive, occupying the position of our Attorney General, as there is in every state of the American Union. This officer will be an officer of the Local Government; but, if the pardoning power is reserved for the Chief Executive, there must, in every case where the exercise of the pardoning power is sought, be a direct communication and report from the local law officer to the Governor General. The practical inconvenience of this was felt to be so great, that it was thought well to propose the arrangement we did, without any desire to infringe upon the prerogatives of the Crown, for our whole action shews that the Conference, in every step they took, were actuated by a desire to guard jealously these prerogatives. (Hear, hear.) It is a subject, however, of Imperial interest, and if the Imperial Government and Imperial Parliament are not convinced by the arguments we will be able to press upon them for the continuation of that clause, then, of course, as the over-ruling power, they may set it aside. (Hear, hear.)

There are numerous subjects which belong, of right, both to the Local and the General Parliaments. In all these cases it is provided, in order to prevent a conflict of authority, that where there is concurrent jurisdiction in the General and Local Parliaments, the same rule should apply as now applies in cases where there is concurrent jurisdiction in the Imperial and in the Provincial Parliaments, and that when the legislation of the one is adverse to or contradictory of the legislation of the other, in all such cases the action of the General Parliament must overrule, ex-necessitate, the action of the Local Legislature. (Hear, hear.) We have introduced also all those provisions which are necessary in order to the full working out of the British Constitution in these provinces. We provide that there shall be no money votes, unless those votes are introduced in the popular branch of the Legislature on the authority of the responsible advisers of the Crown—those with whom the responsibility rests of equalizing revenue and expenditure—that there can be no expenditure or authorization of expenditure by Address or in any other way unless initiated by the Crown on the advice of its responsible advisers. (Hear, hear.)

As regards the financial features of the scheme, the arrangements made as to the present liabilities of the several provinces, and the future liabilities of the Confederation, on these and kindred matters, I have no doubt that my honorable friends, the Finance Minister and the President of the Council, will speak at full length, and that they will be able to shew you that this branch of the subject has received the fullest consideration. I feel I would be intruding myself unnecessarily on the House if, with my inferior knowledge of those subjects I were to detain you by venturing to speak of them, when I know that they will be so ably and fully gone into by my two honorable friends.

The last resolution of any importance is one which, although not affecting the substance of the Constitution, is of interest to us all. It is that "Her Majesty the Queen be solicited to determine the rank and name of the federated provinces." I do not know whether there will be any expression of opinion in this House on this subject—whether we are to be a vice-royalty, or whether we are still to retain our name and rank as a province. But I have no doubt Her Majesty will give the matter Her gracious consideration, that She will give us a name satisfactory to us all, and that the rank She will confer upon us will be a rank worthy of our position, of our resources, and of our future. (Cheers.)

Let me again, before I sit down, impress upon this House the necessity of meeting this question in a spirit of compromise, with a disposition to judge the matter as a whole, to consider whether really it is for the benefit and advantage of the country to form a Confederation of all the provinces; and if honorable gentlemen, whatever may have been their preconceived ideas as to the merits of the details of this measure, whatever may still be their opinions as to these details, if they really believe that the scheme is one by which the prosperity of the country will be increased, and its future progress secured, I ask them to yield their own views, and to deal with the scheme according to its merits as one great whole. (Hear, hear.)

One argument, but not a strong one, has been used against this Confederation, that it is an advance towards independence. Some are apprehensive that the very fact of our forming this union will hasten the time when we shall be severed from the mother country. I have no apprehension of that kind. I believe it will have the contrary effect. I believe that as we grow stronger, that, as it is felt in England we have become a people, able from our union, our strength, our population, and the development of our resources, to take our position among the nations of the world, she will be less willing to part with us than she would be now, when we are broken up into a number of insignificant colonies, subject to attack piece-meal without any concerted action or common organization of defence. I am strongly of opinion that year by year, as we grow in population and strength, England will more see the advantages of maintaining the alliance between British North America and herself. Does any one imagine that, when our population instead of three and a-half, will be seven millions, as it will be ere many years pass, we would be one whit more willing than now to sever the connection with England? Would not those seven millions be just as anxious to maintain their allegiance to the Queen and their connection with the Mother Country, as we are now? Will the addition to our numbers of the people of the Lower Provinces, in any way lessen our desire to continue our connection with the Mother Country? I believe the people of Canada East and West to be truly loyal. But, if they can by possibility be exceeded in loyalty, it is by the inhabitants of the Maritime Provinces. Loyalty with them is an overruling passion. (Hear, hear.) In all parts of the Lower Provinces there is a rivalry between the opposing political parties as to which shall most strongly express and most effectively carry out the principle of loyalty to Her Majesty, and to the British Crown. (Hear, hear.)

When this union takes place, we will be at the outset no inconsiderable people. We find ourselves with a population approaching four millions of souls. Such a population in Europe would make a second, or at least, a third rate power. And with a rapidly increasing population—for I am satisfied that under this union our population will increase in a still greater ratio than ever before—with increased credit—with a higher position in the eyes of Europe—with the increased security we can offer to immigrants, who would naturally prefer to seek a new home in what is known to them as a great country, than in any one little colony or another—with all this I am satisfied that, great as has been our increase in the last twenty-five years since the union between Upper and Lower Canada, our future progress, during the next quarter of a century, will be vastly greater. (Cheers.) And when, by means of this rapid increase, we become a nation of eight or nine millions of inhabitants, our alliance will be worthy of being sought by the great nations of the earth. (Hear, hear.)

I am proud to believe that our desire for a permanent alliance will be reciprocated in England. I know that there is a party in England—but it is inconsiderable in numbers, though strong in intellect and power—which speaks of the desirability of getting rid of the colonies; but I believe such is not the feeling of the statesmen and the people of England. I believe it will never be the deliberately expressed determination of the Government of Great Britain. (Hear, hear.) The colonies are now in a transition state.

Gradually a different colonial system is being developed—and it will become, year by year, less a case of dependence on our part, and of overruling protection on the part of the Mother Country, and more a case of a healthy and cordial alliance. Instead of looking upon us as a merely dependent colony, England will have in us a friendly nation—a subordinate but still a powerful people—to stand by her in North America in peace or in war. (Cheers.) The people of Australia will be such another subordinate nation.* And England will have this advantage, if her colonies progress under the new colonial system, as I believe they will, that, though at war with all the rest of the world, she will be able to look to the subordinate nations in alliance with her, and owning allegiance to the same Sovereign who will assist in enabling her again to meet the whole world in arms, as she has done before. (Cheers) And if, in the great Napoleonic war, with every port in Europe closed against her commerce, she was yet able to hold her own, how much more will that be the case when she has a colonial empire rapidly increasing in power, in wealth, in influence, and in position. (Hear, hear.)

---

* By the mid-1860s, the former penal colonies of Australia were "self-governing democracies" in the British Empire with constitutions modelled on Canada's responsible government. The political federation of the Australian states did not occur until 1901. (Denoon and Wyndham, "Australia and the Western Pacific," *OHBE*, vol 3, 555, 561)

It is true that we stand in danger, as we have stood in danger again and again in Canada, of being plunged into war and suffering all its dreadful consequences, as the result of causes over which we have no control, by reason of their connection. This, however, did not intimidate us. At the very mention of the prospect of a war some time ago, how were the feelings of the people aroused from one extremity of British America to the other, and preparations made for meeting its worst consequences. Although the people of this country are fully aware of the horrors of war—should a war arise, unfortunately, between the United States and England, and we all pray it never may—they are still ready to encounter all perils of that kind, for the sake of the connection with England. There is not one adverse voice, not one adverse opinion on that point. We all feel the advantages we derive from our connection with England. So long as that alliance is maintained, we enjoy, under her protection, the privileges of constitutional liberty according to the British system. We will enjoy here that which is the great test of constitutional freedom—we will have the rights of the minority respected. (Hear, hear.) In all countries the rights of the majority take care of themselves, but it is only in countries like England, enjoying constitutional liberty, and safe from the tyranny of a single despot or of an unbridled democracy, that the rights of minorities are regarded. So long, too, as we form a portion of the British Empire, we shall have the example of her free institutions, of the high standard of the character of her statesmen and public men, of the purity of her legislation, and the upright administration of her laws. In this younger country one great advantage of our connection with Great Britain will be, that, under her auspices, inspired by her example, a portion of her empire, our public men will be actuated by principles similar to those which actuate the statesmen at home. These although not material, physical benefits, of which you can make an arithmetical calculation, are of such overwhelming advantage to our future interests and standing as a nation, that to obtain them is well worthy of any sacrifices we may be called upon to make, and the people of this country are ready to make them. (Cheers.)

We should feel, also, sincerely grateful to beneficent Providence that we have had the opportunity vouchsafed us of calmly considering this great constitutional change, this peaceful revolution—that we have not been hurried into it, like the United States, by the exigencies of war—that we have not had a violent revolutionary period forced on us, as in other nations, by hostile action from without, or by domestic dissensions within. Here we are in peace and prosperity, under the fostering government of Great Britain—a dependent people, with a government having only a limited and delegated authority, and yet allowed, without restriction, and without jealousy on the part of the Mother Country, to legislate for ourselves, and peacefully and deliberately to consider and determine the future of Canada and of British North America.

It is our happiness to know the expression of the will of our Gracious Sovereign, through Her Ministers, that we have her full sanction for our deliberations, that Her only solicitude is that we shall adopt a system which shall be really for our advantage, and that She promises to sanction whatever conclusion after full deliberation we may arrive at as to the best mode of securing the well-being—the present and future prosperity of British America. (Cheers.) It is our privilege and happiness to be in such a position, and we cannot be too grateful for the blessings thus conferred upon us. (Hear, hear.)

I must apologize for having detained you so long—for having gone perhaps too much into tedious details with reference to the questions bearing on the Constitution now submitted to this House.—(Cries of "no, no" and "go on.") In conclusion, I would again implore the House not to let this opportunity to pass. It is an opportunity that may never recur. At the risk of repeating myself, I would say, it was only by a happy concurrence of circumstances, that we were enabled to bring this great question to its present position. If we do not take advantage of the time, if we show ourselves unequal to the occasion, it may never return, and we shall hereafter bitterly and unavailingly regret having failed to embrace the happy opportunity now offered of founding a great nation under the fostering care of Great Britain, and our Sovereign Lady, Queen Victoria. (Loud cheers, amidst which the honorable gentleman resumed his seat.)

"MARTYR TO THE CAUSE," EULOGIZING McGEE, 1868

A bullet stopped the life of Irish nationalist-turned-Confederation-supporter Thomas D'Arcy McGee (1825–1868), early on the morning of April 7, 1868. A conviction against Fenian sympathizer Patrick Whelan was obtained, but no definitive link to the Irish Republican Brotherhood was ever proven. McGee's innovative vision of a "new nationality" for Canada within the imperial yoke had brought him enemies. But grown disenchanted with Irish nationalism, McGee staked his fortunes with Canada, which offered the possibility of transcending differences. McGee contributed an ardent literary output to the new nation and envisioned policies to support the development of a distinctive Canadian literary culture. More practically, McGee focused on the civil service as a route to strengthened national loyalty. He desired to make it less partisan and more merit-based, following the model used in Ireland.

---

* In many instances, McGee's 1863 report condemning the civil service did not reflect the full complexities of its hiring practices and needs. (Burns, "McGee, Thomas D'Arcy," *DCB*; Piva, "Getting Hired: The Civil Service Act of 1857," 98)

Macdonald's eulogy of April 7 in the House of Commons entwined
McGee's life with the national story when Fennings Taylor reproduced
it in his 1868 biography D'Arcy McGee: Sketch of His Life and
Death:

[SIR JOHN A. MACDONALD:] Mr. Speaker [James
Cockburn (1819–1883)], it is with pain amounting to anguish
that I rise to address you. He who last night, nay this morning,
was with us and of us, whose voice is still ringing in our ears,
who charmed us with his marvelous eloquence, elevated us by
his large statesmanship, and instructed us by his wisdom and his
patriotism, is no more—is foully murdered.

If ever a soldier who fell on the field of battle in the front of
the fight, deserved well of his country, Thomas D'Arcy McGee
deserved well of Canada and its people. The blow which has
just fallen is too recent, the shock is too great, for us yet to realize its awful atrocity, or the extent of this most irreparable loss.
I feel, Sir, that our sorrow, our genuine and unaffected sorrow,
prevents us from giving adequate expression to our feelings just
now, but by and by, and at length, this House will have a melan-
choly pleasure in considering the character and position of my
late friend and colleague. To all, the loss is great, to me I may
say inexpressibly so; as the loss is not only of a warm political
friend, who has acted with me for some years, but of one with
whom I enjoyed the intercommunication of his rich and varied
mind; the blow has been overwhelming.

I feel altogether incapable of addressing myself to the subject
just now. Our departed friend was a man of the kindest and
most generous impulse, a man whose hand was open to everyone, whose heart was made for friendship, and whose enmities
were written in water; a man who had no gall, no guile; "in wit

a man, in simplicity a child." He might have lived a long and respected life had he chosen the easy path of popularity rather than the stern one of duty. He has lived a short life, respected and beloved, and died a heroic death; a martyr to the cause of his country. How easy it would have been for him, had he chosen, to have sailed along the full tide of popularity with thousands and hundreds of thousands, without the loss of a single plaudit, but he has been slain, and I fear slain because he preferred the path of duty. I could not help being struck with his language last night, which I will quote from the newspaper report. "He hoped that the mere temporary or local popularity would not in that house, be made the test of qualification for public service; that rested simply on popularity, and he who would risk the right, in hunting for popularity, would soon find that which he hunted for slip away. Base indeed would he be who could not risk popularity in a good cause; that of his country." He has gone from us, and it will be long ere we find such a happy mixture of eloquence, wisdom and impulse. (Hear, hear.) His was no artificial or meretricious eloquence, every word of his was as he believed, and every belief of his was in the direction of what was good and true.

Well may I say now, on behalf of the Government and of the country, that, if he has fallen, he has fallen in our cause, leaving behind him a grateful recollection which will ever live in the hearts and minds of his countrymen. We must remember too that the blow which has fallen so severely on this House and the country will fall more severely on his widowed partner and his bereaved children. He was too good, too generous to be rich. He hast left us, the government, the people, and the representatives of the people, a sacred legacy, and we would be wanting in our duty to this country and to the feeling which will agitate the country from one end to the other, if we do not accept that legacy as a sacred trust, and look upon his widow and children as a widow and children belonging to the State. (Hear, hear.)

FOUNDING A LIBRARY, 1868

HOUSE OF COMMONS, OTTAWA, MAY 11

In the 1st Session of the 1st Parliament, Macdonald rose to speak on the myriad of small details attendant on launching a new nation, including the lending rules for the Library of Parliament. The founding of the Library of Parliament in 1867 brought much needed stability to the national collection. The legislative library of the former United Province of Canada had travelled with the House between Kingston, Montreal, Toronto, and Quebec City. The moves had taken a heavy toll upon the books, which were also decimated by the fires of 1849 in Montreal and 1854 in Quebec.

The library that arrived in Ottawa in 1865 had been restocked and boasted fifty-five thousand volumes. It was the most important repository in Canada of English and French works on science, art, and law, and also contained novels and "books of ordinary reading." One MP complained that "there was so little room" in the "Library accommodation" that "it was impossible to keep the books in good order." This MP thought that the important books should not be allowed to circulate. Novels, however, the members could carry away with them.[8]

The reconstructed Debates of the House of Commons, 1st Parliament, 1st Session, record on May 11, 1868:

SIR JOHN A. MACDONALD: explained that this was a Library for the Dominion, and should not be a circulating Library to be carried home by members, knocked about by their children for a year, and then lost or returned torn and defaced. Let members of Parliament be allowed to get from the Library on an order from the Speaker, and having given a receipt, such books as they really required in following up any study. There could be no objection to that course; but there must be a limit, and every effort must be made to preserve those rare and valuable works of reference without which the Library would be useless. He [Macdonald] would suggest that, as some of the provisions of the report [of the Committee on the Library of Parliament] were too stringent, it should be referred back to the Committee. He also spoke against granting sums to authors to aid in the publication of their works. As a rule, any work of value was pretty sure to be patronized by the public, and nothing was gained by encumbering the Parliamentary shelves with worthless works.

PACIFICATION OF NOVA SCOTIA, 1869

HOUSE OF COMMONS, OTTAWA, APRIL 16

Anti-Confederation feeling had been strong in Nova Scotia. The London Conference of 1866 resolved some issues. Section 93 of the British North America Act guaranteed that the federal government would oversee the provision of separate schools for minority populations in each province.⁹ The then premier of Nova Scotia Charles Tupper had supported Confederation but chosen not to call an election that would put the issue before a voting public who were energized by a vocal anti-Union opposition.

Tupper's key opponent was Joseph Howe, a former premier of Nova Scotia. In the spring of 1868, Howe travelled to London to lobby the British House of Commons as part of a Nova Scotia delegation pressing for a repeal of the British North America Act.¹⁰

After the fait accompli *of Confederation, and Britain's refusal to repeal the Act, Macdonald travelled to Nova Scotia in the summer of 1868 to court Joseph Howe with the promise of new financial terms or "better terms" for Nova Scotia. In 1869, Howe and an ally visited Macdonald in Ottawa. Macdonald again promised "financial relief" for the province by putting it on the same terms as New Brunswick.¹¹ Soon afterward Howe entered the federal cabinet as president of the Privy*

Council.[12] *Nova Scotia's peace with Confederation was announced in the Throne Speech, and Macdonald elaborated upon the events in the formal debate that followed.*

The reconstructed Debates *of the* House of Commons, *1st Parliament, 2nd Session, record on April 16, 1869:*

SIR JOHN A. MACDONALD: said that of late years such explanations were not usually given until an answer had been made to the speech from the Throne. It was right enough to ask for them, but that was not usually the stage to make them; still he would answer the hon. member with regard to the accession of Mr. Howe to office, the question asked was really one *pro forma*, as his hon. friend and the country at large had been informed through the papers very fully of all the circumstances. Mr. Howe could not be considered as being in opposition to the Government last session. His position was different. He was in opposition to all the Governments under Confederation. His position was one of hostility to Confederation and the Confederation Act. On the floor of the House, however, he carefully guarded himself, neither taking the position of a regular supporter nor that of an opponent of Government. His position was one of isolation from the rest of the house. Mr. Howe, as was known, went to England to seek a Repeal of the Confederation Act, and no doubt with his usual zeal and ability left no stone unturned to effect his object. Happily he failed. It became certain that the Confederation Act would not be repealed or modified, and he returned without accomplishing anything. It is also known that the late Colonial Secretary called the attention of the Canadian Government to the representations made by the Anti-Unionists of Nova Scotia, by the Government, by the Legislature, and by deputations; and it was

further set forth in that despatch that, while it was the policy
of the Empire to maintain Confederation, yet the attention of
the Government and the Legislature of Canada should be called
to the strong expediency existing for considering all objections to Union, which could be considered by the Canadian
Government within the bounds of the Constitution.* Canada
was expressly prohibited from interfering so far as regarded any
constitutional changes; but the attention of the Government
was directed to the financial ground of discontent of Nova
Scotia—the objections made by her to the terms of Union.
On that invitation, and in order to ascertain for ourselves the
real basis of discontent in that Province, a deputation of the
Government went to Nova Scotia, had the opportunity of
meeting a great many public men there, of discussing the subject in all its details, and of assuring them that it was the desire
of the House and of the Provinces that there should be justice
and even generosity in dealing with any claims that Nova Scotia
might have. They were assured by the deputation that if any
injustice could be shown—if any hardships pointed out, or it
were made apparent that burdens pressed unduly—Parliament
would gladly remove those hardships and diminish those burdens. As a representative man—one holding a foremost position
in the Province for many years—Mr. Howe was then asked
to come forward and aid the Government in carrying out the
Confederation Act. He declined, saying he thought that would
do no good. He was not prepared, he said, to carry the agitation further. When the Imperial Government rejected all the

* The Colonial Office's official announcement in the summer of 1868 that the request
for the repeal of Confederation on behalf of Nova Scotia had failed was accompanied by
the expressed desire that the province be awarded "pecuniary concession." (Creighton,
Old Chieftain, 17-8; Morton, *Critical Years*, 226-30)

appeals of Nova Scotia, he felt they had to make the best of it.
He was not prepared to invoke foreign assistance against the
decree of the Imperial authorities. Still he thought he could not
then be of use to the Government by becoming a member of it;
but said he would attempt, by moderate counsel, to bring about
such a state of feeling as would admit of the Government of
Canada and people of Nova Scotia conferring together in order
to settle a basis on which Union might be accepted. It was a
matter of notoriety that in pursuance of this understanding that
Mr. Howe and Mr. McLelan came to Ottawa.* The negotiations, which were free, frank and full, had already been made
known through the press, and the papers on the subject would
be laid before the House at the proper time. Having come to
an understanding with these gentlemen as to what was fair to
Nova Scotia, he (Sir John) repeated the invitation which he had
given Mr. Howe months before, to come forward and accept
office. He was reluctant, but felt the appeal to take office, in
order to show that he was satisfied the Government of Canada
had acted fairly, justly and generously by the people of Nova
Scotia. These were the conditions on which he took office, and
he is now before his constituents, asking their sanction to his
act. With regard to the other question, that of the Government
departments, it was not logical to say that, because the head of a
department had not been appointed, the department itself was
not wanted.

---

* Archibald Woodbury McLelan (1824–1890) supported Joseph Howe's opposition to
Confederation. After travelling to Britain with Howe to ask for a repeal of the BNA Act,
he accompanied him as they negotiated "better terms" for Nova Scotia. He became a
senator and a commissioner for the Intercolonial Railway. (Waite, "McLelan, Archibald
Woodbury," *DCB*)

PART FOUR

STEADFAST
VISIONARY

RESISTANCE AT RED RIVER, 1870

Macdonald's discussion in the House of Commons about the conflict at Red River began when John Hillyard Cameron (1817–1876), the Conservative member for Peel, asked if the government had any news.

The promise of the west beckoned. Following Confederation, the Canadian government had negotiated the purchase of Rupert's Land from the Hudson's Bay Company for £300,000. The date of transfer was set for December 1, 1869. Enthusiastic settlers had been slowly establishing agricultural and commercial communities near the historic community at Red River. Some had formed an ultra-Protestant pro-Canada political movement that they dubbed the Canadian Party, which promoted annexation of the Red River Colony by the Canadian government. When the government surveyors upset the Métis by not acknowledging their land rights, Macdonald delayed the transfer of Rupert's Land until the problems had been settled. But he did not have time to stop lieutenant-governor designate William McDougall (1822–1905) from proclaiming the transfer on December 1, 1869, anyway.

Métis leader Louis Riel declared a provisional government in order to block further incursions, and some settlers backed him as the best person to negotiate the region's entry into Canada. Meanwhile, Riel's support-ers stopped members of the Canadian Party that included Thomas Scott (c. 1842–1870), an Irish adventurer and Orangeman. Scott behaved so aggressively in captivity that he fatally alienated his captors. Riel, deep in negotiations with Canada, needed the continued support of the Métis and bowed to pressure among his supporters to punish Scott, whereupon a court martial was struck. Scott was executed on March 4, 1870, and his death was condemned as a "murder" in some quarters.

Macdonald rose to answer questions about the state of affairs in Red River on April 6.[1]

The reconstructed Debates *of the House of Commons, 1st Parliament, 3rd Session, record on April 6, 1870:*

HON SIR JOHN A. MACDONALD: My hon. friend [Hon. John Hillyard Cameron] commenced his remarks by asking the Government and myself, whether we had any later news to give relating to this deplorable event, the murder of this man [Thomas Scott], than we had when I addressed the House last on the subject. I have simply to state that we have no further intelligence, but the intelligence is complete as to the fact of the man having been shot by a party of men calling themselves a Court Martial.

That the man was murdered there can be no doubt. I stated that I would have full information from the [Special] Commissioner [Donald Alexander Smith],* who was sent on behalf of the Government on a mission of conciliation, and for

---

* Donald Alexander Smith, later Baron Strathcona and Mount Royal, had spent his early career in the Hudson's Bay Company, beginning as a factor in the Esquimaux Bay district. In December 1869 Macdonald appointed him special commissioner to investigate the growing conflicts at Red River. (Reford, "Donald Alexander Smith (1820–1914)," *DCB*; Sprague, *Canada and the Métis*, 46

the purpose of assisting Governor Mactavish* to restore order. That gentleman is now in this city, and is preparing a report, and so much of it as can be properly laid before this House will be laid on the table. I suppose that will be done in a very short period. So much for the information.

The hon. gentleman asks me to give further information as to the course the Government is about to pursue. I can only say to my hon. friend and to the House, and both he and the House will fully appreciate the reticence which I feel it my duty to observe in the matter, I can only say that the Government are fully aware of, and appreciate the gravity of the position, and have been so through the whole of this winter, and since the events which occurred about the end of October, they understand and fully appreciate the responsibility that rests upon them. They have been in constant communication with Her Majesty's Government on the subject, and I may say that the two Governments are acting in accord and unison—(hear, hear)—and with the one object in view, that of retaining that country as a portion of Her Majesty's Dominions, and of restoring law and order therein. We are acting in complete unison with Her Majesty's Government, and the line of conduct has been settled upon. What that line of conduct may be, must be for the present withheld from the House. It would simply be giving information at an improper time, and it would soon arrive at improper quarters. But I am glad to say that Her Majesty's Government are acting in accord with us, and have adopted our suggestions and have approved of the course we have devised, and that

---

* William MacTavish (1815–1870), governor of Rupert's Land and governor of Assiniboia at the time of the crisis, believed that the Métis (many of whom were Hudson's Bay Company employees and were the descendants of the colonists sponsored by Selkirk) should be consulted in the transfer of Rupert's Land. (Goossen, "Mactavish, William," *DCB*)

course I am sure will be carried out to a successful completion at no distant day. Further I cannot say. It would be improper for me to say any more, and I am quite sure the House will not ask nor expect me to say more.*

With respect to the delegation† the hon. gentleman has spoken of, I can only say that if they arrive here they will be received and heard, and there will be attentive consideration given to whatever they may say in the matter. One hon. gentleman has spoken—and I see the press has spoken in the same sense—as if this delegation were coming from the persons who are the instigators and accessories of the murder of this man, and therefore should not be received. I do not understand that there are any such persons coming here. (Hear, hear.)

There was a meeting held, as the House and country knows, months ago, composed of representatives elected of the resident inhabitants, both English and French.‡ That meeting was held

---

* Macdonald appears to be referring to the military expedition to Red River then under consideration, which he continued to resist talking about explicitly on April 26, when Antoine-Aimé Dorion inquired "whether any expenditure of public money was going on without the sanction of Parliament." He asked, because "[t]hey knew that East and West preparations had been onfoot for sending an armed expedition into the Territory." Macdonald replied, "I will only make one remark upon that most unfortunate speech of the hon. gentleman opposite [Dorion], and it is this, that the Government are making arrangements of a certain kind, which, however, cannot be carried out, and will not be carried out, without an express vote of Parliament." (House of Commons, *Debates,* 1st Parl., 3rd Sess., vol. 3, 1191)

† A delegation was due to arrive shortly in Ottawa from the North-West to negotiate Manitoba's entry into Confederation. It included Alfred H. Scott (c. 1840–1872), Judge John Black (1817–1879), and Noel-Joseph Ritchot (1825–1905). Ritchot and Scott were promptly arrested by Thomas Scott's brother. Macdonald had promised the Colonial Office that the delegates would be well received, and, embarrassed, personally paid their legal costs. (Sprague, *Canada and the Métis,* 55-6; Morton, "Scott, Alfred Henry," *DCB*)

‡ Macdonald is referring to the convention first held on January 26, 1870, of 40 members of the community elected to discuss their concerns. They created a subcommittee of English- and French-speaking "halfbreeds" and Métis to outline the residents' terms for

for the purpose of conferring—you may call it a conference in fact—as to the state of the country, and what their claims should be before assenting to come into the Union.

That body I believe was elected by the people, and was composed of a respectable body of men as a whole. The delegates I understand were selected by this meeting, and you will at once see there can be no assassin among them when I tell you that Judge Black* is at their head, a gentleman who has presided at the court there of the largest criminal and civil jurisdiction, and who enjoys the confidence and respect of all parties—even of the persons who are now insurgents. He is at the head of the deputation, and any imputation or insinuation that he could in any way countenance any such outrage as that spoken of, is, of course, out of the question.

I may say further, in order to show the character of the delegation, and how it is esteemed by the people there, that when Judge Black thought at first that he could not come here in consequence of private and personal matters, it was settled that the Anglican Bishop of Rupert's Land, Bishop Macrae [Robert Machray (1831–1904)] should go in his place. Of course from his position it would be understood that he is a gentleman of the highest character, and I believe he is regarded as an honour to his Church and his profession. However, Judge Black found it possible to come, and, I believe, he will be here with the rest.

They will be heard; and so much importance, I may say, is

---

entry into Confederation. The convention also chose the delegates to take it to Ottawa. The whole process arose from Donald Smith's reassurances to the people in mid-January, 1870. (Sprague, *Canada and Métis*, 47)

* John Black (1817–1879) was the recorder of Rupert's Land and in the fall of 1869 was the acting governor presiding at the Council of Assiniboia when Riel resisted William McDougall's entry into Red River. (Dorge, "Black, John," *DCB*)

attached to the fact that this body is coming here—this body of *quasi* ambassadors—that Sir Stafford Northcote [1818–1887], who is Governor of the Hudson Bay Company, is coming out here for the very purpose of meeting them. They will be heard, and their representations will receive every consideration, and possibly the result of the conference may be the subject of discussion in this House before the end of the present session. I do not know that it is necessary, or that it would be proper or expedient for me to say anything more in answer to my hon. friend. If there is anything I have omitted I will be very glad to supplement my present statement.

MANITOBA ENTERS CONFEDERATION, 1870

The resistance at Red River in abeyance partly due to the military expedition led by Garnet Joseph Wolseley (1833–1913), Manitoba entered Confederation in 1870. Macdonald negotiated personally with the delegates from Red River. Setting aside the question of a general amnesty for the resistance, they agreed on many issues, including a bilingual legislature and the provision of separate schooling for Catholics. Macdonald also agreed in principle to recognize that the Métis had dual rights to the land as homesteaders and as the descendants of the original Aboriginal occupants of the land. But, the Crown, not the new province, would hold all public land in order to further settlement and the construction of a transcontinental railway.

On May 2, 1870, he rose to present the bill that made Manitoba part of Confederation and outlined its constitutional machinery.[2]

The reconstructed Debates of the House of Commons, 1st Parliament, 3rd Session, record on May 2, 1870:

HON SIR JOHN A. MACDONALD: I rise, sir, with the consent of the House, to submit the result of our deliberations for the framing of a constitution for the country heretofore

known as Rupert's Land and the North-West Territory.* In
moving for leave to introduce this Bill, of which I have given
notice, I may premise by stating that there has been a discussion going on as to whether we should have a Territory or a
Province. The answer we made on behalf of the Canadian
Government was that such a thing as a Territory was not known
to the British colonial system, that the expression was not recognized, that the expression was Colony or Province, and that
we thought it would be better to adhere to the old and well
known form of expression—well known to us as Colonists of
the Empire—and not bring a new description into our statute
book. It was not, of course, a matter of any serious importance
whether the country was called a Province or a Territory. We
have Provinces of all sizes, shapes and constitutions; there are
very few Colonies with precisely the same constitution in all
particulars, so that there could not be anything determined by
the use of the word.

Then the next question discussed was the name of the
Province. It was thought that was a matter of taste and should be
considered with reference to euphony and with reference also as
much as possible to the remembrance of the original inhabitants
of that vast country.† Fortunately the Indian languages of that
section of the country give us a choice of euphonious names

* After creation of Manitoba, the remainder of Rupert's Land and North-West
Territory—from the then borders of Ontario and Quebec to the Arctic Ocean, to the
Rocky Mountains—was incorporated into Canada on July 15, 1870, as the North-West
Territories. After 1870, it would be governed by the North-West Government Act. (Hall,
"North-West Territories," *OCCH*)

† The Plains Cree, an Algonquin-speaking group, was the most populous Aboriginal
people living in the region, alongside smaller groups of Assiniboine, a Sioux-speaking
group; the Salteaux, a branch of the Anishinaabe; and the Dakota, a branch of the Sioux.
The Cree were more recent arrivals to the area, adopting by 1790 the Plains' culture of
the buffalo hunt and its longer agricultural tradition. (Carter, *Lost Harvests*, 25, 31–3, 38)

and it is considered proper that the Province which is to be organized, shall be called Manitoba. The name Assiniboia,* by which it has hitherto been called, is considered to be rather too long, involving confusion, too, between the river Assiniboine and the Province Assiniboia. I suppose, therefore, there will be no objection to the name that has been fixed upon, which is euphonious enough in itself, and is an old Indian name, meaning "The God who speaks—the speaking God." There is a fine lake there called Lake Manitoba, which forms the western boundary of the Province.

A subject of very great importance, which engaged much of our consideration, was the settlement of the boundaries of the Province we are organizing. It is obvious that that vast country could not be formed into one Province. It is obvious that the Dominion Government and the Dominion Parliament must retain, for Dominion purposes, the vast section of that country, which is altogether or nearly without inhabitants, and that the Province must be confined to the more settled country that now exists. We found happily that there was no great difficulty in regard to this matter, that there was no discussion upon the subject, and I may read a description of the boundaries that have been settled upon. "The region which is to form the new Province of Manitoba commences at a point on the frontier of the United States Territory, 96 degrees West of Greenwich, and extends to a point 98 degrees and 15 minutes West, being bounded on the South by 49th parallel of latitude, and on the North by latitude 50 degrees and 30 minutes."

He here placed a map on the table showing the boundaries

---

* Assiniboia was the administrative district of Red River. Later, one of the four provisional districts of the North-West territories established in 1882 was also called Assiniboia. (Brennan, "Assiniboia," OCCH)

of the new Province and the members gathered round to examine it.

HON. COL. [JOHN HAMILTON] GRAY: How many square miles are there in the new Province?

HON SIR JOHN A. MACDONALD: Eleven thousand square miles. It is a small Province as the House will observe, but yet it contains the principal part of the settlements which are ranged, as those who have studied the matter know, along the banks of Red River and the banks of Assiniboine from the point of their confluence at or near Fort Garry up westward towards Lake Manitoba.

One of the clauses of the Bill which I propose to lay before the House, but which is not yet in such a position as to go into the printer's hands preparatory to the second reading, provides that such portions of the North-West Territory, as are not included in this Province, shall be governed as an unorganized tract by the Lieutenant Governor of Manitoba, under a separate Commission under the Great Seal of the Dominion, and that until they are settled and organized they shall be governed by Orders in Council.

MR. [ALEXANDER] MACKENZIE: Does the Bill provide a Constitution for that territory?

HON SIR JOHN A. MACDONALD: No. It simply provides that the Lieutenant Governor of Manitoba shall be Governor of the remaining portion of the Territory under directions of Orders in Council, and action upon separate commission issued under the Great Seal.

In settling the Constitution of the Province the question
of how far representative institutions should be properly conferred at this time has been fully discussed. The House knows
that this subject was discussed last summer by the press in all
parts of Canada, and that there was a good deal of objection
that the Bill of last Session, provisional as it was, and intended
to last only a few months, did not provide representative institutions for the people of that Territory.* That Bill provided that
the Lieutenant Governor should have an Executive Council,
and that that Council should have power to make laws, subject, of course, to the veto power, the paramount power of the
Governor General here. It was passed simply for the purpose of
having something like an organization ready, something like
the rudiments of a Government, from the time the Territory
was admitted into the Dominion, it being understood that the
Act should continue in force only until the end of the present
session of Parliament. On the introduction of that Bill by the
Government, it was received in that particular, and I think
in every particular, with the almost unanimous sanction and
approval of Parliament. The Government felt they were not
in a position from acquaintance with the circumstances of the
country and wants of its people, to settle anything like a fixed
constitution upon the Territory. They thought it, therefore,
better that they should merely pass a temporary Act to last for
a few months providing for the appointment of a Lieutenant
Governor, for which office my hon. friend from North Lanark

---

* Macdonald had desired a waiting period of perhaps a year before Manitoba could be a
province, allowing for the institution of representative government to mature. However,
he conceded to the demands of Noel-Joseph Ritchot (1825–1905) and the negotiators that
the District of Assiniboia would attain provincial status right away. (Sprague, *Canada
and the Métis*, 57)

[William McDougall (1822–1905)] was selected, who, when he arrived upon the spot, would have an opportunity of reporting upon the requirements of the country, and after discussing the matter with the principal men of the settlement, to suggest what kind of institutions were best suited to those requirements.

Unfortunately no opportunity was offered for entering into that discussion or getting that information. One result, however, of the enquiry that was instituted in this country, was to pour a flood of light upon the Territory, and I have no doubt every hon. member of this House has taken advantage of it so as to enable him, with a greater degree of certainty, to approach the subject of what the Constitution ought to be. Besides that we have discussed the proposed Constitution with such persons who have been in the North-West as we have had an opportunity of meeting, and the result has been as I will shortly describe.

In the first place, as regards the representation of the Province of Manitoba in the Dominion Parliament, the proposition of the Government is that the people of the Province shall be represented in the Senate by two members until the Province shall have a population at a decennial census of 50,000. From thenceforth the people there shall have representation in the Senate of three members; and subsequently, when the population shall amount to 75,000, they shall have representation of four members. That will give them the same representation in the upper House of the Dominion Legislature as has been proposed for Prince Edward's Island, and agreed to by the representatives of that Province at the Quebec conference—Prince Edward's Island being the smallest of the Provinces, having a population of about 85,000. The Bill does not provide for any increase of numbers beyond four. It is not likely that, in our day at any rate, the Province will have a population which will entitle it to more. With respect to its representation in the House of Commons, it is proposed that it shall have four members in this House—the Governor General having, for that purpose, power to separate and divide the whole of the Province into four electoral districts, each containing as nearly as possible an equal number of the present community of settlers.

The executive power of the Province will, of course, as in all the other Provinces of the Dominion, be vested in a Lieutenant Governor, who shall be appointed like the other Lieutenant Governors, by Commission from the Governor General, under the Great Seal of the Dominion. He shall have an Executive Council, which shall be composed of seven persons, holding such offices as the Lieutenant Governor shall, from time to time, think fit, and, in the first instance, shall not exceed five in number. The meetings of the Legislature until otherwise ordered by the Legislature itself, shall be held at Fort Garry, or within a mile of it. With respect to the Legislative body, there was considerable difficulty and long discussion whether it should consist of one chamber or two; whether, if one chamber, it should be composed of the representatives of the people and of persons appointed by the Crown, or Local Government, or whether they should be severed and the two chambers constituted—all these questions were fully discussed. After mature consideration, it was agreed that there should be two chambers. I see my hon. friend (Hon. Mr. MacDougall) laughs, but, being a true liberal, he will not object to the people having a voice in the settlement of their own Constitution and to determine whether they shall have one or two chambers or even three if it suits their purpose to have them. It is proposed then to have two chambers, but the Legislative Council is not a very formidable one. It is to be composed in the first place of seven members. After the expiration of four years it may be increased to twelve, but not more than that number. The object of making that provision is this, that we could not well have a smaller Legislative body than seven; and yet it might be well that the Government of the day—the Lieutenant Governor having a responsible Ministry— have the power of meeting the difficulty arising from a possible deadlock between the two chambers—the Legislative Assembly and the Legislative Council. It is therefore proposed that after the end of the first four years—after the first Parliament of the Province, the Lieutenant Governor may if he thinks proper upon the advice of his Executive Council, who have the confidence of the people and of their representatives, increase the number up to twelve. The Legislative Assembly shall be composed of a body of twenty-four members—the Lieutenant Governor dividing the Province for that purpose into twenty-four Electoral Districts having due regard to the various communities into which the settlement is at present divided. All these clauses and stipulations are, of course, subject to alterations by the people themselves, except so far as they relate to the appointment of the Lieutenant Governor, which, of course, rests upon the same authority as in the other Provinces of the Dominion. In all other respects they may alter their Constitutions as they please. It is provided in the Bill that all the clauses of the British North America Act, except- ing as altered by the Bill itself, or excepting those clauses which apply only to one or two Provinces, and not to the whole of the Provinces, shall apply to the new Province. The Bill contains various other clauses with which I will not now trouble the House because they refer to matters of no great interest, except as they are requisite to carry on the machinery of the Executive and Legislative bodies. Until the Legislature otherwise provides, the qualification of voters for members both of the House of

Commons and Local Legislatures shall be the same as provided by the Confederation Act for the District of Algoma. I think the House will agree with me that no other qualification can be provided. The clause runs that every British subject who has attained the age of 21 years, and who is and has been a householder for one year, shall have a right to vote. The duration of the Legislative Assembly shall be four years, as in the other Provinces.

Macdonald's speech continued and outlined the terms agreed upon with the delegates, including the grant of "1,200,000 acres," for "the purpose of extinguishing the Indian title" of the Métis. The ensuing debate focused on this grant. Macdonald retreated from his position of May 2, but the Act still provided for a land grant (1,400,000 acres) and saw no role for the new provincial government in crown land management.[3]

WAITING FOR NEWS OF PEI, 1873

Liberal Alexander Mackenzie began the day's debate about Prince Edward Island by saying "he was astonished to find in the newspapers of that Province, as well as in other eastern newspapers, a statement showing that negotiations had taken place between the two Governments" relating to PEI's entry into Confederation. Having to pay the huge cost of building a railway had made the prospect of joining Confederation more palatable to Islanders, who had rejected it in 1867, and a delegation had been sent to Ottawa to discuss terms. Their conditions for entering Confederation included a final solution to the long-standing problem of reverting to the state the lands of absentee landowners who failed to contribute to the improvement of the Island.4 Macdonald rose to reply.

The reconstructed Debates of the House of Commons, 2nd Parliament, 1st Session, record on March 20, 1873:

HON. SIR JOHN A. MACDONALD said [Mackenzie's] inquiry was a very natural one. The Government of the Island of Prince Edward has sent two of their members to Ottawa, and they have had negotiations with the Government here on the Union of Prince Edward's Island with the Dominion.

Certain conditional arrangements were entered into and these gentlemen went home for the purpose of submitting them to their colleagues, and they in turn had made up their minds to submit them to the people before they would be laid before the Legislature. These terms would therefore be laid before that body after the elections, and it was obviously a matter of importance to that Government that they should choose their own time and their own mode of submitting the propositions of the Dominion Government to their people; therefore he [Macdonald] did not deem it advisable to place these provisional returns before the Parliament here until the Government had ascertained that they had been presented to the public of Prince Edward's Island.

Of course the Government of Prince Edward's Island had the great task of submitting the question to the people and going to the country upon it, and he [Macdonald] thought it might be thwarting greatly the object they all had in view if there were a premature publication. It was a matter of little consequence whether one or the other party published these terms first. He expected information from the Government of Prince Edward's Island in a short time, and after his Government had received that, they would be in a position, without injury to the great cause of union, to submit the papers to this House.

MR. [DAVID] MILLS: said it would be contrary to law for the Government to initiate such a measure. That motion belongs to Parliament and not to the Government.

MR. [TIMOTHY WARREN] ANGLIN: said the people of Prince Edward's Island might receive a very improper impression from the report of the speech of the leader of the Government.

The newspapers of Prince Edward's Island published the proposed terms, and the Government had gone to the country upon these terms. If the people of Prince Edward's Island heard that the Minister of Justice thought it might possibly damage the cause of Confederation in that Province by announcing to the House whether their public statements were correct or incorrect, they might suppose there was some doubt as to their correctness.

HON. SIR JOHN A. MACDONALD: said he had not even seen the statements in the newspapers. All he knew was that provisional arrangement had been entered into by the gentlemen from Prince Edward's Island, who had left here for the purpose of submitting it to their colleagues and afterwards, if they thought proper, to the people. Of course it would be open to Parliament afterwards to decide whether or not these terms should be accepted.

HON. MR. [ALEXANDER] MACKENZIE: said the hon. gentleman could see statements in the newspapers, and he could compare them with the actual facts, and if they were correct, or nearly correct, it would be quite evident they had been communicated and published in Prince Edward's Island by Government.

The moment it was made manifest that there was any official communication, the papers should be laid before the House, accompanied with any documents necessary to enable the House to understand the position taken by the Government. Of course it was quite true, as the member for Bothwell (Mr. Mills) has said, the Government had no right to make any arrangements, but he did not object to the Government endeavouring to enter upon such negotiations as might result in the Union of the remaining provinces still outside the Dominion; and anything that might promote that object would receive the assistance on his side of the House; but he did think it was not treating Parliament with respect due to it, to have such documents as that reach them from such address during the session, and then, when the attention of the Government had been called to it to tell them that as soon as official communications were made with Prince Edward's Island, the Government would place the information before the House. He did not think it was the way to carry on business in relation to such matters.

The terms, of course, would have to receive the consent of the House, and in order that that might be done, the papers should be laid before them on the earliest possible occasion, so that they might judge as to the propriety or impropriety of the course of action proposed.

HON. SIR JOHN A. MACDONALD said he differed from the hon. gentleman. In his view they ought to act upon the newspaper. The statements appeared in the newspapers where members can see them.

MR. MILLS: These statements may be incorrect.

HON. SIR JOHN A. MACDONALD differed from the hon. gentleman's idea that they should act upon newspaper items. The statement might not be correct, and, if incorrect, it would be very improper of the Government to lay the papers before the House until they had received official communication from Prince Edward Island. No unauthenticated documents should be acted upon. The Government of the Island desired that they should have an opportunity of submitting their provisional case in their own way to their own people, before it was brought up in the Dominion Parliament. The House would have every opportunity of considering the resolutions, should there be a necessity to concur in or reject them.

TREATY 1 AND THE
NORTH WEST MOUNTED POLICE, 1873

By 1873, peace had been restored to the west. The Government of Canada had begun negotiating with 1,000 Aboriginal people at Lower Fort Garry in the late summer of 1871. The negotiations took nine days. The resulting treaty, Treaty 1, set out the terms for the agreeing parties to "cede, release, surrender, and yield up to Her Majesty the Queen" huge portions of southern Manitoba in return for reserved areas equivalent to 160 acres (65 hectares) for "a family of five, and an initial payment of $3 per person and an annuity to be paid in goods." However, the agreement had been supplemented by a verbal agreement to provide farming assistance that had not been communicated to the federal government.

In 1873, the original signatories to Treaty 1 and to Treaty 2 (signed August 21, 1871) were drawing attention to the non-fulfilment of agreements and the paltry compensation offered for the land. Several members of the legislature called for an inquiry into the matter so that the unsatisfactory agreement would not become the basis for future treaties.

Macdonald's response here focused upon the creation of the North West Mounted Police, who went on to play an integral role in the treaty-making process that lasted until 1877, and who were active in the North-West Rebellion of 1884–1885 and in the Yukon during the Gold Rush.

Treaties 1 and 2 did provide a model for successive treaties after the Macdonald government adjusted their terms. Having secured the chiefs' formal acceptance, the government in 1875 increased the annuity from $3 to $5, and increased payments to chiefs and band councillors. The new terms also provided the agricultural implements originally promised verbally but not included in the written text of the treaty.[5]

The reconstructed Debates *of the House of Commons; 2nd Parliament, 1st Session, record on March 31, 1873:*

HON SIR JOHN A. MACDONALD: there could be no objection to the proposed Commission. The discussion, however, had taken a wider range, and had been directed more or less towards the policy which it would be better to observe in connection with the Indians of the Northwest.

He [Macdonald] had no objection to the production of papers in connection with the existing Treaty, but if it were to be supposed that no treaty would be made with the Indians except such as they would be satisfied with for all time to come, there would be no end to that sort of thing.

HON MR. [ALEXANDER] MACKENZIE: Hear, hear.

HON SIR JOHN A. MACDONALD said the Indians were always anxious to get all they could, either by brute force or bullying; the object of the Government was to meet all their reasonable requests, to promise them all that they deserved, and to carry out these promises faithfully and to the letter.*

The Treaty now in existence and which was made in 1871, was as much a treaty on the part of the Indians as on our part. They were free to enter into and free to reject it. There was neither fraud nor guile used towards them to induce them to enter it. The House knew themselves, and they had the testimony of more than one gentleman tonight, that these Indians were fully competent to understand what they were asking for; that they were men of good intellectual ability, as well as of superior physique, and that they had among them half-breeds† who, while they threw into their deliberations the advantage of a civilized training, also shared fully the common feelings of the Indians themselves.

It might therefore be fairly believed that in entering into the Treaty with Mr. Archibald,‡ they were quite well aware of what they were doing, and the Treaty itself was fair, just, and honest. It would be a hopeless thing, and unfortunate, if we were called upon to open up this treaty and renew it because the Indians

---

* Macdonald may have been echoing Indian Commissioner Wemyss Simpson's (1824–1894) report that the nine days of negotiation for Treaty saw the Indians making "demands of such an exorbitant nature, that much time was spent in reducing their terms to a basis upon which an arrangement could be made." (Miller, *Compact, Contract, Covenant*, 163)

† The "halfbreed" in the mid-nineteenth century referred to the English-speaking Métis, who were the descendants of Aboriginal women and Scottish or English fur traders. Here Macdonald is referring to the government's reliance on intermediaries such as James McKay (1828–1879) and Peter Erasmus (1833–1931), men of mixed parentage who held the confidence of Canadian, Métis, and Aboriginal peoples to help negotiate the first treaties. By 1874, Erasmus played an important role after being invited by Plains Cree chiefs Ahtahkakoop (c. 1816–1896) and Mistawasis (c. 1813–1896). (Miller, *Compact, Contract, Covenant*, 136, 161-2)

‡ Adams G. Archibald (1814–1892) helped pacify Manitoba following the 1869-1870 resistance and as lieutenant-governor of Manitoba and the North-Western Territory witnessed the negotiations of Treaty 1. (Miller, *Compact, Contract, Covenant*, 163)

are now not satisfied with it. A bargain was a bargain; and no one knew or—and to their credit he would say it—observed it more faithfully than the Indians. They expected contracts made with them to be fairly and faithfully observed, and they in their turn faithfully and fairly carried out their share—or, at least, the Government and people of this country had always found it thus.*

So far as the Treaty of 1871 was concerned, by which a large tract of country in the immediate vicinity of Manitoba was purchased and obtained, and that it be submitted by the most fair and honest means, he would just say that it was the intention to maintain that treaty and hold that property. (Hear, hear.)

As to the other treaties,† that was a matter of very great importance. He, for one, thought it was out of the question that the Government of Canada should be called upon to take the responsibility of charging upon the revenue of the country sums of money to be paid to all the tribes from the western boundary of Ontario to the Rocky Mountains. They had all the rights already that they could be permitted to have. The Dominion of Canada must have the right of way for railways and all the lands wanted for the purpose of settlement.

He [Macdonald] eulogized the management of Indian affairs by the Hudson Bay Company, and thought that one of

---

* Aboriginal groups made clear statements in the 1870s that they expected the government to treat fairly for their homeland. When surveyors arrived unannounced, they summarily turned them away. (Miller, *Compact, Contract, Covenant*, 153-4; Tobias, "Canada's subjugation of the Plains Cree, 1879–1885," 519-20)

† Macdonald is apparently referring to a current treaty process. The government made increased use of the Métis to help negotiations and began yielding on points such as allowing bands to participate in choosing the location of a reserve and in increasing the size of the reserve. Treaty 3 was signed on October 3, 1873. The process of extinguishing Aboriginal title through treaties continued until 1877 and included seven treaties. (Miller, *Compact, Contract, Covenant*, 167-8, 184)

the greatest features connected with the policy of that great Company was its treatment of the Indians. He pointed out the peace and prosperity the people there had enjoyed under that regime, compared with those south of the line, and he thought they must be entrusted with the management of affairs as at present for some time to come.

The Government could not possibly be able to protect all the traders in that country, either those moving about or those remaining stationary. It was the duty of the Government to see the frontier protected, to see that the interior was organized and law introduced and enforced, but the idea of defending the traders and trading posts of that country was a task too great for them to undertake, and was not assumed by the Government of the United States.

The country had been ours only some two years and ever since there had been a force of 300 men there, a force by the way of as fine men as there were to be found in all the world.* (Hear, hear.) The very fact of their presence there in case of anything like war or imminent danger of war was a great security against any outbreak at all.

The Government, however, would go further and would favour a grant of money to organize a mounted police—not a large force, but something after the kind of the Irish country constabulary.† This force would have military discipline, would

---

* The Manitoba Force was formed from the 300 troops remaining in the West following the resistance at Red River in 1870. The next year, the force defended the province against a Fenian threat, and their numbers were augmented. "The Manitoba Force remained responsible for law and order in the province until the North West Mounted Police took over in 1877." (Oliver and Granatstein, "Manitoba Force," *OCCMH*)

† The Irish Constabulary (officially the Royal Irish Constabulary since 1867) was an armed, centralized police force created in 1836 and unusual among police forces in Britain for its paramilitary qualities—the men were armed, wore uniforms, and trained

be mounted on the hardy horses of the country, and could be distributed where required. By being a police force they would also be peace officers. A military force would be deficient in the respect that they could not interfere except when the civil officers had failed to keep the populace in proper order, while the proposed force could have the advantage of a military training and the possession of civil power.

He [Macdonald] hoped this would be the only force which would be required to be placed there by the Dominion, because the country, when settled by the ordinary process, would proceed with the organization of the necessary protective forces for itself, the burden of which would fall upon the country for whose use it was raised, as was the case in the rest of Canada. This mounted police would protect the frontier, prevent smuggling, and do other services in connection with the inland revenue; and in case of any outbreak would, in conjunction with the militia, be sufficient for the military purposes of the Dominion.

The difficulty of settling with the Indians, he [Macdonald] was afraid, was greatly increased by the injurious advice given by the traders who came across the line. They went to and fro, they had no settlement in the country, and they were therefore under no restraint. They traded with the Indians, and for their furs and other wares gave them arms, ammunition, and strong drink. They flattered the Indian and excited him, advising him to ask unreasonable terms from us. These we had to meet with firmness, and to let the Indians understand that they would get fair compensation for what was asked from them and no more.

---

according to a military regime. Small units were stationed throughout Ireland outside of Dublin, "to impose public order." ("Royal Irish Constabulary," *OCIH*)

The Ministry was fully aware of the difficulties they would encounter and all the responsibility they would incur, when they took the country. The only true way to do this was to be just to themselves and just to the Indians. There was no objection to the appointment of the Commission. (Cheers.)

THE PACIFIC SCANDAL, 1873

HOUSE OF COMMONS,
OTTAWA, NOVEMBER 3

On July 4, 1873, Macdonald woke to the realization of his growing misapprehensions. Blazoned across the pages of the Montreal Herald was the private correspondence of the shipping magnate and railway promoter, Sir Hugh Allan*—a correspondence "edited," to suggest that Allan was going forward and building the Canadian railway with American money. The documents did not reflect Macdonald's refusal to countenance Allan's American partnership. Macdonald acted immediately by publishing on July 5 an "affidavit" that included Allan's sworn statement that he had broken off with the Americans. Macdonald began to push for a royal commission to investigate the charges against him and retreated to Rivière-du-Loup for a much needed holiday.

By mid-July, the papers in Toronto and Montreal and Quebec flamed with new material, including a telegram addressed to Allan through his solicitor and marked "immediate, private," followed by the words, "I must

---

* Sir Hugh Allan (1810–1882) was a Scottish-born shipping magnate of the 1850s with close ties to the Conservatives. By the 1870s, Allan was one of Canada's most successful capitalists and he bid for the contract to build the Pacific Railway (Young with Tulchinsky, "Allan, Sir Hugh," *DCB*)

have another ten thousand"; it had been issued by Macdonald and Cartier in August 1872. Writing to Lord Dufferin, Macdonald acknowledged that it was "one of those overwhelming misfortunes that they say every man must meet once in his life. At first it fairly staggered me. . . ." The stolen telegram requested campaign funds from Allan, the very man with whom he was negotiating a contract in the national interest. Macdonald disintegrated into drink. The press speculated widely about his rumoured suicide. Lord Dufferin observed sadly, "Sir John A. has been in a terrible state for sometime past."

Lord Dufferin agreed to follow through with a previously agreed-upon prorogation of Parliament—but only for ten weeks. The commission commenced investigations into the affair on September 4. Lord Dufferin reviewed the material and on October 19 he pointed out to Macdonald, "In acting as you have, I am well convinced that you have only followed a traditional practice and that probably your political opponents have resorted with equal freedom to the same expedients, but as Minister of Justice and the official guardian and protector of the laws, your responsibilities are exceptional and your personal connection with what has passed cannot but fatally affect your position as minister." Despite this judgment, Lord Dufferin, backed by the Colonial Office in England, declined to withdraw confidence from the prime minister.[6]

Parliament opened on October 23, and debate about the Pacific Scandal raged on, breaking Macdonald's majority and apparently his will. Lord Dufferin reported that in a skirmish with Edward Blake, Macdonald said all "the wrong things" and "showed to everyone" that "he was quite tipsy." But then a transformation came over Macdonald. He rose to applause at nine o'clock at night and spoke for five hours. Although his supporters praised the speech, the government resigned on November 6; however, Macdonald did not resign as party leader. He regained a seat, but the Conservatives lost the 1874 election and Macdonald would be in opposition until 1878.

Towards the end of the five hours Macdonald began his summation.[7]
The reconstructed Debates *of the House of Commons, 2nd
Parliament, 2nd Session, record on November 3, 1873:*

[HON. SIR JOHN A. MACDONALD:] Well, Sir, I will state
now what occurred with respect to the Pacific Railway. I was at
Washington bartering my country as some of the hon. gentlemen say, (laughter) attending at all events to the Washington
treaty,* when the resolutions were carried which happily I say
for Canada, brought British Columbia into the union of the
British North American Provinces. (Cheers.) The proposition
included the Pacific Railway, for British Columbia would not
have come in, unless the terms of the union had included
a railway.† Notwithstanding great opposition the resolutions
were carried by my late honoured and lamented colleague,‡
but he only carried them by promising to introduce resolutions
by which the railway would be built, not by the Government
directly, but by private capital, aided by Government grants.

I would not, if I had been here, have willingly assented to
that proposition, but though I was not here yet I am responsible for that act, and I do accept it as perhaps the best proposition to be had; otherwise, perhaps, the Union would not have

---

* Macdonald had been one of the commissioners negotiating the Washington Treaty of
1871, in which his scope of action had been restricted by the relations between the United
States and Britain. (Messamore, "Diplomacy or Duplicity?" 48)

† George-Étienne Cartier, acting in Macdonald's stead as prime minister, negotiated
British Columbia's entry into Confederation in 1871 on the promise that the federal gov-
ernment assume the colony's debt and build a railway to the west coast within ten years.
(Macdonald, "British Columbia," *OCCH*; Young, *Montreal Bourgeois*, 122)

‡ Cartier had died on May 20, 1873, while seeking treatment in London, England, for his
kidney condition. Macdonald wept openly in the House of Commons when he announced
the death of his friend. (Bonenfant, "Cartier, George-Étienne,"*DCB*)

been consummated. The resolutions declared that the Railway should be built by a Railway Company assisted by Government grants of land and money.

The hon. member for Napierville (Hon. Mr. Dorion), however, moved a resolution setting forth that the House did not believe that private capital could be obtained sufficient for the purpose. The whole of the resolutions moved by hon. gentlemen opposite were more for the purpose of defeating the construction of the Pacific Railway; and when Sir George-É. Cartier produced his resolutions and was about to carry them as prepared, he had to give way to the desire of the House, because even those who usually supported the Government were alarmed at the cry which had been raised by gentlemen opposite. Thus if the motion of the hon. member for Napierville had been adopted and Canada was unable to get a Company to build the Railway, the bargain with British Columbia would fall to the ground and be only waste paper and British Columbia would sit out shivering in the cold forever without a Railway.

The policy indicated by that solution of the hon. member for Napierville has been carried out ever since. In March, long after the legislation had taken place, by which Parliament declared that there should be a Pacific Railway built in some way or other, we find the *Globe* urging its friends to still further oppose that scheme; and, Sir, we have had arraigned against us the opposition of those who usually ally themselves against the Government, supported by those gentlemen of the Opposition, many of whom owe their elections to sectional cries. (Cheers.) We have met them, and it is said we met them with money. I believe that the gentlemen opposite spent two pounds to our one. (Opposition cries of no, no.)

I challenge the hon. gentlemen to have a Committee on this subject. Let us have a Committee. (Ministerial cheers.) I read the speech of the hon. member for Bruce South (Hon. Mr. [Edward] Blake) at London, and he suggested the appointment of a Statutory Committee. In God's name let us have it! Let us have a Committee of three, to go from county to county, from constituency to constituency, and let them sift these matters to the bottom, and I tell you on my honour as a man, that I believe I can prove that there are more who owe their elections to money on that side of the House than on this. (Loud Ministerial cheers.) If I be challenged I can go into detail. I can show, and I can prove it that many members owe their election to money, and to money alone. I challenge the hon. gentlemen to agree to the appointment of a Committee, a Statutory Committee, as suggested by the hon. member for Bruce South. Let us put the names of the Judges of all the Provinces into a bag, and draw out three names, who shall form the Committee. (Cheers.)

As I stated in my evidence, and I hope my evidence has been carefully read by every member of this House, and I say here that I tried to be as full and as frank as I could well be. I could not help it if I was not subjected to a rigid cross-examination. I was exceedingly anxious that the hon. member for Shefford* should be there to cross-examine me—(cheers)—and I would willingly have answered his questions. I have little more to say than I said then.

---

* Lucius Seth Huntington (1827–1886) was the Liberal MP who exposed the Pacific Scandal. He had not supported the Great Coalition and the Confederation project, and by the 1870s he advocated cutting diplomatic ties with Great Britain so that Canada would have the power to enter into treaties independently. When the Conservative government fell over the scandal, he formed a syndicate "to acquire the Pacific railway construction contract." (Little, "Huntington, Lucius Seth," *DCB*)

Sir, there was no sale to Sir Hugh Allan of any contract whatever. (Cheers.) Consider for one moment, Mr. Speaker [Hon. James Cockburn], how the case stood. Parliament had passed two Acts, one for Upper Canada and one for Lower Canada, and some two or three subsidiary Acts respecting branch lines. But we will leave these out of the question, and will consider that there were two Acts passed, one for a Company having its centre in Montreal, and the other in Toronto. Now, Sir, although there were Ontario gentlemen connected with the Canada Pacific Company, and although there were Quebec gentlemen connected with the Interoceanic Company yet they were really Acts promoted by men who have Ontario and Quebec interests only, and every one saw that they were essentially sectional.

Before Parliament met, and before either Act was passed, the cry was got up that the Northern Pacific people were desirous of obtaining the control of our railway. At the first, Mr. Speaker, when the first interview took place between the Government and these gentlemen, I was very glad to see them. We had passed in 1871 the Act that British Columbia should be a portion of the Dominion, and we had passed the resolution by which we were to build the railway in ten years. It was understood, then, Sir, that the whole matter should stand over until the ensuing session, and that in the meantime the Government should go on with the survey and be ready in 1872 with the plans. We got through the session of 1872 and we commenced, in order to keep faith with the British Columbians, the survey, and I think they will admit, and everyone must admit, that the greatest energy and the greatest zeal has been exhibited in the survey, and that within two years there has never been so much work so satisfactorily done as in this railway survey by Mr. San[d]ford Fleming.* (Cheers.) The survey was going on, and in midsummer and in the fall all the members of the Government were scattered looking after their several affairs, taking their little holidays, and God knows the public men of this country have little enough holiday.

They were all scattered except Hon. Sir Francis Hincks and myself when Mr. Waddington† called on me. I had known the gentleman before, and I much respected him. He said to me that there were some American gentlemen to see us about the railway. I said to him in my way, "What a fool you were to bring them here. We can do nothing with them." He was very much distressed, and said to me, "But you will not refuse to see them." I said certainly not.

The gentlemen then came, and Hon. Sir Francis Hincks and I met them, and we talked pleasantly, and I said to them that I was glad to see that American capital was looking for investment in Canadian enterprises, but that it was altogether premature as we could not then take any offers or suggestions, or take any action till after we had met Parliament. One of them remarked that they had evidently been brought on a wild-goose errand, and they then went away.

This first brought to my mind very strongly the necessity for looking out for our railway. Parliament had tied down our hands and the railway could only be built by a company, and

---

* At the time of the Pacific Scandal, Sandford Fleming (1827–1915) was the engineer-in-chief of the Intercolonial Railway, a position he held until 1876. He was knighted for his many accomplishments in 1897. (Creet, "Fleming, Sandford," *DCB*)

† Vancouver Island politician Alfred Penderell Waddington (1801–1872) published *Overland communication by land and water through British North America* (Victoria, 1867), *Overland route through British North America; or, the shortest and speediest road to the east* (London, 1868), and *Sketch of the proposed line of overland railroad through British North America* (London, 1869). (Lamb, "Waddington, Alfred Penderell," *DCB*)

there were no other means of carrying out the pledge with British Columbia, and I therefore immediately addressed myself to the matter. And what did I do? I spoke to all that I could, as I have no doubt my colleagues did, and endeavoured to arouse Canadians in the enterprise. I went to Toronto and saw Messrs. Macpherson, Gzowski, Col. Cumberland, Mr. Howland and his son, and Gooderham & Worts, and in fact every one, and endeavoured to induce them to enter into the great enterprise. I told them, as Hon. Sir Francis Hincks told Sir Hugh Allan, that by law there was no other way of building the road but by a company, and that they ought to get up a grand company, get a charter and go to England for any capital they needed.

As I went to Toronto, Hon. Sir Francis Hincks went accidentally to Montreal, and told Sir Hugh about the American gentlemen who had called on us, and the fault I found with my friend Sir Francis, and which I ventured to tell him when he was a member of the Government was, that while merely attempting to stimulate Sir Hugh to go into the work, he had named to him that he had better put himself in communication with the American capitalists. That was the act of Hon. Sir Francis Hincks. That was his concern, and I would not at all object to American capital, or capital from England, or anywhere else, but I told Sir Francis on his return that he had been premature in this, that we ought to have kept to a great Canadian Company before any offer or intimation that Americans might come in was made.

Then Sir Hugh, acting on the hint given by Sir Francis, and it was no more than a hint—it was in no way a Government action—communicated with the Americans, and we had a visit from a number of Americans with Sir Hugh; and Mr. Speaker, I being spokesman on both occasions, gave them precisely the same answer that they were premature; that we were very glad to see them, but we could make no arrangement until Parliament met. I said we would be very glad, however, to hear any proposition, and asked them whether they had any to make. Sir Hugh asked in return whether we were in a position to entertain a proposition; and on our replying in the negative, he rejoined that he had no proposition to make. And these were all the communications between the Canadian Government and these gentlemen. (Cheers.) This statement cannot be controverted, and will not be.

In the meantime a sectional jealousy had arisen, instead of, as I had hoped, a joint action between the capitalists of Montreal and Toronto, and instead of, as I had hoped, there being a rush and anxiety among our moneyed men in the different parts of Canada to form one great Company, for the work required united exertion, there was a jealousy fanned from some quarter, which we know now, and this jealously prevented the two great bodies of capitalists, who ought to have built the road, from joining, and all our hopes were scattered; and a feeling arose in Toronto first, that if the Montreal interest got the preponderance Toronto trade would get the go-by, and second, that Sir Hugh Allan and the Montreal interests were joined with the Americans.

That feeling grew and I am not now in a position to state, after reading the evidence and after reading the letters of Sir Hugh Allan and those published by Mr. McMullen, I am not now in a position to state that jealousy in Toronto was ill founded. I am not in a position to state that they had not some ground of which we knew nothing for believing that the Montreal party were in communication with the Americans. I am not now in a position to state that the people of Toronto and the Interoceanic had not great cause for suspicion and jealousy, whether that suspicion was well or ill founded; but before Parliament met, as I have sworn and as Mr. Abbott* has sworn and as every member of the House knows, the feeling against the introduction of American capital was so great that by no possibility could it be allowed entrance.

We felt, Mr. Speaker, and every member knew it, that it was necessary that every American element must be eliminated from the Acts, or they could not pass—(cheers)—and I appeal to hon. gentlemen who were then in the House if they do not know, as a matter of fact, that it was understood on all sides that the American element was eliminated. I understood it so; the Government understood it so, and the House understood it so, and Mr. Abbott, who undertook the management of the bill of the Montreal Company through this House, made it a special understanding with Sir Hugh Allan that it should be so before he promoted the bill, and so it was by universal consent.

I know, Mr. Speaker, that it will be said, and I may as well speak of it now, that Sir Hugh Allan's letters show that he still kept up his connection with the Americans. I knew it, and I painfully know it, that Sir Hugh Allan behaved badly and acted disingenuously towards the men with whom he was originally connected. I say that when he found that Americans were not to be admitted he ought to have written to them, and informed them that though he had made a contract with them, still so strong a feeling existed in Canada that he must at once and forever sever his connection with them.

Instead of doing so, however, he carried on a correspondence with them, a private correspondence which he has sworn

---

* John Joseph Caldwell Abbott (1821–1893) was Hugh Allan's solicitor. He oversaw the incorporation of the Canada Pacific Railway and was a provisional director until the venture failed in the scandal. (Miller, "Abbott, Sir John Joseph Campbell," *DCB*)

no one else saw, and which he has sworn that not even his colleagues in the Canada Pacific Company knew of, not even Mr. Abbott, his confidential adviser. He says he conducted it as his own personal affair, believing and hoping that in the end the people of Canada would come to a different view, and allow American capital to be used. He has sworn that, and we never knew that he was carrying on communications with the Americans. Mr. Abbott never knew it and the Canada Pacific Company have declared that there was no connection between them and the Americans, but I have heard it said, I think, by the member for Châteauguay (Hon. Mr. [Luther] Holton), is it possible that the Government would give a contract to a man who had behaved so disingenuously, and after this want of ingenuousness had been shown to the Prime Minister, by the exhibition of the correspondence?

Sir, let me say a word about that. After the Act passed and we were working with all our might to form a good company and a strong one, long after, Mr. Speaker, as it appears in the correspondence between Sir Hugh Allan and the Americans, Mr. McMullen came to my office in order to levy blackmail. (Cheers.) He did not show me the correspondence but he flourished certain receipts and drafts which Sir Hugh had drawn at New York. There was nothing, however, in that because he had told us he had gone into that association, and we knew that he had communication with the Americans, and there was nothing extraordinary in my seeing that these gentlemen had subscribed a certain sum of money for preliminary expenses, and I have never known a Company, railway or otherwise, without preliminary expenses being provided for by the promoters. I told Mr. McMullen, therefore, that it was his matter, and that he must go and see Sir Hugh.

I heard no more about the matter until late in January or February, after we had formed the Company, after a correspondence with every Province of the Dominion, after having tried to excite and having successfully excited the capitalists of the different Provinces to subscribe, after we had got everything prepared, after I had drafted the charter and the great seal only required to be affixed, and just when the charter was about to be launched, and the Company to build the road was about to be made a certainty, then Mr. C. M. Smith, Mr. Hurlbut and Mr. McMullen walked into my office.

I do not say that Mr. Smith or Mr. Hurlbut came to levy blackmail. I do not think they did, for they looked respectable gentlemen, and spoke and behaved as such. They told me Sir Hugh Allan had behaved very badly, and they read a good deal of the correspondence which had been published, and I told them then, "Gentlemen if your statement is true, Sir Hugh Allan has behaved badly towards you, but the matter is your own, and Sir Hugh is no doubt able to meet you." They spoke of the seizing of his ships and bringing actions against him both in the United States and Canada, when I repeated to them that they had their proper remedy, and added that Sir Hugh had not the slightest power to give them the contract. (Cheers.) I told them that he ought to have broken off his connection with them long ago, and that if he had kept them in the dark they must take their own remedy against him.

We were then asked how could we admit Sir Hugh into the contract. Mr. Speaker, we had already admitted him. The contract was made. Every Province had been given its Directors. The charter had been drawn, and only waited the signature of the Governor General; and more than all this, the correspondence, whatever may be said of the conduct of Sir Hugh

Allan towards the Americans, proved the existence of hostility between them, and showed that if Sir Hugh were one of the Company who received the contract, we should keep the Americans out altogether.

I had to get that contract let. I had to get a sufficient number of the capitalists of Canada who would take up this subject, and Sir Hugh Allan was the first. He is our greatest capitalist. He was the first man who went into it, and these gentlemen, Mr. McMullen and the rest, proved to me that Sir Hugh Allan had cut the cord of connection, had nothing to do with the Americans, or with Jay Cooke Co., and that they were resolved to follow him to the death as they had done. (Hear, hear.) This, then is the narrative, so far, of our connection with the Pacific Railway.

My evidence states that shortly before the elections I went to Toronto, and Sir George-É. Cartier went to Montreal. I do not wish hon. gentlemen to suppose for one single instant that I would desire to shelter myself or my living colleagues by throwing the blame on my dead colleague. (Cheers.) Whatever Sir George-É. Cartier has done I will assume the responsibility of. (Hear, hear.) Whatever Sir George-É. Cartier has done I must accept as being the honest expression of an individual Minister; but, sir, I do not admit, and I will not admit, and it is not safe for hon. gentlemen opposite to admit, that any one Minister can bind a Ministry. (Cheers.)

I went to Toronto in order to descend to the stern contest that was forced upon me by the course taken by hon. gentlemen opposite, to meet the arguments that were going to be used against me, the sectional questions that were raised against me, the numerous charges which were made against me, and which I had always found operating against me. When I went to Ontario for that purpose, and to meet these charges, it was not for the first time. As long as I have been in Parliament I have been charged by hon. gentlemen opposite with selling Upper Canada, with sacrificing the best interest of Upper Canada, with selling myself to French domination and Catholic influences and Lower Canadian interests.

I had refuted these charges repeatedly, and had convinced the majority in Upper Canada that I held then as I do now the principle of union between Upper and Lower Canada, and that the only way by which that union could be firmly established was by ignoring sectional questions and religious differences. (Cheers.) These cries are still raised. You will hear them before many days in this House, and you will hear them throughout the country whenever it pleases hon. gentlemen opposite to raise them; but as my past history has shown, so my future history will prove that whatever party political exigency may be, I have never, and shall never give up the great principle of keeping intact the union of Upper and Lower Canada by a give and take principle, by a reciprocity of feeling and by surrendering our own religious and political prejudices for the sake of Union.

I went to the West to do what I could during the elections, in fighting the battle of the party and the Government. I had simply said to Sir George-É. Cartier that I should have a very hard fight in Upper Canada, as I had the Government of Ontario against me, and I wished him to help me as far as he could. I went to Toronto, and I tried all I could before the elections took place to procure an amalgamation of the two Companies.

It was of vital importance, in a Party point of view, laying aside the patriotic view, to have a Company to build the road, composed of the Montrealers and the Toronto men, so that I could have gone to the country and said, "Here is a great enterprise. We have formed a great Company. We are carrying out a great scheme. We are forming a great country." I spared no pains to procure an amalgamation; Senator Macpherson, and any one in Toronto connected with the enterprise, will tell you how hard, how earnestly, in season and out of season, I worked to procure that amalgamation. I failed. I thought I had succeeded two or three times.

I abandoned my own constituency; I might have been elected by acclamation, or at all events by a very large majority, but instead of attending to my election I went up to Toronto to attempt to bring about an amalgamation between the two companies. Then they got up a story about me, according to the habit of the Opposition that I considered my constituency a pocket borough, and thought I could afford to pass it by.

I thought at one time I had succeeded in procuring an amalgamation, and Mr. Abbott came up to Toronto in response to a telegram from me. We had an interview with Mr. Macpherson, and almost succeeded in coming to an agreement. The only question was whether there should be seven and six or five and four directors from Ontario and Quebec. The arrangement was so near that I was satisfied when I left Toronto that the amalgamation was complete. I found, however that that was not the case, and in the middle of my election on the 25th, I think, of July, I telegraphed to Mr. Macpherson to come down, and he came down to Kingston and saw me and then I sent that telegram which had been published in the papers, and which was the only arrangement as regards the granting of the charter so far as the Government were concerned, so far as I was concerned. (Hear, hear.) That telegram which was sent on the 26th of July was sent by me to Sir Hugh Allan after seeing Mr. Macpherson, and with the knowledge of Mr. Macpherson.

Now what does that say? I was obliged reluctantly to give up the hope of having an amalgamation before the elections. These little jealousies, these little personal ambitions and the jostling between seventeen and thirteen members on the board had come in the way, and I could not carry out the arrangement I had hoped to complete. I could not spare the time. I was in great danger of losing my election by throwing myself away on this great Pacific Railway. I actually came down to Kingston only on the day of my nomination, trusting to the kindness of my old friends in Kingston.

Well, Sir, what was the telegram which I sent? It said: "I have seen Mr. Macpherson"—he was in the room when I wrote it. "I have seen Mr. Macpherson. He has no personal ambition, but he cannot give up the rights of Upper Canada. I authorise you to state that any influence the Government may have in the event of amalgamation, shall be given to Sir Hugh Allan. The thing must stand over till after the elections. The two gentlemen, Mr. Macpherson and Sir Hugh Allan, will meet in Ottawa and form an amalgamation."

That was the proposition which I made, and just think, Sir, what was involved, think how much I was snubbing, which is a word which had been used by the *Globe* lately, how much I was injuring and prejudicing the interest of my colleague in Montreal, Sir George-É. Cartier. Sir Hugh Allan did not care so much for the Pacific Railway, and Sir George-É. Cartier did not care so much for Sir Hugh Allan. It was not Sir Hugh Allan or the Pacific Railway that he cared so much about; but Sir Hugh Allan had made himself the representative man of Lower Canada with respect to the Northern Colonization Road, the North Shore Road, and the Ottawa and Toronto Road, so that the members from Lower Canada would have stood by Sir

Hugh Allan even to the risk of losing all the elections, because their Montreal interests would be so much affected if Sir Hugh Allan were not sustained with regard to the Pacific Railway.

But with respect to the other railways, my hon. friend from Hochelaga (Mr. [Louis] Beaubien) and other gentlemen can say that if there had been accord between Sir Hugh Allan and the French members of Lower Canada from the Montreal district there would have been a great peril of the Lower Canadian members from that district deserting Sir George-É. Cartier, and supporting Sir Hugh Allan in carrying out the Northern Colonization road.

I was standing by Sir George-É. Cartier, who was most improperly charged with being so much attached to the Grand Trunk Railway that he would not do justice to the other roads. I will ask my friends from Lower Canada if Sir George-É. Cartier's connection with the railway had anything to do with the result of the elections. His prospects were connected with the local roads alone. In order to prove to you how true a man Sir George-É. Cartier was, how perfectly unselfish he was, I may state that he held back on my account. When he said, "I wish to be elected on my own merits, and on my own services, and not on account of the Colonization or any other road," (cheers) and when by a word he could have put an end to the cry of interest, he felt that it was a sectional feeling between Upper and Lower Canada, and that if he pronounced in favour of any railway in Lower Canada, he would injure me in Upper Canada, and he sacrificed himself for my sake in Lower Canada, because he thought that any pronouncements in favour of Sir Hugh Allan, might injure me and my friends in the western elections. (Cheers.) I had only one thing to do and that was to return to him the confidence and trust he had reposed in me. I said "Don't mind me. Fight your own battles. You must make your own arrangements with your friends in respect to the railways," and it was not until he had that communication with me that he said he would help the Northern Colonization road.

It was not because Sir George-É. Cartier had any personal objects to gain, it was not because he was connected with the Grand Trunk Railway, but it was purely from a desire to save me from any possible difficulty in Upper Canada that he held back, and I have here now, when he is dead, the proud opportunity of stating that even in the last moment he was actuated by no selfish feelings, by no desire to promote his own interests, but that he only thought of his colleague, of his comrade of twenty years. He only thought that by appearing to promote a national interest in Lower Canada he might hurt me in Upper Canada and he threw away all his chances, all his hopes, everything like a certainly or a reasonable hope of success, for the purpose of standing by me, and I am proud and happy now to pay this tribute to his memory. (Cheers.)

Well, Sir, on the 26th of July I sent a telegram, and that was the only bargain. No man can make a bargain with the Government, except by an Order in Council, or by the action of the First Minister, recognized and accepted by his colleagues. Any act of a First Minister until it is disavowed is considered equal to a minute of council, equal to an Act of the Government. That telegram of mine of the 26th of July was an Act of Government. My colleagues have not repudiated it; they have accepted it, and it was a fair arrangement as we could not get the amalgamation.

As we could not succeed in going to the country with a perfect scheme for building the Pacific Railway, what else was left to us but to keep the amalgamation of these great capitalists open till after the elections, and then call them together, and the only word of preference for Montreal over Toronto was simply my expression that any influence the Government might have in case of amalgamation, in the case of the two Companies joining and electing a Board of Directors, would be fairly used in favour of Sir Hugh Allan for the Presidency. I think that was due to Sir Hugh Allan, and after all it was no great affair. Everybody knows that the President of a Company is no more than the junior member of the Board of Directors. It depends altogether upon the personal weight of the man. We have seen Boards where the President governed the Board; others where the President was a mere figure head, and others again where the junior member governed the Company. It depends entirely upon the personal figure and authority of the man.

Well, Sir, I made that promise, but I wish the House to remember that at the time of that telegram, in which I simply stated that as we could not form a Company before the elections, we would form one afterwards out of the two, and would do what we could to make Sir Hugh Allan President. At that time there had been not one single word said about money— (cheers)—and there never was one said, as far as I was concerned, between Sir Hugh Allan and me. (Hear, hear.)

I was fighting the battle in Western Canada. I was getting subscriptions, as I have no doubt the hon. member for Lambton (Hon. Mr. [Alexander] Mackenzie) was getting subscriptions, and if he denies it I will be able to prove it. (Cheers.) I state in my place that I will be able to prove it. (Cheers.) I was doing what I could for the purpose of getting money to help the elections, and I was met, not only by individual exertions, but by the whole force, power and influence, legitimate and illegitimate of the Ontario Government. I have no hesitation in saying that in all expenditure, we were met by two dollars to one. (Hear, hear.) I have read with some amusement the attacks that have been made upon the Government, because a member of the Government was a party to this fund. If we had had the same means possessed by hon. gentlemen opposite; if we had spies; if we had thieves; if we had men who went to your desk, picked your lock and stole your note books, we would have much stronger evidence than hon. gentlemen think they have now. (Cheers.) We were fighting an uneven battle. We were simply subscribing as gentlemen, while they were stealing as burglars. (Cheers.) We may trace it out as a conspiracy throughout. I use the word conspiracy advisedly, and I will use the word out of the House as well as in the House. (Cheers.)

The hon. member for Shefford (Hon. Mr. Huntington) said that he had obtained certain documents. He attempted to read them to this House, not much I think to his credit, and certainly contrary to the sense of the House and of the country. Now how did he get these documents. We had Mr. George W. McMullen, who was the American agent of these gentlemen. He had carried on this correspondence with Sir Hugh Allan, and when he came to me in December and tried to levy blackmail on me (hear, hear) I told him to go—well I did not use any improper language, but I told him to step out of my office, (Laughter and cheers) and he went to the hon. gentlemen opposite. (Cheers.) This is no mere hypothesis of mine. Sir Hugh Allan had promised to pay this man $17,000 for these papers, and although he had the money almost in his hand, the hon. gentlemen gave him something more. (Cheers.) The hon. gentlemen cannot deny that he did.

HON. MR. [LUCIUS] HUNTINGTON: I do deny it. (Oppo-sition cheers.) The statement is without foundation.

HON. SIR JOHN A. MACDONALD: If there is one person in the world whom the hon. member for Shefford had as a friend, it is the editor and proprietor of the Montreal *Herald* (hear, hear). I think he takes him to his bosom. I think they sleep together. I think that they have but one thought. He is a guide, philoso-pher, and friend, and when we have the announcement from the Montreal *Herald*, of May the 22nd, 1873, I think we must accept it. "No one can suppose that such a plot could have been laid bare without great labour and large expenditure," (cheers) again, the *Herald* says, speaking of Hon. Mr. Huntington,— "But for the courage with which he assumed it, as well as for the pains and expenditure which it has cost him to expose the mys-tery, he is entitled to the warmest gratitude." (Cheers on both sides of the House.) I judge from the cheers of hon. gentlemen opposite that the hon. member for Shefford has their thanks; but that is an admission that he made the expenditure. (Oh! oh! and cheers.) This man bought Mr. McMullen. It is admitted by the Montreal *Herald* that he bought him. (No! no! and hear, hear.)

HON. MR. HUNTINGTON: I have already stated in the House that the charges were not founded on any information from Mr. McMullen, and that the statements which have appeared were false. I never got any information from McMullen till long after I made the charges. I never paid nor promised him a cent, and the statement of the hon. gentleman is utterly without foundation. (Opposition cheers.)

The statement also that he made a few minutes ago that I have been influenced here by foreign gold, and that foreign gold had been used in my election, is an utterly unfounded statement, false in every particular; and I challenge the hon. gentleman to the combat, and dare him on his responsibility to take the Committee. (Hon. Mr. Huntington was proceeding, when cries of "Order!" were raised on the Government benches, answered by Opposition cheers. The hon. gentleman went on speaking in the midst of an uproar which rendered his remarks perfectly inaudible.) On order being restored,

HON. SIR JOHN A. MACDONALD proceeded. There, Sir, it is very evident that I have hit the spot; that I have hit him on a sore point. (Cheers and No! no!) I have told the hon. gentleman that I am willing to have a Committee to inquire into the whole matter, including the case of the hon. gentleman.

HON. MR. HUNTINGTON: Oh! You can back out as you will.

HON. SIR JOHN A. MACDONALD: I am not backing out, but the hon. gentleman cannot expect to have it all as he likes. I'll read another extract. "Mr. Huntington said that the charter was obtained in the session of 1872, long after the men who furnished the money to him (Sir Hugh Allan) were repudiated and made arrangements with him (Hon. Mr. Huntington) to bring the charges against the Government." (Cheers.)

HON. MR. HUNTINGTON rose to a question of order. The report of my speech is entirely without foundation. (Cries of order, order.) That is a question of fact, and the hon. gentlemen can correct it afterwards.

HON. SIR JOHN A. MACDONALD: I heard it myself. (Cries from Government benches, "We all heard it.") Perhaps the hon. gentleman will deny that he said Jay Cooke would have him in his office without a witness.

HON. MR. HUNTINGTON: That is another falsehood of the *Ottawa Times*. That paper, which is inspired by hon. gentlemen opposite, deliberately falsified my speech from the beginning to the end. I refused to disgrace myself by noticing the malignant statement of the dastard sheet. What I said was that I had not seen Jay Cooke for four years; that I went to a prominent promoter of the Northern Pacific Railway (hear, hear), with that view of conversing with him and found that they were the allies of hon. gentlemen opposite, because they would not even talk to me without people being present. (Hear, hear.)

THE SPEAKER: I must call the hon. member to order. I hope this interruption will cease. The hon. member knows what the rules of debate are as well as any one else in the House, and this plan of interruption can only lead to assembly confusion in the House. The hon. gentleman will ask his opportunity from the House. I am sure it will be given to him, and he can then make his denial on the question of fact.

HON. SIR JOHN A. MACDONALD: I wish to invite the attention of every hon. member of this House who is an honest and candid man, to the statement I am making. There could be no amalgamation before the elections. In my telegram of the 26th of July I stated that the question must stand over until after the elections; that the two companies would stand on perfectly equal footing, and that the arrangements which had been made between Mr. Macpherson and Mr. Abbott should be the guiding line. That arrangement was that Upper Canada should have seven, Lower Canada six, and each of the other Provinces one Director on the Board. Not by any chance or possibility could Sir Hugh Allan by his large capital, or the influence created by that capital, get an undue influence on the Board for Lower Canada or for himself over my own Province.

On the 30th of July I received a letter from Sir Hugh Allan, Sir George-É. Cartier being sick, stating that he had made certain arrangements with Sir George, and it was a bad arrangement, for it was something like this, that if there should not be an amalgamation he thought that Sir Hugh Allan's Company ought to get the charter. I received that message in the middle of my election contest, and I said to myself it is not much consequence whether one company or the other gets the charter if they unite, but it will kill me, it will kill us if the Montreal Company without amalgamation receives it. However, I telegraphed back at once that I would not agree to the arrangement, and I would go down to Montreal that night. Yes, Mr. Speaker, in the midst of a severe election contest, for I was elected only by 130, whereas at the previous election I had a majority of 300, I said I would run down to Montreal on this matter. I telegraphed to Sir George-É. Cartier that I would not consent to the arrangement, and that my telegram of the 26th of July, 1872, would be the decision of the Government, and the Government would be bound thereby, and would be governed by nothing else.

I wish it to be clearly understood, beyond the possibility of doubt, that the Canadian Government had agreed that since it could not obtain an amalgamation of the two companies before the elections, they would try to get an amalgamation after the elections, and in such an amalgamation they would do what was fair, in order to get Sir Hugh Allan made President of the Amalgamated Company. (Cheers.)

I say that that arrangement made by Sir George-É. Cartier was set aside and why? Because it would have killed me in Upper Canada. I telegraphed that even at the risk of my election I would go down to Montreal and put an end to it, and Sir George-É. Cartier, when he got my message, saw what an absurd proposition it was, and there was an end of it, and Sir Hugh Allan telegraphed back that the bargain was ended. At that time there had not been one single word said about money subscriptions.

Sir, it may be very wrong to give subscriptions to election funds at all, but is there any one gentleman opposite who will say that he had not expended money himself, or has been aided in doing so by his friends. (Several members of the Opposition here denied the charge.) Whether those acts had been done by members themselves or their friends, money was spent and always would be spent on elections. I don't hesitate to say—and I state this in the face of this House, of the country and of the world—that I am not aware of any one single farthing having been spent illegitimately and contrary to the law—(Opposition laughter and cheers)—by members on the Government side of the House. I can tell of one man on the other side who spent $26,000; another case I can prove of spending $30,000, and I can also prove cases of spending $5,000, $6,000, $7,000 and $8,000, and when the Committee which the hon. member for Bothwell (Mr. [David] Mills) challenged me to move, and which I intend to move, is appointed, I shall give the proofs. (Laughter, in which Mr. [David] Blain joined.) I can prove the expenditure of money by that gentleman (Mr. Blain) himself.

MR. [DAVID] BLAIN: If the right hon. gentleman refers to me, I say there is not a particle of truth in the statement. Not one single solitary cent came out of my pocket unfairly. (Cheers and laughter.)

HON. SIR JOHN A. MACDONALD: Perhaps the gentleman has not a pocket. Perhaps his wife has. (Laughter, and cries of "Shame" from the Opposition.)

MR. BLAIN rose. (Cries of "Order.") He said the right hon. gentleman had made a charge against him. He would answer it at another time.

HON. SIR JOHN A. MACDONALD: Before the Committee which I propose to move, and which will have power to administer an oath, and which the member for Bothwell (Mr. Mills) has invited, I shall be able to prove the fact I stated. The hon. gentleman will perhaps reserve himself for that. (Interruption.)

HON. MR. [LUTHER] HOLTON: I raise the question of order. I doubt whether the right hon. gentleman is in order in making statements affecting the right of hon. gentlemen to sit in this House without formulating charges to be followed by a motion. The hon. gentleman intimates his intention of making a motion at a future time, but he cannot move a motion of the kind indicated in a debate on the Address. To charge members with having obtained their seats by improper means is therefore a violation of the proprieties of debate, and I believe of other standing orders of the House.

HON. MR. [EDWARD] BLAKE: In the case of the member for York West (Mr. Blain) the proceeding is doubly irregular, for it is interfering with an actual petition pending before an election Committee.

THE SPEAKER: The question before the House really does not properly relate to these subjects. (Hear, hear.) I have not hitherto interfered in any way with this debate. There has been a good deal of language used which is not strictly Parliamentary, and reference made that might better have been avoided, but the subject of the debate is of such a character that I thought I ought not to interfere with free discussion. I have not used any influence to stay the parties who have been marking this charge against the Ministry, and I should have still pursued the same course unless applied to by the other side; but I must say I think it would be better if the Minister of Justice (Hon. Sir John A. Macdonald) would refrain from making direct charges against individual members. (Hear, hear.)

HON. SIR JOHN A. MACDONALD: I submit to your decision, Sir, I would not have alluded to the hon. member if it had not been for the offensive way in which he interrupted me, and my knowledge about his case. The hon. gentlemen opposite will find out that I know a great deal more about their elections than they would care that I should know.

I shall now proceed with the history I am giving to the House as well as I can under these unseemly interruptions. Sir, there never was an occasion, there never was a minute, in which the interests of Canada were sacrificed by the Government of Canada for election purposes. (Loud cheers.) I say that we carry out the law as well as the law could possibly be carried out.

(Cheers.) I say that up to the very last moment we tried to obtain an amalgamation of the two Companies. I almost went on my knees, which is not my habit, I am sorry to say, to my friends in Toronto, for the purpose of securing an amalgamation, and though I did not secure an amalgamation of the two Companies, yet I got an amalgamation of the two interests, and secured the best men in Western Canada.

I have no hesitation in saying that in the Company chartered by the Government, we have the very best men in Canada, considering all the circumstances. Let us go over the whole Board from Upper Canada. There is Mr. Donald McInnes, of Hamilton, I will ask the hon. member for Welland (Mr. [William Alexander] Thomson) if he is not a merchant of standing and respectability, and one of the last men to sell the interests of the Dominion to the Yankees. I asked the Hon. Mr. [John] Carling to come on the Board, but when the House came to the conclusion to exclude members of Parliament from that Board, I obtained Major Walker, representing one of the leading industries in the West. Then there is Col. Cumberland, and can we suppose that Col. Cumberland, who is at the heat of the great railway interests, and is charged with the management of millions of dollars, would sell himself to Sir Hugh Allan or the Yankees. (Cheers.)

I ask if Mr. Fleming, the engineer, the man whose name will live on the continent for his great engineering exploits, and who was objected to with Col. Cumberland and Major Walker by Sir Hugh Allan. Then the last man I asked was Mr. Walter Shanly. To some of you Walter Shanly may be unknown, but in the old Provinces of Canada he is everywhere known as being most highly respected, and as an engineer, the man who formerly managed the Grand Trunk, the man who achieved the great triumph of constructing the Hoosac Tunnel. I asked him as a personal friend of mine, as an old Ontarian, as one who was representing a wealthy constituency, to come on that board, and much against his will he came.

In the same way let us look at the Lower Province members. We look at Mr. E. R. Burpee. That is a truly honoured name, I am told, in New Brunswick. Do you think that E. R. Burpee is going to sell to the Yankees, Jay Cooke Co., or to the member for Shefford. (Laughter and cheers.) Then we come to Lieutenant-Governor Archibald, of Nova Scotia, and is he likely to sell us to the Yankees, the member for Shefford (Hon. Mr. Huntington), or Jay Cooke Co., I appeal to all the members for British Columbia, some of whom were opposed to him in politics, whether the name of Dr. Helmcken did not inspire respect. (Cheers.) With respect to Manitoba, I will only ask you to say whether Mr. McDermott, the richest and oldest merchant in Manitoba, a man who was the last who would sell the interest of this great Dominion to the Yankees, whether that man would sell Canada.* If ever any Government succeeded in accomplishing any particular object, surely this Government tried, and succeeded, to prevent foreigners from obtaining influence in or control over our transcontinental railway. (Cheers.)

By their line of action, the gentlemen opposite have postponed for some years the building of that railway, and they have besmirched unjustly, dishonourably, the character of the Canadian Government and of the Canadian people. (Cheers.) If there be any delay, any postponement in the completion of that great system of railways, I charge it to the hon. gentlemen

---

* Andrew McDermot (1790–1881) was a well-regarded entrepreneur. He was estimated at his death in 1881 to have been "the wealthiest man in Manitoba and one of the most generous." (Hyman, "McDermot, Andrew," *DCB*)

opposite. (Cheers.) Long after this quarrel is over, it will be recorded in the history of this Dominion of Canada that there was one body of men in this country willing to forget self, to forget Party, to forget section to build up a great interest and make a great country, and they will say that there was another Party who fought section against section, province against province, who were unable to rise to the true position of affairs, and I say the history of the future will be our justification and their condemnation. (Loud cheers.)

But, Sir, I have some more to say. I say this Government has been treated with foul wrongs. (Cheers.) I say this Government has been treated as no Government has ever been treated before. It has been met with an Opposition the like of which no Government in any civilized country was ever met. (Loud cheers.) I say we have been opposed not with fair weapons, not by fair argument, not by fair discussion, as a Government ought to be opposed, but opposed in a manner which will throw shame on hon. gentlemen opposite. (Renewed cheers.)

When we first met in this House, and we first discussed the Pacific Railway measures, I told you, Sir, that there was a confirmed plan to kill the Pacific Railway Company. The attack on the Government was a secondary matter. It was comparatively an inferior matter. But those gentlemen opposite went into the attack for the purpose of getting in evidence as quickly as possible for the purpose of sending it across the Atlantic by cable and kill Sir Hugh Allan's enterprise, and afterwards leave the proof of the evidence to chance.

Then we found that Sir Hugh Allan, by a very natural feeling, agreed to pay a certain sum of money to Mr. McMullen for the return of his correspondence, which was accepted, and the whole matter was arranged. Then blackmail was attempted to be levied on me, but I was not subject to be blackmailed. (Laughter.) They did levy blackmail on Sir Hugh Allan in Montreal and McMullen, for surrendering his letters to Sir Hugh, was paid $20,000, and promised $17,000 more on certain conditions being fulfilled. Mr. McMullen got his extra sum from some one.

The hon. gentleman (Hon. Mr. Huntington) would deny that Mr. McMullen was paid by some one. Everyone will believe that man who was to be paid that large sum of $17,000 did not accept it because he was offered some larger sums. (Cheers.) I believe that when we have the Committee which the member for Bothwell (Mr. Mills) challenged to move for, I shall be able to prove more than the $17,000, and I believe I shall be able to prove there were other parties in the purchase of G. W. McMullen, who over-bid Sir Hugh Allan. (Cheers and an Opposition member, "is it not right?") It was never right to buy him in the first place, nor in the second place, but if Sir Hugh Allan by paying $17,000 committed a crime, the man who paid him a larger sum must surely have committed a larger crime. (Laughter and cheers.)

I say that you must have a Committee in order to ascertain who are the gentlemen who went and deliberately bought those documents from Sir Hugh Allan. That may be fair war, but some one said it was striking below the belt. The man who goes deliberately and bribes people to hand a man's private letters, is a man who will be marked as a criminal all his life, and the man who goes and deliberately purchases private letters for any purpose, even though it may do good to the public, and expose a corrupt Government, will be generally condemned. Then we come down to a little more infamy. When I tell you that a letter of mine, addressed to a colleague at Montreal, was deliberately stolen, and when I tell you there was no doubt that it was stolen because it was thought to contain something that could be made politically useful, you can understand what infamy that is.

MR. BLAIN rose to a point of order, and submitted that this question was not before the House.

THE SPEAKER ruled against him stating that it came on the Address, which covers almost every possible question connected with public affairs.

HON. SIR JOHN A. MACDONALD: When I wrote that letter to my colleague, the Minister of Agriculture, I sent, at the same time, three telegrams to three different places, and that telegram was seen by some one acting in the interests of the Opposition, and from it they supposed that the letter would be connected with the Pacific Railway matter. That letter was deliberately stolen, not only stolen, but was stolen by an officer of the Post Office Department. I say stolen by an officer who was bought by some one, and who will some day, not long distant, for the evidence is being followed up and has not been abandoned, be found out, and it will be shown that he, believing that the letter contained something that would criminate the Government, stole it from the office and handed it over to be used in the manner the House was aware of. True it was that the letter contained nothing respecting the Pacific Railway.

I have got evidence beyond the possibility of a doubt, that my telegrams were stolen from Sir Hugh Allan's office, day after day; that a man went to the office night after night, after six o'clock and copied those telegrams and brought them down and sold them to the Opposition; that the safe of the office was not broken, and that after the documents were copied and sworn to by the man, he was paid money for them. I state this in presence of the House and of the country; and there was such a dishonest system of espionage carried on. And I say more than this, I join with the hon. member for Bothwell in asking for the Committee, before which I will prove all that I have said, and will put a credible witness in the box, who will swear he saw it with his own eyes.

You can judge how poorly the Government has been treated. In fact no Government in the world could exist if every drawer is to be searched, if every confidential servant is to be bribed by money offered to them. I may tell you this one thing, that I had got the evidence of this treachery, parties actually approached a secretary in Mr. Abbott's office, and offered him money to tell how much evidence had been obtained. Mr. Abbott is present in the House and will attest the truth of what I state. I can prove that from the beginning to the end of this business there was never a more gross system of espionage, of corruption, of bribing men to steal papers from their employers; and I would ask how any Opposition or Party in this country could stand under such an accusation if it be proved.

Sir, before I sit down I will touch upon one point to which I have not yet adverted, and that is how far a Government or member of a Government may concern themselves in elections, and the necessary expenditure or supposed expenditure of money at elections. I would wish to point out what has taken place in England, not under the old regime, but by the Reform Party in England. It is of some importance, as showing at all events that for everything I have got good authority. The House well remembers the great struggle, almost amounting

to a revolution, which accompanied the passage of the Reform
Bill in England. Well, Mr. Speaker, strange to say, the Reform
Party there, who were going to purify the political atmosphere,
those who were going to put down the old borough mon-
gers, did not hesitate to spend money at elections. They did
not trust to the excellence of their measures, to the justness
of their cause, and the consequence was that before the date
of the Carlton Club and the Reform Club, of which so much
has recently been said, the Reform Party had a Treasurer, and
whom do you think they gave the office to? It was the maker
and unmaker of Whiggery, Edward Ellice.*

Now, Edward Ellice was the man who made the Whig
Government. He was a member of the Government, and acted
as whipper-in of the Party, and was the man ordinarily employed
in making arrangements about elections. But Edward Ellice
was a man incapable of doing anything which he did not think
he was justified in doing. Any man who knew that right hon.
gentleman, who knew what a great influence he had on the history of his country, would know that Edward Ellice was perhaps
a greater man for pulling the strings and making arrangements
for Reform than even Lord John Russell [1792–1878] himself.

Let me tell you a little story about him. In my boyhood, when
I knew him, he often told me stories of this sort. In 1834 there
happened to be a committee on the Inns of Court. Mr. Daniel
O'Connell was the Chairman, and it came out in that investiga-
tion, which involved the seat of a member of Parliament, that
Lord Westham had got five hundred pounds from Mr. Ellice

---

* Edward Ellice (1783–1863) was a British landowner with property in Canada, and a
leading liberal or "Radical" in British politics. Ellice became "chief election manager,
party publicist, and chief whip in the House of Commons when the Whigs took office in
1830 under his brother-in-law, Earl Grey." (Colthart, "Ellice, Edward," DCB)

the Secretary of the Treasury, in order to carry the Liberal candidate. O'Connell felt it his bounden duty to report this matter to the House, and there was a motion of censure moved against Mr. Ellice by Mr. O'Connell. Mr. Ellice resigned his place and I shall read you what he said. At the time he made that speech he was Secretary of War; at the time he expended the money he was Secretary of the Treasury. He was an important man to the Government and might have been Cabinet Minister, had it not been that as every one who knew the history of those times knew, he would not take that position. He was the man who arranged matters for the Whigs, and he was charged with having used the secret service money in elections, as, by the way, I was a short time ago. The right hon. gentleman then quoted from Mr. Ellice's speech, volume 27, Mirror of Parliament, and now said he, I will quote from Sir Charles Buller [1806–1848]. Sir Charles Buller was the head and front of the Philosophical Radicals of England. They formed a Party of their own, and tried to engraft their principles on the politics of England, and, although they did not succeed, they sowed good seed, the results of which are seen at present day. I, who was a boy, remember him, and remember the kindness with which he discussed politics with me, and I am certain that he would have sustained the cause of the Liberal Party by nothing that was wrong. The right hon. gentleman quoted from the speech referred to. The attack was made upon Mr. Ellice that he had spent money out of the Secret Service Fund; but when Mr. Ellice rose and said that he had spent no money out of the Secret Service Fund, and that although a very large sum of money had passed through his hands for election purposes, none of it had been improperly procured, the House passed on without taking any action, though Mr. O'Connell supported the motion with all his great eloquence and ability.

A remark has been made in the newspapers that on one occasion I stated that no money had been expended by the Government on elections, and in answer to the charge, I asked Mr. Kidd, on the hustings at South Perth, whether any money had been expended at his election, and he said no, no statement could have been truer.

Sir, the money that was expended by the Committee, of which I was a member, was not with the purpose or object of endangering any man's seat. (Ironical cheers from the Opposition, and cheers from the Ministerial benches.) I state distinctly, so far as I know, not one single farthing that passed through my hands was expended improperly or contrary to the law. If it is so, the election tribunal of the country will settle that question, and, as I understand it, no improper expenditure has been proved in any election tribunal. (Cheers.) I say distinctly, say it in my place as a member of Parliament, that money was distributed for the purpose of fighting money against money, fire against fire, influence against influence; and we were over-matched by the hon. gentlemen opposite. (Loud cheers.)

There is one more remark that I have to make before I sit down. The Government never gave Sir Hugh Allan any contract that I am aware of. (Cheers.) We never gave him any contract in which he had a controlling influence. We had formed a Committee of thirteen men, chosen carefully and painfully, for the purpose of controlling Sir Hugh Allan from having any undue influence. We promised, we provided, that not one of the board should hold more than one hundred thousand dollars of the stock, that not one single man should have any interest in the contract whatever, which were, of course, only the ordinary provisions in a charter of incorporation. (Cheers.)

Now, Mr. Speaker, I have only one more thing to say on this point. I put it to your own minds. There were thirteen gentlemen, Sir Hugh Allan and others incorporated by that charter. That charter—study it, take it home with you. Is there any single power, privilege or advantage given to Sir Hugh Allan with that contract that has not been given equally to the other twelve? (Cheers.) It is not pretended that any of the other twelve paid money for their positions. It is not contended that the gentlemen gave anything further than their own personal feelings might dictate. (Cheers.) You cannot name a man of these thirteen that has got any advantage over the other except that Sir Hugh Allan has his name down first on this paper. (Cheers.)

Can any one believe that the Government is guilty of the charges made against them. I call upon any one who does to read that charter. Is there anything in that contract? If there is a word in that charter which derogates from the rights of Canada; if there is any undue privilege, or right, or preponderance given to any one of these thirteen Directors, I say, Mr. Speaker, I am condemned. But, Sir, I commit myself, the Government commits itself, to the hands of this House, and far beyond the House, it commits itself to the country at large. (Loud cheers.) We have faithfully done our duty. We have fought the battle of Confederation. We have fought the battle of Union. We have had Party strife setting province against province, and more than all, we have had in the greatest province the preponderating province of the Dominion, every prejudice and sectional feeling that could be arrayed against us.

I have been the victim of that conduct to a great extent; but I have fought the battle of Confederation, the battle of Union, the battle of the Dominion of Canada. I throw myself upon this House; I throw myself upon this country; I throw myself upon posterity, and I believe that I know that, notwithstanding the many failings in my life, I shall have the voice of this county and this House rallying round me. (Cheers.) And, Sir, if I am mistaken in that, I can confidently appeal to a higher Court, to the Court of my own conscience, and to the Court of Posterity. (Cheers.)

I leave it with this House with every confidence. I am equal to either fortune. I can see cast the decision of this House either for or against me, but whether it be against me or for me I know, and it is no vain boast to say so, for even my enemies will admit that I am no boaster, that there does not exist in Canada a man who has given more of his time, more of his heart, more of his wealth, or more of his intellect and power, such as it may be, for the good of this Dominion of Canada. (The right hon. gentleman resumed his seat amid loud and long continued cheering.)

PLACING THE TARIFF PILLAR
OF THE NATIONAL POLICY, 1879

Macdonald's exit from power after the Pacific Scandal in 1873 coincided with the advent of a deep depression among the trading western nations. He spent his years in opposition watching and learning. He became more engaged with the plight of the "working man" in Canada and with devising a plan to help the economy.[8] Charles Tupper advocated a "National Policy" in the 1860s. In the 1870s the Conservatives envisioned a program of promoting Canadian industries, protected by a high tariff wall that would prevent Canada from being flooded with cheaper American products.[9] Such an idea of import substitution had been articulated by John Rae (1796–1872), a Scottish immigrant living in the 1820s in Upper Canada. He published in 1834 an influential critique of Adam Smith and economic liberalism, Statement of some new principles on the subject of political economy, exposing the fallacies of the system of free trade, and of some other doctrines maintained in the "Wealth of Nations."[10] *The protectionism intended by the tariff wall also reflected Canada's failed attempts to renew the Reciprocity Treaty with the United States. Macdonald*

and the Conservatives got back into Parliament in 1878 on the strength
of the tariff and the National Policy, supported by "working-men."[11]
Macdonald soon launched an attack on the election tactics of Alexander
Mackenzie's Liberal government.

The Debates of the House of Commons, 4th Parliament, 1st
Session, record on May 7, 1879:

He [SIR JOHN A. MACDONALD] . . . They all remembered
how, before that hon. gentleman [Mackenzie] was a Minister
at all, before he was a member of this House, and while he was
a member of the Legislature of Ontario, how he hoisted the
"bloody shirt," as it was called in the United States, and invoked
the ghost of the slaughtered [Thomas] Scott; they all remembered
that, and how he tried to rouse up the country on that question,
and how, when he came to be a Minister here, he was willing
to crouch behind his French-Canadian and Catholic supporters.

He [Mackenzie] forgot the "bloody shirt" then, he forgot
the ghost of the murdered Scott; and he got the Governor
General [Lord Dufferin]—they had a right to say so, as he had
said the same of the present Government—he got the Governor
General to intervene and take the responsibility off his shoulders, letting off Riel and Lepine.*

It did not rest in the hon. gentleman's mouth to make
such a charge now, especially when the charge was altogether

---

* Ambroise-Dydime Lépine (1840–1923) was the adjutant general, responsible for
administering justice in Louis Riel's provisional government, and implicated in the
death of Thomas Scott. In 1874 he was tried in Manitoba, and found guilty but recommended for mercy. Canadians, particularly in Quebec, reacted vehemently to the
sentencing. Prime Minister Alexander Mackenzie asked the governor general, Lord
Dufferin, to intervene, and he commuted the sentence to two years in prison and forfeiture of Lépine's civil rights. Shortly afterwards, Riel and Lépine were offered amnesty
in return for a five-year banishment. Lépine served out his term, and Riel left for the
United States. (Ens, "Lépine, Ambroise-Dydime," *DCB*)

unfounded, that this Government [Macdonald's] in any respect, or on any occasion refused to assume the full responsibility of all their acts, of all their advice, and of all their conduct, he [Macdonald] supposed the hon. gentleman did that in consequence of his alliance—rather an entangling alliance he would find it—with the present Ontario Government. For the purpose of assisting that Government in their great straits, he, [Mackenzie] had tried to make political capital of such a dry subject as a tariff.

But now, instead of talking about tea, sugar, wheat and barley, he talked about independence, he talked about ministerial responsibility, he talked about Goldwin Smith, he talked about everything, especially about the hardships of the poor farmers who were going to be crushed by this tariff. Poor farmers.

> "Alas! unconscious of their doom,
> The little victims play;
> Careless they are of ills to come,
> They think but of to-day."*†

The poor farmers were quite unconscious of all the ruin the tariff was going to inflict upon them, and if the hon, gentleman had

---

* Alexander Mackenzie sat in the Ontario legislature between 1871 and 1872; but in 1873 he became leader of the Liberals. The party, favouring free competition and anti-monopoly, found a platform during the Pacific Scandal. It also tried to pursue free-trade policies and courted Canada's farmers whose markets they saw restricted by the tariffs; but financial shortfalls kept the tariffs in place creating party divisions. Goldwin Smith, despite limited support for the National Policy, advocated continental trade links for Canada. (Forster, "Mackenzie, Alexander," *DCB*; Berger, *Sense of Power*, 42, 189)

† Here Macdonald is quoting from "Ode on a Distant Prospect of Eton College," by the poet Thomas Gray (1716–1771). Although a few words have been altered from the original, the lines retain the same meaning. (*Oxford Dictionary of Quotations*, 230)

the correspondence put into his hands that had been received by the hon. the Finance Minister, he would find that whether the letters came from the farmers, the manufacturers, or whatever class it was, the complaints were all, and especially those of the farmers, that the protection was not sufficient.

MR. MACKENZIE: They say, then, it is a failure.

SIR JOHN A. MACDONALD said those who wanted Protection, were like the squaw who said about whiskey that a little too much was just enough.

Those who wanted to get protected wanted all the protection they could get. When his hon. friend was making that exhaustive speech of his—if he were allowed to pay a compliment to his own colleague—whenever he mentioned an increase of duty on any article, he was cheered by the immense majority of this House, and whenever he spoke in hesitating tones, as to the smallness of the duty on any article, —the House sat in silence. The same feeling existed all through the country, and the hon. gentlemen opposite knew that, be the cause well or ill founded, this country had deliberately—not by surprise, not by false pretences, as the hon. gentleman for Centre Huron* had said, but of a full and lengthened discussion for years, of a strong pressure for Protection on the one side, and an able resistance by the hon. gentleman in favour of Free-trade on the other—the country had deliberately accepted a Protective policy.

Therefore the present Ministry [Macdonald's] came into

---

* Sir Richard John Cartwright had regained his seat in November 1878 as MP for Huron Centre. He was knighted in March 1879.

power on that policy, the vast majority of this House were elected on that policy [of the National Policy and the tariff], and, true to their promises, true to their pledges and their principles, they had presented this tariff to Parliament, and the country had gratefully accepted what it considered a boon.

If there were any dissatisfaction in the country at all in the matter, it was they did not go far enough in the right direction. The hon. gentleman from Lambton [Mackenzie] generally argued logically, but sometimes his logic did not follow in easy sequence, for in one breath he stated that there was going to be an increase in prices in consequence of the tariff, and in another breath he said there was no improvement in the country at all, and that he believed more people were employed before the tariff was introduced than since.

But it was well known, that if prices rose on any article, that business became profitable, and more people were employed in it; and yet, the hon. gentleman in one breath, stated the prices had increased—therefore the profits had increased—and in the next breath he stated that the number of employés had decreased in every branch.

But the hon. gentleman had brought in Mr. Goldwin Smith. Now, Mr. Smith was no ally of his (Sir John A. Macdonald's), but he was a member of a celebrated club which, perhaps, the hon. member for Lambton had heard of—the Cobden Club—and he was a Free-trader, like the hon. gentleman. But there was a difference between them; one was a philosophical Cobdenite, and the other a fanatical Cobdenite.[*]

---

[*] Richard Cobden (1804–1865) promoted the idea of free trade in Britain in the 1840s as a route to social progress and regeneration, as well as to peace among nations. After his death, like-minded economic liberals founded a club in his name. (Hilton, *Mad, Bad People*, 240, 245, 636)

There was as great a distinction between the hon. member for Lambton and Mr. Goldwin Smith in that respect, as there was between John Stuart Mill [1806–1873] and the hon. member for Lambton. John Stuart Mill, the great exponent of political economy, pointed out that there might be disturbing causes which made Protection desirable. Goldwin Smith, in that letter, which the hon. gentleman had lugged in by the head and shoulders, said the same thing: that in this country, there were disturbing causes; that as it was a new country, and placed on the ragged edge of this continent—he did not know as that was the phrase—that they suffered a good deal by being excluded from the American market, while the Americans could come in and kill any particular industry whenever they liked; and in that letter he announced that the country was suffering from the causes which John Stuart Mill, in his celebrated work, said justified Protection.

SEVERAL HON. MEMBERS: No, no.

SIR JOHN A. MACDONALD said yes; if the hon. gentleman could show that he was wrong, let him do so in his answer. He [Macdonald] affirmed that John Stuart Mill said there were cases when Protection was allowable, and that meant, he [Macdonald] supposed, protecting struggling industries against heavier capital and established industries.

Goldwin Smith said, in that letter, the same thing—neither more nor less. He began to think that the reason the hon. gentleman brought in that letter, was because Mr. Goldwin Smith, in the same letter, intimated that he thought this country ought to walk alone, that they ought to be either an independent people or a portion of the United States.

He (Sir John A. Macdonald) did not agree with him in that opinion, nor did the hon. member for Lambton [Mackenzie] agree with him either. On that point they both agreed that Goldwin Smith was wrong, but though he might be wrong on that point, he might still be a very good political economist.

It did not lie in the hon. gentleman's mouth [Mackenzie] to speak of Goldwin Smith as the ally of the present Government, when one of that hon gentleman's own colleagues in his Government, had written an essay, and boasted of it, in which he declared that Canada could never be prosperous until she was free from Great Britain.

That was the hon. member for Shefford [Lucius Seth Huntington], and when he was charged with it in this House, he drew himself up and said he did not write that letter as a politician or as a member of the House of Commons, but he did it as a mere literary man.

And so Mr. Goldwin Smith would say the same thing; he was a literary man, and not a politician, he had no responsibilities, he was not a member of Parliament. He had not constituency as the hon. member for Shefford [Huntington] had, when he made that independence speech, and yet the hon. gentleman tried to lug him in, in order to hit us over the shoulders. As long as that hon. gentleman was an opponent of the Government, prior to 1873, he was hail fellow well met with the hon. member for Lambton, they would sleep in the same political crib together, and the hon. gentleman did not then feel he could dispense with his assistance.

We could all remember how his variable letters—some, perhaps not very agreeable to himself personally,—were heralded and quoted with such unction by the hon. gentleman in attempting to hurt us. However, we could leave Mr. Goldwin

Smith to take care of himself, as he was quite able to reply to the attacks made upon him by the hon. member for Lambton.

MR. MACKENZIE: I made no attack upon him.

Macdonald continued his attack upon Mr. Mackenzie.

LAND, MONEY, AND THE
CANADIAN PACIFIC RAILWAY, 1881

HOUSE OF COMMONS,

OTTAWA, JANUARY 17

The lifting of economic gloom in the 1880s turned Macdonald's thoughts back to the great transcontinental railway. By June 1880 George Stephen (1829–1921), Canada's most visionary and successful businessman, had formed the Canadian Pacific Railway syndicate with his cousin Donald Alexander Smith—Macdonald's antagonist from the Pacific Scandal—and Scottish-born entrepreneur Duncan McIntyre (1834–1894). At first the CPR syndicate rejected the government's offer of a $20 million subsidy and 30-million-acre (12-million-hectare) land grant. In July, Macdonald went to London, seeking investors. He found some, but no deal emerged. He returned to the Stephen syndicate, grown more complex now with the addition of some European minority backing. Macdonald sent a triumphant cable to his colleagues: "Best terms can be got are twenty-five million cash and twenty-five million acres . . . Four colleagues concur. Hope you concur. Absolute secrecy. Answer quick. Telegraph Tilley. Sail next Thursday."[12]

The storm of protest that followed was international in scope. The debates in the House of Commons began in earnest when Charles Tupper, minister of railways and canals, introduced the bill for a second reading on January 14. The opposition was outraged that they had "heard nothing about it from the Government." They argued that government "disturb[ed]" the "administration of affairs" of business and that the railway should be placed in the hands of "a commercial company." They said the deal was unfair and monopolistic, and that not enough time had been allowed to consider other bids, such as the one hastily arranged in December 1880 by Sir William Pearce Howland (1811–1907), heading the "second syndicate" which offered to build the CPR for less money, less land, and fewer privileges.[13]

Macdonald's response was impassioned, angry and implacable. He began by reminding the House of the constitutional obligation to complete the CPR, of his government's efforts, of his successor's (Alexander Mackenzie's) lack of effort and of the government's right to conduct the business of the contract.

The Debates of the House of Commons, 4th Parliament, 3rd Session, record on January 17, 1881:

SIR JOHN A. MACDONALD: Well, Mr. Speaker [Hon. Joseph-Godéric Blanchet], Mr. Mackenzie told the hon. gentleman [his Liberal party member Edward Blake] that he had nothing to ask Parliament for, and it was after that, after he found he was going to get the sullen opposition of the hon. gentlemen, and that Cave of Adullam,* which the hon. gentleman had found behind his back, that he whipped Mr. Mackenzie into that statement [that he, Mackenzie, "had

---

* Macdonald is quoting John Bright (1811–1889), a British Radical. (*Oxford Dictionary of Quotations*, 82)

nothing to ask Parliament" in committing the Government to build the railroad from Esquimalt to Nanaimo.]* I cannot be mistaken. The circumstance is deeply impressed upon my mind. The Government I say, had every right to use all their exertions in order to relieve themselves and the country of the obligation of building this road, and the still greater obligation of running it.

Let any one consider for a moment what these obligations are, and how they press upon the Government. We see this in the Intercolonial and in every public work. Why, Sir, it is actually impossible, although my hon. friend has overcome many obstacles with regard to the Intercolonial Railway, for the Government to run that railroad satisfactorily. It is made a political cause of complaint in every way. The men that we put on the railroad from the porter upwards became civil servants. If one of these men is put on from any cause whatever, he is said to be a political hack. If he is removed it is said his removal was on account of his political opinions. If a cow is killed on the road a motion is made in respect to it by the member of the House, who has the owner's vote as support. The responsibility, the expense, the worry and the annoyance of a Government having charge of such a work, are such that for these causes alone it was considered advisable to get rid of the responsibility.

---

* In 1874 Edward Blake and other Liberal Party members clashed with their leader Prime Minister Alexander Mackenzie over British Columbia. Mackenzie, despite having criticized the terms on which the province entered Confederation, felt morally bound to meet them. The Pacific Scandal had scuttled the transcontinental railway promised the province by 1880, helping foment a secessionist movement. Mackenzie committed the federal government to building the Nanaimo-Esquimalt line and to completing a railway from the coast across the Rocky Mountains. (Creighton, *Old Chieftain*, 197; Ormsby, "Prime Minister Mackenzie," 148)

We have had enough evidence of that in this House. With respect to the question raised by my hon. friend from South Bruce [Alexander Shaw], I have the answer here. It is:

"We [Mackenzie said in an earlier debate] have never asked Parliament for the authority but merely communicate to Parliament this decision, and rely upon the House to support us in accepting the terms made through the intervention or mediation of Lord Carnarvon; and that support I do not doubt will be cheerfully accorded."

Well, Sir, we went to England, and though in England we occasionally saw what was going on in the Opposition.[*]

Oh, how frightened they were lest we should succeed, and cablegram after cablegram came to Canada informing the country, with an expression of regret, that we had miserably and wretchedly failed. They said it was an evidence of want of confidence of the people of England in the present Administration. How could any body of capitalists put any confidence or trust in a Government stained with the Pacific Railway scandal?

It was said that if another Government having greater purity of character, and greater ability, and possessing in a great degree the confidence of European capitalists who had undertaken the enterprise, the result would have been different. There were tears, crocodile tears, perhaps, dropped upon the unhappy fate of Canada in having such an incompetent and criminal Government that could, within nine years from the original transaction, carry out a beneficial arrangement by which it was

---

[*] Macdonald is most likely referring to his July 1880 trip to England to seek investors for a transcontinental railway. (Creighton, *Old Chieftain*, 295-9)

proposed to endeavour to get English capitalists to take their place and build the road.

However, Sir, we did. And in the speech at Hochelaga that I hear so much about, a speech that can hardly be dignified by the name of speech, I announced the fact that we had made the contract firm. I say so now. We made the contract firm. The occasion of my making that speech was upon my arrival at Hochelaga. I was presented with an address by Club Cartier, a Conservative institution, and I made that answer. I do not retract a word. I said: "As for the present I hope it will be equally true, and for the future that I may be able to look down by-and-bye on the Pacific Railway as completed," and I hoped it would be done with the assistance of hon. gentlemen opposite as long as we were in the Government, but the project that has been laid on the Table to-day, shows that they have abandoned all idea of ever building the Canadian Pacific Railway.

By a political plot they are trying to put off the blame upon others; but notwithstanding that plot we are going to build that road, and the original treaty will be carried out.

The pledge made to British Columbia, the pledges made in reference to the future of this Dominion will be carried out under the auspices of a Conservative Government, and with the support of a Conservative party.

That road will be constructed, and, notwithstanding all the wiles of the Opposition and the flimsy arrangement which has been concocted, the road is going to be built and proceeded with vigorously, continuously, systematically and successfully to a completion, and the fate of Canada will then, as a Dominion, be sealed. Then will the fate of Canada, as one great body, be fixed beyond the possibility of hon. gentlemen to unsettle. The emigrant from Europe will find here a happy and comfortable home in the great West, by the exertion of the Conservative party.

But then, Sir, comes the interjection. After the arrangements have been made and the Government had made a contract that hon. gentlemen opposite three or four years ago would have laughed at and bragged and boasted of as a wonderful proof of their superior administrative ability—we now have the assertion that the contract was made without due authority.

As long as Mordecai sits at the King's gate he will protest. We have had to take part in this discussion with gentlemen who are accomplished actors—my hon. friends opposite. These hon. gentlemen are perfectly trained histrionics. But, Sir, the best actor is not always successful. We have had tragedy, comedy and farce from the other side.

Sir, it commenced with tragedy. The contract was declared oppressive, and the amount of money to be given was enormous. We were giving away the whole lands of the North-West. Not an acre was to be left for the free and independent foot of the free and independent settler. There was to be a monopoly handed over to this Company.* We had painted the tyranny of this Company that was to over-ride the people by raising a high tariff, and the tyranny of a great monopoly which was to keep in their control a large area of lands—out of which they expect to build this railway—for some hundreds of years, in order that through the exertions of others the value of their acreage might be increased, and this was the tragedy;

---

* The contract with the Stephen syndicate did include a so-called monopoly clause: "For twenty years from the date hereof, no line of railway shall be authorized by the Dominion Parliament to be constructed south of the Canadian Pacific Railway, except such line as shall run south-west, or to the westward of south-west; nor to within fifteen miles of latitude forty-nine." (Creighton, *Old Chieftain*, 303)

and hon. gentlemen opposite played it so well, that if they did not affect the whole audience, we could see tears of pity and sorrow trickling down the cheeks of gentlemen sitting on that side of the House.

Then, Sir, we had the comedy. The comedy was that when every one of the speeches of these hon. gentlemen were read to them, it was proved that last year or the year before, and in previous years, they had thought one way, and that now they spoke in another way. Then it was the most amusing and comic thing in the world. Every hon. gentleman got up and said,

> "I am not bound by that. It is true that I said so a year ago, or it is true that I said so two years ago, but circumstances alter cases, circumstances are changed in two years, or one year, or in eight months in one case, [by] what I said eight months ago I am not bound now."

This was very comic. It amused us all. It amused the House, and the whole country chuckled on a broad grin. These hon. gentlemen said it is true, we were fools eight months ago, and two years ago; but, because we were fools in the past you have no right, being Ministers, to be fools too; you have no right to advocate the follies we advocated then, when now we assert acts of wisdom on our part. This was the comedy.

Now, Sir, the last thing that came was the farce. We had the farce laid on the Table to-day. The tragedy and comedy were pretty successful; but the farce I am afraid, with an impartial audience, in theatrical phrase, will be damned. It is a farce, but still whether it will be farcical in its consequence, I do not know. I do not think, for my part, that it will be farcical in its consequences, because the greatest punishment that a farce writer or a farce actor can get when he has played his farce, is that his farce is unsuccessful, and the audience hisses the act, and this will be the consequence of this charming farce.

It has been played to change the metaphor, Mr. Speaker, I may say it is too thin. It won't catch the blindest. It won't catch the most credulous. It won't catch the most unsuspicious. No one of common sense, no man who can say two and two make four will be caught for one moment by this flimsy scheme, Mr. Speaker. It was concocted here. It was concocted in Ottawa. It was concocted as a political engine, the reason of it was this: Well, the present Government have committed themselves under their hand and seal, and here is the seal of the Minister of Railways, and here is the Order in Council, and here is the contract signed, sealed and delivered. The Government are pledged to it. They cannot get out of it, and we are quite safe. We [the opposition] can make any offer. We can make an offer to build the road for $1,000 a mile. We are quite safe. We can get all these gentlemen to sign, and I think, although I was not here at the time, that my hon. friend from Niagara [Josiah Burr Plumb] showed that the incorporators and petitioners themselves, who make the offer, under this precious document, seven or six—

MR. [JOSIAH] PLUMB: The number is seven.

SIR JOHN A. MACDONALD: Seven of them were disappointed and defeated candidates at former elections. I need not go over their names. I read the speech of my hon. friend, and I find that it is a political plot. I would ask my hon. friend, the member for the West Riding of Durham, (Edward Blake) if John Walker is not a rather remarkable politician. I would ask my hon. friend if H. H. Cook is not also a remarkable politician, and so on, Mr. Speaker. It is a political plot got up here. It was quite easy, oh, so easy to make an offer knowing that the Government cannot, or ought not, or will not accept it.

We [Macdonald's government] made a bargain with a company in good faith, and we promised that it shall be a compact between the Dominion of Canada and them, provided that the Parliament ratifies it. We were bound to submit the agreement to Parliament for ratification, and there it was argued. The Opposition say to themselves:

> "The Government cannot in honor, cannot in decency, if their policy is defeated, remain in office, and, therefore, we will get in, and we will take care of our friends, of these seven or eight political gentlemen and their confreres. We will make things easy for them, and so arrange it that, even if their offer was accepted by us when we go into office, we can let them out of it."

I say that that document shows on its face that it was drawn up here, and for the purpose of removing from these gentlemen apprehension that by any possibility they could get into any scrape, because, on the face of the papers, there is a series of clauses providing that the Government can let them out of it. These hon. gentlemen have made up their minds that we must go, they have made up their minds that we could not respectably remain in office. They said:

> "Well, our sentiments are known; everybody knows what we think about the construction of the Canadian Pacific Railway, and what we will do, and what our

policy is, and what, when we get in, we will carry out, and that is, to let you out of building all the difficult parts of the road."

It is a game all on one side, Sir, but it is too thin. It is in vain for the fowler to spread the net in the eyes of a bird. We must be blind as bats, and the country must be blind as owls in the day, if they do not see that there is a net, and they will avoid the net. They will not be caught by it. No web in the net is going to catch the intelligent community with these papers before them.

Sir, these hon. gentlemen had better have dealt with this matter in general; they could have said other people are ready to make a contract. If they had said in their places, they knew of their own knowledge that certain people were ready to come forward and build the railway for a small sum; then, Sir, some persons, who would not see that it was merely a flank movement to obstruct the formation of the Company, and to obstruct the organization of the Company, and to delay and postpone the construction of the road, might have had their faith shaken, but no man, be he ever so simple, who is fit to be elected to this House, can read else on these papers than that it is a political trick, and a discreditable trick, as I said before, that will redound permanently to the discredit and dishonor of all those who have concocted it, and of all those who have joined it.

I do not believe that the hon. member for the West Riding of Durham (Edward Blake) will get up in his place and advise this Government or this House to accept the proposition of this second Syndicate. I say I defy him to get up and do so. I know he will not give such advice, I will not believe all he has said, and believe all that those who have spoken from that side of the

House have urged respecting the first Syndicate, by advising this House to accept the responsibility of voting for the proposition which has been made by the second Syndicate. These hon. gentlemen cannot do it.

What have they told us, Sir? That this proposition was illegal. The hon. member for Gloucester [Timothy Warren Anglin] told us it was illegal and unconstitutional for the Government to have made this arrangement with the first Syndicate, and how can he vote to give the contract to this second Syndicate? The hon. member for North Norfolk [John Charlton] has told us that some portions of this arrangement are a swindle. Yet those very clauses which he said were a swindle are incorporated in the proposals of the new Syndicate. Those very clauses which the hon. gentleman so eloquently, but rather unparliamentarily, denounced as a swindle and a fraud, he will find here, with the two exceptions. Let me first look over some of these clauses. In the first place our terms were said to be excessive. In comparison with the terms of the present bogus tender there might be a pretence for assuming that. In the next place it was said that we had no right to contract except upon tenders given in reply to an advertisement. But this is the point to which I will call the attention of the hon. member for North Norfolk. The manner of selecting the lands under our proposal was said by him to be a swindle, a fraud and a robbery. Yet these gentlemen, Sir W. P. Howland and Company, say that they must be allowed to perpetrate that swindle and carry out that fraud or they will not undertake the contract. Surely, this being the case, the hon. gentleman will not vote for the second Syndicate.

AN HON. MEMBER: He will do anything.

SIR JOHN A. MACDONALD: Then it was said:

> "Oh, the Government is going to build the road from
> Thunder Bay to Red River; from Kamloops to Yale,
> and from Yale to Port Moody. Why the Government
> will become a partner with the Syndicate, that will
> never do."

Gentlemen who used that argument cannot vote for the new
Syndicate. Then there was an argument used that the scheme
for issuing bonds was wrong, that the contractors would issue
the bonds and leave the bondholders to whistle for their money,
and the people of Canada to whistle for their road. Yet the general principle for the issue of bonds is adopted in the proposal
of Sir W. P. Howland and Company. Then Mr. Speaker, there
was a great grumble at the smallness of the deposit. The offer
is a million of dollars. That is the offer made by the gentlemen of the new Syndicate. I have learned from my hon. friend
since I came into the House that the new Syndicate gentlemen
thought they could go one more—to use the language of my
good friend Mr. H. H. Cook—and they have sent down cer-
tificates to the extent of twelve or thirteen hundred dollars.

SOME HON. MEMBERS: Oh, oh.

SIR JOHN A. MACDONALD: Hon. gentlemen opposite
must not be unparliamentary. I am speaking at some disadvantage, because I am not well, but I will make myself heard.

The proposition just laid on the Table of the House is
that the members of the new Syndicate shall make a deposit
of a million of dollars. I understand that they have sent a

communication by telegraph stating that they have deposited $1,200,000 as security; that when the contract is signed they will deposit the million dollars permanently. Well, Sir, this is a small trick to put up $200,000 over the million, and yet if you look at the contract lying on your Table you will see that the Syndicate have to put up the whole of $5,000,000 by the 1st May, 1882.

MR. [TIMOTHY] ANGLIN: No, no.

SIR JOHN A. MACDONALD: I beg not to be interrupted again. I think that an old speaker ought to know something about decencies of debate.

AN HON. MEMBER: The 1st of December, 1882.

SIR JOHN A. MACDONALD: They are to put $1,000,000 to remain permanently in the hands of the Government. They are to put up the other $4,000,000 by the 1st December, 1882— and that is a sufficient security to the country and to this House that the Syndicate will not find it to its advantage to sell the bonds and then abandon the work. The proposition that they would do so is so absurd, so discreditable to those who make it, that it is almost unworthy of notice.

But, Sir, before I call the attention of the House to the new Syndicate, and show what a complete farce it is—and I do not use a word too strong when I describe it as farcical—I would say that when I intended to speak on Friday* it was simply to state that

---

* Macdonald had been suffering ill health since Parliament had begun in early December 1880 and his doctor recommended he miss the opening ceremonies; he had still been ill after the Christmas break. (Creighton, *Old Chieftain*, 305)

the Government, as a Government, feels itself bound to carry out the contract it has entered into, in good faith, and that it has a right to challenge, and does challenge the vote of this House.

They believe it is the best offer that has been made up to that time. They believe it is one which will be satisfactory to the country.

We believe it is one that will not involve ultimately the expenditure of sixpence by the people of Canada. We believe it will carry out that for which it was intended; that we should carry out the early construction of the railway; and, we are bound to ask, on its own merits and without reference to any attempted obstruction at the eleventh hour, by the bringing out of bogus tenders—and I use the word bogus, notwithstanding the respectability of some of the gentlemen who have signed it—that the contract be adopted and the road built according to the wishes of the people and Parliament of Canada.

It is not constitutional, and I would not say for a moment or hold any threatening language to the House, indicative of what course the Government ought to take, or would take in the matter, if, when they have submitted their best judgment, which becomes a portion of their policy, it were not adopted. But all I can say is, to use an expression which has been rather celebrated in Canada, that I think we should find and be told by hon. gentlemen opposite—and this document is probably prepared for the purpose of giving them the opportunity—that our usefulness was gone.

The hon. gentlemen opposite have not hidden their lights under a bushel; their words have not been spoken in a corner. We knew the governing policy of the Opposition, enunciated on several occasions, and repeated in this House, during the present Session, by the leader of the Opposition. We know he is opposed to the building of the road through British Columbia; that he has, from the time the subject was brought before Parliament, protested against it, using such language to that Province as—erring sister depart in peace.

We know he has ridiculed the idea of forcing a railroad through an inhospitable region, a sea of mountains, that would get no traffic, but be built at an enormous expense and be of no real value.

The hon. gentleman has adhered to that policy. Last Session he moved that the further construction of the road through British Columbia, in allusion to the contract given out by the present Government under advertisements published by the late Government, and for the purpose of carrying out its policy, be postponed, as also all action with that object; and I express my regret at the unavoidable absence of my hon. friend from Lambton [Alexander Mackenzie] on this occasion.

But great as I regret that, I still more greatly regretted his humiliation at the time last Session when the hon. gentleman's motion was in your hands. If I were his worst enemy, and wished to triumph over him, I would not desire a greater humiliation, a sorrier fate, or a more wretched ending of a statesman than that, at the whip of the man who had deposed him—of the man who had removed and supplanted him—he should be obliged to eat his own words and vote in favour of postponing the construction of the road through British Columbia—that he should have to belie—I use not the word in an offensive sense—his own advertisement and all the action of his Government in asking for tenders for the building of that road.

What did that advertisement mean and the calling for tenders? Was it a sham, a fraud—assuming, like those who did not know, that the hon. gentleman went down to the depths of degradation, to use that argument himself, and say that he did not mean anything by that advertisement, but merely wished to ascertain the probable cost of the work? Because it was stated in this House that that was the object of issuing the advertisement so that contractors were called upon to come from not only all parts of the Dominion, but San Francisco, the United States, England and the world to consider this matter, and they were to go over the whole ground with their surveyors and engineers, make their surveys and estimates at the greatest trouble and expense in order to ascertain the character of the work, and that the Canadian Government might be able to say to them afterwards,

> "Gentlemen we are very much obliged to you for the information you have given us, gathered at your expense and not at that of the public."

Not one of the gentlemen of the late Government could have done that, I am sure, or have said that the advertisement was not *bona fide*, was not for the purpose of giving out the work, otherwise it was a mockery, a delusion and a snare, an injury to every man put to expense in connection with it and to all the professional men and capitalists of the world. I must say the policy of the leader of the Opposition was avowed and expressed.

In the first place his policy as a Minister would be to stop all the work in British Columbia—not a mile would be built—not a train would ever run through British Columbia if he could help it. Not an article of trade or commerce would pass over a line through that Province to the East if he had his will, and that Province would be compelled to appeal to the paramount power, to the justice of the British Government and Parliament, where justice is always rendered, to relieve her from connection with a people so devoid of honor, so devoid of character, so unworthy of a place among the nations, and let her renew her immediate connection with Her Majesty's Government, which would see that justice was done to that long suffering people. That was the policy of the leader of the Opposition with regard to the West.

Now, his policy with regard to the East, was hostile to the construction of the road north of Lake Superior. He avows his predilection for the Sault Ste. Marie line, to run off the trade into the United States, to strengthen, to renew, to extend and develop our commerce with the United States, to the utter destruction of the great plan, basis and policy of the Dominion, which is to connect the great counties composing the Dominion from sea to sea by one vast iron chain, which cannot and will never be broken. With our common feelings of loyalty and allegiance to our common sovereign, influenced by all the principles which actuate British subjects to desire to live and die under the British Crown, we should have in favour of this means of connection the pecuniary interests of British Columbia, inclining them to unite more firmly to the rest of the Dominion, all of the Provinces thus becoming one country in principle, loyalty and interest.

That was the policy of hon. gentlemen, and it was supported, and would be supported, by the whole party. It was supported by their organ also. I do not often read it, for I do not think it very wholesome reading, but I am told it now goes in strongly for the Sault Ste. Marie road. Yet we all remember, for I have heard it read many a time, the manner in which that organ in days of old denounced the building of the Sault road as traitorous to the best interests of Canada, and destructive to the future of the Dominion—as calculated to unite as willy-nilly with the States, by a commercial connection, which must be followed by a political connection a little later. Times changed, and I am told that organ strongly supports the hon. leader of the Opposition just as strong as some years ago it vigorously, and in a loyal British sense, opposed him. Other men govern that paper now, and if the chief man who conducted that paper were now living, I do not believe he would so belie his whole life and all his interests as to surround a great connecting principle which, whatever might be the subjects of contention across the floor, kept him always united with the party of which I am a humble member, always united in defending British interest, in defending monarchical institutions, and in trying as far as possible to keep us a free and independent people of all external relations with any country in the world except our grand old Mother Country of England.

Now it is quite clear that this document was prepared here for a political use. I would only call the attention of the House to a very few variations which are made in this contract from the contract that we laid on the Table, and you will see that it is prepared for the express object of enabling the most timid man—including Sir William P. Howland, who would not risk $5,000 unless he were certain of getting it again—it is drawn for the purpose of enabling the most timid man to sign this document, knowing that he was safe. It was—heads, I win; tails, you lose. Those who connected themselves with this expected that the present Government must and would adhere to the first contract, and, therefore, a new Government would take its place, and my hon. friend would take the place which I now unworthily occupy—a place which his individual ability and individual zeal and exertions for his party would enable him to adorn. They knew what his policy would be. He has declared it so recently that I do not think he can change it. To be sure he can change between 1880 and 1881, but then, in this case, the change would be so rapid that even my hon. friend's versatility of talent would not allow him to change so speedily as that.

Well, I come to the new offer, and what is the first proposition?

"The Company also hereby offers, in the event of the Government desiring to withdraw from the proposed construction of the eastern section, that the Company shall reduce the said subsidy in money and land by the amount apportioned by the said eastern section of the railway under the 9th paragraph of this proposal."

Now, the gentlemen who made that tender did not intend to build the Lake Superior section, because they believed that the present Government would insist upon the Lake Superior section being built. They hoped we would be defeated by the proffer of the second Syndicate, and that the hon. gentlemen opposite would come in, and in that event of the Government desiring to withdraw from the proposed construction, they would do it for so much less. They had the previously pledged policy of the hon. gentleman that he would withdraw it. Therefore they were preparing in advance, and these other three clauses, convince me, and will convince every man, that this was politically drawn, that this was a political plot, and that these men—some of more means, some of less, and some of none at all—could not by any possibility run a chance of forfeiting a single sixpence, either by building the Lake Superior section or running it for ten years afterwards. The next section is as follows:

"In the event of the Government desiring to withdraw
the said eastern section from construction hereafter, the
Company hereby offers to construct within three years,
and equip, own and operate as a part of the Canada
Pacific Railway, a branch line from South East Bay,
Lake Nipissing, to Sault Ste. Marie."

The other section likewise, they were put in the tender which
the hon. gentleman opposite would accept, for the purpose of
building under this contract, if they get it, the Sault Ste. Marie
road and throw over the Lake Superior section. It is so clear that
he who runs may read.

Now, Sir, the 21st clause, this relates to my constituency and
the Province which I represent, and I call the attention to it of
my hon. colleague in the representation of Victoria:

"In the event of the Government desiring to postpone
or withdraw from the construction of the western section of the said railway, extending from Kamloops to
Port Moody, they shall be at liberty to do so at and for
a sum of $3,500,000."

There it is again, no chance for a road running towards the sea
to Yale. The hon. gentleman is against a mile of railway being
built in British Columbia, and how gladly he would receive
those gentlemen whenever they came to say:

"Well, you don't want to press us to build this, to go
on with that now"; and the hon. gentleman would say:
"No, we are too glad to get rid of it." The last clause
reads thus: "In the event of the Government desiring

to postpone or withdraw from construction, by the
Company hereunder, of the westerly portion of the
central section of said railway—"

That is to say, the first contract is to build from Kamloops down
to Emory's Bar, that is under contract now; but the remaining
450 miles, from Kamloops through the Rocky Mountains to
Jasper House, is the roughest of any portion of the country:—

"Being the westerly 450 miles thereof, as mentioned in
the 9th clause of this proposal, the Company offers to
reduce the subsidy in money and land by the amount
apportioned to the said 450 miles."

That is, the first clause does away with Lake Superior section,
the second clause provides for the building of the Sault Ste.
Marie road, the third clause provides that the Government
may give up the building of the line from Emory's Bar to Port
Moody, and the fourth section gives up the building of anything West of Jasper House.

Now, Mr. Speaker, it is the policy of the Government to
build all these sections; it is the pledged policy of the Opposition
to wipe them out. It is the pledged policy of the Opposition.
They cannot go back on their pledged policy. It is in fact a
tender for the prairie section of the road, the paying section, the
easiest section, the cheapest section, the most profitable section,
the section that will be built not only inexpensively, but that
will pay whenever population comes in, and population will
follow the building of the road. And this whole scheme which
was ostensibly to assume the responsibility of building and running the whole line from Lake Nipissing to the Pacific Ocean, is

simply an impudent offer to build the prairie section, and to do it by means of political friends, who, when they get in power, will grant them all they want, and allow them to confine their exertions, their responsibilities, and all the liabilities for the future; to building an easy road across the prairies, and so connecting with the American system of railways, and carrying away the trade of the North-West by one or more American channels, to the utter ruin of the great policy under which the Dominion of Canada has been created, to the utter ruin of our hopes of being a great nation, and to the ruin of our prospect of getting possession of the Pacific trade, and connecting Asia with England by a railway passing through the dominions of England. It is as easy as rolling off a log to run a railway across the prairies and work it; but this is an endeavour to deprive this country, to deprive Ontario, to deprive Quebec, to deprive the Maritime Provinces of all connection by railway with the North-West.

MR. ANGLIN: Hear, hear.

SIR JOHN A. MACDONALD: The hon. gentleman says "Hear, hear." Yes; I am proud to say that if our scheme is carried out, the steamer landing at Halifax will discharge its freight and emigrants upon a British railway, which will go through Quebec, and through Ontario to the Far West, on British territory, under the British flag, under Canadian laws, and without any chance of either the immigrant being deluded or seduced from his allegiance or his proposed residence in Canada, or the traffic coming from England or from Asia being subjected to the possible prohibitory or offensive restrictive taxation or customs regulations of a foreign power.

So that it is quite clear that these gentlemen are safe—safe as a cherry. They would be under no obligations to build the very expensive portions of the road. They would be relieved from running any portion of the road that would not pay. Canada might whistle for those connections in her own territory, but the people would gradually see that the colonies would gradually be severed from each other; that we should become a bundle of sticks, as we were before, without a binding cord, and that we should fall, helpless, powerless, and aimless, into the hands of the neighbouring Republic. Let us consider what this offer is. These gentlemen are going to build the prairie road for $7,333 a mile, against our $10,000, and they make a corresponding reduction in the quantity of land. But you must remember that if there is a reduction in the quantity of land, that land will lie right alongside the railway on the prairie. They will get all the land where it is most valuable. It has been variously calculated as worth $5, $4, $3, $2, and $1, but it is quite clear that if the prairie section only is to be built, all the land will be taken from the immediate vicinity of the railway, while if the whole is built, much of the land will be taken far away from the railway at diminished value. George Stephen & Co. must take the land where they can get it. They can only get some 11,000,000 acres from Winnipeg to Jasper House, and the remainder of the 25,000,000 acres they must find elsewhere.

In order to make it worth a dollar—worth anything at all, they must build branch railways to those points, and this House and country would be only too glad to give them this permission, in order that they might open up other sections of country far away from the main line of the railway. But we have the testimony of hon. gentlemen opposite as to what, according to them, the lands in the vicinity of the railway are worth.

The railway will run through the most fertile portion of the land, and still further increase their value, so that the profit to be gained in building the prairie section of the railway out of the lands in the immediate vicinity of the railway which are to be handed over to the new Syndicate, is a much larger profit than all the 25,000,000 will give to a company bound to build the whole line from Lake Nipissing to the Pacific. So it was a very, very safe bargain to make.

There is a little point of difference between these two tenders, to which I cannot refrain from calling the attention of the House. I have already stated that, in going over this second offer, I find they have just cut out of the printed paper most of the clauses of the contract and the schedule, but reducing the price.

But there are some changes, and there is a change of one little word, to which I think, I ought to call the attention of the House. We all remember the discussion between my hon. friend from Lincoln (Mr. [John Charles] Rykert) and the hon. leader of the Opposition upon the question whether there was any power which could force the railway company to construct the railway, and my hon. friend (Mr. Rykert) quoted the Court of Chancery. I stated that if it was merely a permissive contract, it could not, of course, be enforced. The only consequence of a permissive contract not being carried out, would be that either the charter might be cancelled by Parliament, if that was the law, or there might be an action for damages, by way of compensation. But if there was a statutory obligation, if it was not merely permissive but obligatory, not merely a contract between parties but an obligatory statutory obligation, it became a statutory duty imposed by Parliament with a paramount power upon the individual, and if that duty was imposed, it could be enforced by a mandamus. That is my statement. Well, the second clause of the contract made by us is followed, word for word, I may say, except striking out the words "hereby contracted for"—hereby tendered for, they mean of course. It provides that "the contractors immediately after the organization of the Company, will deposit with the Government $1,000,000 in cash or approved securities."

There was an obligation we were told, that they "shall" do it, that they must do it. When I came to the clause about building the road, the word "shall" in the contract that we made, is struck out and the word "will" put in. The parliamentary statutory obligation to pay the money was left, but when we come to the clause saying they shall build the road, the word "shall" is struck out and the word "will" substituted. The word "will" is merely an expression of intention, and the only consequence, if this is carried out, is that the subsequent part of the contract will be inoperative, because it says that on condition of the promise, the Government agree to make certain payments. So if the promise be not carried out, the payments will not be made.

If the word shall is good for "shall deposit," it is good for "shall build," yet it is left in for the deposit and struck out for the road. There must be an object in that; that is a statutory obligation which imposes that duty which the Government of the day can force as it can force all duties thrown on Parliament on the subject. I had forgotten a paper that is placed in my hands to which I shall call your attention. I spoke about the value of the land along the prairie section which, of course, must be of more value than the land which the whole Syndicate would have to take for their additional burden and their additional responsibility along the whole line of railway. We will take the Canadian section. Now, this is the statement based on the new proposal. We will value the land grant for the prairie section at $1.00 an acre, and that everybody must admit is absurdly low.—

MR. [DAVID] MILLS: Hear, hear.

SIR JOHN A. MACDONALD: Yes, it is absurdly low for the land laying twenty-four miles on each side of the prairie section; it must be worth more, when the railway is built, than a dollar an acre. The cash subsidy, 900 miles at $733.33 per mile will be $6,000,000, and the land grant, 10,000 per mile for 900 miles at $1 per acre, will be $9,000,000, making in all, for building the prairie section, at $1 an acre, $15,600,000. If you take the land at $2 an acre, and that is far too low by the estimates of the hon. gentleman opposite, the cash subsidy of the land grant at $2 an acre will make in all $24,600,000. Value the land at $3.18 an acre and it will be worth $28,620,000, making in all, cash and land, $35,220,000, so that for building the prairie section, the cheap section, the easy section, the section which can be run at a profit—at $1 an acre, they will get $17,333.33 per mile; at $2 an acre, they will get $27,333.33 a mile, and $3.18 an acre they will get $39,133 a mile. And this price would be given by hon. gentlemen opposite who say that that section can be built at $8,110 per mile.

SIR ALBERT J. SMITH: How much would they get on your proposition?

SIR JOHN A. MACDONALD: Now, when the House was discussing the sub-division and subsidy, it was alleged that there was a disproportionate sum given to Messrs. Stephen & Co., and this offer was meant to make the public believe that the sum was excessive. I have shown you, that believing as everybody must who looks at this offer, that it is only intended to build the prairie section, the whole thing will vary from $17,000 to $39,000 per mile, according to the various estimates per mile. That is for the prairie section alone. The reason why the sum was put large and full in the original contract for the prairie section, was because that section must be built, first and speedily. That is the portion that can only be built first, and until that is built the population which we believe will readily and eagerly seek shelter and homes in our North-West, cannot get there. It was of the very greatest consequence to the Government that this road should be built at once. This large subsidy was, therefore, given for the prairie section as an inducement for the contractors to push that road there within three years, which they stated they were quite ready to do that, if they got the contract ratified by the 1st of January, and they will build that as shortly after that time as possible. It makes no difference if the security is good; if the capital is in the hands of gentlemen of honor and means, it is of no consequence where the money is expended. The division is made for the purpose of hurrying up the 1,000 miles across the fertile prairies of the North-West, so as to enable the population to go in at once. And, Sir, you must remember they can get no lands near Lake Superior nor in British Columbia, which had been described by hon. gentlemen opposite as value-less, that Province being a "sea of mountains." Therefore all the land to be given is concentrated in the prairie country, and we endeavour to induce them to build the road and as many branches as possible by grants in that region. The great object was not only to have the line running from east to west, but to assign the Company lands to be selected by the joint action of the Government and themselves. To encourage them to build branches, we give them a large and valuable allowance, so that that whole country may not only be opened up east and west, but be penetrated by herring-bone lines running northward and southward far into the interior.

I hear a voice behind me saying that they are to build the Lake Superior section at the same time. We took good care of that. I believe that the men who signed the first contract are men of honor and great wealth, who cannot afford to lose their character, prestige and credit in the markets of the world by breaking a contract. But we felt we had no right to take their word for it, and therefore stipulated in the contract that the Government commence from the beginning of the Canadian Pacific line, possibly at Callandar Station, and proceed vigorously and continuously, and in such a manner that the annual progress shall not secure completion at the end of ten years but shall be such as to show the Government that the Lake Superior road could be finished in ten years. You must remember that this is one contract, and not a separable contract, to build the eastern or the western section. It is a contract to build both, and if the Company failed in performing their contract in carrying out their obligations as to the Lake Superior road, or the prairie road, they have no right to claim a subsidy in land or money because of having done so much work on the prairie section. If they fail on one section, although they may have built twice the number of miles that they promised across the prairie, and may have finished them to our thorough satisfaction, when they come to demand the land and the money, if they have not worked vigorously and continuously on the Lake Superior section, achieving a rate of annual progress, assuring us that it will be finished within the proper time, then we shall say:

"No you don't—you shall not have this money; true, you have built the prairie section, but you have failed at other parts of the road which must go on *pari passu*, and we will not give you a dollar or an acre, because, though you have done the full amount on the prairies, you have made a failure to a great extent elsewhere."

In order to make a great flourish on the new sections or proposals, the opponents of the old scheme have struck out the 15th clause as follows:—

"For 20 years from the date hereof, no line of railway shall be authorized by the Dominion Parliament to be constructed South of the Canadian Pacific Railway, from any point at or near the Canadian Pacific Railway except such line as shall run South West or to the Westward of South West; nor to within fifteen miles of Latitude 49. And in the establishment of any new Province in the North-West Territories, provisions shall be made for continuing such prohibition after such establishment until the expiration of the said period."

That was a clause put in deliberately for the same reason that we asked Parliament to build the Canadian Pacific at all. We desire, the country desires, that the road, when built, should be a Canadian road; the main channel for Canadian traffic for the carriage of the treasures and traffic of the west to the seaboard through Canada. So far as we can, we shall not allow it to be built for the benefit of the United States lines. Why a train starting from the foot of the Rocky Mountains—and I am glad to know perhaps one of the most fertile, if not the most fertile section, lies directly at the eastern slope of the Rocky Mountains—with freight from British Columbia for the east, we desire to keep on our own railroad as long as we legitimately can. We believe it will carry freight as cheaply and satisfy the wants of the country as fairly as any American railway.

But, Sir, we desire to have the trade kept on our own side—that not one of the trains that passes over the Canadian Pacific Railway will run into the United States if we can help it, but may, instead, pass through our own country, that we may build up Montreal, Quebec, Toronto, Halifax and St. John by means of one great Canadian line, carrying as much traffic as possible by the course of trade through our own country. I do not mean to say we can prevent cheaper channels being opened. There is nothing to prevent other railroads running across the continent through our own country. Our Dominion is as big as all Europe, and we might as well say that the railways running from Paris to Moscow might supply the wants of all Europe as that this railway might supply the wants of the whole North-West. There will be room for as many railways in that country by-and-bye as there are in Europe; and if there be any attempt—the attempt would be futile—on the part of the Canadian Pacific Railway to impose excessive prices and rates, it is folly that would soon be exposed by the construction of rival lines east and west, which would open up our country in all directions and prove amply sufficient to prevent the possibility of a monopoly which has been made such a bugbear of by hon. gentlemen opposite. I was going to say that a train starting from the foot of the Rocky Mountains might obtain connections by a line running through in a south-easterly direction with roads in the United States. The hon. gentleman says it is only for 20 years; but I was going to say, that a train starting from the foot of the Rocky Mountains, might be bled by a line from any southerly direction connected with the United States, and so much traffic will be carried off to the United States; and a few miles further another line might connect with another American line, and so on, Sir, until long before we got to Winnipeg or Red River the main portion of the trade would be carried off from our line into American channels. That magnificent river, the Rhine, starting with pride from its source, runs through the finest portions of Europe, and yet has a miserable, wretched end, being lost in the sands as it approaches the sea; and such would be the fate of the Canadian Pacific Railway if we allowed it to be bled by subsidiary lines, feeding foreign railways, adding to foreign wealth and increasing foreign revenue by carrying off our trade until, before we arrived at the terminal points in Ontario, and at Montreal, it would be so depleted that it would almost die of inanition. No men in their senses would undertake to build the 450 miles through that stern country to the north of Lake Superior and run it for ten long years, when they knew that unless there was some check placed upon those lines, not a pound of freight would go to the North-West, but it would almost all go to the United States. Some of it would come to us, but the great portion of the trade would go through the United States by the favored line of hon. gentlemen opposite, without any hope of getting it back to Canada at Sault Ste. Marie. Sir, we know what a great amount, what an enormous amount of capital American capitalists possess who are connected with the railways of the United States. We have seen evidences of the mad rivalry which has existed occasionally between some great railway lines of that country. We have seen them run railways at ruinous rates, in the hope of breaking each other down.

Sir, with our road, backed by a country of scarcely 4,000,000, with our infant country and with our infant capitalists, what chances would they have against the whole of the United States capitalists? What chance would they have? The Americans would offer to carry freight for nothing and aye to pay shippers for sending freight that way. It would not all come by Sault Ste. Marie. It would come to Duluth. It would come to Chicago. It would come through a hundred different channels. It would percolate through the United States, to New York and Boston, and to the other ports, and, Sir, after our railway was proved to be useless, they might, perhaps, come into the market and buy up our line as they have bought up other lines.

Railway and telegraph lines are under no protection from foreign capitalists coming in and buying them up, getting control of our markets, and cutting us off from the trade which should come from the great West and by Canadian railways to the River St. Lawrence. They could afford for a series of years with their enormous wealth, with their enormous capital, exceeding the revenue of many, many first-class Governments in Europe, to put their rates for freight down to such a figure as would ruin our road, as would ruin the contractors, as would ruin the Company, and render them utterly impossible to continue in competition, and, Sir, what can be more wretched, or more miserable, in any country, than an insolvent railway. What could be more wretched and miserable and destructive to the future of a country than the offering on the market of the stock of insolvent railways?

They cannot supply, they cannot renew the rails, they cannot maintain the road-bed in repair, they cannot keep the line supplied with railway stock. Sir, the road would become shrunken, shrunken, shrunken until it fell an easy prey to this ring. We cannot afford to run such a risk. We saw what a wheat ring did in Chicago. They raised the price of the necessaries of life,—the ring in Chicago raised the price of the poor man's loaf for a whole year in order to make a profit at the expense of the laboring poor of Europe, and of all the rest of the world, and a similar combination, but infinitely richer, with infinitely more capital, and infinitely more unscrupulous—and no men are so unscrupulous and so reckless, and are proven to be so unscrupulous and reckless, as the railway speculators and proprietors in the United States—would be found in this case.

Sir, it was essentially as a matter of precaution, a matter of necessity, and a matter of self-defence, that we provided that this road should not be depleted of its traffic in the manner which I have mentioned.

That road shall be allowed fair play for twenty years from now, and only ten years after construction; and that it should be protected from the chance of being robbed of all the profits, robbed of all the gain, the legitimate gain, which the Company expects to get from this enterprise, and the employment of their capital. This was done only to protect them for the first ten years of their infant traffic. We know perfectly well, it will take many years before that country is filled up with a large population, and the first ten years will be most unprofitable; we know perfectly well that it will require all the exertion, and all the skill, and all the management of the Company to make the eastern and western sections of this road fully compensate them, and fairly compensate them for their responsibility, and for their expenditure during these ten years. In order to give them a chance, we have provided that the Dominion Parliament—mind you the Dominion Parliament: we cannot check any other Parliament; we cannot check Ontario, we cannot check Manitoba—shall for the first ten years after the construction of the road, give their own road into which they are putting so much money and so much land, a fair chance of existence.

The very fact, Sir, that these gentlemen are willing to strike that bargain, and the very fact that they are willing to have their road built so, shows that they do not mean to run the line east of Red River. They can well afford, Mr. Speaker, to allow railways to run into the prairie line. Any railway as a local colonization line, as a line to supply the wants of the country lying along the line from east to west, the local traffic, and the trade which the road will obtain from Jasper House to Red River, will be amply sufficient to keep it up, and therefore, these gentlemen can well afford to say: "We do not want any such exemptions."

Macdonald, aware that a probable election loomed in 1883, continued his implacable attack on Mackenzie's railway record. He finally concluded his speech with an "appeal to the patriotism of the people of Canada."

"We can tell them," he continued, "that we want a line that will connect Halifax with the Pacific Ocean. We can tell them, even from the mouth of our enemies, that out of our lands we can pay off every single farthing, every cent taken out of the pockets of the people, twenty-fold, and we will have a great Pacific Railway. This is what we will have." He vowed to create "a great, an united, a rich, an improving, a developing Canada, instead of making us tributary to American laws, to American railways, to American bondage, to American tolls, to American freights, to all the little tricks and big tricks that American railways are addicted to for the purpose of destroying our road."

Later Macdonald would say, "I was luckily strong and well when I spoke, which I did in the fashion of twenty years ago." A Toronto friend wrote to tell him that "your speech was the whole topic of conversation through the whole city" the next day, and that "the champagne corks were flying like a humming fire of artillery." The House sat through the night more than once debating the bill, but on February 1, 1881, it passed, 128 votes to 49.[14]

ANALYZING THE
NORTH-WEST REBELLION, 1885

In 1884, Louis Riel returned from exile to Saskatchewan. The world-wide economic depression of the 1870s, crop failure, and the disappearance of the buffalo brought distress to the Métis, the Plains Indians, and the other settlers. The lack of immediate solutions to the Métis concerns about their title to river lots and the extinguishment of the Aboriginal title created frustration. The Indian Department's attempt to control the Plains Cree and the Assiniboine by ignoring treaties and using the law to reshape their culture raised tensions. The promise of the west, of Manitoba, the treaties, and the North West Mounted Police had fallen short.

Riel's messianic religious views alienated the settler population, the Aboriginals, and the missionaries. Nevertheless, backed by many Métis, Riel established another provisional government in 1885. Tensions came to a head in May at Batoche, where government forces defeated the Métis. Very few Aboriginals had participated. Mistahimaskwa (c. 1825–1888), the Plains Cree chief known as Big Bear, had attempted unsuccessfully to keep his warriors from participating in the conflict at

Frog Lake; and at Cut Knife the military had attacked the Plains Cree of Pītikwahanapiwīyin (c. 1842–1886) and Minahikosis (c. 1830–1885), known respectively as Poundmaker and Little Pine. Riel was executed on November 16, 1885, while Big Bear, Poundmaker, and other Plains Cree were convicted of treason-felony.[15]

On July 6, Edward Blake delivered a seven-hour condemnation of Macdonald's delayed response to the rising concerns in the West, citing document after document. The dominant issue in this excerpt was Edward Blake's accusation that Macdonald delayed responding to a December 20, 1878, report by then deputy minister of the interior Colonel John Stoughton Dennis (1820–1885), recommending that the government attend to the Métis concerns and consider an agricultural settlement scheme. Macdonald stood up to give an account of the department's actions since he had regained office in 1878 to take up the portfolio of minister of the interior that included the role of superintendent general of Indian affairs branch—often known as the Indian Department.

In 1879, Macdonald's government created the legal authority to distribute the grant in the North-West Territories—the Dominion Lands Act of 1879. Then he turned his attention to the economy and other matters, but launched some inquiries into the best fashion of distributing the grant, beginning with a request to Colonel John Stoughton Dennis to investigate and write a memo—which he did, endorsing a proposal popular with the council of the North-West Territories. Other experts were consulted. Agreement on how to distribute the land was divided and the matter sat until 1884. In January 1885, Macdonald and his minister of the interior since 1883, David Lewis Macpherson (1818–1896), agreed to offer the Métis of the North-West Territories the same settlement as provided by the Manitoba Act (in its many revisions), which granted them land as settlers and in extinguishment of their Aboriginal title to the land possibly in scrip—a promissory note potentially redeemable in land or money. It went against the personal judgment of Macdonald to reproduce the Manitoba experience because most of the scrip had ended up in the hands of speculators. Notwithstanding the Métis' reasons for the request, Macdonald believed (as he explained moments earlier in this July 6 debate) that the request was "for the purpose of enabling the land grabbers and speculators, who have a hold on these poor people," meaning the Métis.[16]

The Debates of the House of Commons, 5th Parliament, 3rd Session, July 6, 1885, record:

[SIR JOHN A. MACDONALD:] When we took office, in 1878, we had to consider this question. The Government before us had altogether ignored the rights of the half-breeds; they had refused to listen to the representations of their own agent, Mr. Matthew Ryan, made under his own hand. Until 1879 there was no legal power, and the Government before us did not ask that power to deal honestly or fairly with the claims of the half-breeds. We only came in in November, 1878, but in the Parliament of 1879 we took power to deal with that subject, according to the best of our discretion. We wished to do the best for the North-West; we wished to do the best for the half-breeds and the country generally; we could have no other object in view. We had just come into power, after a defeated, a discredited Administration had gone out, with the united voice of the majority of the people. We had everything to gain by doing what was right, and we attempted to do what was right. What did we do? We wrote to the leading men of the North-West. We wrote to Archbishop Taché* and to the other bishops, of whom the hon. gentleman has spoken; we wrote to

---

* Alexandre-Antonin Taché (1823–1894) was a missionary who had participated in the Oblate missions of Hudson Bay and James Bay since 1844. (Hamelin, "Taché, Alexandre-Antonin," DCB)

Mr. Laird,* and we got their opinions, and their opinions were united against the granting of scrip; their opinions were united against giving patents to the half-breeds. The hon. gentleman did not read that Col. Dennis, my respected, and worthy, and able deputy, who now, I am sorry to say, is retired, wrote that remarkable despatch to which the hon. gentleman alluded, a despatch creditable to him in some degree creditable to me, as sanctioning every word he wrote, asking the best advice we could get as to what we would do with these people, to save them from their own improvidence and grant them their rights, so far as was consistent with the general prosperity of the country. At the expense of being a little tedious, I will look over what these hon. gentlemen have said. The confidential despatch or letter of Col. Dennis I need not read, because it has been alluded to with sufficient fulness by the hon. gentleman, but let us take the answer of Archbishop Taché. Nobody can doubt that he was a friend of the Indian; nobody can doubt that he was a friend of the half-breeds, and that, when he was writing back to the Department, he was pleading the cause of the half-breeds and fighting their battles, and pointing out, whether pleasing or unpleasing to them, their interests. And what does he say? Does he advocate the granting of the scrip? Does he advocate the giving away of the lands? No; his opinion was quite the reverse. The hon. gentleman read a portion of this letter, in which he stated that the half-breeds are a highly sensitive race, that they feel and resent injury or insult; in fact, that they were

---

* David Laird (1833–1914) was a Prince Edward Island–born minister of the interior between 1873 and 1876, under Alexander Mackenzie's Liberal government, and the lieutenant-governor of the North-West Territories between 1876 and 1881, which role also included that of superintendent of Indian Affairs until 1879. (Robb, "Laird, David," *DCB*)

daily humiliated in regard to their origin, and so on. Let us see what the Archbishop says:

"Every one acknowledges the desirability for the half-breeds to settle definitively on lands, to cultivate them. Here is a scheme I take the liberty to propose:

"a. I estimate the half-breed population actually in the North-West to number about twelve hundred families. Let the Government make twelve reserves for them, in the very places the half-breeds themselves will like to have them.

"b. Each reserve should be for one hundred families at least, and contain an area of twelve square miles of available land, that is to say, the extent of four townships.

"c. All the half-breeds, men, women and children, residing in the North-West on the 1st January, 1879, ought to receive two more negotiable scrips for eighty acres of land each, to be located by them in anyone of the twelve above-mentioned reserves.

"d. Said lands could neither be sold, mortgaged nor taxed, before they should have passed through the hands of, at least, the third generation of those who receive them, or of their representatives. I say, at least, because I am strongly inclined to believe that it is desirable that such land be entirely unalienable; and such an idea cannot seem unreasonable to those who consider the advantages deriving from a similar policy, with regard to real and unalienable estates of noble men."

Now, every half-breed in the North-West, if he does not claim as an Indian and has not accepted as an Indian, belonging to an Indian band and enjoying all the advantages of an Indian, and they are great, because the treaties are liberal, the annuities are large, the supply of implements, cattle, seeds, and so on, is very generous, on the whole—and any half-breed who chooses to be an Indian can go with his tribe—but any half-breed who says I will be considered a white man has all the privileges of a white man; he can get his 160 acres, and after three years' cultivation he gets his land. Here is the friend of the half-breeds, Archbishop Taché, who says he shall not get that, but shall only have a claim to land, shall not have the use of it, unless he cultivates it himself, but he shall not be able to alienate it, that he cannot mortgage it or sell it; and who would take the land under these restrictions, when, under the more liberal law of the Dominion of Canada, every half-breed can enter himself for 160 acres and get his patent after three years, the same as an emigrant from Ontario and Quebec? So, when the Government took up the question which had been left on their hands unsettled, what was best to do for the half-breeds, they were told by Archbishop Taché that the half-breeds would get no land, no matter whether they settled upon it, no matter whether they built a house of marble or a house of clay, that they should have no rights upon it till the third generation. When that was presented to us, do you not think we should consider and pause before we handed over those lands to these people? Archbishop Taché, knowing and believing, having well ascertained that the granting of land to these people would lead to their alienating [i.e., selling] it for a few dollars, if a man wanted to make a present to his wife of a dress, or if the husband could get the present of a few dollars, or, perhaps, in some cases, a few gallons of whiskey. If we look over the various recommendations of the various bodies, in the North-West we get the same result. Bishop MacLean* who knew the country well, was not in favor of granting the patent for this land to these men. The bishop of Rupert's Land, who has lately gone there, honestly says he has been too short a time there to judge, and therefore he gives no opinion. But what does the North-West council of 1878 say? The hon. gentleman [Edward Blake] quoted a portion but not the whole of it. I have not the original document, but I will read it from a letter of Mr. Matthew Ryan, who was a member of the council that passed the order. This was the resolution passed by the North-West council:—

"That in view of the fact that grants of land and issues of scrip were made to the half-breeds of Manitoba towards the extinction of the Indian title for the lands of that Province, there will be dissatisfaction among the half-breeds of the Territories unless they receive some like consideration; that this consideration would most tend to the advantage of the half-breeds were it given in the form of a non-transferable location ticket for, say, 160 acres to each half-breed head of a family, and to each half-breed child at the time of the transfer to Canada, the ticket to be issued immediately to any half-breed of eighteen years or over, who furnishes

---

* John McLean (1828–1886) was Church of England bishop of Rupert's Land in 1865 and in 1874 became the first bishop of Saskatchewan. (Thomas, "McLean, John," *DCB*)

evidence of his claim; that each half-breed obtaining such location ticket should be allowed to locate it upon any unoccupied Dominion lands, but the title of the land so entered should remain in the Crown for ten years."

The recommendation of Archbishop Taché was that the title should be kept away from the half-breeds for three generations. The recommendation of the council was that it should be kept away for ten years. What was the policy of the Government? Go, take your 160 acres; take your pre-emption for 160 acres more, and you shall stand as well as a white man, and shall get your patent after three years, no matter what the Archbishop or the North-West council have told us. We, the Government of the Dominion of Canada, have more confidence in the half-breeds even than their own Archbishop and their own council. We say: We give you the land; occupy it, cultivate it, live on it, be happy on it, and at the end of three years you will get 160 acres, and you will stand free and independent, a freeholder, a yeoman, a free man in the North-West. You shall not be subject to this paternal Government which has been urged upon you by your own friends in the North-West. Although we are so far away, although we do not know you, although we are charged with dealing unjustly by you, we have more confidence in you than your own friends. We will not ask you to remain for three generations as slaves of the soil—to remain ten years without your deed. We tell you that in three years you may go and occupy your land, and may God's blessing be with you.

Sir, that is the policy of the Government, and that is the policy the hon. gentleman has maligned, that he has condemned, that

he would curse. The policy of the Government has been generous, it has been free, it has been considerate, and mind you, Mr.
Speaker [Hon. George Airey Kirkpatrick], the Government
have held that the land that he has is found in occupation of,
and that he had the right to on the 15th July, 1870 [as set out in
the Manitoba Act] that it was his, and the Government could
not deprive him of it. The Dominion Act gave it to him. Every
man, woman and child, under the Dominion laws, passed, I do
not know whether originally by us and afterwards amended by
the hon. gentleman opposite, the Dominion Acts, one and all,
declare that being in occupation of land before the Act passed
they have now an inalienable right to their lands, no matter
whether they are on odd-numbered or even-numbered sections. The Act says that in all unsurveyed lands the party, found
in possession shall retain possession of that land, not only the
half-breeds, whether English or French, but every white settler, every man in the North-West, whether he is a Hudson Bay
factor, or clerk, or runner—every one of them had their rights
under the Dominion Lands Act. It did not, in any way, interfere
with the rights of the settlers. Everyone of those men may say
to us: We have occupied this land; this is ours; we will get out
a deed for that, and that is secured to us by the Dominion Lands
Act; but we will take up, as settlers, 160 acres of land elsewhere.
Every half-breed has that right. No one could deprive him of
it. No one could say: If you are going to take your 160 acres
as a homestead, you will lose your land as an old settler. They
had a right to both, and those claims have been rejected; those
claims are now inherent. And I tell you this, as I said before,
that no one, no man, no woman, has been dispossessed or distressed since the Government of Canada came into possession
of that country.

Well, Sir, what had the Government to do? We had all our friends; we had the Archbishop; we had even Mr. Jackson, of whom the hon. gentleman has spoken, who now represents the half-breeds in the North-West council; we had him stating that there should be no grant given to the half-breeds, except on condition of five years of continuous occupation. There was a conflict of opinion; I will not trouble the House with showing that there was an infinity of opinions; an infinity of advice was offered to the Government, how best to deal with the half-breeds, and the Government had only one thing to think of—what was the best for the people, what was it best to do for them, to save them even against their own improvidence, and at the same time not to keep back the settlement of the country. This, Mr. Speaker, may account, to any reasonable man, for what the hon. gentleman talks of as delay. They were not suffering anything. The half-breed had his own lot, he was not cultivating the land that he had. Giving him his land and giving him more land was giving him nothing. The nomadic half-breed, who had been brought up to hunt, having had merely his shanty to repair to in the dead season, when there was no game—what advantage was it to him to give him 160 or 240 acres more? It was of no use to him whatever, but it would have been of great use to the speculators who were working on him and telling him that he was suffering. Oh! How awfully he was suffering, ruined, destroyed, starving, because he did not get 240 acres somewhere else, or the scrip for it, that he might sell it for $50! No, Sir; the whole thing is a farce. Now, Mr. Speaker, we, at the last moment, made concessions, and we did it for the sake of peace. The Government knew, my hon. friend, Sir David Macpherson, the Minister of Interior, knew that we were not acting in the interests of the half-breeds in granting them scrip, in granting him the land. We had tried, after consulting man after man, expert after expert, to find what was best for the country, and we found, without one single exception, they were all opposed to granting unlimited scrip and immediate patents to the half-breeds.

But, Sir, an agitation arose [the outbreak of hostilities], and the hon. gentleman has rung the changes on Riel being brought into that country. Who brought him into the country? Not the Indians; not the half-breeds. The half-breeds did not pay the money. The white speculators in Prince Albert gave their money to Gabriel Dumont,* and gave it to Lepine [Maxime Lépine (1837–1897)], and gave it to others. They had all got their assignments from the half-breeds; they had all got in their pockets the scrip or the assignment, and they sent down [to Montana] to bring Riel in as an agent to be a means of attaining their unhallowed ends. It is to the white men, it is to men of our own race and lineage, and not to the half-breeds, nor yet to the Indians, that we are to attribute the war, the loss of life, the loss of money, and the discredit that this country would have suffered had it not been for the gallant conduct of our volunteers. Now, Mr. Speaker, I am able to prove that

---

* Gabriel Dumont (1837–1906) was a well-established Métis leader and led them during the hostilities. Throughout the 1870s and early 1880s, Dumont had helped create structures of local government and organized requests to the government to help the Métis adjust to life after the disappearance of the buffalo, requesting in particular the recognition, as they had been in St. Albert, of Métis river lots, long strips of land that did not fit into the grid survey of the west. In March 1884, mistakes and miscommunications had worn thin Dumont's patience and he agreed with other Métis to ask Riel to return from Montana. Not convinced by the subsequent negotiations with the government, Dumont helped rally Métis to take up arms. Maxime Lépine (c.1837–1897) was Riel's brother-in-law and a member of Manitoba's legislative assembly in the mid-1870s until he moved to Saskatchewan in the North-West Territories. He supported Riel after his return and throughout the unrest, although being "not keen on war," as he put it. (Macleod, "Dumont, Gabriel," DCB; Payment, "Lépine, Maxime," DCB)

there has been a deep-laid conspiracy. I am able to establish that the cry of the half-breed grievances was merely a pretext. I am able to show that white man after white man has entered into it. And I tell you this, further, Mr. Speaker—I do not mean in the least degree to impugn the hon. member for West Durham [Edward Blake]; I do not at all mean to say that he was in any way a party to it; but I tell him this, and I can prove this, that they have unscrupulously used his name and used the name of his party, and they have used that name, not only in the North-West with the half-breeds, not only along the frontier, but they have used it at Washington; at Washington his name has been quoted. I do not believe the hon. gentleman is liable to the charge; but it only shows that you cannot touch pitch without becoming fouled. The hon. gentleman, I know, in his anxiety to get evidence against this Government, in his anxiety to get evidence, no matter from whom or in what way—I can show, if need be, under his own handwriting and signature, that he has gone very far.

MR. [EDWARD] BLAKE: Show it.

SIR JOHN A. MACDONALD: I will prove it, with very great reluctance. I do not know whether the hon. gentleman ever heard of a person called J. E. Brown.

MR. BLAKE: Yes.

SIR JOHN A. MACDONALD: Very well. J. E. Brown was a man formerly in the Mounted Police in the North-West. J. E. Brown living in that country employed himself in the very useful but perhaps unpopular occupation of trying to be a detective.* J. E. Brown, in his anxiety, not only to extol the merits of the North-West but also, perhaps, to do a little in a pecuniary way, wrote to the hon. member for the west riding of Durham, and told him he could give him a good deal of information—and he would like to get a pass. The hon. gentleman said he could not give him a pass, but he would try to see him in Toronto, and if he could not do so, he would try and get a confidential friend to see him. I have not the man's letter, but I have the hon. gentleman's reply. The man must have written saying: I am going to apply for a survey from the Dominion Government; it will prove rather inconvenient to me if I lost the office, and therefore, perhaps, you will not use my name in that connection, but treat it confidentially, until after I get the appointment. Then, of course, I will give you the information. The hon. gentleman answered him, that he would keep all his communications confidential until after he had got the office. J. E. Brown was to come to the Government here, and was to go on his knees and say he was a friend of the Government, and appeal to the Government and get employment on a survey, and then supply the hon. gentleman with information. The hon. gentleman indicates that I have not got those letters.

MR. BLAKE: I do not say you have not got these letters.

SIR JOHN A. MACDONALD: Then we will read them. Mr. Blake writes:

------

* By the mid-1880s, Macdonald had developed a fairly sophisticated secret service and information-gathering networks in Canada through the auspices of the Dominion Police (created in 1868, and which provided him, for example, with excellent advance knowledge of Fenian activities) and the North West Mounted Police in 1873. (Kealey, "Empire Strikes Back," 15-7)

"OTTAWA, 7th May.

"I have your letter of the 6th, and should be very glad indeed to learn from you any facts connected with the management of affairs in the North-West Territories. I would willingly comply with your request for a pass to Ottawa if it were in my power, but I have no means of procuring railway passes. It is possible, though by no means certain, I may be in Toronto for a few hours within the next few days, and if so I would try to arrange an interview with you, or if I am unable to manage that, I can arrange an interview with a confidential friend of mine, who would note down, for my own ear only, all you should choose to communicate, if this would be agreeable to you.

"Yours faithfully,
"EDWARD BLAKE."

That is the prologue to the play.

"OTTAWA, 12th May, 1885.

"DEAR SIR,—I have your letter, and will ask a friend to make an appointment with you. I will take care, as you desire, that your name shall not be used to your prejudice. I will not disclose it until you have had ample opportunity of securing an appointment for the surveys this year, if you are fortunate enough to do so. But I fancy there will not be a great deal of surveying done. I should gladly assist you in procuring employment if

it were in my power, but I have no means of forward-
ing your interests in this respect. With thanks for your
good wishes,

"I am, yours faithfully,
"EDWARD BLAKE."

In the hon. gentleman's anxiety to show what a wicked Government this is, to prove how derelict it is in its duty, that it deserves
the censure of the country, he tells this man to go on, apply
for a position on the surveys, get it if he can, although he does
not think there will be many surveys this year, and he will not
reveal his name until after he has got the appointment. Then
information is to be given by this man who came on his knees
to the Government, to show how the Government were injuri-
ously affecting the interests of the country. That is not the way
an hon. member usually gets information.

We find, in consequence of the continual pressure of the
white men, in consequence of the fact that the half-breeds at
Prince Albert were the slaves of the white men, of the fact that
they held meetings and might rise in arms or might do whatever the white men chose to ask them to do—we made up our
mind that although we did not consider it for the interest of
the people in the Territories, yet if they would accept nothing
else, and we offered them 160 acres of land—if they would
place themselves at the mercy of cormorants, who were ruining
them and holding them as slaves, and continually keeping up an
agitation, we cannot help it; we will give you scrip, although
we know it is not in your interest, and it will be thrown away,
and will be secured by people who will give you the smallest
possible sum for it; but we cannot help it; this matter must

be settled. I do not hesitate to say that I did it with the greatest reluctance. I do not easily yield, if there is a better course open; but at the very last moment I yielded, and I said: "Well, for God's sake let them have the scrip; they will either drink it or waste it or sell it; but let us have peace." And my successor, my respected and able successor, Sir David Macpherson, acted upon that decision, which was carried out in January. At that time we know there was a discontented people; that the white people were making trouble.

I say, and I appeal to the judgment of the House to say, if we did not act as we ought to have acted when, in 1879, when we took possession of the Government, when we found that the Government who were behind us had taken not a single step to settle this question; when we found that the Government had denied the right of the half-breed; when the whole thing was thrown upon us—if we did not act wisely, afterwards when we took power, when we went to the chief men of the country, to the men who were known to be friends of the half-breeds, when we went to the hierarchy and the clergy, both Catholic and Protestant; we went to everybody who could give us information, and they were unanimous in saying that it was wrong that this scrip should be used in this way, and that the land could be got possession of for little or nothing. We held out as long as we could, but such was the influence of the half-breeds, who already got a share of their lands in Manitoba, that they went to the North-West, they became dwellers on the plains, they played Indians, and pretended that they had lived in Manitoba; that they were suffering; that their Manitoba friends had got lands and scrip; and nine-tenths of the men claiming it had already got scrip, and were attempting to put up bargains in the North-West. Fourteen out of seventeen petitioners, in one

case, were shown to have got lands already in Manitoba. Isidore
Dumont, brother of Gabriel Dumont, had land; he applied
again, and it was one of his grievances that he did not get
more land in the North-West. Gabriel Dumont got not only his
160 acres, as promised, but he had the best house in Batoche;
and so it was with very many of these men—they had already
got their lands and scrip, but they were greedy to get more.
Appetite grew with eating; and though they had got all much
more than originally by law they ought to have got, they are
clamoring for more. If time would permit, I could prove many
such cases; but perhaps, I may take another occasion, as the hon.
gentleman has said we are going to hear from him again on this
subject—I may take another occasion to show that the fact of
the half-breed not getting, at the moment he wants it, his scrip
or his claim for 240 acres, was a mere pretence; yet Riel, from
the beginning, when he went into the country until he left,
went there for the purpose of making money. He came there
for the most sordid purposes possible, and he told all kinds of
lies. Among other things, he said that the hon. member for East
York [Alexander Mackenzie], when he was in the Government
offered him $20,000, and I offered him $30,000—he remembered perhaps, the old matter, when he got some money on the
frontier, in order to clear away.*

One of the letters read to-day by the hon. gentleman was
that he had been promised a senatorship or a seat in the Cabinet.
He came there, and he ruled these men for the most sordid
purposes. The white men in Prince Albert and the vicinity, or
many of them, subscribed to bring him there, and encouraged

---

* Louis Riel's acceptance of an indemnity by Alexander Mackenzie and Macdonald is a
matter of historical discussion. (Flanagan, *Riel and the Rebellions*, 118)

him there, for the sake of making a little fuss and drawing attention to Prince Albert and for the sake of threatening the Government into settling the claims of the half-breeds, or, in other words, putting money into their pockets. Sir, I shall not detain the House any longer on the subject. As the hon. gentleman has stated, it is a subject which cannot rest here. This subject must be fully dealt with. I have not alluded to the statements of the hon. gentleman, with respect to the land regulations, the treatment of the whites; and these questions the hon. gentleman has ingeniously mixed up with the question he brought before the House. He has been preparing himself for, I will not say how long, while this House was studiously and earnestly discussing the Franchise Bill; while they were occupied night and day working out that great problem, the hon. gentleman was diving into this question. Well, he has dived into it, and he has gone pretty low into its depths. The hon. gentleman first took up the half-breeds, then the land laws, then the whites, then the colonisation companies—and I do not know what else. But let him take each subject separately, clause by clause, sentence by sentence, impeachment by impeachment, charge by charge, and deal with them, and I shall meet him, and convince this House that the charges are groundless, that the Government are safe and sound, in the opinions of the people and of the country, because they have done what they believed to be the best in their judgment, ought to be done; and because I know that although perhaps they may have made occasional mistakes, although in the tentative process of settling a new country, they have committed, perhaps, an occasional error, they were not too proud to change; and when they came to the conclusion that they had committed an error, they did not indulge in the miserable vanity of thinking they could do no wrong. When

they found that any of their conclusions, from their own judgment or on reference to their responsible officers, had better be
altered, they were brave enough and honest enough to admit
the error, and cure the error, and make amendment. What was
the consequence? Sir, I believe we stand well among the whites
of the North-West. I know we stand well with the red men of
the North-West.

MR. [DAVID] MILLS: Hear, hear.

SIR JOHN A. MACDONALD: The hon. gentleman says
hear, hear, but I can prove by the testimony of every Indian that
has been in arms—of Poundmaker, and Big Bear, and Beardy,
and Little Pine, and Little Poplar, and all those Indians—I can
show to you, not only that they have been well treated, but that
those who have been their guardians, their clergy, and those
who watched over them, admit that the Indians had no wrongs
to redress; and if you will read the press of the North-West, read
such papers as the Saskatchewan *Herald*, and will find that we
were wrong—that we have been pampering and coaxing the
Indians; that we must take a new course, we must vindicate the
position of the white man, we must teach the Indians what law
is; we must not pauperise them, as they say we have been doing.*

---

* The Canadian west, compared to the American west, did benefit from the law and
order provided by the government. But in the mid-1880s the relative peace was as much
due to the forbearance of many Plains Indian leaders, such as Mistahimaskwa (known as
Big Bear), who tried to avoid violence while resisting the tactics of the Indian Department
to withhold provisions in exchange for cooperation, or to prevent them from choosing
contiguous reserves to strengthen their alliance. (Miller, *Compact, Contract, Covenant*,
159, 190-1, 192; Miller, "Owen Glendower, Hotspur, and Canadian Indian Policy," 34-6;
Smith, "John A. Macdonald, and Aboriginal Canada," 21; Tobias, "Canada's Subjugation
of the Plains Cree," 523, 533, 536, 548)

MR. MILLS: Hear, hear.

SIR JOHN A. MACDONALD: The hon. gentleman says hear, hear. Why, Sir, I have come to this House again and again and stated the case of the Indians. I have said it was a case of hardship, and we could not, as Christian men, allow them to starve. We have done all we could to put them on themselves; we have done all we could to make them work as agriculturists; we have done all we could, by the supply of cattle, agricultural implements and instruction, to change them from a nomadic to an agricultural life.*

We have had very considerable success; we have had infinitely more success during our short period, than the United States have had during twenty-five years. We have had a wonderful success; but still we have had the Indians; and then in these half-breeds, enticed by white men, the savage instinct was awakened; the desire of plunder—aye, and, perhaps, the desire of scalping—the savage idea of a warlike glory, which pervades the breast of most men, civilised or uncivilised, was aroused in them, and forgetting all the kindness that had been bestowed upon them, forgetting all the gifts that had been given to them, forgetting all that the Government, the white people and the Parliament of Canada had been doing for them, in trying to rescue them from barbarity; forgetting that we had given them

---

* Agriculture was part of the Plains Indians' culture and many viewed agricultural support as an important part of the 1870s treaties. Delivery of this support was slow and on occasion non-existent. By the late 1870s, the government instituted a scheme to provide a few years of tools and supplies and a permanent farm instructor to the reserves in order to encourage self-supporting farmers. The results of the initiative were mixed, due to the difficulties of prairie farming and the complexities of surviving the farms' initial years of unproductivity without buffalo to provide essential material support, such as clothing. Within a few years, the government had turned its attention to industrial schooling focused upon a younger generation. (Carter, *Lost Harvests*, 39, 72-3, 79, 106-7)

reserves, the means to cultivate those reserves, and the means of education how to cultivate them—forgetting all these things, they rose against us.

Why, Sir, we are not responsible for that; we cannot change the barbarian, the savage, into a civilised man. Look at the United States; consider the millions that they have expended in defending their frontier; look at the war that is now going on on the south-western frontier, where there is infinitely more loss of life among the tribes of Apaches than has occurred in all our North-West. It is an inglorious war, and there has been a great loss of life; but Americans do not take the part of the rebel and the traitor; that is reserved for the leader of the Opposition in the Parliament of Canada. We acquired the North-West country in 1870. Not a life was lost, not a blow was struck, not a pound nor a dollar was spent in warfare, in that long period that has since intervened. I have not hesitated to tell this House, again and again, that we could not always hope to maintain peace with the Indians; that the savage was still a savage, and that until he ceased to be savage, we were always in danger of a collision, in danger of war, in danger of an outbreak. I am only surprised that we have been able so long to maintain peace—that from 1870 until 1885 not one single blow, not one single murder, not one single loss of life, has taken place. Look at the United States; along the whole frontier of the United States there has been war; millions have been expended there; their best and their bravest have fallen. I personally knew General Custer [1839–1876], and admired the gallant soldier, the American hero; yet he went, and he fell with his band, and not a man was left to tell the tale—they were all swept away. The American army have suffered by hundreds; the American Treasury has been depleted by millions. We have, from a combination of unfortunate circumstances, had one war inconsiderately commenced, wickedly commenced, criminally commenced by the instigators. We put that down speedily and gallantly; and, Sir, it is one consolation, that if we have seen young men sacrificed, if we have lost from this House, as a consequence of that war, one of the most respected members, they went up there of their own accord to fight the battle of their country; they have gained glory and distinction, and they have convinced, not only us—we do not want that conviction—but the mother country, in whose good opinion we take so much pride, that we have as good a militia as their own, that we have men who, untrained as they are, still can listen to the voice of discipline, and will do everything they are called upon to do to maintain the credit of their country. Their action has raised the credit of Canada, not only among the right-minded thinking men of the world, but even in the sordid purlieus of the stock exchange. The credit of Canada has risen, because Canada has shown, as a vindicator of herself, that she is worthy of being a nation, and worthy of the credit of the world.

WADING AGAINST THE
RIVERS AND STREAMS ACT, 1882

In the 1880s, a threat arose to Confederation, from Ontario. The "Provincial Rights" movement emerged to resist the strong centralizing powers of reservation and disallowance accorded to the federal government. In the case of the province of Ontario's Act for Protecting the Public Interests in Rivers, Streams and Creeks, Macdonald was adamant. Three times, Macdonald disallowed it; three times Oliver Mowat, his former schoolmate, and longtime antagonist, now premier of Ontario, passed it again. Partisan politics muddied the waters. Macdonald first struck down the law in 1881. A partisan dispute between two men lay at the root of the Act—Mr. McLaren (a Conservative supporter), who had improved the river and owned his improvements, and Mr. Caldwell (a Liberal supporter), who believed he was free to float his logs down the river. Macdonald chose to support McLaren and wrote the official report recommending disallowance of the "Rivers and Streams Act." The Judicial Committee of the Privy Council in Britain served as a court of arbitration, and its decisions in the 1880s and early 1890s by and large supported the claims of the provinces.[17]

In 1882, the Act had arisen again in the House of Commons. Macdonald, challenged by Edward Blake, pointed to a history of consistent and unbiased application of the power of disallowance.[18]

The Debates *of the House of Commons, 4th Parliament, 4th Session, record on April 14, 1882:*

SIR JOHN A. MACDONALD: Then, although some of the reasons given by the Minister of the Interior were bad, and although he did not approve of them, yet he comes to the same conclusion, and he insults the Legislature of Manitoba. He trampled on their autonomy. He snuffed them out, because, forsooth, in their own opinion, overriding the opinion of the Legislature of Manitoba, he thought they were better off with the old Bill than with the new one. These are the gentlemen who are protecting the rights and the autonomy of the different Provinces. Why, Mr. Speaker [Hon. Joseph Godéric Blanchet], the whole House laughed at him. You can see the absurdity of the Opposition in which the hon. gentlemen are placing themselves in their endeavor to make political capital in this wretched way, as they have no merits of their own, no acts of their own, by which they can claim the confidence of the people; they must raise these little questions; but when we find written before us that they have done the same things, that they have contrary to their speeches, contrary to their press, and contrary to the attacks which they have made on this Government, again and again carried out that policy, what can be said of them; and we are compelled to use the term which was employed with regard to them the other night, and declare that they are an organized hypocrisy. Sir, this Bill is retroactive. Oh, but it is a general Bill. It was introduced as a general Bill; otherwise it could not have been got through at all. A Private Bill must be introduced by petition; notice must be given of it. As a Private Bill, Mr. McLaren must be heard before the Committee on Private Bills, and it was, even for that Government, too strong a measure to pass a law expressly to take one man's property and hand it over to another; and so the Government introduced this Bill. The greatest proof of fraud is shown by the style of the Bill. What would be said, Mr. Speaker, if the Legislature of Quebec some years ago—and perhaps it is the case now—when the Magdalen Islands all belonged to Admiral Coffin,* who was sole proprietor, had legislated against Admiral Coffin. He was sole freeholder, and the Islands were covered by his tenants; and suppose they wished to make Admiral Coffin pay all the taxes, and would say: We cannot directly say that he shall pay all the taxes of all the people of the Island, but we will pass a Bill stating that it is proper to declare that all the taxes on the Magdalen Islands shall be paid and defrayed by the freeholders on the Island, there being only one freeholder. That would look very much like fraud. This was the same kind of fraud, and it was done with the same fraudulent intent.

Mr. Speaker, in the first place, I would say that the report was made by the Minister of Justice, the present Chief Justice of Nova Scotia, my namesake Mr. McDonald. I heartily approve of it. I take the responsibility for it, and my colleagues will join me in doing so. We were protecting a man from a great wrong, from a great loss and injury, from a course which, if pursued, would destroy the confidence of the whole civilized world in the law of the land. What property would be safe? What man would make an investment in this country? Would capitalists

---

* Sir Isaac Coffin (1759–1839), an officer in the British Navy, acquired the seigneury of the Îles-de-la-Madeleine in 1798 and failed to develop it as a settlement despite his efforts. (Douglas, "Coffin, Sir Isaac," *DCB*)

come to Canada if the rights of property were taken away, as was attempted under this Bill? This was one of the grounds on which in that paper of mine of 1867, I declared that, in my opinion, all Bills should be disallowed if they affected general interests. Sir, we are not half a-dozen Provinces. We are one great Dominion. If we commit an offence against the laws of property, or any other atrocity in legislation, it will be widely known. England is so far off that she is not affected by it; she is not so likely to disallow our Bills, however bad they may be, because the consequences fall on our own heads. But here where we are one country and altogether, we go from one Province to another as we do from one county to another and from one town to another, is it to be borne that laws which bind civilized society, which distinguish civilization from barbarism, which protect life, reputation and property, should be dissimilar; that what should be a merit in one Province should be a crime in another, and that different laws should prevail. There may be differences in the laws in detail, but the great grand principle that every man should have the right to occupy his own house and property, sit under his own fig-tree, cultivate his own vine, and be protected in all this, is the common law of all civilized countries and must prevail throughout the Dominion. The hon. gentleman has threatened us with an appeal to the people. Sir, we have no objection to go to the people. If I told these hon. gentlemen that the elections were to take place on the 17th of September, 1883, why, Sir, Grit stock would go up 20 per cent. Their faces have been lengthened so that their longitude is almost at long as their speeches. From the reading of the amendment it is clear that the hon. member for South Huron is not to be fully trusted. Sir, I have no doubt that the honest men of the country will vote to support the

Government in this measure. I do not mean to say the hon. gentlemen are going to vote against their consciences, but the country will believe that they were fully conscious of what they were voting.

BEING AN AUXILIARY KINGDOM, 1886

Newfoundland ("the key to our front door," as Macdonald put it) remained aloof from Confederation, and the provinces were restive, but for all that, the North-West territories gained representation in the House of Commons. British Columbia, Manitoba, and Prince Edward Island were all part of Confederation and the Canadian Pacific Railway had been completed. Foreign affairs and Canada's place in the world dominated remarks upon the Speech from the Throne.[19]

Edward Blake responded to the address by twitting Macdonald for putting words in the governor general's mouth and for a speech Macdonald had given at the St. George's Club in London. Macdonald had gone "in the middle of a general election" to establish a High Commission for Canada and had announced in Britain that Canadians "are forming a navy and will assist the mother country in enforcing the peace of the world." Macdonald, he said, was taking Canada "to join the mother country in an offensive and defensive league; to sacrifice ourselves, to risk our last man and last shilling in defence of the Empire and the flag."[20]

In the mid-1880s, free-trade ideas continued to dominate and the "self-reliance" of the colonies in the 1860s had matured, but the surging

industrial strength of other world powers had diminished Britain's position. The idea of a "constructive imperialism" emerged, touting the
Empire, not just Britain, as the basis of public policy, and efforts were
made to create a coordinated entity. High-level meetings of the colonies
were discussed and the first Colonial Conference convened in 1887. Such
conferences became a place to discuss the laying of the "all red route" of
underwater transoceanic cables to join all the colonies of the British Empire,
and other matters ranging from defence to the Imperial penny post.[21]

Macdonald opened his remarks by pointing out that Edward Blake
too had been to London and given a speech, at which point Liberal MP
George Landerkin (Grey South) said they were "proud of it."[22]

The Debates of the House of Commons, 5th Parliament, 4th
Session, record on February 26, 1886:

SIR JOHN A. MACDONALD: Well, I dare say the hon.
gentleman [Mr. Landerkin] is proud of it. But the hon. gentleman [Edward Blake] thought my speech at the St. George's Club
was worthy of some remark, and he spoke about my exaggeration when I said that every acre in the Dominion of Canada was
in a healthful climate; the hon. gentleman foisted in the word
"beautiful." If the word beautiful is in my speech as reported, I
never used that word. I spoke of the Dominion of Canada being
a beautiful country, and so it is notwithstanding the disparagement of the honorable gentleman. I spoke of the country as fit
for the settlement of Englishmen, Irishmen and Scotchmen, and
so it is, notwithstanding the speeches of the hon. gentleman,
which sent so many to Kansas and other parts of the United
States. I spoke of the climate of Canada; I said up to the North
Pole—aye, Sir, from the boundary line to the North Pole, be
the climate frosty or genial, or be the soil fertile or unfertile,
there is no portion of the Dominion of Canada that is liable to

the malignant fevers which exist in other countries. We have no
Texas fever in Canada; we have no Kansas complaints; our very
animals seem to be protected by Providence from the diseases
that ravage the herds and flocks of other countries. It is the style
of the hon. gentleman, as it is of those who support him, to
take every opportunity to lessen the reputation and the position
of Canada in the world. Sir, I spoke the simple truth when I
said that every acre of the Dominion of Canada had a healthful
climate, which man, woman and child could emigrate to and
could prosper in.

The hon. gentleman also alluded to my over-patriotic
views. He intimated, in fact, that I was kotowing to the Mother
Country—seeking favor there by saying that Canada would
expend her last man in the defence of the Empire. I know that
hon. gentleman would not be one of those who would spend his
shilling or put his musket to his shoulder for that purpose, no
more than the hon. member for Centre Quebec (Mr. [Wilfrid]
Laurier) would do so; I know neither of them would do so; and
they laugh, I dare say, in their sleeves at my quixotry in saying
that England, in case of distress, in case of danger, in case of
the perils of war, would find Canadians ready to do what they
could to back the sovereignty of England. But, Sir, my speech
was not simply an expression that we would spend our last shilling and our last man.

My speech was in favor of having such an arrangement
between the central United Kingdom and all the colonies—
having an arrangement made by which the auxiliary kingdom
of Canada and the auxiliary kingdom of Australasia should
together form one great empire, and by uniting their forces, by
uniting their men and their money, should together be so strong
as an empire that they would control the world in arms.

That was my statement; I have made it in this House; I have made it in former Houses. Whenever I have had an opportunity of speaking on that subject, I have stated that the future of the Empire of Great Britain depended upon a close and intimate alliance between the central power and the dependencies, the auxiliary kingdoms; and, Sir, I believe if it were put to the electors at the polls in the Dominion of Canada—if they were polled men and women—and on that point the women ought to get the franchise, because they would be the most loyal of all—the hon. gentleman would find that he would be in a miserable minority if he proposed to draw back from any well organised scheme by which the Mother Country and the children kingdoms were united in one great force to maintain the civilisation of the world—to maintain the superior civilisation of those people who are contained within the bounds of the great Empire to which we are proud to belong.

The hon. gentleman also tried to get a cheer by stating that I said the French would not come here because if they did we would appeal to the United States to protect us. I said no such thing; that was a garbling of what I stated. What I stated was this: that in consequence of sensational articles that were published in England, emanating from the press of the United States, apprehensions prevailed in England—that fostered by these articles distrust was raised in the minds of the English people, the English Government and the English Parliament. I found when I got to England that they had made some impression on the minds of the people there. They said: "Is it true what the New York *Herald* and other papers say, that the French Canadians are going to rise in arms, that they are watching an opportunity of severing their connection with Canada and that no dependence can be placed on their loyalty?"*

I took upon myself, from a knowledge of 40 years of the French Canadians, to deny that statement. I stated then that there was no portion of Her Majesty's subjects, no matter what their origin or their language might be, more loyal to this Empire, more loyal to the Crown of England, than the French Canadians; and I stated further, in answer to the apprehension that was entertained and expressed again and again, in some of the English press, that even if the French Canadians were loyal, even if they did not desire to sever the connection between England and Canada, yet that at this moment the French republic were seeking colonies restlessly, opening, new and extensive, a restless and an aggressive colonial policy, there was no need to fear that France would attempt to intrigue with the French Canadians, because French statesmen know too well, from the experience they found in Mexico, when Maximilian† came over, with a generous but mistaken ambition, to found a State in Mexico, what the consequence was. The United States said to the French Government: "You must retire; no European monarchy can get a new footing on this continent; no European Government can come in this North America."

---

* After the hanging of Louis Riel on November 16, 1885, Montrealers flooded Champ de Mars in angry demonstrations and gave their support to Honoré Mercier, uniting political divides in Quebec against the federal government. (Dufour and Hamelin, "Mercier, Honoré," *DCB*; Wade, *The French Canadians*, vol. 1, 417)

† Ferdinand Maximilian Joseph (1832–1867) was Emperor of Mexico (1864–1867); he was supported by France until internal pressures and resistance from the United States forced the French to retreat. Maximilian I was executed by his opponents in June 1867. ("Maximilian," *Dictionary of World History*)

That was the Monroe doctrine,* and the knowledge of that would prevent the possibility of the French Government or Frenchmen, instigated by the French Government, trying to intrigue and raise a spirit of disloyalty which is now unexistent among the descendants of Frenchmen happily living in Canada. That was the language I used, and I must ask my French Canadian friends, those opposed to the Government as well as those supporting it, if I do not express the sentiments of the French Canadians. Certainly, I may not express the sentiments of one of them, the hon. member for Quebec.

MR. LAURIER: Order; the hon. gentleman has no reason to impute to me such imputations as he does.

SIR JOHN A. MACDONALD: I impute no imputations.

The debate continued.

---

* James Monroe (1758–1831), president of the United States from 1817 to 1825, declared the country free from further colonization "by Europe, and promised no U.S. interference with existing European possessions." (Jones, "Monroe Doctrine," *OCUSH*)

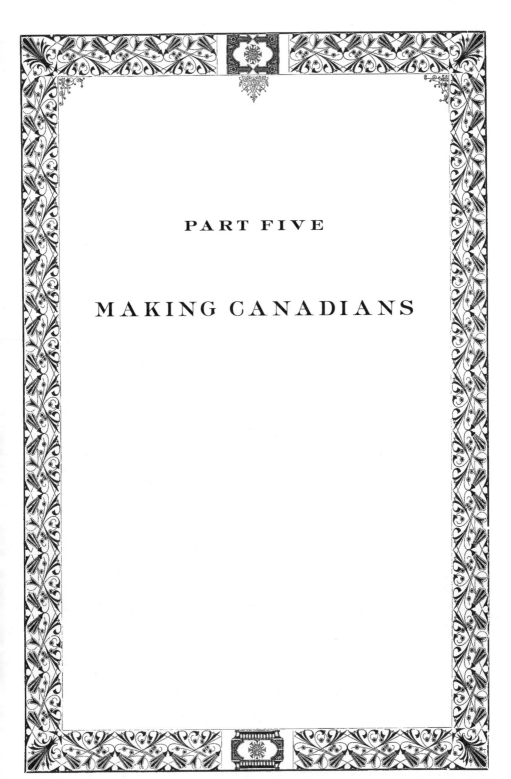

PART FIVE

MAKING CANADIANS

NEW BRUNSWICK SCHOOLS, 1873

One of the British North America Act's first tests of strengths in balancing provincial and national concerns to create a common Canadian culture came in 1873. The New Brunswick Common Schools Act of 1871, attempting to stabilize funding for province-wide schooling, secularized the whole system. The province's large minority population of Catholics deplored this move. John Costigan (1835–1916), the member for Victoria, New Brunswick, proposed that the House resolve to advise the governor general to disallow the legislation passed to enable the Act and to seek judicial review of its constitutionality.[1] Macdonald rose to defend the federal system.

The reconstructed Debates of the House of Commons, 2nd Parliament, 1st Session, record on May 14, 1873:

HON. SIR JOHN A. MACDONALD, after expressing an opinion that it would have been desirable if the hon. gentleman had had this resolution printed and distributed a sufficient time to enable the members to consider its provisions, said he must express to the hon. mover of the resolution his appreciation *quantum valet* of the moderation with which he had made his motion. (Hear, hear.) He could not express too strongly his feeling that the hon. gentleman had distinguished himself alike by his ability in stating the case of his co-religionists, his constancy in fighting their battle, in which he (Hon. Sir John A. Macdonald) sincerely sympathized, and his good sense, notwithstanding the strong feelings he must entertain, in not deviating in the slightest degree from the strictest Parliamentary rules. In doing so he had done more to further the cause of his co-religionists than by any other course which he could have adopted. (Hear, hear.)

To those hon. gentlemen who had done him (Hon. Sir John A. Macdonald) the honour to pay any attention to his political career and his political opinions, he need not say that he sincerely sympathized with the feelings of the hon. gentleman, and that he believed it would have been for the best interests of New Brunswick, and for the best interests of education, had the system which prevailed in Ontario and Quebec been extended to New Brunswick. He had had great pleasure in voting for the resolution which was carried last session, on the motion of the hon. member for Stanstead [Charles Carroll Colby], expressing a desire that some modification might be made of the law to meet the just wishes and expectations of the Roman Catholics of New Brunswick; but the question now arose as it had arisen then, not as a matter of sympathy, but as a matter of constitutional principle.

If he [Macdonald] had much pride in the success of his opinions he might feel gratified at these continued attempts to upset the federal character of the British North American Provinces. He had been from the first in favour of a legislative union, and had believed that the best interests of the country might have been promoted by a legislative union of all the

Provinces, aided by a subordinate system of municipal institutions with large powers. However, he had been overruled in that respect by large majorities in the old Parliament of Canada. The feeling had been unmistakeable, not only in Canada but also in the other Provinces, that we could have only reunion on the federal principle, and as he had thought then, as he thought still, that the union of the four Provinces was essential to the future development and progress of British North America, he yielded his own opinions and went in with the Government of which he was a member for the establishment of one great Dominion on the principle of a federal union, and he had loyally and to the best of his judgment, power and ability endeavoured to carry out that principle faithfully.

It was true that he had been charged by some hon. gentlemen with a desire to strengthen the central power, to the disadvantage of the Provincial Governments and Legislatures; that he had given any doubt resting his mind against the authority of the Local Legislatures, and to strengthen the central power, it might be so, though he had endeavoured to prevent his own predilection for a Legislature over a Federal Union from preventing it.

Still it might be that he had rather leaned in favour of centralisation, but if a resolution like this was adopted formally and solemnly by the Dominion Legislature, he must say that his original ideas had been fully carried out; that a federal union of the Provinces was at an end; that the legislative union had commenced, and the whole real power and authority of all the powers of government had been transferred from the Provincial Legislatures to the Dominion Parliament. (Hear, hear.)

They could not draw the line. It might be, and he did not hesitate to say, that from his own point of view it was so in this case, that the minority, the Catholic minority in New Brunswick, suffered a wrong by this legislation, but there might be wrongs not only in questions of education or religion, but in questions of finance, of civil liberty, and in questions of every possible kind. And if the ultimate power of decision as to what is right and what was wrong was to be vested in this Parliament, where was there a vestige of the use of power, of the benefit, or advantage, of all our paraphernalia of Provincial Governments and Provincial Legislatures. (Hear, hear.)

If they were to deal here authoritatively and to order the Governor General, the representative of the Queen, to disallow such bills as they thought the Local Legislature ought not to have passed, they would have wiped off the slate as with a wet sponge, the influences and authority of the Local Governments, and Legislatures, and have centred it all in the Canadian Parliament. Was this House prepared for this? Was it prepared to assume that new responsibility and to alter in spirit and constitution? It might be that they might keep up the sham of Provincial Legislatures, but what would they be but sham, if at any time the member of the other Provinces disagreeing with the policy deliberately adopted by the Legislature of any one Province could alter that policy?

Take the Province of Quebec which was the most obvious instance he quoted, he believed we might have had a Legislative Union instead of a Federal Union if it had not been for the Province of Quebec. The other Provinces were of one race of Anglo-Saxon ancestry. To a great degree the majority in the other Provinces were Protestants and their laws were based upon the common law and institution of England. Lower Canada contained a different race and used a different language. The majority had a religion which was in the minority in the whole

Dominion, and they claimed and justly claimed as a protection to them, to those institutions which they held so dear, to their old associations, to their religion, and to the education which in that Province was based on religion, that we should not have a Legislative Union; but that in all the questions relating to the tenure of their land, their property, their institutions, and so on, they should have a Legislature having the power to act as they pleased; as they thought they ought to act in consonance with the wishes of their people. The Lower Canadians drew themselves up, and said, if the constitution were not so drawn up as to give them the power to protect beyond a doubt their institutions, their religion, their language, and their laws, in which they had so great a pride, they would never consent to a union; and if they had not been agreed to, we should not now have the Dominion of Canada.

The same principle applied to all the Provinces. They had their rights, and the question was not whether this House thought a Local Legislature was right or wrong. But the whole question for this House to consider, whenever such a question as this was brought up, was that they should say at once that they had no right to interfere so long as the different Provincial Legislatures acted within the bounds of the authority which the constitution gave them. (Hear, hear.) There was this fixed principle, that every Provincial Legislature should feel that when it was legislating, it was legislating in the reality and not in the sham. If they did not know and feel that the measures they were arguing, discussing and amending and modifying to suit their own people, would become law it was all sham. The Federal system was gone forever and the system which he had vindicated was adopted.

He [Macdonald] did not hesitate to say that it would have given him great pleasure if he could have come to the conclusion that the Act was beyond the competence of the New Brunswick Legislature. He believed they had made a great mistake, and many others agreed with him that they had better have left the law as it was. He spoke *sub judice*, because those who passed the law had a right to maintain its wisdom; but from his own point of view he believed it was a great mistake to have repealed the law and raised this question, for but little purpose. (Hear, hear.) But that was a question for the Local Legislature. The question of education, except under the peculiar circumstances of the establishment of separate schools in Upper and Lower Canada, was left exclusively in the control of the Local Legislatures. It was withdrawn altogether from the supervision of the general Legislature, so that the people in each of the Provinces might educate their children after their own fashion.

The British North America Act provided that the Governor General might disallow a bill coming from a Local Legislature. That prerogative he exercised as the representative of the Sovereign. Before Confederation the Governor in each Province was the direct representative of the Sovereign. But in consequence of Confederation the Lieutenant-Governors were appointed by the Governor General, who was the only immediate representative of the Sovereign.

This House by passing this resolution, would assume the power and invade the prerogative of the Executive. The British North America Act said that the Queen might at any time within two years exercise the Royal prerogative in disallowing an Act of this Parliament, and that the Governor General, as her representative, might at any time within one year exercise the Royal prerogative in the disallowance of a bill from the Local Legislatures. They must assume that this provision was inserted in the constitution for wise purposes, and it gave His

Excellency a year to decide. But this resolution said that one year was too long, and that the Governor General must disallow the Act at once. What right had this House to break the constitution, and to give any such command or suggestion? It was distinctly an attempt to using a branch of the prerogative. On the two grounds, therefore, that this resolution was an unwarrantable invasion of the prerogative of the Crown, and that this Legislature ought not to interfere or dictate the exercise of that prerogative in a matter within the competence of the Local Legislature, he thought the resolution was faulty and ought not to receive the assent of this House.

Of course it would not be a vote of want of confidence in the Administration, because that was not an expression of opinion that the House had no confidence in the Government in their administration of the affairs of the Dominion. But this was an appeal to the Government to take a certain course. The Governor General had his instructions which applied as well to the Acts passed by Local Legislatures as to those passed by this Legislature, and he would ask if His Excellency, supposing this address were adopted, were to ask the advice of Her Majesty's Government at Home, what instructions he would be likely to receive? Her Majesty's Government would refuse to interfere with any bill which was within the competence of the Local Legislature.

The question would be asked whether these laws were a fair expression of the views of the Legislature of New Brunswick? There could be no doubt that whether they were right or wrong they were carried by sufficient majorities in the New Brunswick Legislature. It would also be asked if there had been an appeal to the people of that Province, and if they had expressed their dissatisfaction with the action of their representative in regard to these Acts? The answer would be in the negative, and Her Majesty's Government would naturally reply that there should be an appeal to the people before there could be any semblance of right in applying to the Sovereign to use the extreme exercise of the Royal prerogative of disallowance.

Although the hon. gentleman had no doubt under strong pressure from those whose interests he so ably advocated, made this motion, he (Hon. Sir John A. Macdonald) believed the passage of such resolutions were not in the interests of the Roman Catholics of New Brunswick. He believed they ought to get their demands—(hear, hear)—that they ought to get separate schools—(hear, hear)—and if any New Brunswick members were now in the House he would desire, in his humble way, to impress upon them his strong belief, that they would never have comfort, peace, or quiet or a complete educational system until they adopted the system which experience had shown in Quebec and Ontario had been entirely successful—that of separate schools—(cheers)—and he would tell the people of New Brunswick, so far as his voice would go to them, that they had the same battle to fight for years in Ontario; that steadily and for many years he had voted in favour of separate schools, and had, perhaps, got some abuse and been occasionally, if not systematically and continuously, maligned in consequence of the course which he had taken on that question; and that, although the parties were arrayed against each other in Ontario, apparently far more than they were now in New Brunswick, there had been no man in the Legislature of Ontario since the passage of the Separate Schools Act who had even proposed its repeal. (Hear, hear.) It had worked like a charm. (Hear, hear.)

They saw the schools side by side working harmoniously in honourable competition with each other, and there had been

removed from the Catholic minority of Upper Canada that
feeling of injustice which had rankled in their breasts until that
bill was passed. They stood on equal terms with their broth-
ers now. There was no forcing on them of a system which was
abhorrent to their principles or their prejudices. There was no
attempt to coerce them, and the result was that in Western
Canada, there were comparatively few separate schools for the
Catholics. Now they were safe, and if any attempt was made
to force religious instruction on their children they had the
remedy in their own hands, of establishing a separate school. So
completely had the religious division and rivalry and dissension
disappeared that there were no less than 600 Catholic teachers
in Ontario alone teaching in the common schools. (Hear, hear.)

He hoped to see that system introduced in the Maritime
Provinces, but only by the calm deliberation and decision of
the majority in the two legislatures of Nova Scotia and New
Brunswick. In Nova Scotia there was practically no difficulty,
because the common school system had been worked with such
liberality that no question had hitherto arisen. (Hear, hear.)

But the moment there was any attempt to coerce the New
Brunswick majority, all hope for the Catholic minority was
gone forever. That minority was a strong minority, being a
third of the whole population; and if they advocated their cause
with the same persistence and ability as the Catholic minority in the old Province of Canada, victory was certain in the
long run. If they appealed to the justice and liberality of the
Protestant majority, and endeavoured to carry their object by
constitutional means, they would be certain of ultimate success; but if they attacked the institutions of their own county,
if they sapped the very foundation of the Legislature of New
Brunswick, then the majority, like freemen conscious of their

right and of their constitutional position, would be deaf to any arguments addressed to their reason.

What had been the effect of the well meant resolution of the House last session in which, while expressing a hope that the New Brunswick Legislature would modify the law so as to relieve the Ministry, they had vindicated the rights of the Legislature by recognizing that only through it could that relief be obtained? It was not received in a kindly spirit, but was regarded as an attempt to coerce them. What then would be the feeling if they went still further and asked the Governor General to disallow measures which were within the competence of the Local Legislature? Last session the question of the competence and incompetence of the Legislature of New Brunswick in this matter was one of great doubt, and it rested only on his (Hon. Sir John A. Macdonald's) opinion. Since that time, after careful consideration, that opinion had been approved of by Her Majesty's Government, and also, he believed, by the unanimous judgment of the Court of Supreme Jurisdiction in the Province of New Brunswick. They might, therefore, assume that the law of 1871 was within the competence of the Local Legislature, and was valid in every respect. So that they stood in quite a different position from that in which they stood last year. He thought it would have been well if the latter Act had not been passed, if the decision of the Supreme Court of New Brunswick had not been interfered with, and if any small pecuniary loss which might have resulted had been borne. But they found in all the Provinces Acts passed confirmatory of previous Acts, and removing technical difficulties. The statute book of Ontario, for instance, teemed with Acts legislating by-laws of every kind. He supposed that the New Brunswick Legislature took the ground that the laws were really intended to carry out the general law of the land, and if there was any technical irregularities these laws should be confirmed.

If this House adopted this resolution it would be a great misfortune for the constitution that we now lived under. He believed it would affect the constitution of the country and the permanence of our institutions. He believed it would destroy the independence of the Provincial Legislatures. He believed that the institutions and laws of no Province would be safer hereafter. For all these considerations he hoped that this resolution would not be adopted. (Hear, hear.) If it were adopted, if this House undertook the great responsibility of interfering with the local laws, they must be prepared to discuss the justice or injustice of every law passed by every Provincial Legislature— (hear, hear)—and this Legislature, instead of being as now the general court of Parliament for the decision of great Dominion questions, would be simply a court of appeal to try whether the Provincial Legislatures were right or wrong in the conclusions that they came to. (Hear, hear.)

If this House was prepared to take that course and adopt that principle, then the Government of the day, while it would have much more responsibility, would also have much more power; for, besides conducting, and administering the affairs of the whole Dominion as one great country it would also have the power, the authority, and the control of a majority over every bill, every Act, every conclusion, every institution, every right of every Province in Canada. (Cheers.)

A SUN RUN ITS COURSE, 1873

RUSSELL'S HOTEL,
OTTAWA, NOVEMBER 13

Macdonald and his government resigned on November 5, 1873, having lost the majority in the House following the Pacific Scandal. When the Conservative caucus met the next day, Macdonald urged them to choose a younger leader. They refused. Instead, on November 13, the Ottawa Conservatives gathered by torch light and proceeded to a public dinner at Russell's Hotel where they honoured their members and heard Macdonald speak.[2]

The Toronto Mail *of November 17, 1873, reprinted the account from Ottawa's* Daily Citizen:

[SIR JOHN MACDONALD] said—Mr. Mayor, and Gentlemen,—Can I believe my scores? Is it true? Am I a defeated man or am I a victorious Minister? (Cheers.) If I were to judge by your plaudits—and they say the world only applauds success—I might suppose I was at this moment leading a successful band of followers—a majority both in and out of Parliament. (Cheers and cries of "You are!") This assembly proves to me that the common saying that mankind only worships success is a falsehood. You are not here to worship success. You are not here to aid in still further elevating men who, by the force of circumstances, have attained, and are now keeping, a high position in the country. You are following a fallen Minister. (Cries of "Never!" and "No!") Aye, Sir, it is too true. Your leaders have fallen, but your voice and the voice in this room, and the voice heard outside of this house, and the voices that are now ringing through the country, tell me that this fall is but the precursor of a second triumph. (Cheers.) There is a sect, a most respectable sect, of religionists that came in old times from the East, and still exists—those who worship the rising sun only. You are not Parsons, gentlemen. (Laughter and applause.) You can say with the poet—

"Let others hail the rising sun,
We bow to that whose course is run."*

(Cheers.)

The sun has run his course and set in the west, but your cheers show you have a confident expectation, an assurance beyond a doubt, that he will rise hereafter with unmitigated splendour in the east, and then you will be ready to cheer and sympathize with that luminary in his setting hours. (Cheers.)

A VOICE—He will rise more brilliant than ever.

---

* Macdonald is citing the opening lines from "An Ode on the Death of Mr. Pelham," by the celebrated eighteenth-century actor David Garrick (1717–1779), about the British prime minister Henry Pelham (1694–1754). Macdonald has altered the pronoun in the second line from *I* to *we*. (Retzer, ed. *Choice of the Best Poetical Pieces of the Most Eminent English Poets*, vol. 3, 3–8)

SIR JOHN MACDONALD—You, Mr. Mayor have made an agreeable allusion to myself and my departed colleague, Sir George-E. Cartier with respect to what we have done for Ottawa. I am proud, as a member of the Administration of that day, of the share we had in bringing the seat of Government to this city. Allow me to remind you of the circumstances connected with that very important movement. The city which I then represented and I now represent in Parliament [Kingston], had been the seat of Government and hoped to be again. Montreal, Toronto, Hamilton and Quebec all strove for the honour, and we finally left it to her Majesty the Queen to decide the question. When we went to parliament and asked to have the decision left to her Majesty, we came forward, Sir George Cartier as a representative of Montreal, I as a member for Kingston and pledge our honours that we would not attempt one way or another, to sway her decision, and that she should be left to act upon such light and guidance as she might seek for. Her majesty chose this city. (Cheers.) The other side were disappointed; my own constituents were very naturally disappointed at the choice. The very next session of Parliament, a gentleman from the district of Montreal, actuated by the desire, of course, to aid his section, moved in Parliament that Ottawa was not a fit place for the seat of Government. The Ministry, of which I was a member, voted against that resolution as one man, because if it were carried, we considered it would be an insult to Her Majesty. The motion was carried and we resigned our offices. (Cheers.) At the time of the fall of that Administration, I was Premier of the late Province of Canada, as at the recent change I was Premier of the Dominion. We gave not a hope that we would submit; we did not lower our flag for one moment. We knew what was before us. We knew that the path of honour demanded that, having left the decision to the Queen, we must abide by it under all circumstances, and no matter who might be disappointed, no matter what effect it might have upon us, we were bound to carry out that decision. (Cheers.) And the consequence was, year after year, we fought that battle until we had the proud satisfaction of seeing the Government that had first left it to the Queen and fallen because we sustained her decision, returned to power in consequence of the character we obtained for defending her Majesty. We were, in 186[0], present to see the son of her Majesty lay the corner stone of the Parliament Buildings.* (Cheers.) I say this, not by way of boast, but simply as a very interesting reminiscence, as a bond of connection between myself and my political friends and the city of Ottawa, which, I hope will never be severed. (Cheers.) The prudence, the propriety, not to say the honour, of that decision is shown by the magnificent results. Look at this city, which, with its environs, has upwards of 20,000 inhabitants; look at the magnificent structures which are the envy of our neighbours, and a town grown to its present magnificent proportion while yet only in its swaddling clothes. (Cheers.) If we acted our part rightly as statesmen and gentlemen of honour, by sustaining the decision of bringing the Government to Ottawa, we have been richly repaid for it, for no truer body of supporters in and out of Parliament of the Ministry of which I have been a member, can be found, than in the city and district of Ottawa. (Cheers.) We have received our reward, and it is a pleasure to me, because, sometimes, good deeds do not get their reward in this world. Not only in this social assembly, but in the confidence, in the

---

* The Prince of Wales laid the cornerstone in September 1860, on the occasion of his tour of Canada. (Creighton, *Young Politician*, 301)

sympathy, in the warm approbation and happy support not only of Ottawa, but of the surrounding district, have I found my reward at once. If I have cast my bread upon the waters, it has returned at once, and not after many days. (Cheers.) Yes here, gentlemen, as I said, assembled to do honour to a fallen Minister—a man who is now reduced to the ranks (Laughter, and cries of "No!"), but I am like many an honest fellow in the army who has risen to a certain position, and who has, through some eccentricity or other, been reduced to the ranks, and prepares to rise again, first to the rank of sergeant-major, and afterwards to the position which he held before. I am as confident as I can be at this moment, that the party that supported the late Government will be excluded from power for but a short time. That their reverse is but momentary is as certain as that I now address you. (Loud Cheers.) It may be that the future Government, composed from the Party to which we all belong, may not be the same as that which lately resigned. I hope myself to be able to be relieved of the responsibility of even being a Minister again. (Cries of "No! No!") I hope, out of the Party to which I belong, there will rise a strong and successful Administration. I have no doubt there will, but I hope I will never be a member of any administration again. You have heard it said by my enemies that I cling to power, that the whole aim and object of my existence is to govern. On addressing the House at one time, I took occasion to show that was not the case. Through circumstances not in my own control, my desire to retire from the cares of office—not from Parliament—was defeated by the united action of my Party . . .

Macdonald went on to recall the fall of the government in 1858 on the "seat-of-government" question. He had offered to withdraw from the party leadership on that occasion. But, "told by my supporters," he explained, that "I would be untrue to myself and to the Party if I did not return, I to the enormous sacrifice of my personal and pecuniary interests, consented." It was the main theme of his speech that evening.

ELECTION SPEECH TO
THE WORKINGMEN, 1882

"THE AMPHITHEATRE," TORONTO, MAY 30

The new industrial reality of Canada was not lost on Macdonald, nor were its social consequences. Early in the 1870s, Macdonald had made it his business to understand working men. Then in 1873, a desperate economic depression gripped the world markets. Toronto workers depending upon wages in Canadian industries grew more militant. Some labour groups promoted their interests independently, but many still sought political solutions through the Conservative party organizations such as the Workingmen's Liberal-Conservative Associations.[3]

By the 1880s, economic conditions had improved vastly. Labour politics evolved with the advent of organizations such as the US-based Knights of Labor and the Canadian-based Trades and Labor Congress. Chapters from both helped to draw unskilled workers, women, and the Irish into the labour movement with an increasingly political voice; the Chinese workers remained vigorously excluded from their folds. Macdonald, however, continued to provide political leadership. His government passed factory acts, began collecting labour statistics, and instituted other measures that recognized the working man. In 1886, Macdonald convened the Royal

Commission on Relations of Labor and Capital, whose 1889 report revealed the dire working conditions of many Canadians. Macdonald saw the election of 1882 as an opportunity to solidify the support of the "workingmen," and to trumpet the positive economic effects of the National Policy. He addressed the National Workingman's Union of Canada in Toronto at the "Amphitheatre on the night of Tuesday, May 30th."[4]

The pamphlet, The Dominion Campaign! Sir John Macdonald on the Questions at Issue Before the People—The Premier's Great Speech before the Workingmen of Toronto, *published in 1882, records that:*

[SIR JOHN MACDONALD:] Mr. Chairman and gentlemen—When I stand in this place and see this crowded amphitheatre, I begin to think that I must be a regular old Rip Van Winkle (loud laughter) that I have been asleep for three years; but that I now come to find the same place, the same crowd, the same friends, the same enthusiasm, the same supporters as I had on this same ground in 1878. (Loud cheers.)

Yes; as a friend says behind me, a larger crowd; because, thanks to the N.P.,* Toronto has grown larger, the population has increased, you are all richer, you have better looking hats— (Laughter)—and better looking coats. (Cheers and laughter.) And, I really must say as a bloated aristocrat and office-holder, that I myself am not a bit the worse for my three years' salary.† (Renewed laughter.) I therefore congratulate myself, you, and

---

* The National Policy was often casually referred to as the N.P.

† Macdonald's financial straits were well known. He was not a privately wealthy man, and while he was in office his law practice suffered. His various government positions often did not pay enough to support his family. Early in the 1870s, a friend organized the Testimonial Fund to provide a supplemental income and help him to pay considerable debts. (Johnson and Waite, "Macdonald, Sir John Alexander," *DCB*)

the country, that after three years I come back and find enthusiasm, hope—not only hope, but certainty—of the future.
(Great cheering.) Let us look back to the year before the 17th
of September, 1878.* Let us remember the time of depression,
the time of sinking hearts, empty pockets, and empty larders—
(Hear, hear, and applause)—and let us bear in mind that since
the National Policy has been inaugurated we see in the country a prosperous, contented, and happy people, and we find
Canada standing amongst the first of the nations in the world in
credit, in resources, in standing, in reputation, and in fruition.
(Cheers.) Mr. Chairman, I owe much, and those who act with
me owe much, to the people of Toronto, to the workingmen
of Toronto. (Loud cheers.)

It was here on this platform that the first spark was lighted.
(Applause.) It was here that the wave of enthusiasm which spread
over the whole Dominion originated. (Cheers.) It was here that
the foundations of the National Policy were laid. (Cheers.)
And I ask you if there has not been a noble, magnificent super-
structure raised on the foundation which you, the workingmen of Toronto, so successfully prepared in 1878. (Applause.)
You gave me your confidence, gentlemen—and although it
was said by those who were opposed to me that my policy was
only a pretence, that the line I had taken in Parliament, the line
that the Conservative Opposition had taken in Parliament with
a view to rescuing the country from the depression was only
a political cry, that when we came into power we would not
carry out our policy, that there would be no National Policy,
no readjustment of the tariff, no attempt to encourage our

---

* September 17, 1878, was the day Alexander Gunn beat him in the Kingston polls by
144 votes and Macdonald lost his seat. (Creighton, *Old Chieftain*, 242)

industries, agricultural, manufacturing, and mining, that our policy was a mere political dodge, and that we were not in earnest—although all this was said, we did carry out our policy. (Cheers.) And I appeal to you as workingmen to witness whether I have not fully carried out the pledges I made before I took office, whether the tariff you expected has not been adopted, whether the industries which I said ought to be encouraged have not been developed, and whether instead of despondency there is not now hope, enterprise, and activity in every branch of business, public and private? (Cheers.) It is true, gentlemen, we see yet but the infancy of the manufactures and industries which we have established, or have tried to establish. These things cannot be established in a hurry. You cannot plant the seed to-day and get the crop to-morrow. But we have sown the seed; and much more rapidly, much more speedily, than even I—sanguine as I was of the success of the policy—expected, it has grown; and it now shows the certainty of a future crop which will make this country envied and looked up to by every other country in the world. (Cheers.)

Mr. Chairman, although our progress is great, we are still in the bud, hoping and believing that there will be an early flower and early maturity. And why are we not in maturity already? Three years is a short time, but in three years much has been done. Why, then, I ask, has not more been done? Because we have had an unscrupulous Opposition; because we have had an unpatriotic Opposition. (Loud cheers.) The gentlemen composing that Opposition have told capitalists, "It is no use your investing your money in manufactures in Canada, because the present Government will never last more than five years. A new vote of the people will sweep away all that, and we will return to power and adopt a free trade policy, and reverse that under which the country prospers today." That, in effect, has been their statement, and I tell you—and this is not a matter of supposition, but of certainty and knowledge on my part—that there are millions of dollars waiting to be invested in Canada; millions in England, and large sums in the United States, waiting to come to Canada, waiting to be invested in every kind of industry, in mines and in manufactures of every kind; but the capitalists say, "Your Opposition say that your policy is only the result of a temporary madness on the part of the people of Canada in 1878, because times were bad then, and that it will be reversed at the next election." (Cries of "never, never.") They say that after the next election Sir John Macdonald and the National Policy will disappear, and we will have Reform purity, and economy, and free trade. (Renewed cries of "never.") I hear you, gentlemen, and I know that you are right. Capitalists, men who have by hard work and great industry, but by slow degrees, collected capital, are naturally timid with reference to the investments they make. They do not like to put their money in an uncertain enterprise; and they have written to me, and to Sir Leonard Tilley, saying, "We are ready to invest large sums of money; Canada is a great field for enterprise; it is a country of all others where manufactures can be most successfully introduced and carried on, but we are told by Mr. [Alexander] Mackenzie"—and, sir, this was said in the Parliament of Canada in my hearing, and you will find it in the published debate—"that protection is a national folly and a national crime, and that it must be abandoned." Sir Richard Cartwright too, the mixer and muddler of figures ("Hear, hear" and laughter) who kept the financial conscience of Mr. Mackenzie, and expects to keep the financial conscience of Edward Blake, said "what?" That all protection was legalized robbery. (Laughter.) So capitalists are afraid to invest money in this country. Mr. Blake says in his address, "Why did these gentlemen dissolve and go to the country? Why did they ask the people to give a verdict when they might have remained in power eighteen months longer?" Our answer was this: That we wanted to let the people declare after three years' experience whether they were resolved to adhere to that policy or whether they were willing to reverse it. (Cries of "never.") It shows at all events, that we, the office-seekers, we, the bloated aristocrats, were disinterested for once. (Loud laughter and cheers.) Yes, I take out of your pockets a salary of $8,000 a year as Prime Minister—(cries of "You deserve it")—and I might have remained in office quietly for eighteen months longer. There was no compulsion to go to the country, but I have given up $12,000 of salary in order that I may come before you, the people of Canada, to know whether you want the N.P. to be maintained or not. (Loud cheers.) I have no doubt from the enthusiastic voices I hear around me that the people will stand by the National Policy. (Cheers.)

These voices are merely repetitions, affirming the same sound as will be heard at every poll in the whole Dominion. I am confident the result of the elections will be that the country will declare that the policy which the people calmly, coolly, and deliberately adopted in 1878 shall be the policy of Canada for the next five years. That is the reason we have appealed to the country, because, as I have said already, we know money is waiting for investment, and all that is wanted by capitalists in Canada, England and the United States, aye, in France and Germany, is to learn whether this country is of the fixed, constant opinion that the National Policy shall be continued as in 1878. (Cheers.) If, as I am sure it will be, the national voice confirms the decision given by the people in 1878, I can retire on my laurels. (Cries of "no.") I have fought the good fight, and I can then make way for younger and stronger men. (Renewed cries of "no.") I have carried out the policy which I believed, and I believe now, was for the interest of the country. (Loud cheers.) I have carried out that policy, and the country has sustained me. And at the end of five years the manufacturers will have generated so much capital, while the workingmen, the skilled and unskilled labor that surround those varied industries, will have become so powerful, the capitalists will be linked together in associations, and workingmen will be bound together in trades unions, and they will fight the battle together. (Loud cheers.) Capital and labor will go hand in hand, and they will put down all attempts to make this country what it was before, a mere agricultural country, from which all skilled labor went to the United States to find employment, and that skilled labor will remain in the country. ("Hear, hear.") Capital and labor will join together, and at the end of five years I defy Sir Richard Cartwright, if he had half a dozen titles, or Mr. Blake, or all the free-traders from John Stuart Mill* down to David Mills [member for Bothwell]—(loud laughter and cheers)—to take the edifice that the people of Canada will have raised. (Renewed cheers.) This country, blessed in every respect, with a fertile soil, a fine climate, an industrious people, with a manufacturing population consuming the products of the farmer, will go forward, and not all the attempts of theorisers and philosophers—(laughter)—will set aside the actual state of facts, that Canada will become, like the Mother Country, great in manufacturing industries of all kinds and great in agricultural

---

* John Stuart Mill (1806–1873) was a philosopher and political scientist. (Harris, "John Stuart Mill," *ODNB*)

development, for it possesses all the elements that make a great nation. (Loud cheers, and a voice, "No more soup kitchens.")

I hear the remark that we shall want no more soup kitchens. Gentlemen, I addressed a body of workingmen at Ottawa the other day, and I had to contrast the state of affairs there five years ago, when Mr. Mackenzie was in power, and at the present time. I stated, and you may remember it was mentioned in all the newspapers at the time, that there was actually no employment for labor, and that the Parliament Buildings and the Government offices were surrounded by men asking for the means of earning their bread, asking for half or quarter time and half or quarter wages in order to support their families. I have seen it myself at Ottawa. I was in Opposition, but I lived there a year and a half before I came to Toronto, and I had my house besieged by persons asking employment, and that I would give them some work to prevent them from being compelled to beg. Now a different state of things prevails. The boot is on the other leg. (Cheers.) I told the Ottawa workingmen this story. Years ago, when Parliament was sitting in Toronto, we had a five months' session. I was in the Government, and I had a very hard fight, because the Opposition was led by a *man*—George Brown—by a strong man, who made a strong fight of it. We got through at last, and when the guns were firing, telling us that the Governor General was coming down to prorogue the House, a great friend of mine came up to me and said: "John A., you do not care a farthing for us now; when the Governor comes we have to go, and you no longer care." "No, my good friend," I said. "I have been kissing your feet for the last five months, and now you may kiss mine for the next seven." (Laughter.) So it was with the workingmen of Ottawa. For four years they were wandering round imploring the people to give them work. Now, in Ottawa the boot is on the other leg, and if I want any work done I cannot get it done because the men are so fully employed—(loud cheers)—and I think it is the same in Toronto, Hamilton, and elsewhere. The boot is on the other leg, and long may it remain there. (Enthusiastic cheers.)

Every session during the last three years of Mr. Mackenzie's Government I moved an amendment in favor of the National Policy, but it was derided, laughed at, and voted down. I was treated contemptuously, as a theorist, as a man of no practical policy, and as merely getting up clap-trap notions for clap-trap purposes. The moment we came into power we carried the National Policy. For one whole month, night and day, Messrs. Mackenzie, Blake, Mills, Sir Richard Cartwright, and the whole of their party opposed every step we took, every motion we made, every readjustment we suggested, and opposed our tariff, both in principle and detail. The *Globe*, gentlemen, which is the able exponent of the principle of the Opposition, has been a free trade journal and is so now. Up to three weeks ago it advanced arguments in favor of free trade. Now, at the last moment, these gentlemen, finding that they are going to the people, that they want their votes, come to you, cap in hand, and say, "Gentlemen, we don't intend at all to interfere with the manufacturers." (Laughter.) Well, gentlemen, they were either fools or rogues; fools if they opposed a policy which they now admit was correct, or rogues for opposing it for factious purposes. What say they now? Mr. Mackenzie says, "We don't intend to disturb the manufacturers; we are going to educate them to free trade by slow degrees; we will show the people the fallacies of protection." This is something like the Dutchman who tried to reduce the feed of his horse by slow degrees from half a bushel of oats to a single wisp of straw, and thus do away with what he called the extravagance of the oats. Unfortunately for his experiment, just as he was about to succeed, the horse died. (Laughter.) So it is with Mr. Mackenzie's proposition, with the proposition of Mr. Blake, in the address which he published to the electors of West Durham. But perhaps Mr. Blake is not going to get in. He has got a man, a *Mail* to oppose him. (Laughter and cheers.) Mr. Blake says: "Of course the expenses of the country are so great that we shall have to keep up the taxation for the present, but by-and-bye we will reduce them, and take off all the burdens from the people." But, gentlemen, the horse will die, the manufactures will be abolished, and we shall be driven back to where we were in 1875-7, and you will suffer this great loss when I shall be too old to try to remedy matters again. (Voice—"I hope you will never get old.") Well, they say in Parliament I am too old for my friends in Opposition. (Laughter.)

You, the people of Canada, know the party that laid down the great principle of national protection, and you put a Government in power to carry it out. You know that the present Government have honestly and sincerely carried that policy out, although they have been attacked in England for so doing. We all desire to stand well with the great old Mother Country, but her people are the judges of their interests and we of ours. (Cheers.) Although free trade prevails in England just now, although we have been reproved and I have been abused in the English papers, which said that Sir John ought to know better than to support any such faded old fallacy as protection and fair trade, nevertheless we have honestly and fairly carried that policy out. We have stood all the obloquy heaped upon us, and shall continue to do so, if we have your support. (Cheers.) I am not going to speak to you at any length to-night. (Cries of "Go on" and "We like to hear you.") Like many old persons, I like to hear myself—(laughter)—but still I must make way for others, and although I may not think their speeches are so interesting as my own—(laughter)—I must affect to be modest and let them come forward and address you. Besides, you are reading men, and must be well acquainted with a subject which has been discussed for the last five years. It would be an insult to your intelligence now to discuss the abstract doctrines of protection and a National Policy. You have made up your minds on this subject, and my feeble arguments are not wanted. You know and have felt the benefit of the National Policy, are resolved they shall be retained for the country, for yourselves, and for your children. (Cheers.)

Macdonald continued expounding on the Dominion's conflicts with Ontario over the provincial boundary and over the disallowance of the Rivers and Streams Acts. He railed against the accusations of gerrymandering levelled against him for his proposed redistribution of seats in the 1882 Representation Bill. He appealed to the working men as taxpayers, as men who had a stake in the community, and he concluded gamely:*

Gentlemen, I feel great pride in occupying the position that has been awarded me by the people of this country. I can, at my age, have no other wish than to live well in the minds of my fellow-countrymen, and when I die to live well in their

---

* The British North America Act stipulated that population was the basis of representation and that constituencies (or seats) would be added to the House of Commons as the population grew according to the ratio set by Quebec's fixed 65 seats and its population. The census of 1881 clearly indicated the need for an increase in representation in the House. Macdonald opted for "strict numerical equality," but in the process created new constituencies across the local units of the county or the municipality, and effectively "hiv[ed] the Grits where they had been concentrated." (Creighton, *Old Chieftain*, 334-5)

recollection. (Cheers.) I have had a long life of politics, a long life of official duties. I have committed many mistakes. Looking back with the light of experience, there are many things I have done wrongly, and many things I have neglected that I should have done. These rise to me; I know them, I recognize them; but I would be more than human if I had not committed errors; I say this to you, and I believe the majority of the country will believe me when I state that whatever I have done, in every act of legislation and administration, I have tried, according to the best of my judgment, to do what I could for the well-being of good government and the future prosperity of this my beloved country.

CELEBRATING FORTY YEARS
IN POLITICS, 1885

The faithful travelled from Toronto to Montreal to celebrate Macdonald's fortieth anniversary in politics on January 12. The "Streets Thronged with Multitudes of People," trumpeted the Toronto Daily Mail. *They marched in triumph next to "Sir John's carriage" on the slow procession to the drill shed, at the Champ de Mars, the "largest covered space in Canada," where a dinner in his honour awaited. Fireworks exploded about the streets as the procession passed; the "coloured fires" illuminated "in fine relief" the "graceful statue of her Majesty the Queen" in Victoria Square. At Place d'Armes an "imitation of a golden fountain" stood "with batteries of Roman candles throwing myriads of brilliant stars far up into the air," and it "captivated all who witnessed the lovely sight." In the drill shed, an audience of "ten or twelve thousand" responded with "deafening" applause as Macdonald took the stage and spoke. The next day Macdonald attended a mock parliament held by an association of young men and he "humorously contrasted the mock Parliament at Ottawa with the real Parliament at Montreal in such a lively and entertaining way that all present were pleased beyond measure."*

The reporter for Toronto's Daily Mail *summarized his speech at* Champ de Mars *for the January 13, 1885, edition:*

[SIR JOHN MACDONALD:] In commencing, Sir John remarked that he could not expect his feeble voice would reach such a vast assembly as that he stood in presence of, but he only wished he could speak like a trumpet to convey his heartfelt gratitude for such a testimonial of respect as he had received from the citizens of Montreal on his seventieth birthday and the fortieth anniversary of his political birth, which was all the more gratifying to him because it came from a city where his public life had its origin, and where he made his first maiden political speech in the Parliament of Canada, which was held in Montreal forty years ago. He admitted that he had committed errors in his long experience of public life, but the spontaneous demonstration tendered him this evening led him to think that he had not lived in vain, but that he had devoted all the abilities God had endowed him with to the service and benefit of his country. He referred to Montreal being only a village, when he commenced public life in it, compared with being the leading commercial city of the Dominion now, which it had developed into, and he predicted in glowing terms what it would become hereafter. After again expressing his gratitude and thanks for the reception and kindness showered upon him he retired amidst a thrilling and prolonged ovation.

UNVEILING GEORGE-ÉTIENNE
CARTIER'S STATUE, 1885

PARLIAMENT HILL, OTTAWA, JANUARY 29

In 1885 Macdonald unveiled the first monument on Parliament Hill, a statue of Sir George-Étienne Cartier. The statue represented more than Cartier's impress on the heart of a nation and on a friend. It showed a Canadian people self-consciously taking their place in history. By the late nineteenth century, western nations increasingly erected public commemorations as statements of identity. La Minerve *newspaper of Montreal speculated that this was the first public statue erected of "someone of purely Canadian fame." The government wanted the best possible sculptor and held an international competition; Louis-Philippe Hébert (1850–1917) from Quebec won the commission.⁵ Macdonald's speech on the occasion itself entered the Canadian historical consciousness.*

Macdonald's words survived to be reproduced by John Boyd's Sir George-Étienne Cartier, Bart: His Life and Times, *published in 1914:*

[SIR JOHN A. MACDONALD:] We are assembled here to-day to do honour to the memory of a great and good man.

The parliament of Canada has voted a sum of money for the purpose of defraying the cost of erecting a fitting statue to Sir George Cartier. In doing so I believe parliament truly represented the desires and wishes of the whole people of the Dominion to do honour to the memory of that statesman.

That lamented gentleman, during the whole of his official life, was my colleague. As we acted together for years from the time he took office in 1855 until 1873, when he was cut off, it is almost impossible for me to allude to his services to the country without at the same time passing, in some degree, a laudation on the Government of which he and I were both members.

But there is no necessity for me to recall to your memory the deeds of Sir George Cartier. He served his country faithfully and well. Indeed, his life was cut short by his unremitting exertions in the cause of this country. I believe no public man, since Canada has been Canada, has retained during the whole of his life, as was the case of Sir George Cartier, in such an eminent degree the respect of both the parties into which this great country was divided. He was a strong constant Lower Canadian. He never disguised his principles; he carried them faithfully and honestly into practice. But while he did this he allowed others the same liberty he claimed for himself and approved of the principle that each man should do according to his conscience what he thought best for the good of the country. The consequence was that even those gentlemen who were strongly opposed to his political course and views gave due credence to his honesty of purpose, and believed that whether right or wrong he was acting according to the best of his judgment and the impulses of his conscience. As for myself, when the tie between us was broken, no man could have suffered more keenly than I did at the loss of my colleague and my friend. I shall leave it to others to expatiate upon his labours more particularly. Sufficient for me to say that he did what he regarded to be in the interests not of a section but of the whole country.

Nevertheless he was a French-Canadian. From the time he entered parliament he was true to his province, his people, his race, and his religion. At the same time he had no trace of bigotry, no trace of fanaticism. Why, those who were opposed to him in his own province used to call him a French-speaking Englishman. He was as popular among the English-speaking people as he was among his own countrymen, and justly so, because he dealt out even justice to the whole people of Canada, without regard to race, origin or principles. Gentlemen, he was true to his province, he was true to the institutions of his province, and if he had done nothing else than see to the complete codification of the law of his native province, if he had done nothing else but give to Quebec the most perfect code of law that exists in the whole world, that was enough to make him immortal amongst civilized people who knew his merits, knew his exertions, and knew the value of the great code of civil law he conferred on his country.*

I shall say no more in respect of what he did, but I will speak of him as a man truthful, honest and sincere; his word was as good as his bond, and his bond was priceless. A true friend, he never deserted a friend. Brave as a lion, he was afraid

---

* Cartier focused his vision of a commercial French Canada by helping to reform "the basic institutions of Quebec society." The abolition of the seigneurial tenure helped reshape key Quebec institutions with investment in the transportation system and the establishment of a compulsory, comprehensive, and bicultural education system. Cartier organized the province's contradictory and unwieldy mass of British laws and French civil law dating back to the French régime into the Civil Code of Lower Canada of 1866, which he called "the most pregnant source of national greatness." (Young, *George-Étienne Cartier*, 86–100)

of nothing. He did not fear a face of clay. But whilst he was bold, as I have said, in the assertion of his own principles, and he carried them irrespective of consequences, he respected the convictions of others.

I can speak of him perfectly because I knew his great value, his great value as a statesman, his great value as a friend. I loved him whilst he was living; I regretted and wept for him whilst he died. I shall not keep you here longer by any remarks of mine. Others coming from his own province will speak of his merits.

Gentlemen, I shall now unveil the statue. It is, I believe, a fine work of art, and we have the satisfaction of knowing that in the hands of the sculptor it has been a labour of love; that the statue has been moulded, framed and carried into successful execution by one of his own countrymen, Mr. Hébert. It is a credit to Canadian art, and it shows he was a true Canadian when he felt his work was a labour of love and cut such a beautiful statue as I shall now have the pleasure of showing you. I think those who knew Sir George Cartier and were familiar with his features will acknowledge it a fine portrait of the man.

I can only conclude in the words of the song he used to sing to us so often when he was with us in society: "Il y a longtemps que je t'aime, jamais je ne t'oublierai."

THE FRANCHISE DEBATES, 1885

Since Confederation, Macdonald had promoted the need to pass a federal franchise law to regularize voting rights across the nation. Attempts in the intervening years failed. In 1885, however, Macdonald proposed Bill 103, which enfranchised propertied, unmarried women (spinsters and widows) and, while allowing them to retain their treaty rights, Indians who met specified qualifications as owners of improved lands. Macdonald called the bill "the greatest triumph of my life." [6]

Since 1867, the franchise had been open to all male property holders twenty-one years of age, about twenty percent of the population, who together created the "political nation." This threshold reflected the idea that maleness, legal majority, and property ownership shielded an individual from influence or coercion by others—be it an employer or a legal guardian such as a husband, a parent, or the state. Owning property also meant having a "stake in the community." [7]

But changing social and economic conditions challenged the existing "political nation." By the 1880s the fight for women's rights had gained visibility. Chinese immigrants and sojourners established communities in British Columbia and in small pockets across Canada and they advocated for their civic rights. Unions emerged to make working men aware of their class interests and to ask for the right to vote. The reserve system incorporated the "Indians" and defined their new relationship with the state. In addition, some—but not all—groups among Canada's Indian population desired a "representative or voice in the Dominion Parliament." For the legislators—already members of the "political nation"—the fundamental question was: Were these newly visible segments of society ready and able to be members of the "political nation"? Were women too dominated by men, workers by employers, the Chinese by ties to a foreign country and ruler, and Indians by the state? Had they earned the right to political participation by their contributions to the nation and its economic growth? Were they capable of making disinterested decisions on behalf of the polity? The House debated the bill between March and June of 1885. It became law on July 4, 1885, after significant amendment.[8]

The House of Commons Debates of the 5th Parliament, 3rd Session, record on April 16, 1885:

SIR JOHN A. MACDONALD: There is one question, however, in this Bill in which, personally, I may be considered to be interested, and that is women's franchise. I have always and am now strongly in favor of that franchise. I believe that is coming as certainly as came the gradual enfranchisement of women from being the slaves of men until she attained her present position, almost the equal of man. I believe that time is coming, though perhaps we are not any more than the United States or England quite educated up to it, I believe the time will come, and I shall be very proud and glad to see it, when the final step towards giving women full enfranchisement is carried in Canada.

We know that Mr. [William Ewart] Gladstone, the head of

the present [Liberal] Administration in England, is strongly in favor of women franchise, although he would not hazard and peril his late Franchise Bill by introducing that question. He said it was a separate question and must be dealt with separately, and therefore he resisted on that ground, and on that ground only, the extension of the franchise to women.

We also know that the leaders of the Opposition in England in both Houses, the Marquis of Salisbury* and Sir Stafford Northcote, are strongly in favor of extending the franchise to women, to the extent set forth in my Bill; that is to say, that widows and unmarried ladies† who have the property qualification should have a vote. Following those illustrious examples, I shall not peril the Bill on that point. I do not mean to say I would strike it out, but when we go into committee we shall have a vote in the House upon that subject, but I have already prepared the Bill in case that the House is not in favor of extending in this Bill the franchise to women—I have prepared the Bill in anticipation of perhaps a hostile vote, which I would be sorry to see on that question.

When this Bill is sanctioned by the adoption of the second reading we shall go into committee—I hope early next week—and I invite the fullest discussion in the House on the various clauses—the enfranchising clauses, and the disfranchising clauses of this measure. I move the second reading of the Bill.

---

* Robert Arthur Talbot Gascoyne-Cecil, third marquess of Salisbury (1830–1903), Conservative prime minister of Britain for two terms in the latter half of the 1880s, did believe that if the working classes were capable of voting, then women should be as well. (Smith, "Cecil, Robert Arthur Talbot Gascoyne,"*ODNB*)

† Veronica Strong-Boag explains that "[e]very suffrage bill Macdonald introduced in the 1880s included provision for widow and spinster suffrage." (Strong-Boag, "The Citizenship Debates," 93, fn 37)

Sir Richard Cartwright, member for Huron South, wondered why Macdonald had "br[ought] down a measure of this enormous importance, and that he thought it worth just eight and a half minutes' discussion by the clock." The franchise debates continued.[9]

Macdonald's further thoughts on extending the franchise to women were recorded in the House of Commons Debates, *5th Parliament, 3rd Session, on April 27, 1885:*

SIR JOHN A. MACDONALD: My hon. friend [Mr. Townshend] has moved this amendment ["of striking out woman suffrage"] in order to test the question of female suffrage, and I think it is very important to test it now as, if female suffrage is denied, it will cause a change in very many portions of the Bill, and it would be well to settle the question as early as possible. As that question affects most other clauses of the Bill, it should be settled first. There can be no objection, of course, to any other amendment being moved to any of the phrases before it.

MR. [EDWARD] BLAKE: Very well. On that understanding it is all right.

MR. [FRANÇOIS] LANGELIER: Is this amendment intended to do away with woman suffrage only for the Province of Quebec? As I understand the amendment it is confined to the Province of Quebec, because the portion of the clause which it is proposed to strike out only refers to that Province.

MR. [DÉSIRÉ] GIROUARD: But it involves the question of woman suffrage.

SIR JOHN A. MACDONALD: It is true that portion of the clause refers specially to woman suffrage in the Province of Quebec, but the Government does not propose, or the Bill does not propose, and I am sure my hon. friend from Cumberland (Mr. Townshend) does not propose in his amendment, that the ladies of Quebec only should be excluded.

My hon. friend takes the earliest opportunity of testing the question as to the female franchise, by moving to amend that portion of this clause which presupports that female suffrage is to be carried in the Bill. Well, Mr. Chairman, with respect to female suffrage, I can only say that, personally, I am strongly convinced, and every year, for many years, I have become more strongly convinced, of the justice of giving women otherwise qualified the suffrage. I am strongly of that opinion, and have been for a good many years, and I had hoped that Canada would have the honor of first placing women in the position that she is certain eventually, after centuries of oppression, to obtain.

It is merely a question of time all over the civilised world. In England the question has made marvellous progress, as we all know who have paid any attention to that subject. By slow degrees women have become owners of their own property; they are protected as much as if they were unmarried—protected in all their rights, not only against all the world, but against their own husbands. They have obtained a *quasi* political position on school boards, in vestries, and in municipal elections, I believe, to a certain extent; and in every position in which they have made an advance towards equality with men, they have proved themselves so efficient that there has not been the slightest attempt to retroactive legislation to deprive them of any privileges or advantages that, after centuries of denial, they have at last obtained.

I had hoped that we in Canada would have had the great honour of leading in the cause of securing the complete emancipation of women, of completely establishing her equality as a human being and a member of society with man. I say it is a mere matter of time.

It is known—at least, it is believed, though I cannot speak positively on that point—but it is generally understood that the present Premier of England is in favor of female franchise. He did not allow female franchise to be imported into his late Franchise or Representation Bill, for fear it might harm the Bill as a whole. He stated that the question was to be judged on its own merits as a separate question; and upon his statement the motion for the extension of the franchise to women was defeated by a large majority. But it was a majority obtained in consequence of that statement made by the Premier, who, as head of the Government and as leader of the House of Commons, was carrying through the Franchise Bill; and when there was a separate motion, standing by itself, moved by Mr. Mason, it was defeated in the House of Commons by a majority of only sixteen votes. I need not enlarge upon this subject, because I am fighting *contra spem*. I believe a majority of this House is opposed to female suffrage.

SOME HON. MEMBERS: No, no.

SIR JOHN A. MACDONALD: Then I am not fighting *contra spem*; but I think I am better informed on this point than those hon. gentlemen who say "no, no." The Government are exceedingly anxious, and are resolved so far as it lies in their power, to persuade the House to give effect to their resolution to have this Bill become law during the present Session, and, therefore wish that this question, which is a very important one, but not the all important one, should be settled as early as possible on this motion.

And after this is disposed of, we shall be better able to judge of the remainder of the measure, especially of the qualification and disqualification of voters. I have nothing more to say, only I hope that my anticipation will not be realised, and that this House will adopt the cause by which unmarried women and widows will have the franchise. The argument has been used with some speciousness in the discussions on this measure that it is illogical, that we must give the vote to every woman if we give it to any.

This matter of the franchise is not a matter of logic, but of expediency; and it does not at all follow that because we go a certain length we have to go the whole length. The argument was pressed so far in this House the other night that it was said: If you grant the privilege of electing, you must grant the privilege and right of being elected. That does not at all follow. We have at this moment various qualifications of electors here who could not themselves be elected. Government contractors and civil servants can all vote, but cannot be elected. Persons receiving money from the public treasury can all vote, but cannot be elected. In the same way in England Church of England clergymen are all voters, but they are ineligible for election to Parliament. So that the logical argument that if you grant one thing, you must go still further, I do not think amounts to much. Then with respect to the argument that because the Bill gives the right to vote to unmarried women and widows, who are unmarried women, you are doing an injustice to married women. If it be a matter of justice and injustice, you are committing an injustice by omitting all women, and if you admit a certain portion you do not do a greater injustice than prevailed when ladies, married and unmarried, were all omitted.

I am, however, in favor of giving ladies, married and unmarried, the franchise. But I am candid enough, as one who has to look at the whole subject, to admit that they do not stand on exactly the same footing. A woman who has no husband, and who is compelled to pay taxes on her property, and assume most of the responsibilities of men, she should have the right to vote for laws, and the most important of which, in any country, are for the protection of property. It seems very hard to argue that a lady who has a large property should not have a vote when her servants may have votes.

A lady of large wealth and property said to me when I was in England a short time ago: I have no vote. My butler has a vote, my steward has a vote, my coachman has a vote and at least fifty of my servants have votes; but I have no vote. She thought it was rather an injustice to her that she had not a vote when so many who derived their means of living from her had votes, and were her superiors in that regard.

Then I must admit that married women stand in a different position on the family ground, which I do not think ought to prevail, but which certainly separates the question of unmarried women from that with respect to those who are wives. They are supposed to have great community of interest with their husbands. Some people are apprehensive that if the wife holds one political view and the husband a different political view there might be family discord. It is an argument that has very great weight with society, and I believe it is the chief argument that is used against giving married women votes. I do not believe in its force. If married women have a right to own property, to invest their money, to spend their money whether the husband is pleased or displeased, and if that law which allows women to have separate property* has not produced such social discord as to evoke a suggestion that the right should be taken away from women, I do not think that the fear of domestic discord on account of exercising the franchise ought to prevail.

Macdonald continued to explore this idea. He said that "we see" husbands and wives "live happily together, one being a Catholic and the other a Protestant, and in England frequently, one being a Christian and the other a Jew." He pointed to other differences between husbands and wives. When "you see," he said, "that all those variances in thought and opinion, and in action—consequent upon difference of opinion—does not produce family discord," then "I must say that I personally am of the opinion that married women ought to have votes." He concluded by saying, "No, sir, I hope that this amendment will fail."[10] The debates continued.

Macdonald's attitude toward Chinese enfranchisement is recorded in the House of Commons Debates, 5th Parliament, 3rd Session, on May 4, 1885:

SIR JOHN A. MACDONALD: I propose to insert after the word "Indian" the words "and excluding a Chinaman." I do not know that I need discuss, at any length, the reasons for this amendment. The Chinese are not like the Indians, sons of the soil. They come from a foreign country; they have no intention, as a people, of making a domicile of any portion of Canada; they come and work or trade, and when they are tired of it they go away, taking with them their profits. They are, besides, natives

---

* Veronica Strong-Boag explains that Macdonald was probably referring to "the Ontario Married Women's Property Act of 1884, which provided that women marrying after July 1, 1881, or acquiring property after that date, held this as 'femmes soles.'" ("The Citizenship Debates," 93)

of a country where representative institutions are unknown, and I think we cannot safely give them the elective franchise.

MR. [DAVID] MILLS: I would like to ask the hon. gentleman, after the observations he made about Charles James Fox, whether it is his intention to strike out property qualification altogether, since he holds that property is no indication of intelligence or capacity.

MR. [PETER] MITCHELL: Would it not be better for the right hon. gentleman to make a distinct clause about Chinamen, because some of us may entertain different opinions on that subject, and may want to vote for this Indian clause.

SIR JOHN A. MACDONALD: What do you mean?

MR. MITCHELL: While I would be quite prepared to vote for this paragraph as it stands, I do not feel that I would be acting consistently in excluding Chinamen. I am in favor of Chinamen being placed on an equal footing with all other persons. Certainly a Chinaman is quite as good as an Indian.

SIR JOHN A. MACDONALD: I cannot agree with my hon. friend at all. Indians are sons of the soil; they are Canadians and British subjects; and, therefore, if they have the property qualification, I think they ought to be treated as other British subjects.

The Chinese are foreigners. If they come to this country, after three years' residence, they may, if they choose, be naturalised. But still we know that when the Chinaman comes here he intends to return to his own country; he does not bring his family with him; he is a stranger, a sojourner in a strange land, for his own purposes for a while; he has no common interest with us, and while he gives us his labor and is paid for it, and is valuable, the same as a threshing machine or any other agricultural implement which we may borrow from the United States on hire and return it to the owner on the south side of the line; a Chinaman gives us his labor and gets his money, but that money does not fructify in Canada; he does not invest it here, but takes it with him and returns to China; and if he cannot, his executors or his friends send his body back to the flowery land. But he has no British instincts or British feelings or aspirations, and therefore ought not to have a vote.

MR. MITCHELL: The idea I have is that every person who comes and lives in the country, and labors and spends his money in the country, even if he is a foreigner—a Chinaman if you like, the most disliked class of foreigners—if he comes to make Canada his home, we ought to make Canada free enough to include even the Chinaman. I would like to see the Bill harmonious in its character. While it is desired to make it comprehensive, I can see no reason why we should exclude the Chinamen. Of course, I know there are gentlemen here who are prejudiced against the Chinamen.

MR. [NOAH] SHAKESPEARE: No.

MR. MITCHELL: Yes; there are hon. gentlemen here who are prejudiced against the Chinamen; there is a strong feeling on the Pacific coast against them. Perhaps they know more about them than we do; but we have a number of them in the city of Montreal, and they are spoken of as a respectable body of men—good, peace-loving citizens. True, they are economical, and some of them are penurious; but what they do with their money after they earn it is not our business. If we can make Canada sufficiently attractive to them, I am not sure that they will go back to China; and we should make our laws comprehensive enough to include all classes of foreigners. So long as they comply with the naturalisation laws, they can become British subjects, and I would give them a vote.

MR. [GEORGE] CASEY: I would ask the hon. gentleman what is the technical meaning of the word Chinaman. As I understand, there is nothing to prevent a Chinaman being a British subject; would he be called a Chinaman? Of course, while he is an alien he cannot vote, whether he is excluded expressly by this Act or not. But the case may arise when a Chinaman becomes naturalised. Would a naturalised Chinaman be a Chinaman, in the meaning of this clause, or would he be a Canadian or a British subject? I should think he ceased to be a Chinaman when he became a British subject.

SIR JOHN A. MACDONALD: If I thought so, I would alter the words. I used the word Chinaman to designate a race. However, I am obliged to the hon. gentleman for the suggestion, and I shall word it—"Excluding a person of Mongolian or Chinese race."

MR. EDGAR: Would that cover the case of a Chinaman born in Hong Kong, who is a British subject by birth, although he is of the Mongolian race?

SIR JOHN A. MACDONALD: The Australians exclude the Chinese from Hong Kong as well as other Chinese. If they are born in Hong Kong they are in one sense British subjects; but the objection applies just as well to the Hong Kong Chinese as to any others.

MR. CASEY: Many maintain that the Indians of British Columbia are of the Mongolian race.

SIR JOHN A. MACDONALD: That is an ethnological question that I will leave the hon. gentleman to settle with Henry Bancroff.

MR. [MATTHEW] GAULT: There are a number of Chinamen in Montreal who are industrious people. I believe they voted at the last election, and I think they should not be deprived of their votes.

The debate continued in this manner, several members from the Maritimes speaking in favour of enfranchising the Chinese. Mr. Arthur Hill Gillmor for Charlotte (N.B.) said, "I do not think myself they are the most desirable class of citizens, but we have them here and they have been a great service to this country," and he pointed to their contribution to the Pacific Railway. As to the Chinese themselves, "[t]hey were a civilised race when your ancestors were barbarians. They have one kind of civilisation one sort of habits, and you have another." But he also thought that they could assimilate; but what chance did they have "when they have been murdered, shot down like dogs, and that in a civilised and Christian society." After an analysis of their economic conditions contained in the commission report, Gillmor concluded that*

---

* Presumably the commission being discussed in the debate was the *Report of the Royal Commission on Chinese Immigration: Report and Evidence* (Ottawa: Canada, 1885).

the Chinese should be allowed to vote, seeing as many had become "rich" merchants and paid taxes.[11]

House members rose to disagree. Should the members of one province "interfere" in the questions facing another province?

The member for Norfolk North, John Charlton, picked up the thread of Gillmor's comments, admitting that "the Chinese civilisation is a wonderful civilisation." Looking back over history, he said, "I realise the fact that 3,000 years ago, when our race was in barbarism, the Chinese civilisation was as far advanced and thoroughly developed as it is to-day." But he thought it was a "stereotyped civilisation," that was "neither advancing nor receding." He thought that "no other people have the pride of race they possess. No other people look down on all other races with the supreme contempt with which the Chinese look down on other races." He did not believe they would "assimilate with other populations. . . ." He thought that it was disgraceful that Chinese had been cruelly used. Their "rights, under the law, should be carefully observed." But it did "not follow that the Chinese should be enfranchised." He speculated that "if they are allowed to enter the commonwealth faster than the process of assimilation can be carried on, that immigration becomes, not a benefit, but a detriment to the country."[12]

SIR JOHN A. MACDONALD: I cannot quite understand the argument of the hon. gentleman from North Norfolk (Mr. Charlton), or the conclusion he has come to. He commenced by stating that each Province should have the making of its own franchise, and I presume that each Province should exercise its own franchise as well at Dominion as at provincial elections. At the same time, he says it is a wise precaution in this Bill to exclude the Chinese. He said that was a wholesome policy; that there were strong reasons for excluding them from the right to vote.

Suppose that, for economic reasons, British Columbia desired to introduce the Chinese population, desired to have them as workingmen, laborers and settlers, and in order to encourage this introduction, was prepared to give them a vote. I quite agree with hon. gentlemen opposite, it would be well to give them a vote *quoad* British Columbia, but they have given the strongest reason why we should retain the settlement of the franchise, as regards Dominion interest.

They state the Chinese should not have the franchise, that there are moral, political and social reasons against their having a vote, and it is a wise and just precaution that we should exclude them. Of course we ought to exclude them, because if they came in great numbers and settled on the Pacific coast they might control the vote of that whole Province, and they would send Chinese representatives to sit here, who would represent Chinese eccentricities, Chinese immorality, Asiatic principles altogether opposite to our wishes; and, in the even balance of parties, they might enforce those Asiatic principles, those immoralities which he speaks of, the eccentricities which are abhorrent to the Aryan race and Aryan principles, upon this House. That is a convincing reason, and they approve of it.

The hon. member for Charlotte (Mr. Gillmor) spoke very ably, as he does, very instructively as well as amusingly, on this point, but he concluded that he did not think they were desirable citizens. To be citizens they must exercise the franchise. He did not consider they ought to do so. At the same time he argued very strongly that they were a very superior race to the whites in British Columbia, and if they are superior in intellect, in morality, and in education, I do not see how he came to that conclusion.

The truth is, that all natural history, all ethnology, shows that, while the crosses of the Aryan races are successful—while a mixture of all those races which are known or believed to spring from a common origin is more or less successful—they will amalgamate. If you look around the world you will see that the Aryan races will not wholesomely amalgamate with the Africans or the Asiatics. It is not to be desired that they should come; that we should have a mongrel race; that the Aryan character of the future of British America should be destroyed by a cross or crosses of that kind.

The world is filling up fast enough. We can be in no very great hurry to have our hundred millions in British America. That will come fast enough. Let us encourage all the races which are cognate races, which cross and amalgamate naturally, and we shall see that such an amalgamation will produce, as the result, a race, equal, if not superior, to the two races which mingle. But the cross of those races, like the cross of the dog and the fox, is not successful; it cannot be, and never will be.

We know that the Chinese have broken through their ancient exclusive system.* They are now spreading themselves wherever they can. They have burst the boundaries of China; they are seeking foreign opportunities of labor and employment, principally because of the over-population of their own country; but wherever they go, there is something antagonistic to the races that they go to intermingle with. Go where you will, where the Anglo-Saxon race predominates, you will find that they unite in the east and in the west in opposition to having a fixed population of Chinamen amongst them. All

---

* The Ch'ing government in China (1644–1912) attempted to prevent emigration, but in 1859 the governor of Kwangtung made emigration legal in order "to control human trafficking." In the 1860s and the 1870s the treaties of the Imperial Court with France, Britain, the United States, Spain, and Peru ratified this decision. The ban on emigration was only lifted in 1893. (Woon, "The Voluntary Sojourner," 677)

the Australian colonists agree upon that. Although the Chinese were invited at first, for very obvious reasons, in the paucity of labor and the sparseness of population in California, when they were valuable as working machines for a time, they soon began to crowd in there, to be formidable there, and they would swarm over into California, and if they were allowed in British Columbia, they would swarm over there in large numbers, and we would have an Asiatic population, alien in spirit, alien in feeling, alien in everything, and after they attained formidable proportions in their numbers, you could not keep them out. Look at what has happened in the Malaccas; look at what has happened in Singapore. There England had a colony of Malays. The aborigines are Malays, as generous, active, pleasant people, as there are in Asia. England threw open the Malaccas, threw open Malaya generally to the Chinese. They have swarmed in there, and the Malays are now virtually aliens in their own country, slaves and serfs to the Chinese, who have swarmed in there, and are absorbing the aboriginal race.

The feeling is not confined to British Columbia. You see all through the Province of Ontario especially, and in Quebec to some degree, wherever there is a meeting of working-men, they make a solemn protest against the introduction of Chinese labor. They are afraid of it, even in the few that have already come. They see in the distant future this foreign race coming in, disturbing the labor market and shouldering out our own people, when there is no necessity for it.* We are in the course

---

* Beginning in 1880, labour leaders across Canada began to complain loudly about the entry of Chinese labourers. In 1883, the newly formed Trades and Labor Congress debated a motion against Chinese immigration in harsh terms, calling the Chinese "unsanitary" and slavish. They also claimed that Chinese workers were "forcing the working people out of industries" due to the "cheapness of their labor." The roughness of the "Chinatowns" intensified the apprehensions of working-class Canadians about their

of progress; this country is going on and developing, and we will have plenty of labor of our own kindred races, without introducing this element of a mongrel race to disturb the labor market, and certainly we ought not to allow them to share the Government of the country.

Macdonald's views on extending the franchise to the "Indians" are recorded in the House of Commons Debates, 5th Parliament, 3rd Session, on June 8, 1885:

SIR JOHN A. MACDONALD: Of course I understood that the hon. member for [South] Brant [William Paterson] was going to oppose, and would oppose the Indian franchise at a subsequent stage of this Bill. When he mentioned, however, that he was going to move an amendment in committee, I said that of course he would have every opportunity of doing so. It is a matter of but little importance what clause this may be attached to, so that it does not interfere with the symmetry of the Bill, if it should be adopted.

I hope, however, that it will not be adopted. I think the hon. gentleman will see that if, an Indian on a reserve is to have the franchise under the conditions which have already been agreed to in this Act, he should have it unshackled by anything which would draw an invidious distinction between him and

---

own living standards if Chinese labour eroded wages. Historians suggest that the fear of what the Chinese represented, more than their actual effect on wages, better explains the vigorous anti-Chinese sentiments of the era; the Chinese demonstrated, more than created, "slave wages" in the industrial era. Moreover, anti-Chinese sentiment and laws predated the rise of organized labour. Tax evasion was widespread in the 1870s, but Canadians focused on Chinese evasions, interpreting them as a forfeited entry into the "political nation" and a refusal to hold "a stake in the community." (Goutor, *Guarding the Gates*, 35; Heaman, "'The Whites Are Wild about It,'" 354-7; Wang, *"His Dominion" and the "Yellow Peril,"* 11-2)

his brother of the white race. The moment it is admitted that the red man should be allowed to vote, there should be as little distinction as possible drawn.

It would only be a cause of irritation and a mark of inferiority planted upon their brows by an assembly like this, composed altogether of white men. I think that the provision in the Bill which was already adopted after very long discussion, quite sufficiently meets the view of the hon. gentleman without stamping inferiority on the Indian. Under the qualifying clauses, the Indian, as a person having the necessary property or other qualification, has the right to vote. Under the disqualifying clauses, it is provided that Indians in Manitoba, British Columbia, Keewatin and the North-West Territories, and any Indian on any reserve elsewhere in Canada who is not in possession and occupation of a separate and distinct tract of land in such reserve shall not be allowed to vote.

The hon. gentleman wants the reserve to be surveyed, laid out in lots, and numbered, I take it, and that the parties living on the reserve should be altogether disqualified until that expensive process is gone through.

If the Indian has a distinct and separate tract of land marked off, with his house and improvements upon it, I think that is all that can be required. The Indian is obliged to prove his qualifications, and to prove that he comes within the Act, the same as a white man. He is obliged to go before the revising officer, and, in case the revising officer is not a judge, there will be an appeal from his decision. There is already a difference in the clause as against the Indian compared with the white man. If the white man has a separate and distinct tract of land of which he is the occupant, and that is of a certain value, he has the right to vote. But the Indian in such a case has not the right to vote.

The value of the distinct tract of land is not taken into account at all in regard to the Indian.

I have regretted in one aspect being induced to put that in the Bill, because it is a mark of distinction between the white man and the Indian. If the white man has a vacant lot and he is the occupant or the owner of that lot, although there are no improvements whatever on it, if it is of the value of $150, he has a vote; but, in consequence of the strong arguments, the strong expression of opinion of many gentlemen on the other side of the house, that, in consequence of the tribal relations, and in consequence of the reserve belonging to the whole tribe and not to any individual Indian, and because no portion of it was alleged to belong to the individual Indian, the distinction was drawn against the Indian when compared with the franchise of the white man; because it is provided that no Indian is qualified who is not in possession and occupation of a separate and distinct tract of land in such reserve, and whose improvements on such separate tract are not of the value of $150.

The land on which he has his house, on which he has his improvements, his cattle, fences and stables, is not to be taken into account at all, and he must have not only a distinct holding but improvements belonging to himself of the value of $150.

I think it would be exceedingly unwise, if we are going to give the franchise to the Indians at all, that we should draw any further invidious distinction between the white man and the Indian. It would decidedly be a grievance in the mind of the Indian; he would feel it as such; and I would say to my hon. friend that I am quite sure that this provision will be felt in his own riding to be rather an affront offered by the hon. gentleman to the Indians.

I do not believe that the hon. gentleman has any such feeling. I believe, however, that he has an exaggerated opinion in his own mind about the danger of the Indian vote without these checks; but I can assure the hon. gentleman, and I think the majority of the House on both sides will agree with me, that there is a sufficient protection now, and that it would be felt as an annoyance, an insult perhaps, and a grievance to the Indians to have a further distinction drawn against them. I took occasion some time ago to speak on this subject to Mr. Plummer, whom I have no doubt the hon. gentleman knows, a very old officer of the Indian Department, who is highly respected by everyone who knows him, and whom I should be very sorry to see the Department lose, though perhaps we shall have to, for he is an elderly man now. He has been inspector for very many years, and he knows nearly all the reserves in the Province of Ontario. I asked him about this matter, and he wrote me as follows:

"Sir,—As regards the question of the title under which the Indians hold the lands they occupy. The reserve occupied by the Mohawks of the Bay of Quinté has been sub-divided into lots and concessions, and each Indian of proper age has been located or allotted by the band in council for at least one lot, averaging from 50 to 150 acres, on which he resides with his family. These several claims have been entered into a book which are recognized and confirmed by the Department. Some of these Indians have been in possession of their lands and homesteads, from father to son, for nearly 100 years, and as they have complied with the regulations of the Department, and the provisions of the several Indian

Acts, no power can legally dispossess them. The Six Nation Indians hold their lands in the same manner as that of the Mohawks of the Bay of Quinté, and the same may be said of all the other Indians in the Provinces of Ontario and Quebec, as well as those of the Lower Provinces. Most of the Indians in the Upper Provinces hold their lands not only by right of allotment by the several bands in council, as provided under the 17th section of the Indian Act, but they also hold location titles as provided by the 18th section. All of the Indians here referred to have not only the undisputed right to hold their lands while they live, but to the right to devise the same by will, provided it be to a relative not further removed than a second cousin. To all intents and purposes the Indian is the absolute owner of his land (although he cannot sell it), and no power on earth can lawfully dispossess him."

That is really the situation of these Indians. By a uniform practice amounting to law, from father to son, they do hold their land by much more than the occupancy that whites are allowed to vote upon. I have received a very interesting letter from Dr. [Peter Edmund] Jones [Kahkewāquonāby],* who is one of the

---

* Peter Edmund Jones (1843–1909) had a background, according to historian Donald Smith, unlike that of many Aboriginal people in Canada. His father, Peter Jones, or Kahkewāquonāby (1802–1856), was part Mississauga and part Welsh, and bridged two worlds in the early nineteenth century as he turned to Methodism to help his people. He also visited England many times to advocate for his people; there he met Peter Edmund's mother, Elizabeth Field (1804–1890), an Englishwoman. Peter Edmund had benefited from his integration into colonial society and from an excellent education; he trained as a physician. Peter Edmund continued to advocate for Indians as a people and to seek their inclusion into the new "political nation," while preserving their cultural distinctiveness. Like his father, he also had the name Kahkewāquonāby. (Smith, "Jones, Peter Edward (Kahkewāquonāby)," *DCB*)

chiefs of the Six Nation Indians, and who is a very intelligent man. He writes me thus:

Hagersville, 30th May, 1885

"My Dear Sir John,—I should have written to you some time ago to thank you for making the Indian a 'person' in the Franchise Bill. Other affairs, however, have prevented me from performing my duty.

"I now thank you, on the part of the 'Grand Council of Ontario,' of which body I am secretary, and at the meeting in September last the vice-president, Chief Solomon Jones, introduced the subject, having previously given me notice by the enclosed letter, which kindly return to me. The matter was fully, and, I must say, ably, discussed, and the unanimous decision of the council was that the time had arrived when we should insist upon a representation or voice in the Dominion Parliament. I was instructed to take action in the matter, and Mr. Plummer is able to show the nature of my ideas and work. This council was composed of delegates from nearly every reserve in Ontario.

"I now, as head chief, thank you on the part of my own band, the Mississaugas of the Credit, who, in council, have heartily and with cheers approved of the step the Government are taking.

"I now thank you on the part of the memory of my father and on the part of myself, as for many years we advocated and urged this step as the one most likely to elevate the aborigines to a position more approaching the independence of the whites.

"There is not an Indian in this neighborhood, there is not a Conservative, but what approves of the noble stand you have taken in this affair, in spite of the bitter opposition you are meeting with in the House, and I have spoken to several Reformers who also approve of the measure, so that the 'seething excitement' has not reached this part of the Province where the Indians are so well known.

"There is one feature of the debate of a personal character in respect to myself and my band, and a reply to which I think is due by me through you to the House.

"I refer to the remarks made by Mr. [David] Mills [member for Bothwell] on Thursday last, that the payment of a claim urged last year by my band, was made to influence our votes anticipating this Franchise Bill.

"Allow me to say, dear sir, that my band are fully aware of every cent we have invested with this Government, that we know the exact amount of interest it bears, and that we are not receiving any bounty or support from the Government more than what we have earned by the sale and surrender of our lands, and far more than this interest do we expend yearly in our local municipal tax and in the purchase of dutiable goods, the revenue upon which goes back to you to support the Dominion Government.

"My band also know perfectly well that even if the vote were not by ballot and nine-tenths of them should vote the Reform ticket, it could by no possibility affect our financial standing with the Government. But as nine-tenths can and do read the newspapers, there is every probability that they will come to the conclusion

to cast their votes against the party which is not holding meetings from one end of the Province to the other
with the express purpose of degrading the character
of the Indian in the eyes of the people, and to raise a
political excitement to deprive us of our just dues. This
is rather a long letter, Sir John, but you have been so
accustomed to lengthy harangues in the House upon
this subject that I hope the five minutes' views of an
Indian will be acceptable and not make you 'tired.'

"I am, my dear Sir John,
"Your obedient servant,
"KAHKWAQUONABY, M.D., Chief."

*The member for Lambton West, James Frederick Lister, responded
immediately. He dismissed Dr. Jones as nothing more than "a strong
supporter of the Conservative party," and rejected Mr. Plummer's evidence because he was "not a lawyer and probably knows very little about
law regulating the holding of real property."*

*Lister continued to question Macdonald about his government's
Indian policy. "Only five short years ago the First Minister [Macdonald]
who has read that letter to-day with such unction, in his report stated
that the Indians were not fit to attempt the simplest duties of municipal
government, and yet to-day he stands up and tells us that in five short
years the Indians, who were then not fit to exercise or enjoy the simplest
form of municipal government, are now so far advanced that they are
capable of exercising intelligently the highest privilege of free men."*

*Lister opined that the "Indian tribes" of Canada were under
Macdonald's thumb. He pointed out that others in the House had
said that "it is improper to give the Indians a vote in the condition of
semi-slavery in which they are living," because, as Lister had intimated*

earlier, the "Government of the day continue[d] to be the custodians of the money belonging to the Indian tribes[.]"[13]

After Bill 103 had been debated and amended, women were still excluded from the franchise. So too were all "Indians" not living in the "old provinces," as were those regarded as "Asiatics." Though lowered, a property threshold continued to limit the vote for many industrial workers. But a fisherman's franchise was introduced.[14]

THE SCIENCE OF MODEL FARMS, 1885

HOUSE OF COMMONS, OTTAWA, JULY 16

Macdonald maintained an interest in science throughout his life. He consistently supported the Geological Survey of Canada. He was among the first members of the Botanical Society of Canada. He attended the first meeting of the Royal Society of Canada, held in the Senate Chambers. By 1885, he became personally involved in establishing a scientific model farm along the lines he had proposed in the 1840s. His perspective was, as always, practical.[15]

The House of Commons Debates of the 5th Parliament, 3rd Session, record on July 16, 1885:

SIR JOHN A. MACDONALD: So far as any plan has been formed by the Government, it is this: We think there should be a site obtained, situated somewhere in Canada, where the climate will represent our average climate of the settled portions of Canada. It will not do to have it down in Gaspé or in Niagara. We do not want to get the best farm in the world, or the richest, or an arid farm, but a farm where the pupil students can really be employed profitably, where they will have some difficulties to overcome, and which will require some skill on their part to bring into proper cultivation. I think the money cannot be better spent than having a first rate model farm, and in order to carry the project out, I must agree the proportions will have to be liberal. There must be a careful choice of superintendent and those who manage the farm, men able to teach and to understand the whole subject.

MR. [JAMES] TROW: In establishing a model farm, if it must be established, a great deal of jealousy will be created as to where it shall be situated. If too far to the east, the climate will be very severe, and if too far to the west, it will be too mild. If the Government are to undertake to purchase Berkshire Pigs and Shropshires and Downs, it seems to me it will be traveling out of the record.

MR. [EDWARD] BLAKE: We ought to know what the scheme of the Government really is. It is important we should know, both with reference to the financial and utilitarian aspects of the whole business. We must get a farm in which the climate is not too severe and also not too mild, in which the soil is not too good and not too bad; it must not be a desert, nor must it be very fertile; it must be a farm which has capability, but it must be one which will also contain difficulties to be contended against, in order that the scholars may have something to learn. Besides being a model farm and an exemplar to the farmers, provided by a paternal Government, it is also to be a college of a more or less ample character, a school in which to teach the young the art of farming. If that is part of the work of the model farm, and it is not necessarily a part of a model farm at all, we are going into a scheme of an agricultural college. We ought to know what we are going into; we ought to know the system under which young men are to be taught the art of farming by Government instructors. What is the extent of the farm proposed? What is the number of instructors to be appointed? How many young men are to be admitted? We are asked to vote $20,000 and are not informed, in the slightest degree, as to how it is to be spent.

SIR JOHN A. MACDONALD: We intend to have a model farm; we will obtain teachers, and the farm is intended to be worked by the pupils. Those pupils will be self-sustaining. The hon. gentleman knows there are a great number of young men who are anxious to be educated as farmers, and who pay considerable fees to private teachers at this moment, in various portions of the country. There are gentlemen agriculturalists who give handsome fees to be taught farming. No doubt, a Government farm, conducted on scientific principles, with competent teachers and a sufficient area to employ students, will be well attended, and the pupils will pay a reasonable amount for their education. There is a very successful model farm conducted by Major Strickland, in Peterboro' district; he has a large number of pupils, and receives very handsome fees.

DISALLOWANCE AND THE
JESUITS' ESTATES ACT, 1889

Macdonald dreaded this debate when it came on March 26, 1889. Honoré Mercier's Jesuits' Estates Act had passed through the Quebec legislature in 1888 to growing opposition in Ontario. The Quebec premier had asked Pope Leo XIII (1810–1903) to arbitrate the disputed disposal of the estates, and the provincial government finally settled $160,000 on the Jesuits and further sums on educational initiatives in the province.* *But the Pope's foreign involvement offended the separation of church and state, so fundamental to the beliefs of so many Ontarian Protestants. Some Conservatives pressed Macdonald to disallow the Act, which was within the powers of the federal government. Macdonald refused. The Act affected no other province, he argued.*[16]

After three days of wearying debate, Macdonald rose on the evening of March 28. He recalled his personal struggle to overcome religious factionalism in the Province of Canada. He dwelled on his commitment to

---

* In addition to the $160,000 settled on the Jesuits, a further $140,000 was given to Laval University, $100,000 to various Catholic dioceses in Quebec, and $60,000 to Protestant educational institutes. (Sylvain, "Jesuits' Estates Act," *Canadian Encyclopedia*)

tolerance and overcoming prejudice to create Canada. He recounted the
virulent anti-Catholic "agitation" he had seen in England during the
debates over the "Papal Aggression Bill" in 1850.

The House of Commons Debates of the 6th Parliament, 3rd
Session, records on March 28, 1889:

SIR JOHN A. MACDONALD: Everybody, as the hon.
member for the West Durham (Mr. Blake) says, was ashamed
of it [the "Papal Aggression Bill"]. The Bill was scouted out
of Parliament, although the excitement had been originally so
enormous. I cannot convey to you the excitement that existed
in England at that time. I hope and believe that when this
matter is fully understood in the Province of Ontario, when
the exhaustive speeches that were made upon it are read and
discussed and weighed, the country will see that their apprehensions are unfounded, and that the country is safe [from the
Catholic threat].

Why, there are in all the Dominion of Canada 71 Jesuits. Are
they going to conquer the whole of Canada? Is Protestantism
to be subdued? Is the Dominion to be seduced from its faith
by 71 Jesuit priests? They are armed with a string of beads, a
sash around their waists and a mass book or missal. What harm
can they do? I told my reverend and eloquent friend, Dr. Potts
of Toronto, that I would match him physically and spiritually,

---

* Macdonald is referring to the passing of Britain's Ecclesiastical Titles Act of 1850 to
resist the restoration of the Catholic hierarchy in England announced by Pope Pius IX
(1792–1878). The move, an internal matter for the Church, sparked the latent anti-
Catholic feeling by rousing the spectre of foreign domination. The Act may have been
an attempt on the part of an unpopular government to gain votes; Queen Victoria had
not been alarmed by the Pope's announcement. By the time the Bill had passed through
Parliament, it had been considerably diluted by amendments, and it was eventually
repealed in 1871. (House of Commons, *Debates*, 6th Parl., 3rd Sess., 907; Conacher,
"The Politics of the 'Papal Aggression,'" 13-4, 17, 22, 23, 29)

against any follower of Ignatius Loyola in the whole Dominion of Canada.*

Now, only think of it. The Jesuits claim, and claimed with an appearance of right, that the effect of their restoration should be to give them back all their own property.† They contended for that, and they had the right to fight the best battle they could. Look at the papers. They said that the value of the property was $2,000,000, but they came down, however, graciously, and said they would take $1,000,000, or, to be accurate, I think, $900,000. But the Government of the Province of Quebec said: No, you cannot have that; you can only have $400,000—not a very large sum. Why, Mr. Mercier has been granting, in the interest of his country, sums as big as that for railways here and there through Quebec. We do the same thing here. It is no very large sum. But not only did Mr. Mercier confine the vote to $400,000 but be said: You shall have not the whole of it; perhaps you shall have none of it. The other ecclesiastic institutions, Catholic colleges, said they had a right to their share.

Now, it was a family matter, it was in *foro domestico*, and, as the hon. member for Bothwell (Mr. Mills) truly said, it was their own money, it was the property of the Province of Quebec and they could do with it as they liked. There is almost no subject to which the Quebec Government could

---

* Unlike some commentators at the time, Macdonald does not appear to make a distinction between the original Jesuit holders of the estates in Quebec—the Society of Jesus, founded by Ignatius Loyola in 1540 and suppressed by Pope Clement XIV in 1773—and the Society of Jesus restored by Pope Pius VII in 1814. (Creighton, *Old Chieftain*, 515)

† In 1842, the restored Society of Jesus returned to Quebec and in 1871, with the authority of Rome, began to press the Quebec government for the estates' return, which (following the death of the last Jesuit in 1800) had reverted to the British Crown, and were awarded in 1831 to the Government of Lower Canada, and passed at Confederation to the Government of Quebec. (Sylvain, "Jesuits' Estates Act," *Canadian Encyclopedia*)

not apply these moneys under the general phrase of "property and civil rights."*

The lands [the Jesuits' Estates] themselves, if they came to the old Province of Canada by escheat, the moment that Upper and Lower Canada were severed, those lands, by the terms of the British North America Act, became, like any other public lands in the Province of Quebec, subject to be sold or kept or retained or applied for any purpose the Government of that Province chose. You cannot bind any Province to carry out the original intentions of the donors. This land became their property, and the representatives of the people, the legislators of the Province, have a right to apply their own property and the proceeds of their property for any purpose they have a right to deal with under the powers of the Act.

How does it turn out? It was left to the Pope† to settle in what proportion the different collegiate institutions should have this $400,000; and his Holiness, instead of being the special supporter of the Jesuit Order, instead of pressing their interests on the people of Canada, instead of giving them wealth in order to advance their insidious designs against the Crown and dignity of Canada, cut them down to the miserable sum of $160,000. He has given the rest of it to the other collegiate institutions and to the bishops for the purposes of higher education.

I hear the argument stated that it is not stated, in so many words, that the money going to the Jesuits shall be devoted to

---

* A provincial jurisdiction in the British North America Act, outlined in Section 92 (13).

† Honoré Mercier asked Pope Leo XIII (1810–1903) to arbitrate when the Catholic Church in Quebec could not agree on how to dispose of the Jesuits' Estates. (Sylvain, "Jesuits' Estates," *Canadian Encyclopedia*)

educational purposes. Why, they are a teaching body in Canada exclusively now. There is not a single parish in the whole Province of Quebec which has a Jesuit as its *curé*; there is not a single parish in which the Jesuits have any control. They are a teaching body in the Province of Quebec. They have a mission in which education and Christianity go hand-in-hand among the Indians and the Esquimaux on the Labrador coast, where they are doing a great deal of good, where they are suffering the hardships and miseries which we read in Parkman* they were always ready to suffer in the cause of religion and humanity.

And, strange to say, if we go west, leaving the Eastern Province of Quebec, to the Province of Manitoba, we find there the College of St. Boniface with Archbishop Taché at its head, and the professors are six Jesuit priests.

We do not hear of Manitoba raising up a cry against that institution. We know how easily popular excitement in a young country like that, full of ardent spirits, can be raised. I have occasion to know something about that. Well, they submit to the enormous wrong of having six Jesuit priests teaching in Manitoba with as much apathy as the Protestants in the Province of Quebec; and more than that, strange to say, there is the Anglican clergy under the charge of the Bishop of the Church of England, there is the Presbyterian clergy under the charge of the Presbyterian body, and they are so recreant to their Protestantism, they are so apathetic, that they have joined hand-in-hand in forming a common university, that common university giving degrees, and the governing body of that university is composed of Catholics, Presbyterians, Anglicans.

---

* Macdonald is referring to Francis Parkman (1823–1893), a historian celebrated in the nineteenth century for his seven-volume work, *France and England in North America*, published between 1865 and 1892. (Eccles, "Parkman, Francis," *DCB*)

And all this cry is for some $160,000, which, at four per cent, amounts to some $6,000 a year. I cannot but remember the story of the Jew going into an eating house and being seduced by a slice of ham. When he came out, it so happened there was a crash of thunder, and he said: Good heavens, what a row about a little bit of pork. It is a little bit of pork, and as the poor Jew escaped being crushed by the thunderbolt, I have no doubt Canada will escape from the enormous sum of $6,000 a year.

If this Bill had been introduced in other terms it would have been fortunate. I agree with those gentlemen who say that the framers of the Bill, by the way it is drawn and the insertion of these recitals, almost court the opposition of the member for Muskoka. I agree that that is so, and, if the Bill had not mentioned the Society of Jesus, it would have passed without any opposition. If the money had been given to the Sulpicians, the money had been given to the University of Laval, if the money had been given to the bishops of the different dioceses for higher education, no one would have objected to it, this Bill would not have excited any attention; but, it is just because the Jesuits have got historically a bad name from Protestant history, and it was simply because their name was in the Bill that all this agitation has been aroused.

This subject is not a new one. Years and years ago, long before Confederation, the subject was discussed in Parliament, and strong arguments were used against the recognition of the claim for Jesuits' estates, and the feeling of opposition was shown and emphasised in the sentence which was used by a worthy member of Parliament—a good Grit he was, by the way, and a very respectable and honest man, strange to say—but he exemplified the feeling of the country in one sentence. His speech was a very effective one. It was this: "Mr. Speaker, I don't like them there Jesuits." That was the feeling. There was a prejudice against the Jesuits, and it is from that same prejudice that all this agitation has been aroused.

Now, I can only repeat that the Government would have performed an act of tyranny if they had disallowed the Bill. Believing as we do that it is perfectly within the competence of that Legislature, and does not in any way affect any other portion of Her Majesty's dominions, there would be no excuse for our interfering, even according to the rigid principles which my hon. friend opposite thinks govern us. I agree strongly with the language used by the hon. member for North York (Mr. Mulock).

Supposing this Bill had been disallowed, Mr. Mercier would have gained a great object. He would have been the champion of his church. The moment it was announced that this Bill was disallowed there would have been a summons for a meeting of the Legislature of Quebec. They would have passed that Bill unanimously, and would have sent it back here, and what would have been the consequence?

No Government can be formed in Canada, either by myself, or by the hon. member who moves this resolution (Mr. O'Brien), or by my hon. friend who sits opposite (Mr. Laurier), having in view the disallowance of such a measure. What would be the consequence of a disallowance? Agitation, a quarrel—a racial and a religious war would be aroused. The best interests of the country would be prejudiced, our credit would be ruined abroad, and our social relations destroyed at home. I cannot sufficiently picture, in my faint language, the misery and the wretchedness which would have been heaped upon Canada if this question, having been agitated as it has been, and would be, had culminated in a series of disallowances of this Act.

Ontario's opposition to the Jesuits' Estates Act grew. Meetings were held, the newspapers chattered. The Equal Rights Association was founded in June 1889. D'Alton McCarthy (1836–1898), member for Simcoe North, joined forces with the new association to oppose bilingualism in the West, so threatening to undo the tolerant accommodation Macdonald had so prized.[17]

PORTRAIT-UNVEILING CEREMONY, 1890

HOUSE OF COMMONS,
OTTAWA, FEBRUARY 27

Macdonald spoke in late February, on the occasion of the unveiling of his portrait. Just over a year earlier, Macdonald had been thinking about history and commemoration. One evening, after the death of his sister, he told his private secretary, Joseph Pope, an anecdote from the Duke of Wellington's life. There had been a monk living in Europe, he said, a custodian of a portrait gallery, who observed one day, "I sometimes feel as if after all, they," the portraits, "were the realities, and we are the shadows."*

On its unveiling, Macdonald expressed gratification at his portrait in a speech that reflected upon the events he had witnessed and which would outlive all who were present.

As a copy of this speech in the collections of the curator of the House of Commons in Ottawa records:

[SIR JOHN A. MACDONALD:] I would indeed be insensitive if I were not deeply affected by the address, the too flattering

---

* The scene was, according to Pope, recalled from Stanhope's *Conversations with the Duke of Wellington*. (Pope, *Memoirs of Sir John*, vol. 2, 292)

address, that has been read, and by your kind friendship and confidence in me. You have alluded to the services that I have been able to render Canada, and while I cannot lay claim to all the merit that you been kind enough in your address to state was mine, I am vain enough to believe that I have not been a lagging or unfaithful representative of the great principles of the great party to which we all belong.

I have always felt since I entered public life that the interests, the future prosperity of Canada, rests upon the development of that party. (Applause.)

If you look back upon the history of Canada since 1841 you will find that all the real progress that has been made by Canada, be it material or social, was made during the time when the Conservative influence was predominant. (Applause.) The party to which we belong is not an exclusive party, and we have shown that to be the case from the commencement of the period where the old name of Tory was given up as being rather restricted in its application. It is a name of which nobody need be ashamed— (Applause)—at all events I am not ashamed of it. (Applause.) My father before me was a Tory, and a Tory I will die. (Applause.)

The aim of the Conservatives of 1841, when Upper and Lower Canada were united, was to be a proselytizing body, not to be an exclusive body. They wanted to widen our bounds, to endeavor to enlist all good men, all men who had the real interests of this country at heart, within our ranks.[*]

We were exceedingly successful. If you go back to 1841 you will remember that the great leader of the Reform party in the Province of Upper Canada was the late revered Robert

---

[*] Macdonald is providing a positive interpretation of the aims of the British Colonial Office for the Union Act of 1841, which united Upper and Lower Canada into the United Province of Canada.

Baldwin. In the Province of Lower Canada the leader was equally revered and respected—Louis Lafontaine. (Applause.) These men, from the accidental fact that the Liberal party were fighting for responsible government, were reckoned among the Reform party* and opposed to the old Tory (party). But these men were as truly Conservative as any one of you and when they had fought the battle of responsible government, when they had succeeded in gaining from the Imperial authorities the right of self-government to the fullest extent, their Conservative principles shone out without any check or party obligations to prevent them from uniting in spirit, if not in actual political bond, with the great Liberal-Conservative party. The consequence was that the great body of the Baldwin Reformers joined the Conservative party, and if you look round the Province of Ontario you will find that among the truest Conservatives that are to be found in the province will be reckoned in the Baldwin Reformers.

So in the Province of Lower Canada, now Quebec. The moment the principle for which the Baldwin-Lafontaine Administration fought and was granted, the whole body of followers of Sir Louis Lafontaine, headed by the lieutenant and disciple, Sir George Cartier, joined the Conservative party and have been united with it ever since. (Applause.) The federation of the provinces to which you allude was, however, not the act of the Liberal-Conservatives alone.

---

* The Clear Grits emerged in the late 1840s and followed George Brown's platform for constitutional reform against "Lower Canadian domination." The remainder of the Reform movement had joined Macdonald's Conservatives by the early 1850s. By the late 1860s, however, Brown also moved closer to the Conservatives as part of the Great Coalition. The basic Reform platform of resisting the imposition of Quebec French Catholics' interests on Ontario survived into succeeding decades. (Romney, "Reformers," OCCH)

The late George Brown, who was then the leader of the Reform party, an extreme partisan, a man of great ability, but also a man of very extreme views, which he was desirous of pressing to the utmost, caused such disturbance between the two sections of the United Canada that he himself was appalled at the consequences of his own violence. He found that anarchy was imminent. A Conservative government was tried and it failed. A Reform government was tried, and it failed; and at last it was found there could be no permanent government for the United Canada unless some great step was taken, and, frightened at the consequences of his own partisan violence, and being, I am bound to give him credit for it, anxious to restore something like peace and prosperity to Canada, he united with myself and those who acted with me in carrying the Confederation of the provinces.

We succeeded but he did not long remain with us. Having helped almost to carry the Confederation Act to England, he withdrew for reasons which we need not discuss, and from the time when he withdrew the whole weight of the inauguration and carrying out and development of the Confederation scheme fell upon the Conservatives of Upper and Lower Canada and their allies from the Maritime provinces; and I must say to you that I look back with great pleasure and with great admiration at the single-hearted and earnest way in which the delegates from the Maritime provinces addressed themselves to the great project, and how much they sacrificed of personal ambitions and personal status in consenting that their provinces, formerly equal in rank and stature within Canada, should be merged with Canada by the Confederation Act. But they have got their reward. If you look back over the list of these gentlemen who united with us in 1866 and 1867 in carrying Confederation, you will see that what I say is true. Some of them have gone to join the majority, but they died honoured and respected by those whose councils they guided into Confederation. Others have held high positions ever since, and they are now in their old age enjoying the reward of seeing Canada a united, a great and a prosperous country. (Great Applause.)

Let me thank you very much for this Crowning proof of your kindness and confidence. On the downward hill of life, which I am slow descending, it is gratifying to know that I have that which Shakespeare speaks of, 'Honour, respect and troops of friends.' (Applause.) If I have been successful, and if my efforts in any way added towards the great advancement of our great country, I owe it to the brave men, the stout-hearted and loyal and true, who stood by me through good reports and evil reports since I entered public life.

I am proud to feel and to know that in my 75th year I am surrounded by the representatives of the people from all parts of the Dominion. I am confidently and without flattery telling you in no single Parliament that I have sat can I reckon upon a greater number of able men, of honest, of men truly loyal and patriotic. (Applause.)

It is a great satisfaction to me to think that when I leave the Parliament of Canada I leave its destinies in the hands of as able a body of men as ever made up any Parliament in its existence. Pardon me for occupying your time so long. My heart is full when I think of your kindness and of the honour that have conferred upon me. My children behind me will look upon this token of your kindness with veneration, and it will make them think the more of their parent when he is gone, when they have here such striking evidence of the high esteem of those men whose approbation is worth seeking. (Applause.)

ELECTION MANIFESTO OF 1891

EARNSCLIFFE,* OTTAWA, FEBRUARY 7

By the time of the 1891 election Macdonald was seventy-six years old. The government decided to dissolve Parliament and go to the people in late January. A political storm was brewing over Britain's hand in pushing Canada into a wide-ranging economic treaty with the United States and over Newfoundland's continued separation from Canada. As he explained to his colleagues, if the British government were to succeed, it "will sacrifice Canada without scruple. We must face the fight at our next election, and it is only the conviction that the battle will be better fought under my guidance than under another's that makes me undertake the task, handicapped as I am, with the infirmities of old age . . . If left to ourselves, I have no doubt of a decision in our favour, but I have serious apprehensions. . . ." So, as an intense economic depression continued to grip world markets, Macdonald hoped that Canadians would support his vision against the Canadian free-traders.[18]

Macdonald published a pamphlet titled Address to the People of Canada *that records his 1891 manifesto:*

---

* Macdonald's private residence in Ottawa.

To the Electors of Canada,

GENTLEMEN,

The momentous questions now engaging public attention having, in the opinion of the Ministry, reached that stage when it is desirable that an opportunity should be given to the people of expressing, at the polls, their views thereon, the Governor General* has been advised to terminate the existence of the present House of Commons, and to issue writs summoning a new Parliament. This advice His Excellency has seen fit to approve, and you, therefore, will be called upon within a short time to elect members to represent you in the great council of the nation. I shall be a candidate for the representation of my old constituency, the city of Kingston.

In soliciting at your hands a renewal of the confidence which I have enjoyed, as a Minister of the Crown, for thirty years, it is, I think, convenient that I should take advantage of the occasion to define the attitude of the Government, in which I am First Minister, towards the leading political issues of the day.

As in 1878, in 1882, and again in 1887, so in 1891, do questions relating to the trade and commerce of the country occupy a foremost place in the public mind. Our policy in respect thereto is to-day what it has been for the past thirteen years, and is directed by a firm determination to foster and develop the varied resources of the Dominion, by every means in our power, consistent with Canada's position as an integral portion of the British Empire. To that end we have laboured in the past, and we propose to continue in the work to which we have

---

* Lord Stanley founded the Ontario Hockey Association in 1890 and in 1893 he presented to the reigning Canadian amateur ice hockey team a trophy that would later become known as the Stanley Cup. (Waite, "Stanley, Frederick Arthur, 1st Baron Stanley and 16th Earl of Derby," *DCB*)

applied ourselves, of building up on this continent, under the flag of England, a great and powerful nation.

When, in 1878, we were called upon to administer the affairs of the Dominion, Canada occupied a position in the eyes of the world very different from that which she enjoys to-day. At that time a profound depression hung like a pall over the whole country, from the Atlantic ocean to the western limits of the province of Ontario, beyond which to the Rocky Mountains stretched a vast and almost unknown wilderness. Trade was depressed, manufactures languished, and, exposed to ruinous competition, Canadians were fast sinking into the position of being mere hewers of wood and drawers of water for the great nation dwelling to the south of us. We determined to change this unhappy state of things. We felt that Canada, with its agricultural resources, rich in its fisheries, timber, and mineral wealth, was worthy of a nobler position than that of being a slaughter market for the United States. We said to the Americans:—"We are perfectly willing to trade with you on equal terms. We are desirous of having a fair reciprocity treaty, but we will not consent to open our markets to you while yours remain closed to us."

So we inaugurated the National Policy. You all know what followed. Almost as if by magic, the whole face of the country underwent a change. Stagnation and apathy and gloom—aye, and want and misery too—gave place to activity and enterprise and prosperity. The miners of Nova Scotia took courage; the manufacturing industries in our great centres revived and multiplied; the farmer found a market for his produce; the artisan and labourer employment at good wages, and all Canada rejoiced under the quickening impulse of a newfound life. The age of deficits was past, and an overflowing treasury gave to the

Government the means of carrying forward those great works necessary to the realization of our purpose to make this country a homogeneous whole.

To that end we undertook that stupendous work, the Canadian Pacific Railway.* Undeterred by the pessimistic views of our opponents, nay, in spite of their strenuous, and even malignant opposition, we pushed forward that great enterprise through the wilds north of Lake Superior, across the western prairies, over the Rocky Mountains to the shores of the Pacific, with such inflexible resolution, that, in seven years after the assumption of office by the present administration, the dream of our public men was an accomplished fact, and I myself experienced the proud satisfaction of looking back from the steps of my car upon the Rocky Mountains fringing the eastern sky.†

The Canadian Pacific Railway now extends from ocean to ocean, opening up and developing the country at a marvellous rate, and forming an Imperial highway to the east, over which the trade of the Indies is destined to reach the markets of Europe. We have subsidized steamship lines on both oceans—to Europe, China, Japan, Australia, and the West Indies. We have spent millions on the extension and improvement of our canal system. We have, by liberal grants of subsidies, promoted the building of railways, now become an absolute necessity, until the whole country is covered as with a network; and we

---

* Donald Alexander Smith hammered in the last spike of the Canadian Pacific Railway at Craigellachie, British Columbia, on November 7, 1885. The railway began regular passenger service between Montreal and Port Moody on June 28, 1886, in the evening. (Den Otter, "Canadian Pacific Railway," *OCCH;* Creighton, *Old Chieftain*, 458)

† Sometime in July 1886, Macdonald sat with his wife on the "cowcatcher," the iron buffer of the Canadian Pacific train *Jamaica*, somewhere past Calgary on one of the line's first "ocean-to-ocean" trips. (Creighton, *Old Chieftain*, 458-61)

have done all this with such prudence and caution, that our credit in the money market of the world is higher to-day than it has ever been, and the rate of interest on our debt, which is a true measure of the public burdens, is less than it was when we took office in 1878.

During all this time what has been the attitude of the Reform Party? Vacillating in their policy and inconstancy itself as regards their leaders, they have, at least, been consistent in this particular, that they have uniformly opposed every measure which had for its object the development of our common country. The National Policy was a failure before it had been tried. Under it we could not possibly raise a revenue sufficient for the public requirements. Time exposed that fallacy. Then we were to pay more for the home-manufactured article than we used to when we bought everything abroad. We were to be the prey of rings and monopolies, and the manufacturers were to extort their own prices. When these fears had been proved unfounded, we were assured that over-competition would inevitably prove the ruin of the manufacturing industries, and thus bring about a state of affairs worse than that which the National Policy had been designed to meet. It was the same with the Canadian Pacific Railway. The whole project, according to our opponents, was a chimera. The engineering difficulties were insuperable, the road, even if constructed, would never pay. Well, gentlemen, the project was feasible, the engineering difficulties were overcome, and the road does pay.

Disappointed by the failure of all their predictions, and convinced that nothing is to be gained by further opposition on the old lines, the Reform Party has taken a new departure, and has announced its policy to be Unrestricted Reciprocity—that is (as defined by its author, Mr. Wiman,* in the *North American Review* a few days ago), free trade with the United States, and a common tariff with the United States against the rest of the world.

The adoption of this policy would involve, among other grave evils, discrimination against the Mother Country. This fact is admitted by no less a personage than Sir Richard Cartwright, who, in his speech at Pembroke on October 21, 1890, is reported to have said:—"Some men, whose opinions I respect, entertain objections to this (unrestricted reciprocity) proposition. They argue, and argue with force, that it will be necessary for us, if we enter into such an arrangement, to admit the goods of the United States on more favorable terms than those of the mother country. Nor do I deny that that is an objection, and not a light one." It would, in my [Macdonald's] opinion, inevitably result in the annexation of this Dominion to the United States. The advocates of unrestricted reciprocity on this side of the line deny that it would have such an effect, though its friends in the United States urge, as the chief reason for its adoption, that unrestricted reciprocity would be the first step in the direction of Political Union.

There is, however, one obvious consequence of this scheme which nobody has the hardihood to dispute, and that is, that unrestricted reciprocity would necessitate the imposition of direct taxation amounting to not less than fourteen millions of dollars annually upon the people of this country. This fact is clearly set forth in a remarkable letter, addressed a few days

---

* Erastus Wiman (1834–1904) worked for George Brown as a young man, as the *Globe's* commercial editor. By the 1890s he had established himself on Staten Island, in the United States, but maintained a strong presence in Canada and helped articulate the ideas at the centre of the Liberal Party's platform of Unrestricted Reciprocity. (Brown, "Wiman, Erastus," *DCB*)

ago by Mr. E. W. Thomson—a Radical and free-trader—to the Toronto *Globe*, on the staff of which paper he was lately an editorial writer, which notwithstanding the *Globe*, with characteristic unfairness, refused to publish, but which, nevertheless, reached the public through another source. Mr. Thomson points out, with great clearness, that the loss of customs revenue levied upon articles now entering this country from the United States, in the event of the adoption of the policy of unrestricted reciprocity, would amount to not less than seven millions of dollars annually. Moreover, this by no means represents the total loss to the revenue which the adoption of such a policy would entail. If American manufactures now compete favourably with British goods, despite an equal duty, what do you suppose would happen if the duty were removed from the American, and retained, or as is very probable, increased, on the British articles? Would not the inevitable result be a displacement of the duty-paying goods of the mother country by those of the United States? And this would mean an additional loss to the revenue of many millions more.

Electors of Canada, I appeal to you to consider well the full meaning of this proposition. You—I speak now more particularly to the people of this Province of Ontario—are already taxed directly for school purposes, for township purposes, for county purposes, while to the Provincial Government there is expressly given by the constitution the right to impose direct taxation. This latter evil you have so far escaped, but as the material resources of the province diminish, as they are now diminishing, the Local Government will be driven to supplement its revenue derived from fixed sources by a direct tax. And is not this enough, think you, without your being called on by a Dominion tax-gatherer, with a yearly demand of $15 a family, to meet the obligations of the Central Government? Gentlemen, this is what unrestricted reciprocity involves. Do you like the prospect? This is what we are opposing, and what we ask you to condemn by your votes.

Under our present system a man may largely determine the amount of his contributions to the Dominion exchequer. The amount of his tax is always in direct proportion to his means. If he is rich, and can afford to drink champagne, he has to pay a tax of $1.50 for every bottle he buys. If he be a poor man, he contents himself with a cup of tea, on which there is no duty. And so on all through the list. If he is able to afford all manner of luxuries, he pays a large sum into the coffers of the Government. If he is a man of moderate means, and able to enjoy an occasional luxury, he pays accordingly. If he is a poor man his contributions to the treasury are reduced to a minimum. With direct taxation, no matter what may be the pecuniary position of the taxpayer—times may be hard—crops may have failed—sickness or other calamity may have fallen on the family, still the inexorable tax-collector comes and exacts his tribute. Does not ours seem to be the more equitable plan? It is the one under which we have lived and thrived, and to which the Government I lead proposes to adhere.

I have pointed out to you a few of the material objections to this scheme of unrestricted reciprocity, to which Mr. [Wilfrid] Laurier and Sir Richard Cartwright have committed the Liberal party, but they are not the only objections, nor in my opinion are they the most vital. For a century and a half this country has grown and flourished under the protecting aegis of the British Crown. The gallant race who first bore to our shores the blessings of civilization passed by an easy transition from French to English rule, and now form one of the most law-abiding portions of the community. These pioneers were speedily recruited by the advent of a loyal band of British subjects, who gave up everything that men most prize, and were content to begin life anew in the wilderness rather than forego allegiance to their sovereign. To the descendants of these men, and of the multitude of Englishmen, Irishmen, and Scotchmen who emigrated to Canada, that they might build up new homes without ceasing to be British subjects—to you Canadians I appeal, and I ask you what have you to gain by surrendering that which your fathers held most dear? Under the broad folds of the Union Jack, we enjoy the most ample liberty to govern ourselves as we please, and at the same time we participate in the advantages which flow from association with the mightiest empire the world has ever seen. Not only are we free to manage our domestic concerns, but, practically, we possess the privilege of making our own treaties with foreign countries, and, in our relations with the outside world, we enjoy the prestige inspired by a consciousness of the fact that behind us towers the majesty of England.

The question which you will shortly be called upon to determine resolves itself into this; shall we endanger our possession of the great heritage bequeathed to us by our fathers, and submit ourselves to direct taxation for the privilege of having our tariff fixed at Washington, with a prospect of ultimately becoming a portion of the American Union?

I commend these issues to your determination, and to the judgment of the whole people of Canada, with an unclouded confidence that you will proclaim to the world your resolve to show yourselves not unworthy of the proud distinction that you enjoy, of being numbered among the most dutiful and loyal subjects of our beloved Queen.

As for myself, my course is clear. A British subject I was born—a British subject I will die. With my utmost effort, with my latest breath, will I oppose the "veiled treason" which attempts by sordid means and mercenary proffers to lure our people from their allegiance. During my long public service of nearly half a century, I have been true to my country and its best interests, and I appeal with equal confidence to the men who have trusted me in the past, and to the young hope of the country, with whom rests its destinies for the future, to give me their united and strenuous aid in this, my last effort, for the unity of the Empire and the preservation of our commercial and political freedom.

I remain, gentlemen,

Your faithful servant,

JOHN A. MACDONALD.

LAST WORDS, 1891

The new Parliament was only two weeks old when Macdonald lost his words. It happened by degree. He had charmed his last crowd in the Napanee town hall in late February. He ended his career as a politician in the same town where he had begun his career as a lawyer at the age of seventeen. When he grew dizzy and disoriented in the crush of the crowd, further campaigning was cancelled. But Macdonald still won his seat in Kingston. Even Queen Victoria was said to have "expressed her great gratification at the results of the election."[19]

While his health fluctuated, the business of the nation ground on. Sir Charles Tupper, Canada's salaried high commissioner in London since 1884, had weighed into the election, causing controversy.[20]

The House of Commons Debates of the 7th Parliament, 1st Session, record on May 22, 1891:

MR. [WILLIAM] PATERSON: With reference to these contingencies. I wish to ask for information to which I think we are entitled. When the High Commissioner [Sir Charles Tupper] was taking his tour through Canada, it was stated in the press that he travelled by special train. I would like to know whether that was the case, and if so, what was the cost of that train and out of what fund it was defrayed?

SIR JOHN A. MACDONALD: I am not aware that any of the High Commissioner's expenses were paid out of the public service, but I will enquire.

MR. PATERSON: I suppose his trips from England to this country and back again find a place in the expenses?

SIR JOHN A. MACDONALD: That may be, but I cannot say.

MR. [JAMES] MCMULLEN: We have a right to know whether he came out on the special invitation of the First Minister and for what particular purpose. Did he come out for the purpose of attending to elections or other matters of an official character?

SIR JOHN A. MACDONALD: I have already stated what I asked him to come out for.

SIR [RICHARD] CARTWRIGHT: The right hon. gentleman stated candidly that he came out to attend the elections. The First Minister has been, however, altogether too modest. I, as a citizen of Kingston, beg to state that it was to the First Minister's own special and earnest care of his constituents, he was indebted for his increased majority. The First Minister had been a good nursing father or mother, whichever he prefers to be called, to the citizens of Kingston for the last three or four years. Such has been his care that a short time ago, when I had to go down to that constituency on private business of my own, the first I thing I heard was that the hon. gentleman, in his anxiety to prevent the people from suffering from distress and destitution, caused no less, I think, than one hundred and twenty cars to be built, about the 5th or 10th of February last, in certain car works in that city. About the same time likewise, the hon. gentleman, in his disinterested regard for the welfare of my fellow citizens, was solicitous in procuring some important railway subsidies for projected railways in the neighbourhood of that city. Well, they have as good a right to it—no more and no less—than a good many other roads the hon. gentleman has subsidized.

SIR JOHN A. MACDONALD: You did not do much for them.

EULOGIZING MACDONALD, 1891

The House was sitting late the night of May 29, still discussing Charles Tupper's involvement in the election, when Sir Hector-Louis Langevin, minister of public works, and Macdonald's long-time ally, read out a note from Macdonald's doctor. Macdonald was in "critical condition." The House adjourned. Macdonald died at his home in Ottawa, on the night of June 6, at twenty-four minutes past ten. Two days later, Langevin rose to remember him, as did Wilfrid Laurier, hope of the Liberals.[21]

Their eulogies are recorded in the House of Commons Debates for 7th Parliament, 1st Session, on June 8, 1891:

SIR HECTOR LANGEVIN: Mr. Speaker [Hon. Peter White], having to announce to the House the sad event that has been known for two days now, I was afraid I could not trust to my memory, and I, therefore, thought it desirable to place in writing what I wished to say. Accordingly I will now read the observations I desire to offer. Mr. Speaker, as the oldest Privy Councillor it falls to my lot to announce to the House that our dear old chief, the First Minister of Canada, is no more. After a painful illness of two weeks, death put an end to his earthly career on Saturday evening last. To tell you, Mr. Speaker, my feelings under the circumstances is more than I can do. I feel that by the death of Sir John A. Macdonald, Canada has lost its greatest statesman, a great patriot, a man of whom any country in the world would be justly proud. Her Gracious Majesty the Queen never had a more devoted and loyal subject than the grand old man, whose loss we all deplore and regret from the bottom of our hearts. For nearly fifty years he has directed the public affairs of this country. He was among the fathers of Confederation the most prominent and distinguished. He put his whole soul into that great undertaking, knowing full well that the confederation of all the British North American Provinces would give to our people a country and institutions to be glorious of, and to the Empire not only a right arm, but a great and safe highway to her Indian and other possessions. He told me more than once how grateful he was to the people of Canada to have allowed him to have consolidated that great work. The fact is, his love for Canada was equal to that he had for his own mother country.

Mr. Speaker, when the historians of Canada write the history of the last fifty years, they will have to write the life of Sir John Macdonald, and, in writing his life, they may not agree with all his public acts, but they cannot fail to say that he was a great man, a most distinguished statesman, and that his whole life was spent in the service of his country, dying in the midst of his official duty, not having had a day's rest before he passed to a better world. I need not express, Mr. Speaker, my own personal feelings. Having spent half of my life with him as his follower and as his friend, his departure is the same as if I lost half of my existence. I remember how devoted he was, not only to the old Province of Canada, but how chivalrous he showed himself to the Province of Quebec, and especially to my French Canadian countrymen. He had only a word to say, and instead of being at the head of a small band of seventeen Upper Canada members, he would have had all the representatives of his province behind him. But, as he told me several times, he preferred to be just to his French compatriots and allies, and the result was that when Confederation came, the Province of Quebec had confidence in him, and on his death-bed our great chief could see that his just policy has secured peace and happiness to all. Mr. Speaker, I would have wished to continue to speak of our dear departed friend, and spoken to you about his goodness of heart, the witness of which I have been so often, but I feel that I must stop: my heart is full of tears. I cannot proceed further. I move:

> That, in the opinion of this House, the mortal remains of the Right Hon. Sir John A. Macdonald, G.C.B., should be publicly interred, and that this House will concur in giving to the ceremony a fitting degree of solemnity and importance.

MR. [WILFRID] LAURIER: Mr. Speaker, I fully realize the emotion which chokes the hon. gentleman. His silence, under the circumstances, is far more eloquent than any human language could be. I fully appreciate the intensity of the grief which fills the souls of all those who were the friends and followers of Sir John Macdonald, at the loss of the great leader whose whole life has been so closely identified with their party; a party upon which he has thrown such brilliancy and lustre. We on this side of the House who were his opponents, who did not believe in his policy, nor in his methods of Government;

we take our full share of their grief—for the loss which they deplore to-day is far and away beyond and above the ordinary compass of party range. It is in every respect a great national loss, for he who is no more was, in many respects, Canada's most illustrious son, and in every sense Canada's most foremost citizen and statesman.

At the period of life to which Sir John Macdonald had arrived, death, whenever it comes, cannot be said to come unexpected. Some few months ago, during the turmoil of the late election, when the country was made aware that on a certain day the physical strength of the veteran Premier had not been equal to his courage, and that his intense labour for the time being had prostrated his singularly wiry frame, everybody, with the exception, perhaps, of his buoyant self, was painfully anxious lest perhaps the angel of death had touched him with his wing.

When, a few days ago in the heat of an angry discussion the news spread in this House, that of a sudden his condition had become alarming, the surging waves of angry discussion were at once hushed, and every one, friend and foe, realized that this time for a certainty the angel of death had appeared and had crossed the threshold of his home.

Thus we were not taken by surprise, and although we were prepared for the sad event, yet it is almost impossible to convince the unwilling mind, that it is true, that Sir John Macdonald is no more, that the chair which we now see vacant shall remain forever vacant; that the face so familiar in this Parliament for the last forty years, shall be seen no more, and that the voice so well known shall be heard no more, whether in solemn debate or in pleasant and mirthful tones. In fact, the place of Sir John Macdonald in this country was so large and so absorbing, that it is almost impossible to conceive that the political life of this country, the fate of this country, can continue without him. His loss overwhelms us. For my part, I say with all truth, his loss overwhelms me, and it also overwhelms this Parliament, as if indeed one of the institutions of the land had given way.

Sir John Macdonald now belongs to the ages, and it can be said with certainty, that the career which has just been closed is one of the most remarkable careers of this century. It would be premature at this time to attempt to fix or anticipate what will be the final judgment of history upon him: but there were in his career and in his life, features so prominent and so conspicuous that already they shine with a glow which time cannot alter, which even now appear before the eye such as they will appear to the end in history. I think it can be asserted that for the supreme art of governing men, Sir John Macdonald was gifted as few men in any land or in any age were gifted: gifted with the most high of all qualities, qualities which would have made him famous wherever exercised and which would have shone all the more conspicuously the larger the theatre. The fact that he could congregate together elements the most heterogeneous and blend them into one compact party, and to the end of his life keep them steadily under his hand, is perhaps altogether unprecedented. The fact that during all those years he retained unimpaired not only the confidence, but the devotion and the ardent devotion—the ardent devotion and affection of his party, is evidence that beside those higher qualities of statesmanship to which we were the daily witnesses, he was also endowed with those inner, subtile, undefinable graces of soul which win and keep the hearts of men.

As to his statesmanship, it is written in the history of Canada. It may be said without any exaggeration whatever, that the life of

Sir John Macdonald, from the date he entered Parliament, is the history of Canada, for he was connected and associated with all the events, all the facts which brought Canada from the position Canada then occupied—the position of two small provinces, having nothing in common but a common allegiance, united by a bond of paper, and united by nothing else—to the present state of development which Canada has reached. Although my political views compel me to say that, in my judgment, his actions were not always the best that could have been taken in the interest of Canada, although my conscience compels me to say that of late he has imputed to his opponents motives as to which I must say in my heart he has misconceived, yet I am only too glad here to sink these differences, and to remember only the great services he has performed for our country—to remember that his actions always displayed great originality of views, unbounded fertility of resources, a high level of intellectual conceptions, and, above all, a far-reaching vision beyond the event of the day, and still higher, permeating the whole, a broad patriotism—a devotion to Canada's welfare, Canada's advancement, and Canada's glory.

The life of a statesman is always an arduous one, and very often it is an ungrateful one. More often than otherwise his actions do not mature until he is in his grave. Not so, however, in the case of Sir John Macdonald. His career has been a singularly fortunate one. His reverses were few and of short duration. He was fond of power, and, in my judgment, if I may say so, that may be the turning point of the judgment of history. He was fond of power, and he never made any secret of it. Many times we have heard him avow it on the floor of this Parliament, and his ambition in this respect was gratified, as perhaps, no other man's ambition ever was. In my judgment, even the career of William Pitt* can hardly compare with that of Sir John Macdonald in this respect; for, although William Pitt, moving in a higher sphere, had to deal with problems greater than our problems, yet I doubt if in the intricate management of a party William Pitt had to contend with difficulties equal to those that Sir John Macdonald had to contend with.

In his death, too, he seems to have been singularly happy. Twenty years ago I was told by one who at that time was a close personal and political friend of Sir John Macdonald, that in the intimacy of his domestic circle he was fond of repeating that his end would be as the end of Lord Chatham—that he would be carried away from the floor of Parliament to die.

How true that vision into the future was we now know, for we saw him to the last, with enfeebled health and declining strength struggling on the floor of Parliament until the hand of fate pinned him to his bed to die. And thus to die with his armour on was probably his ambition. Sir, death is the law— the supreme law. Although we see it every day in every form, although session after session we have seen it in this Parliament striking right and left without any discrimination as to age or station, yet the ever-recurring spectacle does not in any way remove the bitterness of the sting. Death always carries with it an incredible sense of pain; but the one thing sad in death is that which is involved in the word separation—separation from all we love in life. This is what makes death so poignant when it strikes a man of intellect in middle age. But when death is the

---

* William Pitt (1708–1778), the first Earl of Chatham, was prime minister of Britain from 1766 to 1768. He led the politically fractious nation during the Seven Years War and rose to power on the strength of his oratory skills. He fell to the ground in the House of Lords after delivering an incoherent speech and died shortly afterwards. (Peters, "Pitt, William, 1st Earl of Chatham," *ODNB*)

natural termination of a full life, in which he who disappears has given the full measure of his capacity, has performed everything required from him, and more, the sadness of death is not for him who goes but for those who love him and remain. In this sense I am sure the Canadian people will extend unbounded sympathy to the friends of Sir John Macdonald, to his sorrowing children, and, above all, to the brave and noble woman, his companion in life and his chief helpmate.

Thus, Mr. Speaker, one after another we see those who have been instrumental in bringing Canada to its present stage of development, removed from amongst us. To-day, we deplore the loss of him who, we all unite in saying, was the foremost Canadian of his time, and who filled the largest place in Canadian history.

Only last week, was buried in the city of Montreal, another son of Canada, one who at one time had been a tower of strength to the Liberal Party, one who will ever be remembered as one of the noblest, purest, and greatest characters that Canada has ever produced, Sir Antoine-Aimé Dorion.[*] Sir Antoine-Aimé Dorion had not been in favour of Confederation. Not that he was opposed to the principle; but he believed that the Union of these provinces, at that day, was premature. When, however, Confederation had become a fact, he gave the best of his mind and heart to make it a success. It may indeed happen, Sir, that when the Canadian people see the ranks thus gradually reduced and thinned of those upon whom they have been in the habit of relying for guidance, that a feeling of apprehension will creep into the heart lest, perhaps, the institutions of Canada may be imperilled.

---

[*] Antoine-Aimé Dorion died May 31, 1891, at age 73, and was accorded a state funeral. (Soulard, "Dorion, Sir Antoine-Aimé," *DCB*)

Before the grave of him who, above all, was the father of Confederation, let not grief be barren grief; but let grief be coupled with the resolution, the determination that the work in which the Liberals and Conservatives, in which Brown and Macdonald united, shall not perish, but that though United Canada may be deprived of the services of her greatest men, still Canada shall and will live. I agree to the motion.

ACKNOWLEDGEMENTS

Ryan Zade, an experienced researcher and scholar, provided the initial compilation of addresses for the Sir John A. Macdonald Bicentennial Commission and SALON Theatre. Our first thanks go to him for his diligence and skill.

The Department of Canadian Heritage provided funding to enable Mr. Zade to complete his work and we are indebted to Ministers James Moore and Shelley Glover, and their officials, for their support and encouragement. SALON Theatre Kingston was the Commission's governing body and we would like to thank SALON for its constant support for and belief in this project.

A debt of gratitude is due to John and Katherine Gibson for invaluable, manifold, and varied contributions to this volume. Alison Bogle also deserves special recognition. We are also very much indebted to Doug Pepper, Elizabeth Kribs, Jennifer Lum, Sean Tai, Brittany Larkin, Max Arambulo, Lynn Schellenberg, and the team at McClelland & Stewart. We extend special thanks to the librarians and staff at the St. Catharines Public Library, MacOdrum Library (Carleton University), and at the Joseph S. Stauffer Library and the W. D. Jordan Special Collections & Music Library (Queen's University). Appreciation and thanks are also extended to the history departments at Carleton and Queen's universities, and in particular to Jeffrey McNairn and James Carson. All errors, omissions, and other unintentional infelicities, are, of course, the responsibility of the editors.

WORKS CITED

ABBREVIATIONS

CHR	*Canadian Historical Review*
DCB	*Dictionary of Canadian Biography*
DEAP	*Dictionary of Early American Philosophy*
OCBH	*Oxford Companion to British History*
OCCH	*Oxford Companion to Canadian History*
OCCMH	*Oxford Companion to Canadian Military History*
OCIH	*Oxford Companion to Irish History*
OCUSH	*Oxford Companion to United States History*
ODNB	*Oxford Dictionary of National Biography*
OHBE	*Oxford History of the British Empire*

HISTORICAL SOURCES FOR SIR JOHN A. MACDONALD'S SPEECHES

HISTORICAL NEWSPAPERS

Chronicle and News (1847–1899, Kingston)

Chronicle and Gazette (1835–1837, 1841–1847, Kingston)

Citizen/Daily Citizen/Ottawa Citizen (1859–, Ottawa)

Gazette (1792–, Montreal)

Globe (1844–1936, Toronto)

The Leader (1853–1878, Toronto)

Mail/Daily Mail (1872–1895, Toronto)

PARLIAMENTARY SOURCES

Mirror of Parliament of the Province of Canada: From March 20th, to June 9th, 1846, Being the Second Session of the Second Parliament. Montréal: M. Reynolds, 1846.

Thompson's Mirror of Parliament: Being a Report of the Debates in Both Houses of the Canadian Legislature, 3rd Session, 6th Parliament. Quebec: Thompson, 1860.

Canada. Legislative Assembly. *Debates of the Legislative Assembly of United Canada, 1841–1867.* Edited by Elizabeth Abbott Gibbs. 13 vols. Montréal: Centre de recherche en histoire économique et sociale du Québec, 1970–1995.

Canada. Parliament. *Historical Debates of the Parliament of Canada.* Ottawa: Library of Parliament, 2013–. Online edition. Accessed April 14, 2014. http://parl.canadiana.ca/.

PRINTED WORKS

Boyd, John. *Sir George-Étienne Cartier, Bart: His Life and Times.* Toronto: MacMillan Company of Canada, 1914.

Collins, Joseph Edmund. *The Life and Times of the Right Honourable Sir John A. Macdonald.* Toronto: Rose Publishing Company, 1883.

Hodgins, George. *Documentary History of Upper Canada,* vol. 7: *1847–48.* Toronto: I. K. Cameron, 1900.

Macdonald, John A. *Address of the Hon. John A. Macdonald to the Electors of the City of Kingston with Extracts from Mr. Macdonald's Speeches Delivered on Different Occasions in the Years 1860 and 1861.* [s.l. s.n] c. 1861.

———. *The Dominion Campaign!: Sir John Macdonald on the questions at issue before the people. The Premier's Great Speech Before the Workingmen of Toronto.* [Toronto?: s.n., 1881?]. Internal evidence suggests the publication date is 1882: May 30 fell on a Tuesday in 1882.

———. *Address to the People of Canada.* [Ottawa?: s.n., 1891]. Date of 1881 printed on page 7 is considered a typographical error, given that 1891 cited within document.

Pope, Joseph. *Memoirs of the Right Honourable Sir John Alexander MacDonald, G.C.B.,* 2 vols. Ottawa: J. Durie and Son [1894?].

Taylor, Fennings. *Sketch of the Life and Death of Thomas D'Arcy McGee.* Montreal: John Lovell, 1868.

Whelan, Edward. *Union of the British Provinces: A Brief Account of the Several Conferences Held in the Maritime Provinces and in Canada in September and October 1864 on the Proposed Confederation of the Provinces together with a report of the speeches delivered by delegates from the provinces on important public occasions.* Charlottetown: G. T. Haszard, 1865.

REFERENCE WORKS

Canadian Encyclopedia. [Toronto]: Historica Foundation of Canada, 1999–. Online edition. Accessed April 15, 2014. http://www.thecanadianencyclopedia.ca/en/.

Dictionary of Canadian Biography, 25 vols. University of Toronto/Université Laval. Online edition, 2003–. Accessed April 14, 2014. http://www.biographi.ca/en/index.php.

Dictionary of Early American Philosophy. Edited by John R. Shook. New York: Continuum. Online edition, 2013. Accessed April 15, 2014. http://www.oxfordreference.com/view/10.1093/acref/9780199797745.001.0001/acref-9780199797745.

Dictionary of Political Thought by Roger Scruton. Third edition. New York: Palgrave Macmillan, 2007.

Dictionary of World History. Oxford: Oxford University Press. Online edition, 2013. Accessed April 14, 2014. http://www.oxfordreference.com/view/10.1093/acref/9780192807007.001.0001/acref-9780192807007

Oxford Companion to Canadian History. Edited by Gerald Hallowell. Oxford: Oxford University Press, 2004.

Oxford Companion to Canadian Military History. Edited by J. L. Granatstein and Dean F. Oliver. New York: Oxford University Press, 2011.

Oxford Companion to Irish History. Edited by S. J. Connolly. Oxford: Oxford University Press, 1998.

Oxford Companion to United States History. Edited by Paul S. Boyer. Oxford: Oxford University Press. Online edition, 2004–. Accessed April 15, 2014. http://www.oxfordreference.com/view/10.1093/acref/9780195082098.001.0001/acref-9780195082098

Oxford Dictionary of National Biography. Oxford: Oxford University Press. Online edition, 2009–. Accessed April 14, 2014. http://www.oxforddnb.com.

Oxford Dictionary of Quotations, Second edition. London: Oxford University Press, 1966.

World Encyclopedia. Seattle: Philips, 2004–. Accessed April 15, 2014. http://www.oxfordreference.com

BOOKS AND ARTICLES

Ajzenstat, Janet. *The Canadian Founding: John Locke and Parliament.* Montreal and Kingston: McGill-Queen's University Press, 2007.

Barker-Benfield, G. J. "Sensibility," in *An Oxford Companion to the Romantic Age: British Culture 1776–1832,* edited by Iain McCalman, 102–114. Oxford: Oxford University Press, 1999.

Berger, Carl. *The Sense of Power: Studies in the Ideas of Canadian Imperialism 1867–1914.* Toronto: University of Toronto Press, Second edition. 2013.

Bliss, Michael. *Right Honourable Men: The Descent of Canadian Politics from Macdonald to Mulroney.* Toronto: HarperCollins, 1994.

Buckner, Phillip. *The Transition to Responsible Government: British Policy in British North America, 1815–1850.* Westport, CT: Greenwood Press, 1985.

Burroughs, Peter. "Defence and Imperial Disunity," in *Oxford History of the British Empire,* vol. 3: *The Nineteenth Century,* edited by Andrew Porter, 320-5. Oxford: Oxford University Press, 1999.

Careless, J. M. S. *The Union of the Canadas: The Growth of Canadian Institutions 1841–1857.* Toronto: McClelland and Stewart, 1967.

Carter, Sarah. *Lost Harvests: Prairie Indian Reserve Farmers and Government Policy.* Montreal and Kingston: McGill-Queen's University Press, 1990.

Conacher, J. B. "The Politics of the 'Papal Aggression' Crisis of 1850–1851." *Canadian Catholic Historical Association Report* (26) 1959: 13-27.

Cornell, Paul Grant. "The Alignment of Political Groups in the United Province of Canada, 1854-64." *Canadian Historical Review* 30(1) 1949: 22-46.

Cragoe, Matthew. "Sir Robert Peel and the 'Moral Authority' of the House of Commons, 1832-41." *English Historical Review* 128(530) 2013: 55-77.

Craig, Gerald M. *Upper Canada: The Formative Years 1784–1841.* Toronto: McClelland and Stewart, 1963.

Creighton, Donald. *The Young Politician* and *The Old Chieftain.* Vols. 1 and 2 of *John A Macdonald.* Toronto: Macmillan, 1952 and 1955. Reprinted with an introduction by P. B. Waite. Toronto: University of Toronto Press, 1998.

———. *The Road to Confederation: The Emergence of Canada, 1863–1867.* Toronto: Macmillan, 1964. Facsimile reproduction with an introduction by Donald Wright. Oxford: Oxford University Press, 2012.

Curtis, Bruce. *The Politics of Population: State Formation, Statistics, and the Census of Canada, 1840–1875.* Toronto: University of Toronto Press, 2001.

Dalziel, Raewyn. "Southern Islands: New Zealand and Polynesia," in *Oxford History of the British Empire,* vol. 3: *The Nineteenth-Century,* edited by Andrew Porter, 573-96. Oxford: Oxford University Press, 1999.

Denoon and Wyndham, "Australia and the Western Pacific," in *Oxford History of the British Empire, vol. 3: The Nineteenth-Century,* edited by Andrew Porter, 546-572. Oxford: Oxford University Press, 1999.

Den Otter, A. A. *Philosophy of Railways: The Transcontinental Railway Idea in British North America*. Toronto: University of Toronto Press, 1997.

Dwyer, John. *Virtuous Discourse: Sensibility and Community in Late Eighteenth-Century Scotland*. Edinburgh: J. Donald, 1987.

Ferry, Darren. "'To the Interests and Conscience of the Great Mass of the Community': The Evolution of Temperance Societies in Nineteenth-Century Central Canada." *Journal of the Canadian Historical Association* 14, 2003: 137-63.

Flanagan, Thomas. *Riel and the Rebellion: 1885 Reconsidered*. Second Edition. Toronto: University of Toronto Press, 2000.

Garner, John. *The Franchise and Politics in British North America, 1755–1867*. Toronto: University of Toronto Press, 1969.

Gordon, Ross. "Libraries for Government," in *History of the Book in Canada*, vol. 2: *1840–1918*, edited by Yvan Lamonde, Patricia Lockhart Fleming, and Fiona A. Black, 273-8. Toronto: University of Toronto Press, 2005.

Goutor, David. *Guarding the Gates: The Canadian Labour Movement and Immigration, 1872–1934*. Vancouver: University of British Columbia Press, 2007.

Green, E. H. H. "The Political Economy of Empire, 1880–1914," in *Oxford History of the British Empire*, vol. 3: *The Nineteenth Century*, edited by Andrew Porter, 346-68. Oxford: University of Oxford Press, 1999.

Greer, Allan. "1837-38: Rebellion Reconsidered." *Canadian Historical Review* 76(1) 1995: 1-18.

Greer, Allan, and Ian Radforth. "Introduction," in *Colonial Leviathan: State Formation in Mid-Nineteenth-Century Canada*, 192-229. Toronto: University of Toronto Press, 1992.

Gwyn, Richard. *John A: The Man Who Made Us: The Life and Times of John A. Macdonald*. Toronto: Random House Canada, 2007.

Hawkins, Angus. *British Party Politics, 1852–1886*. New York: St. Martin's Press, 1997.

Heaman, Elsbeth. "'The Whites Are Wild about It': Taxation and Racialization in Mid-Victorian British Columbia." *Journal of Policy History* 25(3) 2013: 354-84.

Hilton, Boyd. *A Mad, Bad, and Dangerous People?: England, 1783–1846.* Oxford: Oxford University Press, 2006.

Hobsbawm, E. J. *Nations and Nationalism Since 1780: Programme, Myth, Reality.* Second edition. Cambridge: Cambridge University Press, 1992.

Johns, Adrian. *Nature of the Book: Print and Knowledge in the Making.* Chicago: University of Chicago Press, 1998.

Kealey, Gregory S. "Presidential Address: The Empire Strikes Back: The Nineteenth-Century Origins of the Canadian Secret Service." *Journal of the Canadian Historical Association* 10(1) 1999: 3-18.

——. *Toronto Workers Respond to Industrial Capitalism, 1867–1892.* Reprinted. Toronto: University of Toronto Press, 1991.

Lamonde, Yvan. *Histoire sociale des idées au Québec, 1760–1896,* vol. 1. Saint-Laurent, QC: Fides, 2000.

Martin, Ged. "1849: Year One in the History of British North America?" in *Canada 1849,* edited by Derek Pollard and Ged Martin, 7-27. Edinburgh: University of Edinburgh Centre of Canadian Studies, 2001.

——. *Britain and the Origins of Canadian Confederation, 1837–1867.* Vancouver: University of British Columbia Press, 1995.

McArthur, Duncan. *History of Canada for High Schools.* Toronto: Gage & Co., 1927.

McCalla, Douglas. "Railways and Development of Canada West, 1850-1870," in *Colonial Leviathan: State Formation in Mid-Nineteenth-Century Canada,* 3-16. Toronto: University of Toronto Press, 1992.

McInnis, Marvin. "The Population of Canada in the Nineteenth Century," in *A Population History of North America,* edited by Michael R. Haines and Richard H. Steckel, 371-432. New York: Cambridge University Press, 2000.

McNairn, Jeffrey L. *The Capacity to Judge: Public Opinion and Deliberative Democracy in Upper Canada, 1791–1854.* Toronto: University of Toronto Press, 2000.

———. "'A Just and Obvious Distinction': The Meaning of Imprisonment for Debt and the Criminal Law in Upper Canada's Age of Reform," in *Quebec and the Canadas: Essays in the History of Canadian Law,* edited by G. Blaine Baker and Donald Fyson, 163-210. Toronto: University of Toronto Press, 2013.

Messamore, Barbara Jane. *Canada's Governors General, 1847–1878: Biography and Constitutional Evolution.* Toronto: University of Toronto Press, 2006.

———. "Diplomacy or duplicity? Lord Lisgar, John A. Macdonald, and the Treaty of Washington, 1871." *Journal of Imperial and Commonwealth History* 32(2) 2004: 29-53.

Miller, J. R. *Compact, Contract, Covenant: Aboriginal Treaty-Making in Canada.* Toronto: University of Toronto Press, 2009.

———. "Owen Glendower, Hotspur, and Canadian Indian Policy." *Ethnohistory* 37(4) 1990: 386-415.

Moir, John. *Church and State in Canada West: Three Studies in the Relation of Denominationalism and Nationalism, 1841–1867.* Toronto: University of Toronto Press, 1959.

———. "The Settlement of the Clergy Reserves, 1840–1855." *Canadian Historical Review* 37(1) 1956: 46-62.

Moore, Christopher. *1867: How the Fathers Made a Deal.* Toronto: McClelland & Stewart, 1997.

Morgan, Cecilia. "'In Search of the Phantom Misnamed Honour': Duelling in Upper Canada." *Canadian Historical Review* 76(4) 1995: 529-61.

Morton, W. L. *The Critical Years: The Union of British North America, 1857–1873.* Toronto: McClelland and Stewart, 1964.

Nish, Elizabeth. "Canadian *Hansard* 1841: Interpreting the Canadian Parliamentary Press," introduction to *Debates of the Legislative Assembly of United Canada, 1841–1867,* vol. 1, *1841.*

Montréal: Centre de recherche en histoire économique et sociale du Québec, 1970, xiii-lxvii.

Ormsby, Margaret. "Prime Minister Mackenzie, the Liberal Party, and the Bargain with British Columbia." *Canadian Historical Review* 26(2) 1945: 149-173.

Owram, Doug. *Promise of Eden: The Canadian Expansionist Movement and the Idea of the West, 1856–1900.* Reprinted with a new preface. Toronto: University of Toronto Press, 1992.

Palmer, Bryan D. *Working-Class Experience: The Rise and Reconstruction of Canadian Labour, 1800–1980.* Toronto: Butterworth & Co., 1983.

Piva, Michael. *The Borrowing Process: Public Finance in the Province of Canada 1840–1867.* Ottawa: University of Ottawa Press, 1992.

———. "Getting Hired: The Civil Service Act of 1857." *Journal of the Canadian Historical Association* 3(1) 1992: 95-127.

Purviance, Susan. "Intersubjectivity and Sociable Relations in the Philosophy of Francis Hutcheson." *Eighteenth-Century Life* 15(1991): 23-38.

Radforth, Ian. "Political Demonstrations and Spectacles during the Rebellion Losses Controversy in Upper Canada." *Canadian Historical Review* 92(1) 2011: 1-41.

———. "Performance, Politics and Representation: Aboriginal People and the 1860 Royal Tour of Canada." *Canadian Historical Review* 83(1) 2003: 1-32.

Reid, John G. *Six Crucial Decades: Times of Change in the History of the Maritimes.* Halifax: Nimbus Publishing, 1987.

Retzer, Joseph, ed. *Choice of the Best Poetical Pieces of the Most Eminent English Poets, vol. 3.* Vienna: John David Hoerling, 1783.

Rudin, Ronald. *Founding Fathers: The Celebration of Champlain and Laval in Streets of Quebec, 1878–1908.* Toronto: University of Toronto Press, 2003.

Russell, Peter H. *Constitutional Odyssey: Can Canadians Become a Sovereign People?* Second edition. Toronto: University of Toronto Press, 1993.

Rutherford, Paul. *A Victorian Authority: The Daily Press in Late Nineteenth-Century Canada.* Toronto: University of Toronto Press, 1982.

See, Scott. "Rethinking 1849: Collective Conflict in British North America," in *Canada 1849,* edited by Derek Pollard and Ged Martin, 209-223. Edinburgh: University of Edinburgh Centre of Canadian Studies, 2001.

Senior, Elinor Kyte. *British Regulars in Montreal: An Imperial Garrison, 1832–1854.* Montreal: McGill-Queen's University Press, 1981.

Smith, Andrew. "The Reaction of the City of London to the Quebec Resolutions, 1864–1886." *Journal of the Canadian Historical Association* 17(1) 2006: 1-24.

Smith, Donald. "John A. Macdonald and Aboriginal Canada." *Historic Kingston* 50 (2002): 1-18.

Smith, Jennifer. "Canadian Confederation and the Influence of American Federalism." *Canadian Journal of Political Science* 21(3) 1988: 443-63.

Sprague, D. N. *Canada and the Métis, 1869–1885.* Waterloo: Wilfrid Laurier University Press, 1988.

Strong-Boag, Veronica. "The Citizenship Debates: The 1885 Franchise Act," in *Contesting Canadian Citizenship: Historical Readings,* edited by Robert Adamoski, Dorothy E. Chunn, and Robert Menzies, 69-94. Peterborough, ON: Broadview Press, 2002.

Sylvain, Philippe. "Jesuits' Estates Act," in *Canadian Encyclopedia,* Historica Canada/Mel Hurtig, 2001–. Accessed April 15, 2014. http://www.thecanadianencyclopedia.ca/en/article/jesuits-estates-act-1/.

Titley, Brian. *The Indian Commissioners: Agents of the State and Indian Policy in Canada's Prairie West, 1873–1932.* Alberta: University of Alberta Press, 2009.

Tobias, John L. "Protection, Civilization, Assimilation: An Outline History of Canada's Indian Policy," in *Sweet Promises: A Reader on Indian-White Relations in Canada,* edited by J. R.

Miller, 127-44. Toronto: University of Toronto Press, 1991.

———. "Canada's Subjugation of the Plains Cree, 1879–1885." *Canadian Historical Review* 64(4) 1983: 519-48.

Tough, Frank. *'As Their Resources Fail:' Native Peoples and the Economic History of Northern Manitoba, 1870–1930.* Vancouver: University of Vancouver Press, 1996.

Vipond, Robert C. *Liberty and Community: Canadian Federalism and the Failure of the Constitution.* Albany: State University of New York Press, 1991.

Wade, Mason. *The French Canadians 1760–1967,* vol. 1: *1760–1911.* Revised edition. Toronto: Macmillan Company of Canada, 1968.

Waite, Peter B. *The Life and Times of Confederation 1864–1867: Politics, newspapers and the union of British North America.* Third edition. Toronto: Robin Brass Studio, 2001.

———. *Canada, 1874–1896: Arduous Destiny.* Toronto: McClelland and Stewart, 1971.

———. "Introduction," to the Canadian House of Commons *Debates, 1st Parliament, 1st Session.* Ottawa: Printers to the Crown, 1967: vii-ix.

Wang, Jiwi. *'His Dominion' and the 'Yellow Peril': Protestant Missions to the Chinese Immigrants in Canada, 1859–1967.* Waterloo, ON: Wilfrid Laurier University Press, 2006.

Wearing, Joseph. "Pressure Group Politics in Canada West Before Confederation." *Historical Papers* 2(1) 1967: 75-94.

Westfall, William. *Two Worlds: The Protestant Culture of Nineteenth Century Ontario.* Montreal and Kingston: McGill-Queen's University Press, 1989.

Williams, Raymond. *Culture and Society 1780–1950.* Second edition. New York: Columbia University Press, 1983.

Winks, Robin. *The Blacks in Canada: A History.* Second edition. Montreal and Kingston: McGill-Queen's University Press, 1997.

Woon, Yuen-fong. "The Voluntary Sojourner Among the Overseas Chinese: Myth or Reality?" *Pacific Affairs* 56(4) 1983: 673-90.

Young, Brian. *George-Étienne Cartier: Montreal Bourgeois*. Montreal and Kingston: McGill-Queen's University Press, 1981.

Zeller, Suzanne. *Inventing Canada: Early Victorian Science and the Idea of a Transcontinental Nation*. Reissued with a new introduction. Montreal and Kingston: McGill-Queen's University Press, 2009.

NOTES

EDITOR'S NOTE

1. Creighton, *Young Politician*, 300.

2. *The Leader*, April 25, 1861.

3. As is evident from Donald Creighton's *Young Politician* and *Old Chieftain*.

4. See the speeches in this volume, "Portrait-Unveiling Ceremony, 1890" and "Eulogizing Macdonald, 1891."

5. Pope, *Memoirs of Macdonald*, vol. 1, 41.

6. Greer and Radforth, "Introduction," 4-10.

7. McCalla, "Railways and the Development of Canada West 1850–1870," 197.

8. Creighton, *Young Politician*, 222; Morton, *Critical Years*, 11-20; Greer and Radforth, "Introduction," 9-10; Martin, *Britain and the Origins of Canadian Confederation*, 47.

9. Ajzenstat, *Canada's Founding*, 7; Moore, *1867*, ix-xiv, 95-8; Martin, *Britain and the Origins of Confederation*, 294-6; Waite, *The Life and Times of Confederation*, 1-16; Barkley, "Taylor, John Fennings," *DCB*.

10. The editors acknowledge a tremendous intellectual debt to Donald Creighton and his two-volume biography of John A. Macdonald, *The Young Politician* and *The Old Chieftain*, in pointing the way to some of Macdonald's lesser-known but important speeches.

11. For example, Macdonald did not speak during the 1886 debate about Riel's execution. Waite, *Canada, 1874–1896*, 172.

12. Nish, "Canadian *Hansard* 1841," xv, xlviii-xlix, lvi-lix, lxii, lxiii; Waite, "Introduction," vii.

13. Nish, "Canadian *Hansard* 1841," lxi.

14. Nish, "Canadian *Hansard* 1841," lx.

15. Rutherford, *A Victorian Authority*, 3, 38.

16. Nish, "Canadian *Hansard* 1841," xxxviii-xxxix.

17. McNairn, *Capacity to Judge*, 31.

18. Buckner, *Transition to Responsible Government*, 257; Hilton, *A Mad, Bad People?*, 20-5.

19. Courtney and Macfarlane, "Francise," *OCCH*.

20. Radforth, "Political Demonstrations and Spectacles," 5; McNairn, *Capacity to Judge*, 31, 304-5; Ajzenstat, *Canada's Founding*, 7-8.

21. Quoted in Moore, *1867*, 77; Bliss, *Right Honourable Men*, 11, with citation.

22. Johns, *Nature of the Book*, 266-323; see for example, Bliss, *Right Honourable Men*, 3; Johnson and Waite, "Macdonald, Sir John Alexander," *DCB*.

23. *The Leader*, April 25, 1861.

24. Purviance, "Intersubjectivity and Francis Hutcheson," 38; Dwyer, *Virtuous Discourse*, 6, 53; Barker-Benfield, "Sensibility," 109.

25. Collins, *Life and Times of Sir John A. Macdonald*, 63.

26. Creighton, *Young Politician*, 136-8; Gwyn, *John A*, 267; *Mail*, November 17, 1873.

27. Ajzenstat, *Canada's Founding*, 8-19.

28. Cited in Nish, "Canadian *Hansard* 1841," xliv.

29. Nish, "Canadian *Hansard* 1841," xliii; Waite, "Introduction," viii.

30. Waite, "Introduction," xvii-ix.

31. Pope, *Memoirs of Macdonald*, vol. 2, 349.

32. Williams, *Culture and Society*, xvi; Berger, *Sense of Power*, 117.

PART ONE: BIRTH OF A PARLIAMENTARIAN

1. Creighton, *Young Politician*, 92-4; Buckner, *Transition to Responsible Government*, 263-4, 266-9.

2. Creighton, *Young Politician*, 101.

3. Pope, *Memoirs of Macdonald*, vol. 1, 41; Creighton, *Young Politician*, 106-7; Tulchinsky, "Moffatt, George," *DCB*; In Collaboration, "Sabrevois de Bleury, Clement-Charles," *DCB*.

4. Quoted in Creighton, *Young Politician*, 106-7.

5. McNairn, *Capacity to Judge*, 360-1, including quoted material; Creighton, *Young Politician*, 107.

6. Pope, *Memoirs of Macdonald*, vol. 1, 41-2; Hilton, *A Mad, Bad, People?*, 234; McNairn, *"A Just and Obvious Distinction,"* 198.

7. Careless, *Union of the Canadas*, 109-11; *Mirror of Parliament*, April 28, 1846, 109; Creighton, *Young Politician*, 115.

8. Garner, *Franchise and Politics in BNA*, 99-103; Senior, *British Regulars in Montreal*, 60-4, 70.

9. Creighton, *Young Politician*, 120-4, with citation; Moir, *Church and State*, 88-9, 96-7; Westfall, *Two Worlds*, 106.

10. Hodgins, *Documentary History*, vol. 7, 6-7, including the bracketed editorial notes.

11. Creighton, *Young Politician*, 127-9; Gwyn, *John A.*, 112.

12. Messamore, *Canada's Governors General*, 49, 58; Buckner, *Transition to Responsible Government*, 312; Martin, "1849: Year One in the History of British North America?," 7, 15; see, "Rethinking 1849: Collective Conflict in British North America," 209; Careless, *Union of the Canadas*, 124-6, 170; Creighton, *Young Politician*, 136-7; Radforth, "Political Demonstrations and Spectacles," 2-3.

13. *Gazette* (Montreal), February 19, 1848.

14. Creighton, *Young Politician*, 138-9.

15. Careless, *Union of the Canadas*, 124-6; Creighton, *Young Politician*, 139; Radforth, "Political Demonstrations and Spectacles," 4, 12, 41.

16. Ferry, "To the Interests and Conscience of the Great Mass of the Community," 148-9; Hilton, *A Mad, Bad, People?*, 577.

17. Careless, "Brown, George," *DCB*.

18. Paradis, "Morin, Augustin-Norbert," *DCB*.

PART TWO: RISE OF A STATESMAN

1. Creighton, *Young Politician*, 209-10, 215; Westfall, "Clergy Reserves," *OCCH*; Westfall, *Two Worlds*, 106-7, 111.

2. Creighton, *Young Politician*, 220-1.

3. Wearing, "Pressure Group Politics in Canada West," 77; Nicholson and Moir, "Charbonnel, Armand-François-Marie de," *DCB*; Moir, *Church and State in Canada West*, 132, 134, 136, 139-40, 142, 143, 152-3, 161.

4. Morton, *Critical Years*, 13; Tobias, "Protection, Civilization, Assimilation," 130.

5. Morton, *Critical Years*, 11, 16; Careless, *Union of the Canadas*, 212; Cornell, "Political Groups in the Province of Canada," 29; *The Globe*, July 20, 1858.

6. Creighton, *Young Politician*, 236-7.

7. Creighton, *Young Politician*, 248-9.

8. Messamore, *Canada's Governors General*, 80.

9. Messamore, *Canada's Governors General*, 92.

10. Creighton, *Young Politician*, 299-301.

11. Radforth, "Performance, Politics, and Representation: Aboriginal People and the 1860 Royal Tour of Canada," 2, 10-11; Houston, "Orange Order," *DCB*; "Orange Order," *OCIH*.

12. Creighton, *Young Politician*, 301-3.

13. Creighton, *Young Politician*, 305-6, 314; Messamore, *Canada's Governors General*, 94.

14. Messamore, *Canada's Governors General*, 81-4; Creighton, *Young Politician*, 265-71; Morton, *Critical Years*, 19.

15. *The Leader*, April 25, 1861; Creighton, *Young Politician*, 308-9; Curtis, *The Politics of Population*, 151, 221-5.

PART THREE: NATION MAKER

1. Creighton, *Road to Confederation*, 105, 126; Welan, *Union of British Provinces*, 18, vii, 42-7.

2. Smith, "Canadian Confederation and the Influence of American Federalism," 444.

3. Smith, "Canadian Confederation and the Influence of American Federalism," 444-5, 451; Russell, *Constitutional Odyssey*, 38; Vipond, *Liberty and Community*, 22.

4. Burroughs, "Defence and Imperial Disunity," *OHBE*, vol. 3, 327.

5. Smith, "Canadian Confederation and the Influence of American Federalism," 451; Russell, *Constitutional Odyssey*, 38.

6. Vipond, *Liberty and Community*, 24, 30-1.

7. Ajzenstat, *Canada's Founding*, 7.

8. Gordon, "Libraries for Government," 273-4; House of Commons, *Debates,* 1st Parl., 1st Sess., 666.

9. Reid, *Six Crucial Decades*, 108; Vipond, *Liberty and Community*, 22.

10. Reid, *Six Crucial Decades*, 111; Morton, *Critical Years*, 226.

11. Creighton, *Old Chieftain*, 30-1.

12. Beck, "Howe, Joseph," *DCB*.

PART FOUR: STEADFAST VISIONARY

1. Rea, "Scott, Thomas," *DCB*; Bumsted, "Red River Resistance," *OCCH*; House of Commons, *Debates*, 1st Parl, 3rd Sess., 890-3; Sprague, *Canada and the Métis*, 44-7.

2. Sprague, *Canada and the Métis*, 57-60; Flanagan, *Riel and the Rebellions*, 65.

3. Sprague, *Canada and the Métis*, 59; Flanagan, *Riel and the Rebellions*, 64, 66.

4. House of Commons, *Debates*, 2nd Parl., 1st Sess., 88; Robertson, "Prince Edward Island," *OCCH*.

5. Miller, *Compact, Contract Covenant*, 159, 163-5 and note 22; House of Commons *Debates*, 2nd Parl., 1st Sess., 152; Oliver and Granatstein, "North West Mounted Police," *OCCMH*.

6. Creighton, *Old Chieftain,* 161-73.

7. Creighton, *Old Chieftain*, 174-9, 180-3.

8. Palmer, *Working-Class Experience*, 93; Creighton, *Old Chieftain*, 119.

9. Creighton, *Old Chieftain*, 120, 184-5; Buckner, "Tupper, Sir Charles," *DCB*.

10. James, "Rae, John (1796–1872)," *DCB*; Hobsbawm, *Nations and Nationalism*, 29.

11. Forster, "National Policy," *OCCH*.

12. Sweeny, "McIntyre, Duncan," *DCB*; Creighton, *Old Chieftain*, 294-9.

13. House of Commons, *Debates*, 4th Parl., 3rd Sess., 448, 450; Creighton, *Old Chieftain*, 305-7; Fleming, "Howland, Sir William Pearce," *DCB*.

14. Creighton, *Old Chieftain*, 309; House of Commons, *Debates*, 4th Parl., 3rd Sess., 494-5.

15. Tobias, "Protection, Civilization, Assimilation," 133; Carter, *Lost Harvests*, 124-6; Owram, *Promise of Eden*, 173; Miller, *Compact, Contract, Covenant*, 193; Macleod, "North-West Rebellion," *OCCH*.

16. House of Commons, *Debates*, 5th Parl. 3rd Sess., 3077-9, 3110, 3115; Sprague, *Canada and the Métis*, 182; Cruikshank, "Macpherson, David Lewis," *DCB*; Titley, *Indian Commissioners*, 7; Flanagan, *Riel and the Rebellions*, 76-9; Tough, *As Their Natural Resources Fail*, 116, 117-8.

17. Russell, *Constitutional Odyssey*, 35-6, 42; Vipond, *Liberty and Community*, 77, 127.

18. House of Commons, *Debates*, 4th Parl., 4th Sess., 923.

19. Creighton, *Old Chieftain*, 445; Waite, *Canada 1874–1896*, 173.

20. House of Commons, *Debates*, 5th Parl., 4th Sess., 12.

21. Green, "Political Economy of Empire, 1880–1914," *OHBE*, vol. 3, 347.

22. House of Commons, *Debates*, 5th Parl., 4th Sess., 19.

PART FIVE: MAKING CANADIANS

1. Vipond, *Liberty and Community*, 119-25; House of Commons, *Debates*, 2nd Parl., 1st Sess., 558.

2. Creighton, *Old Chieftain*, 180-2; *Daily Citizen* (Ottawa), November 14, 1878.

3. Kealey, *Toronto Workers*, 216; Creighton, *Old Chieftain*, 336; Palmer, *Working-Class Experience*, 93, 95.

4. Goutor, *Guarding the Gates*, 13-4; Creighton, *Old Chieftain*, 275.

5. Lacasse, "Hébert, Louis-Philippe," *DCB*; Rudin, *Founding Fathers*, 3.

6. Strong-Boag, "The Citizenship Debates," 69, 75-6.

7. Strong-Boag, "The Citizenship Debates," 71, 76; Courtney and Macfarlane, "Franchise," *OCCH*.

8. Strong-Boag, "The Citizenship Debates," 69, 70, 72-4.

9. House of Commons, *Debates*, 5th Parl., 3rd Sess., 1384.

10. House of Commons, *Debates*, 5th Parl., 3rd Sess., 1389.

11. House of Commons, *Debates*, 5th Parl., 3rd Sess., 1585-6.

12. House of Commons, *Debates*, 5th Parl., 3rd Sess., 1587-8.

13. House of Commons, *Debates*, 5th Parl., 3rd Sess., 2371.

14. Strong-Boag, "The Citizenship Debates," 80, 83, 87; Kealey, *Toronto Workers*, 368, fn4.

15. Zeller, *Inventing Canada*, 93, 233; Creighton, *Old Chieftain*, 337.

16. Creighton, *Old Chieftain*, 513-7; Sylvain, "Jesuits' Estates Act," *Canadian Encyclopedia*.

17. Miller, "Equal Rights Association," *OCCH*.

18. Creighton, *Old Chieftain*, 547-52; Pope, *Memoirs of Macdonald*, vol. 2, 336.

19. Creighton, *Old Chieftain*, 557-8, 561.

20. Buckner, "Tupper, Sir Charles," *DCB*.

21. Creighton, *Old Chieftain*, 569-71, 576.

INDEX

Abbott, John J., 252, 253, 257, 266, 275

Aboriginal peoples, xxvii, xxx, xl, 67, 77, 223, 223n, 230, 329, 342-44; enfranchisement of, 394, 401, 402, 410-13, 415, 416, 417-18; and North-West Rebellion, 324-25; reserve system, 394, 411, 413-14; treaty negotiations, 236-39, 241-42

Ahtahkakoop, 238

Ajzenstat, Janet, xli

Allan, Hugh, xi, 243-44, 248, 250-55, 257-62, 266, 267, 270, 272-73, 278-79

American Civil War, 105, 113, 120, 126-27, 130, 142, 146n, 148, 153n, 170, 173-74

Anderson, John, 104, 104n

Anglin, Timothy W., 232-33, 299, 301, 310

Archibald, Adams G., xx, 238, 238n, 271

Arendt, Hannah, xxxi

Australia, 201, 353, 404, 409

Aylwin, Thomas C., 6, 15

Baldwin, Robert, x, xiv, 2, 5, 8, 19n, 24-25, 27, 29, 31, 57, 108, 431

Bancroft, Henry, 405

Beaubien, Louis, 259

Bentham, Jeremy, 12-13

Big Bear (Mistahimaskwa), 324, 342, 342n

Bill 103. See Franchise Bill (1885)

Birkbeck, Morris, 9

Black, John, 219n, 220-21

Blackwood's Magazine, 9

Blain, David, 267-69, 274

Blake, Edward, x, 290, 291n, 298, 347, 351, 352, 353, 379-80, 384, 396; on model farms, 420-21; North-West Rebellion debate, 325, 330, 335, 336-38, 340-41; on Pacific Scandal, 244, 247, 268-69

Blake, William H., xl, 32-33

Blanchet, Joseph-Godéric, 290, 347

BNA Act. See British North America Act (1867)

Bowell, Mackenzie, xxiv

Boyd, John, 389

Bright, John, 153n, 290n

Britain, 3, 60, 115, 131, 132; Abolition of Slavery Bill, 50-51, 50n; and Canadian Confederation, 145, 153n, 199-201; Catholic Emancipation Bill, 59, 59n; colonial reformers in, 146, 146n, 149; Ecclesiastical Titles Act, 423, 423n; enfranchisement of women, 394, 395, 397, 398, 400; and free trade, 14, 15n, 36, 384; House of Lords, 182-83; immigrants from, 159, 159n, 160; Judicial Committee of the Privy Council, 346; primogeniture in, 10-11; Reform Bill of 1832, 45, 182, 275; usury laws, 12

British Columbia, 315, 351, 403, 407, 409; entry into Confederation of, 245, 245n, 246, 248, 291, 291n, 293, 304-05

British Empire, 149, 201, 202, 213, 351-54, 355, 436, 443, 444, 449

British North America Act (1867), viii, 211, 212-14, 229, 358, 363-64, 368, 385, 425, 425n. *See also* Quebec Resolutions

Brown, George, 41, 42, 58, 103, 140, 382; coalition with Macdonald and Cartier, 155n, 432n, 433; and "double-majority" principle, 67-70; and representation by population issue, 105, 129, 133-34; and royal tour (1860), 84, 89, 97-98; "Two-Day Administration" of, xii, 72, 99, 100-02

Brown, J.E., 335-38

Buller, Charles, 277

Burke, Edmund, xxxvii

Burpee, E.R., 271

Burton, Francis H., 132

Caldwell, Boyd, 346

California, 409

Cameron, John H., 55, 216, 217

Canada, Dominion of (1867-), viii; economic depression of 1873, 375, 382, 437; farming in, 419-21; foreign investment in, 379-80; franchise, 393-418; immigration to, 159n, 401-06, 408, 409, 409n; Indian Department, 324, 325, 342n, 413; population, 159n; position in Empire, 351-54, 436; school system, 358-59, 363, 365; tariff wall, 281, 283-86, 377, 378, 379; unions, 394; women's suffrage, 393, 394, 395, 396-401, 418

Canada, United Province of (1841-1867), viii, xxxiv; as ally of Britain, 138; census of 1861, 105, 142; dissolution of, 135-36, 137, 160-61; "double majority," 67-70; duelling in, 39-40, 40n; election

law, 5-7; import duties, 14-15; jury laws, 118-20; legislative library, 209; militia, 147, 147n; religious factionalism in, 256, 366, 422-23, 427-28; representation by population issue, 105, 106-107, 108-17, 120-38, 152, 160, 161-62; responsible government in, xxxv, xxxvi, 3, 8, 31, 35, 68, 180; royal tour (1860), 77-98; seat of government issue, 2, 36, 71-73, 100, 371-72, 373-74; secret ballot in, 16-17; temperance movement, 37, 39n; university endowment issue, 18-19, 20-30; usury laws, 121

Canada East. *See* Lower Canada; Quebec

Canada West. *See* Upper Canada; Ontario

Canadian Pacific Railway (CPR), xxix, xxxiii, 159n, 248, 252n, 253, 289-94, 296-98, 302, 309-23, 351, 438, 439

Canadian Party, xx, 216, 217

Carling, John, 270

Cartier, George-Étienne, xi, xliii, 78, 85, 133, 140, 246, 255, 258, 259-60, 266, 267, 371, 432; co-leader of Macdonald-Cartier government, 67, 71, 98-99, 152, 244, 245n; death of, 245, 245n; Macdonald's tribute to, 389-92

Cartwright, Richard, xi-xii, 284, 284n, 379, 381, 440, 442, 446

Casey, George, 404, 405

Castlereagh, Lord (Robert Stewart), 44

Cathcart, Lord (Charles Murray Cathcart), ix

Catholic Church, 26, 28, 42, 64-65, 151n, 422n, 423n, 425n, 426

Cauchon, Joseph-Édouard, 89
Charbonnel, Armand-François-
    Marie de, 64-65
Charles I, 59, 59n
Charlottetown Conference (1864),
    140, 143, 157-58
Charlton, John, 299, 406
Chauveau, Pierre-Joseph-Olivier,
    109, 109n, 110-11
Chicago, 321
China, 408, 408n
Chinese Canadians, xxx, xli, xlv,
    159n, 375, 409-410n; enfranchise-
    ment of, 393-94, 401-07, 410, 418
Chronicle and Gazette (Kingston),
    xlii, 2
Chronicle and News (Kingston), xlii, 20
Church of England, 25-26, 28, 55,
    60, 61, 399
Church of Scotland, 26, 60, 61
Clear Grits Party, 42, 67, 432, 432n
Clement XIV, Pope, 424n
Clergy Reserves Act (1854), 54-63,
    117-18
Cobbett, William, 10
Cobden, Richard, 285, 285n
Cockburn, James, 206, 248
Coffin, Isaac, 348
Colby, Charles C., 359
College of St. Boniface, 426
Colonial Conferences, 352
Confederation, xxxiii, 140-47,
    151-54, 162, 204, 433-34; costs
    and savings of, 164-65; and
    defence system, 142, 145, 192-93;
    fathers of, xli, 140, 449; govern-
    ment model, 148-49, 163, 167,
    171, 172, 173, 174-79, 181, 183-88,
    189-92, 195, 196-97; and legal
    system, 193-95; name of federated
    provinces, 198; opposition to, 151,

15In, 164, 199; and relationship
    with Britain, 145-47, 199-203;
    and relationship with United
    States, 170-71; vs. legislative
    union, 162-63, 359-60, 361. *See
    also* British North America Act;
    Quebec Resolutions
Connor, Skeffington, 111, 119, 128
Conservative Party, xi, xiii, xxxii, 5,
    18, 30, 35, 42, 54, 55, 57, 77, 131,
    293-94, 306, 373, 431, 432, 432n;
    and electoral reform, 105, 108,
    110; and Pacific Scandal, 243-44,
    369. *See also* National Policy
Cook, H.H., 297, 300
Cooke, Jay, 255, 265, 265, 271
Costigan, John, 358-59, 365
CPR. *See* Canadian Pacific Railway
Cumberland, Frederic, 270
Custer, George A., 344

Dennis, John S., 325, 327
Derby, Lord (Edward Smith-
    Stanley), 50-51, 68, 69
Dominion Lands Act (1879), 325, 332
Dominion Police, 336n
Dorion, Antoine-Aimé, xii, 73, 97, 99,
    102, 133, 15In, 174, 219n, 246, 455
Dorion, Jean-Baptiste-Éric, 15In
Draper, William H., xii-xiii, 14,
    23n, 25
Drummond, Lewis T., xxxviii, 46n,
    74, 133
Dufferin, Lord (Frederick Hamilton-
    Temple-Blackwood), ix, 244,
    282, 282n
Dumont, Gabriel, 334, 340
Dumont, Isidore, 339
Durham, Lord (John Lambton),
    xxxv, 56n
Dwyer, John, xxxix

Smith, Donald, xxi, 217-18, 220n, 289, 438n

Smith, Goldwin, xxi-xxii, 153n, 283, 285, 286-88

Smith, Sidney, 103, 103n, 132-33

Society of Jesus, 424n, 427

Stanley, Lord (Edward Smith-Stanley, 14th Earl of Derby), 50-51, 68-69

Stanley, Lord (Frederick Arthur Stanley, 16th Earl of Derby), x, 436

Stephen, George, xxi, 289, 294n, 311, 314

Strickland, Samuel, 421

Strickland, Susannah (Moodie), xxxv

Strong-Boag, Veronica, 395n, 401n

Taché, Alexandre-Antonin, 326, 327-29, 331, 426

Taché, Étienne-Paschal, xliii, 64, 67, 71, 150

Taylor, Fennings, 206

Tchegus, Robert P., xxviii

Temperance Bill (1853), 37-41

Tessier, Ulric-Joseph, 150

Theory of Moral Sentiments (Smith), xxxix

Thibaudeau, Joseph-Élie, 133, 134

Thomson, E.W., 441

Thomson, William A., 270

Thompson's Mirror of Parliament, xlii, 74

Tilley, Samuel L., xxii-xxiii, 140, 379

Toronto, 36, 107, 251, 255, 261, 322-23, 375-77, 382

Toronto Daily Mail, 387, 388

Trades and Labor Congress, 375, 409n

Treaty 1, 236, 237, 238, 238n

Treaty 2, 236, 237

Treaty 3, 239, 239n

Trent affair (1861), 146, 146n

Trow, James, 420

Tupper, Charles, xxiii-xxiv, 140, 211, 281, 290, 445-46, 448

Union Act (1841), viii, 46, 189, 431, 432

United States: and aboriginal peoples, 343-44; annexation of Canada, xii, 311, 440, 443; constitution, 171-72, 173, 174, 194, 195; and France, 355-56; government of, 142-43, 148, 149, 186 193; railways, 319-21, 322; trade with Canada, 14, 15, 170, 170n, 171, 281-82, 435, 437, 440-41, 442; war with Britain, 145, 145n, 146, 202. See also American Civil War

University of Toronto, 24, 27

Upper Canada, 200; benefits of union with Lower Canada, 137, 156, 161; and compensation to seigneurs, 47-51; education in, 24, 64, 65; electoral reform in, 16, 42, 105, 116-17; inheritance laws, 8, 9; immigration to, 74, 75; newspapers in, xxxv, 151n. See also Ontario

VanKoughnet, Philip, 97, 103, 103n

Victoria, Queen of the United Kingdom, ix, 71, 72, 79-80, 81-82, 203, 371-72, 423n, 445

Victoria College, 18, 19, 26, 28

Waddington, Alfred P., 249, 249n

Waite, Peter, xlii

Walker, John, 296